THE MAN BORN TO
BE KING

THE MAN
BORN TO BE KING

A Play-Cycle on the Life
of Our Lord and Saviour
JESUS CHRIST

Written for broadcasting by
DOROTHY L. SAYERS

IGNATIUS PRESS   SAN FRANCISCO

Cover by Christopher J. Pelicano

these plays are for
VAL GIELGUD
who has made them
his
already

CONTENTS

THE MAKERS

The Architect stood forth and said:
   "I am the master of the art:
I have a thought within my head,
   I have a dream within my heart.

"Come now, good craftsman, ply your trade
   With tool and stone obediently;
Behold the plan that I have made—
   I am the master; serve you me."

The Craftsman answered: "Sir, I will,
   Yet look to it that this your draft
Be of a sort to serve my skill—
   You are not master of the craft.

"It is by me the towers grow tall,
   I lay the course, I shape and hew;
You make a little inky scrawl,
   And that is all that you can do.

"Account me, then, the master man,
   Laying my rigid rule upon
The plan, and that which serves the plan—
   The uncomplaining, helpless stone."

The Stone made answer: "Masters mine,
   Know this: that I can bless or damn
The thing that both of you design
   By being but the thing I am;

"For I am granite and not gold,
   For I am marble and not clay,
You may not hammer me nor mould—
   I am the master of the way.

"Yet once that mastery bestowed
   Then I will suffer patiently
The cleaving steel, the crushing load,
   That make a calvary of me;

"And you may carve me with your hand
 To arch and buttress, roof and wall,
Until the dream rise up and stand—
 Serve but the stone, the stone serves all.

"Let each do well what each knows best,
 Nothing refuse and nothing shirk,
Since none is master of the rest,
 But all are servants of the work—

"The work no master may subject
 Save He to whom the whole is known,
Being Himself the Architect,
 The Craftsman and the Corner-stone.

"Then, when the greatest and the least
 Have finished all their labouring
And sit together at the feast,
 You shall behold a wonder thing:

"The Maker of the men that make
 Will stoop between the cherubim,
The towel and the basin take,
 And serve the servants who serve Him."

The Architect and Craftsman both
 Agreed, the Stone had spoken well;
Bound them to service by an oath
 And each to his own labour fell.

INTRODUCTION

Historical reality ... is above all a concrete and not an abstract reality; and no concrete reality other than the historical does or can exist. ... Everything genuinely historical has both a particular and a concrete character. Carlyle, the most concrete and particular of the historians, says that John Lackland came upon this earth on such and such a day. This indeed is the very substance of history — BERDYAEV.

Very God of very God ... incarnate by the Holy Ghost of the Virgin Mary. ... He suffered under Pontius Pilate.

There is a dialectic in Christian sacred art which impels it to stress, from time to time, now the eternal, and now the temporal elements in the Divine drama. The crucifix displays in one period the everlasting Son reigning from the tree; in another, the human Jesus disfigured with blood and grief. For various reasons, some of which will appear in this introduction, "it seemed good to the Holy Ghost and to us" that our Life of Christ should depict, primarily, not so much the eternal sacrifice, as the "one oblation of Himself once offered"; that is, it should be handled, not liturgically or symbolically, but realistically and historically: "this is a thing that actually happened".

This decision presented the playwright with a set of conditions literally unique, and of extraordinary technical interest.

There were, to begin with, no modern precedents to offer a guide as to treatment, or to prepare the minds of critics and audience for what they were to hear. Few out of the millions in this country could be supposed to have visited Oberammergau; and the mediaeval mysteries were too remote in period and atmosphere to serve as a model, even allowing them to be familiar to one listener in ten thousand. The law forbidding[1] the representation on the stage of any Person of the Holy Trinity had helped to foster the notion that all such representations were intrinsically wicked, and had encouraged a tendency, already sufficiently widespread, towards that Docetic and totally heretical Christology which denies the full Humanity of Our Lord. The thing was therefore a quite new experiment, undertaken in the face of a good deal of prejudice, and in the absence of any adequate standards of comparison.

The material also was unique. All drama is religious in origin, and Greek

---

[1] Reasonably enough, in view of the very inelastic powers in Great Britain at the Lord Chamberlain's disposal. He has no authority to licence *a particular production;* a licence, once granted, is *generally* valid, and the play can thenceforward be presented by any persons, under any conditions, without safeguards of any kind as to the style and quality of the performance. It is thus delivered over, lock, stock, and barrel, to the tender mercies of commercialism, unless the author (if alive) is sufficiently public-spirited to interpose a veto. This state of things could be remedied by permitting the grant, in certain cases, of a limited licence, covering one production only, the play to come up for re-licence on each subsequent occasion when it is sought to produce it. As it is, many plays which would be wholly without offence in the reverent and decent hands of Messrs. A _____ or Mr. B _____ have to be withheld from the public for fear of what they might only too easily become under the sensational management of Mr. X _____, or Messrs. Y _____ & Z _____, Ltd.

tragedy in particular dealt with divine stories whose details were perfectly familiar to every person in the audience. A performance of the *Oresteia* was not only an entertainment but an act of communal worship, recognised as such. So far, there was a parallel (though, here again, one could not count upon the recognition, by an English audience, of this age-old, intimate connection between the theatre and the heavenly places). But the Greek tragic poet, though he was expected to follow the outlines of the accepted legends, was not riveted to the text of a sacred book, nor to the exposition of a rigid theology.

Something must be said on both these points. The knowledge which the British public has of the New Testament is extensive, but in many respects peculiar. The books are, on the whole, far better known as a collection of disjointed texts and moral aphorisms wrenched from their contexts than as a coherent history made up of coherent episodes. Most people are aware that Jesus was born at Bethlehem, and that after a short ministry of teaching and healing He was judicially murdered at Jerusalem, only to rise from the dead on the third day. But for all except the diminishing company of the instructed, the intervening period is left in the jumbled chronology of the Synoptists—a string of parables, a bunch of miracles, a discourse, a set of "sayings", a flash of apocalyptic thunder—here a little and there a little. And although many scattered fragments of teaching are commonly remembered and quoted (to the exclusion of as many more, less palatable to the taste of the times), they are remembered chiefly as detached pronouncements unrelated to the circumstances that called them forth. A multitude of people will recall that "the devil is the father of lies" for one who could state on what occasion the words were spoken and to whom, or make a précis of the argument developed in the long, pugnacious, and provocative piece of dialectic in which they occur.

Moreover, the words of the books, in or out of their context, are by great numbers of British Christians held to be sacrosanct in such a sense that they must not be expanded, interpreted, or added to, even in order to set the scene, supply obvious gaps in the narrative, or elucidate the sense. And this sacrosanctity is attributed, not to the Greek of the original and only authentic documents, but to every syllable of a translation made three hundred years ago (and that not always with perfect accuracy) in an idiom so old-fashioned that, even as English, it is often obscure to us or positively misleading. The editor of a newspaper expressed this point of view very naively when he said: "In quoting the Bible we must take the Authorised Version, and not the interpretations of scholars, however wise." That is to say, we are to pay attention, not to the ascertainable meaning of what the Evangelist wrote, but only to the words (however inexact or unintelligible) used by King James's translators—who, incidentally, were themselves mere "scholars, however wise." (Presumably, those of our fellow-Christians who happen not to speak English are debarred from quoting the Bible at all, since this gentleman—who is typical—will allow authority neither to the Greek nor to the Vulgate, but only to "the sacred English original".)[2] Of this singular piece of idolatry I will say only that it imposes difficulties upon the English playwright from which the Greek tragic poets were free. Nor are things made any easier by the existence, side by side with the instructed and the bibliolaters, of a large and mostly youthful public to whom the whole story of Jesus is *terra incognita* — children who do not know the meaning of Christmas, men and women to whom the name of Christ is only a swear-word — besides a considerable body of agnostics and semi-Christians who accept some incidents of the story and firmly disbelieve the rest, or who propose to follow the teaching of Jesus while rejecting the authority on which He founded it.

This brings us to the theology, which is a very different matter. From the purely dramatic point of view the theology is enormously advantageous, because it locks the whole structure into a massive intellectual coherence. It is scarcely possible to build up anything lop-sided, trivial, or unsound on that steely and gigantic framework. Always provided, of course, that two conditions are observed. It must be a *complete* theology; never was there a truer word than that "except a man believe rightly he cannot" — at any rate, his artistic structure cannot possibly — "be saved". A loose and sentimental theology begets loose and sentimental art-forms; an illogical theology lands one in illogical situations; an ill-balanced theology issues in false emphasis and absurdity. Conversely; there is no more searching test of a theology than to submit it to dramatic handling; nothing so glaringly exposes inconsistencies in a character, a story, or a philosophy as to put it upon the stage and allow it to speak for itself. Any theology that will stand the rigorous pulling and hauling of the dramatist is pretty tough in its texture. Having subjected Catholic theology to this treatment, I am bound to bear witness that it is very tough indeed. As I once made a character say in another context: "Right in art is right in practice"; and I can only affirm that at no point have I yet found artistic truth and theological truth at variance.

The second condition appears at first sight to contradict the first, though in fact it does not. It is this: that in writing a play on this particular subject, the dramatist must begin by ridding himself of all edificatory and theological intentions. He must set out, not to instruct but to show forth; not to point a moral but to tell a story; not to produce a Divinity Lesson with illustrations in dialogue but to write a good piece of theatre. It was assumed by many pious persons who approved the project that my object in writing *The Man Born to Be King* was "to do good" — and indeed the same assumption was also made by impious persons who feared lest it might "do good" in the Christian sense, as well as by pious but disapproving persons who thought it could only do harm. But that was in fact not my object at all, though it was quite properly

---

[2] The dispute in this case arose from the fact that the editor in question, misunderstanding a common Jacobean idiom, had placed upon a saying of Our Lord an interpretation which involved a violent wresting of the English text, and could not legitimately be derived from the Greek at all.

the object of those who commissioned the plays in the first place. My object was *to tell that story* to the best of my ability, within the medium at my disposal—in short to make as good a work of art as I could. For a work of art that is not good and true *in art* is not good or true in any other respect, and is useless for any purpose whatsoever—even for edification—because it is a lie, and the devil is the father of all such. As drama, these plays stand or fall. The idea that religious plays are not to be judged by the proper standard of drama derives from a narrow and lop-sided theology which will not allow that all truth—including the artist's truth—is in Christ, but persists in excluding the Lord of Truth from His own dominions.

What this actually means is that the theology—the dogma—must be taken by the writer as part of the material with which he works, and not as an exterior end towards which his work is directed. Dogma is the grammar and vocabulary of his art. If he regards it as something extrinsic to his subject, he will produce at best something analogous to those harmless but inartistic mnemonics which inculcate grammatical rules:—

> Abstract nouns in *io* call
> *Feminina* one and all;
> Masculine will only be
> Things that you may touch or see....

At worst, he will fabricate the cheap and pretentious, like those verses which, purporting to illustrate the musical richness of the English vocabulary, issue only in a jingling and artificial syllabic pattern—Poe's *The Bells,* for example. The music of English can indeed be abundantly illustrated from English poetry, but only from those poems which are created *by that means* and not *to that end.* Indeed, the effort to make language indulge in this kind of exhibition-ism defeats its own object; and the same is true of any work of art which sets up a part of its own material as a thesis external to itself. Accordingly, it is the business of the dramatist not to subordinate the drama to the theology, but to approach the job of truth-telling from his own end, and trust the theology to emerge undistorted from the dramatic presentation of the story. This it can scarcely help doing, if the playwright is faithful to his material, since the history and the theology of Christ are one thing: His life is theology in action, and the drama of His life is dogma shown as dramatic action.

For Jesus Christ is unique—unique among gods and men. There have been incarnate gods a-plenty, and slain-and-resurrected gods not a few; but He is the only God who has a date in history. And plenty of founders of religions have had dates, and some of them have been prophets or avatars of the Divine; but only this one of them was personally God. There is no more astonishing collocation of phrases than that which, in the Nicene Creed, sets these two statements flatly side by side: "Very God of very God.... He suffered under Pontius Pilate." All over the world, thousands of times a day, Christians recite the name of a rather undistinguished Roman pro-consul—not in execration (Judas and Caiaphas, more guilty, get off with fewer reminders of their iniquities), but merely because that name fixes within a few years the date of the death of God.

In the light of that remarkable piece of chronology we can see an additional reason why the writer of realistic Gospel plays has to eschew the didactic approach to his subject. He has to display the words and actions of actual people engaged in living through a piece of recorded history. He cannot, like the writer of purely liturgical or symbolic religious drama, confine himself to the abstract and universal aspect of the life of Christ. He is brought up face to face with the "scandal of particularity". *Ecce homo*—not only Man-in-general and God-in-His-thusness, but also God-in-His-thisness, and *this* Man, *this* person, of a reasonable soul and human flesh subsisting, who walked and talked *then* and *there,* surrounded, not by human types, but by *those* individual people. This story of the life and murder and resurrection of God-in-Man is not only the symbol and epitome of the relations of God and man throughout time; it is also a series of events that took place at a particular point *in time. And the people of that time had not the faintest idea that it was happening.*

Of all examples of the classical tragic irony in fact or fiction, this is the greatest—the classic of classics. Beside it, the doom of Oedipus is trifling, and the nemesis of the Oresteian blood-bath a mere domestic incident. For the Christian affirmation is that a number of quite commonplace human beings, in an obscure province of the Roman Empire, killed and murdered God Almighty—quite casually, almost as a matter of religious and political routine, and certainly with no notion that they were doing anything out of the way. Their motives, on the whole, were defensible, and in some respects praiseworthy. There was some malice, some weakness, and no doubt some wresting of the law—but no more than we are accustomed to find in the conduct of human affairs. By no jugglings of fate, by no unforeseeable coincidence, by no supernatural machinations, but by that destiny which is character, and by the unimaginative following of their ordinary standards of behaviour, they were led, with a ghastly inevitability, to the commission of the crime of crimes. We, the audience, know what they were doing; the whole point and poignancy of the tragedy is lost unless we realise that they did not. It is in this knowledge by the audience of the appalling truth which is hidden from all the agonists in the drama that the tragic irony consists.

Consequently, it is necessary for the playwright to work with a divided mind. He must be able at will to strip off his knowledge of what is actually taking place, and present, through his characters, the events and people as they appeared to themselves at the time. This would seem obvious and elementary; but its results are in fact the very thing that gives offence to unimaginative piety. We are so much accustomed to viewing the whole story from a post-Resurrection, and indeed from a post-Nicene, point of view, that we are apt, without realising it, to attribute to all the New Testament characters the same kind of detailed theological awareness which we have ourselves. We judge their behaviour as though all of them—disciples, Pharisees, Romans, and men-in-the-street—had known with Whom they were dealing and what the meaning of all the events actually was. But they did not know it. The disciples had only the foggiest inkling of it, and nobody else came anywhere near grasping what it was all about. If the Chief Priests and the Roman Governor had been aware that they were engaged in crucifying God—if Herod the Great had ordered his famous massacre with the express intention of doing away with God—then they would have been quite exceptionally and diabolically wicked people. And indeed, we like to think that they were: it gives us a reassuring sensation that "it can't happen here". And to this comfortable persuasion we are assisted by the stately and ancient language of the Authorised Version, and by the general air of stained-glass-window decorum with which the tale is usually presented to us.[3] The characters are not men and women: they are all "sacred personages", standing about in symbolic attitudes, and self-consciously awaiting the fulfilment of prophecies. That is how they were seen, for example, by a certain gentleman from Stoke Newington, who complained that the Centurion who was commended for building a Jewish synagogue had been made by me to "refer to the sacred building in a conversation, in a levitous (sic) and jocular manner". For him, the Centurion was not a Roman N.C.O., stationed in a foreign province, and looking on the local worship with such amiable indulgence as a British sergeant-major in India might extend to a Hindu cult. He was a sacred Centurion, whose lightest word was sacred, and the little Jewish edifice was sacred to him, as though he had no gods of his own. Still odder is the attitude of another correspondent, who objected to Herod's telling his court, "keep your mouths shut", on the grounds that such coarse expressions were jarring on the lips of any one "so closely connected with our Lord".

Sacred personages, living in a far-off land and time, using dignified rhythms of speech, making from time to time restrained gestures symbolic of brutality. They mocked and railed on Him and smote Him, they scourged and crucified Him. Well, they were people very remote from ourselves, and no doubt it was all done in the noblest and most beautiful manner. We should not like to think otherwise.

Unhappily, if we think about it at all, we must think otherwise. God was executed by people painfully like us, in a society very similar to our own—in the over-ripeness of the most splendid and sophisticated Empire the world has ever seen. In a nation famous for its religious genius and under a government renowned for its efficiency, He was executed by a corrupt church, a timid politician, and a fickle proletariat led by professional agitators. His execu-

---

[3] "In which saintly figures are bound to colour one's view of outward things."—*Times* Cross-word clue to the words STAINED GLASS. *Et ille respondens ait: Tu dicis.*

tioners made vulgar jokes about Him, called Him filthy names, taunted Him, smacked Him in the face, flogged Him with the cat, and hanged Him on the common gibbet—a bloody, dusty, sweaty, and sordid business.

If you show people that, they are shocked. So they should be. If that does not shock them, nothing can. If the mere representation of it has an air of irreverence, what is to be said about the deed? It is curious that people who are filled with horrified indignation whenever a cat kills a sparrow can hear that story of the killing of God told Sunday after Sunday and not experience any shock at all.

Technically, the swiftest way to produce the desirable sense of shock is the use in drama of modern speech and a determined historical realism about the characters. Herod the Great was no monstrous enemy of God: he was a soldier of fortune and a political genius—a savage but capable autocrat, whose jealousy and ungovernable temper had involved him in a prolonged domestic wretchedness. Matthew the Publican was a contemptible little quisling official, fleecing his own countrymen in the service of the occupying power and enriching himself in the process, until something came to change his heart (though not, presumably, his social status or his pronunciation). Pontius Pilate was a provincial governor, with a very proper desire to carry out Imperial justice, but terrified (as better men than he have been before and since) of questions in the House, commissions of inquiry and what may be generically called "Whitehall". Caiaphas was the ecclesiastical politician, appointed, like one of Hitler's bishops, by a heathen government, expressly that he might collaborate with the New Order and see that the Church toed the line drawn by the State; we have seen something of Caiaphas lately. As for the Elders of the Synagogue, they are to be found on every Parish Council—always highly respectable, often quarrelsome, and sometimes in a crucifying mood.

So with all of them. Tear off the disguise of the Jacobean idiom, go back to the homely and vigorous Greek of Mark or John, translate it into its current English counterpart, and there every man may see his own face. We played the parts in that tragedy, nineteen and a half centuries since, and perhaps are playing them to-day, in the same good faith and in the same ironic ignorance. But to-day we cannot see the irony, for we the audience are now the actors and do not know the end of the play. But it may assist us to know what we are doing if the original drama is shown to us again, with ourselves in the original parts.

This process is not, of course, the same thing as "doing the Gospel story in a modern setting". It was at a particular point in history that the Timeless irrupted into time. The technique is to keep the ancient setting, and to give the modern equivalent of the contemporary speech and manners. Thus we may, for example, represent the Sanhedrim as "passing resolutions" and "making entries in the minute-book", for every official assembly since officialdom began has had some machinery for "agreeing together" and recording the result. We may make a Roman officer address his squad with modern military words of command, since some similar verbal technique must always and everywhere have been used to start and turn and stop bodies of soldiery, or to inspect their kit and parade-order. We may make a military policeman or a tax-collector lard his speech with scraps of American slang; for the local speech must have been full of catch-phrases picked up from the foreign soldiers and merchants who swarmed along the great trade-routes of the Empire; and for these bits and pieces of vulgar Latin, bastard Greek, and Syriac dialects the language of Hollywood is the modern equivalent. Nor was the Roman Imperium at all unlike some types of the New Order advocated for the world to-day. But there are limits. Financial trickery, "big business" methods, and the "rake-off" of the middle-man were as familiar then as now; but it would be a mistake to make 1st-century people talk in terms of the Limited Liability Company and the Stock Exchange. The liberal virtues were known and practised, but not the thing we know as "Liberal Humanism"; a Roman was only too well acquainted with the dole and divorce and the Married Women's Property Act, but not with "democratic institutions" as we know them, nor did he share our feelings about slavery. The men of a past epoch spoke and thought about certain things as we do: about others, quite differently. But nothing is gained by making them use obsolete forms of speech as though they seemed old-fashioned to themselves. For to themselves they seemed, and were, "modern"—like us, they had all the latest improvements.

There is one further complication. The rhythm of speech chosen to represent this ancient modernity has to be such that it can, from time to time, lift itself without too much of a jolt into the language of prophecy. For at that date the snobbery of the banal had not yet imposed itself. You might still speak nobly without being sneered at for a highbrow. Fortunately, the English language, with its wide, flexible, and doubletongued vocabulary, lends itself readily to the juxtaposition of the sublime and the commonplace, and can be stepped up and down between the two along an inclined plane which has one end on the flat pavement—

<blockquote>In the south suburbs at the Elephant</blockquote>

and the other among

<blockquote>The cloud-capped towers, the gorgeous palaces.</blockquote>

The smooth execution of this movement is the technician's job.

When, however, we listen to the language of Shakespeare's time, the movement is to a great extent hidden from our ears, because even the commonest words and most pedestrian phrases of that period have acquired a patina of "nobility" through sheer lapse of time; the back-chat of the tavern has become quaint, the coarse abuse sterilised, the jokes antiquarian, the current slang "poetical"; that which was written in fustian is heard in cloth of gold. And even in its own day, the English of the Authorised Version was a little formal and old-fashioned—partly because it is a translation bearing the impress of a foreign speech-rhythm, and also because of the lingering influence of Wycliffe's Bible—though, if one compares the two versions it is easy to see how the language has been brought up to date: King James's scholars did not cultivate archaism for its own sake. Consequently, the 20th-century writer appears to take a longer step in moving from the common man's idiom to the idiom of prophecy. But this is largely due to the effects of perspective: as the landscape recedes into the distant past, the planes are foreshortened and blurred by an atmospheric haze of antiquity in which distinctions are lost. It is this misty, pleasant, picturesque obscurity which people miss when they complain, in the words of one correspondent, that in the modern presentation "the atmosphere created seems so different from that of the original story . . . where it is all so impressively and wonderfully told". So it is. The question is, are we at this time of day sufficiently wondering and impressed? Above all, are we sufficiently disturbed by this extremely disturbing story? Sometimes the blunt new word will impress us more than the beautiful and old. "Except ye eat the flesh of the Son of Man", said Jesus—and then, seeing perhaps that the reaction to this statement was less vigorous than it might have been, He repeated it, but this time using a strong and rather vulgar word, meaning "to eat noisily, like an animal"—chew? munch? crunch? champ? chump? (But in the end, I was pusillanimous, and left it at "eat", not liking to offend the ears of the faithful with what Christ actually said.)

Thus far, then, concerning the language. I should add that no attempt has been made at a niggling antiquarian accuracy in trifles. The general effect aimed at has been rather that of a Renaissance painting, where figures in their modern habits mingle familiarly with others whose dress and behaviour are sufficiently orientalised to give a flavour of the time and place and conform with the requirements of the story. Thus the incidents of the Wedding at Cana and the tale of the Ten Virgins demand some knowledge of Jewish marriage-customs; the Last Supper, of Eastern table-manners and of the Passover ritual; and these have been given with just sufficient accuracy to make the action intelligible. But it is immaterial whether or not Martha and Mary would have had a spit in their kitchen or served sherbet to their guests; and if young listeners suppose that the Wise Bridesmaids filled their lamps with paraffin, or that the vinegar provided for condemned felons was the domestic malted article, what does it matter? the distinction between vegetable and mineral, grapes and barley in no way affects faith or morals. Marching songs have been made to sound like marching songs, not "wrapped in soft Lydian airs" for the benefit of the sticklers for modality; and when it was desired to present the picture of a gentleman mounting a horse in a hurry, he was allowed to cry, "My stirrup, Eleazar!" regardless of the date at which stirrups were introduced into Palestine. The limitations of the microphone have also to be borne in mind. It is doubtless true, as somebody pointed out, that a yoke of oxen would be driven, not with a whip but with a goad; but the lash of a whip can be heard on the air, whereas it is useless to ask the studio-effects-man to stand by making a noise like an ox-goad.

From the linguistic material we may pass to the architectural material. The structure of the Gospel drama is interesting. Up to and including the Crucifixion it has, as I have said, the strict form of classical tragedy, though not of what Aristotle would consider a tragedy of the best type. For it depicts the fall of a good man to undeserved misfortune, and this he reckons only the second worst of the four possible forms. Nor would Aristotle have altogether approved the character of the Protagonist, for "the hero of a tragedy should be a mixed character, neither perfectly good nor perfectly bad." The Hero is, indeed, one of the major difficulties in this particular drama, since perfect goodness is apt to be unsympathetic, and generally speaking permits of little development. But this Hero's goodness was not of the static kind; He was a lively person. He excited people. Wherever He went He brought not peace but a sword, and fire in the earth; that is why they killed Him. He said surprising things, in language ranging from the loftiest poetry to the most lucid narrative and the raciest repartee. (If we did not know all His retorts by heart, if we had not taken the sting out of them by incessant repetition in the accents of the pulpit, and if we had not somehow got it into our heads that brains were rather reprehensible, we should reckon Him among the greatest wits of all time. Nobody else, in three brief years, has achieved such an output of epigram.) And if He had no *hamartia* in the literal sense, there was at any rate that clash between His environment and Himself which is the mainspring of drama. He suffered misfortune because He was what He was and could not be otherwise; and since His time tragedy has become the tragedy of will and character, and not of an external and arbitrary destiny.

Thus far, then, a classical tragedy. But in the fifth act there occurs a *peripeteia*, again of the classical kind, brought about by an *anagnorisis*. The Hero is recognised for what He is: and immediately, what was the blackest human tragedy turns into Divine Comedy.

In the light of this fact, the interesting question arises whether such a thing as a Christian tragedy is possible. It has been said on the one hand that it is of the essence of Christianity to take a deeply tragic view of human nature. So indeed it is. Seen from the earthly end, mankind, haunted from the womb to the grave by a *hamartia* that sets him at odds with himself, with society, and with the very nature of things, is a being whose every action is fraught with tragic significance. His native virtues are but "splendid sins", issuing in ineluctable judgment; his divine graces involve him in a disharmony with his fellow-men that can end only in his crucifixion. Either way he is—like Oedipus, like the House of Atreus—doomed to self-destruction. But, viewed from the other end, his worst sins are redeemable by his worst suffering; his evil is not merely purged—it is in the literal sense made good. The iron necessity that binds him is the working of the Divine will—and lo! the gods are friendly.

Short of damnation, it seems, there can be no Christian tragedy. Indeed, if a man is going to write a tragedy of the classic type, he must be careful to keep Christianity out of it. At least, it will not do to introduce a complete Catholic theology; where Christ is, cheerfulness will keep breaking in. Marlowe the atheist did indeed write a Christian tragedy, and by a just instinct chose the only possible subject for unrelieved Christian gloom: *Dr. Faustus* is a tragedy of damnation. But it is not classical. Faustus is not the victim of fate: he has what he chooses; his hell is bought and paid for. Moreover, it is an individual catastrophe; his damnation is not shown in any relation to the Divine Economy; whereas the sin of Judas played its part in the great Comedy of Redemption, and if he damned himself, it was because he did not choose to wait for the last act.

What Christian tragedies are there? No tragedy of Shakespeare possesses a definite Christian theology, or even a well-defined Christian atmosphere (Shakespeare knew better than to introduce this wrecking element). Corneille's *Polyeucte* is a tragedy only in the sense that his hero is finally killed; but he dies in sure and certain hope of everlasting life—there is no tragic frustration. In T. S. Eliot's *The Family Reunion,* the soul is stripped of its last worldly holding, only to find that the curse of sin is lifted, and that the Furies have become the Eumenides. Something of the same transformation occurs, indeed, in the *Oresteia;* here, it is connected with Zeus the Saviour, "who established Learning by Suffering to be an abiding law", and whose saving wisdom is

the gift of One by strife
Lifted to the throne of life.[4]

In the *Prometheus* also, and in the *Supplices* there is the conception of a God who can reconcile because He understands, and can understand because He has in some way shared the suffering due to sin.[5] It seems that wherever there is a suffering God, there is an end of tragic futility, and a transvaluation of all values. To this conclusion many races of men were guided by that Spirit *qui et semper aderat generi humano* — if it could be thus, they felt, all would yet be well. The disciples of Jesus, plunged into cowardice and despondency by the human tragedy of the Crucifixion, needed only to be convinced by the Resurrection that that which had suffered and died was in actual historical fact the true Being of all things, to recover their courage and spirits in a manner quite unparalleled, and to proclaim the Divine Comedy loudly and cheerfully,

[4] *Agamemnon:* Gilbert Murray's translation.
[5] One must not, of course, push the parallel too far. It is doubtful whether any heathen soteriology knows of a God who can redeem sin by sharing its suffering without also sharing its guilt. Christianity alone ascribes this supreme value to the suffering of the innocent, though it is, of course, to some extent implicit in all sacrificial religions. Christianity places a new interpretation upon those rites which a deeply rooted instinct had felt to be proper and satisfying—an interpretation which is obscured and distorted by the use of terms such as "substitution" and "propitiation" borrowed from the older religions. But, so far as it goes, the parallel is significant.

with the utmost disregard for their own safety. Why and how the suffering of God should have this exhilarating effect upon the human spirit is a question for Atonement theology; that it had this effect on those who believed in it is plain. Under Pontius Pilate, the prophecies of the poets had become furnished with a name, a date, and an address; thenceforward the tragic Muse could survive only by resolutely closing her eyes to this series of events. To those first Apostles, the Resurrection seemed important, not because it held out a promise of "personal survival"—St. Peter's Pentecostal sermon contains nothing about "pie in the sky when you die"; it was important *because it established the identity of the Slain:* "God hath made that same Jesus whom ye crucified both Lord and Christ". Earlier than that, the identification had been made in terms still more emphatic and unequivocal: ὁ κύριός μου καὶ ὁ Θεός μου—"my Lord and my God". All the prophecies were fulfilled. Those who make it a reproach to Christianity that it taught no new morality and invented no new kind of Deity could not be more laughably wide of the mark. What it did was to guarantee that the old morality was actually valid, and the old beliefs literally true. "Ye worship ye know not what, but we know what we worship", "that which we have seen with our eyes and our hands have handled"—"He suffered under Pontius Pilate". God died—not in a legend, not in a symbol, not in a distant past nor in a realm unknown, but here, a few weeks ago—*you saw it happen;* the whole great cloudy castle of natural religion and poetic prophecy is brought down to earth and firmly cemented upon that angular and solid cornerstone.

Which brings us to the records themselves.

They were not compiled by modern historians, nor yet (needless to say) with an eye to the convenience of a radio-dramatist some nineteen centuries later. The Evangelists, particularly the Synoptists, are concerned to write down what Jesus said and did; not to provide "local colour" (which their readers knew all about) or sketches of contemporary personalities. Nor are they as much interested as we should be in a precise chronology—except, of course, as regards Holy Week. *That* was the important date, and there they are substantially agreed about the outline of events. St. Luke also takes a good deal of pains to fix the birth-date. But between these points, as Archbishop Temple has pointed out,[6] only St. John has any real chronology at all. Frequently the material seems to have been arranged according to subject-matter rather than to the logical or chronological succession of events. Thus St. Matthew takes a number of sayings which in St. Luke are distributed over a dozen different contexts, and arranges them in the one long discourse which we know as the "Sermon on the Mount". On the other hand we find in St. Luke the three parables of forgiveness (the Lost Piece of Silver, the Lost Sheep, and the Prodigal Son) grouped together, followed—without any more transition than a brief "and he said also to his disciples"—by the parable of the

[6] *Readings in St. John's Gospel:* Introduction.

Unjust Steward; after which come a set of detached "sayings" on various subjects, then the parable of Dives and Lazarus, and then another string of sayings without any context at all, leading up to the miracle of the Ten Lepers and a passage of prophecy about the end of the world. St. Luke rather likes to put together little bundles of aphorisms, in the manner of those who compile volumes of "Sayings of Dr. Johnston" or "Epigrams of Oscar Wilde". St. Mark tends to present us with successions of miracles joined together by some such vague formula as "and straightway", or "and forthwith", or "and again", or "in those days". St. John is different. He is always anxious to show a logical connection, and very often the chronological order as well.

In presenting this material dramatically, it was necessary always to bear in mind the conditions imposed by the medium. There were to be twelve plays, separated by intervals of four weeks. Some people might be able to listen to all the plays; some would hear only a few here and there. Each play had therefore to fit into its place as a logical unit in the architecture of the series as a whole; every word, line, and episode bearing a proper relation to what had preceded and what was about to follow. Characters and "plot-structure" must be consistent throughout—otherwise, not only the audience but the actors would be confused and disconcerted. But also, each separate instalment had to stand on its own feet as a play-in-itself, with some kind of structural unity and a proper beginning, middle, and end to its action; otherwise, we should have no *plays* at all, but only lengths arbitrarily cut from an interminable Scripture lesson. All this involved the taking of some liberties with the Gospel text—the omission of some incidents, the insertion and expansion of others, the provision of backgrounds and what are technically called "bridges" to link the episodes, and occasional transpositions. For most of these activities there was ample precedent in the Gospels themselves: Matthew and Luke are the great "transposers"; John, the provider of glosses, backgrounds, and bridges.

The Nativity story stands, of course, by itself as ready-made dramatic material with a shape of its own; and the five Passion-plays, from the Entry into Jerusalem, also fell conveniently into self-contained episodes, needing only to have the various narratives conflated into a coherent story. The period of the Ministry naturally presented the greatest difficulty, partly because the matter itself was not so clearly arranged, and partly because it is always difficult to make the *middle* of any story self-contained for the reader or listener who comes to it as to a detached item of entertainment.

First, as regards the linking of all the episodes to the main story. This involved two threads of development. Apart from the general theological argument, there was a theme-structure, chosen as being that aspect of the story which was bound to loom large in the minds of both writer and audience at this moment, namely: its bearing upon the nature of earthly and spiritual kingdoms. This question, which supplied the title for the series and dictated the emphasis and line of approach throughout, was just as acute for the men of the first century as it is for us; under the pressure of the Roman

Imperium, their minds were exercised as ours are by problems about the derivation of authority, the conflict between centralised and decentralised government, the sanctions behind power-politics, and the place of national independence within a world-civilisation. No force of any kind was needed to bring the story into a form that was sharply topical.

Theme-structure by itself will not, however, make a play. There must also be a plot-structure, and this was provided by bringing out certain implications in the story and centring them about the character of Judas. The unexplained incident of the ass and the pass-word will be found more fully dealt with in the Notes to Play VIII. As it stands in the text, it is unlike anything else in the Gospels, and appears to need something more to account for it than the deliberate, and rather theatrical, "staging" by Jesus of a fulfilment of prophecy. It is very possible that the disciples themselves never knew how the ass came to be there. I have suggested a reason, using for this purpose the character of Baruch the Zealot—the only main character of any importance who is of my own invention. His connection with Judas supplies the main-spring of the plot-machinery.

Judas in the Gospels is an enigma. He is introduced suddenly, at a late moment in the action, "all set" for villainy. We are not told how he came to be a disciple, nor what motives drove him to betray his Master. St. John says he was a thief; he certainly took payment for his treason; Jesus called him *"diabolos"*—the enemy—and "the son of perdition"; when he had done his worst and saw what he had done, he brought back the reward of iniquity and went out and hanged himself. He seems a strange mixture of the sensitive and the insensitive. One thing is certain: he cannot have been the creeping, crawling, patently worthless villain that some simple-minded people would like to make out; that would be to cast too grave a slur upon the brains or the character of Jesus. To choose an obvious crook as one's follower, in ignorance of what he was like, would be the act of a fool; and Jesus of Nazareth was no fool, and indeed St. John expressly says that "He knew what was in" Judas from the beginning. But to choose an obvious crook for the express purpose of letting him damn himself would be the act of a devil; for a man, *a fortiori* for a God, who behaved like that, nobody—except perhaps Machiavelli—could feel any kind of respect. But also (and this is far more important for our purpose), either of these sorts of behaviour would be totally irreconcilable with the rest of the character of Jesus as recorded. You might write an anti-Christian tract making Him out to be weak-minded and stupid; you might even write a theological treatise of the pre-destinarian sort making Him out to be beyond morality; but there is no means whatever by which you could combine either of these theories with the rest of His words and deeds *and make a play of them.* The glaring inconsistencies in the character would wreck the show; no honest dramatist could write such a part; no actor could play it; no intelligent audience could accept it. That is what I mean by saying that dramatic handling is a stern test of theology, and that the dramatist must tackle the material from his own end of the job. No; the obviously villainous Judas will not do, either dramatically or theologically—the most damnable of all sins is a subtler thing than any crude ambition or avarice. The worst evil in the world is brought about, not by the open and self-confessed vices, but by the deadly corruption of the proud virtues. Pride, which cast Lucifer the Archangel out of Heaven and Adam out of the Eden of primal innocence, is the head and front of all sin, and the besetting sin of highly virtuous and intelligent people. Jesus, who dealt gently with "publicans and sinners", was hard as nails about the lofty-minded sins; He was a consistent person, and if He spoke of Judas with almost unexampled sternness, it is likely that the sin of Judas was of a peculiarly over-weening loftiness. What his familiar devil precisely was, we are at liberty to conjecture; I have conjectured that it was an intellectual devil of a very insidious kind, very active in these days and remarkably skilful in disguising itself as an angel of light. The fact that various persons have written angrily to say that the Judas I have depicted seems to them to be a person of the utmost nobility, actuated by extremely worthy motives, confirms my impression that this particular agent of hell is at present doing his master's work with singular thoroughness and success. His exploits go unrecognized—which is just what the devil likes best.

The continuity of the plot-structure was thus secured by linking it all on to the Judas-Baruch political intrigue, and by "planting" Judas at the very outset of the Ministry as a disciple of John the Baptist. Equally important, both for theme and plot, was the Roman element in the story. It was essential that the enormous fact of the Imperium should be present at every moment to the audience as it was to the persons of the time: the persistent pressure, the perpetual menace, the power and prestige of Caesar. Accordingly, another "tie-rod" was run through the series in the person of Proclus, the Roman Centurion. All that was required here was the identification of the Centurion whose servant was healed with the "Believing Centurion" at the Crucifixion—a thing not unreasonable in itself, and making the final expression of belief much more dramatically convincing. Once that had been done, it was easy to introduce the young Proclus among the Roman bodyguard which was, in historical fact, assigned to Herod the Great, and so tie together the first scene of the tragedy and the last, by bringing Proclus and Balthazar together again at the foot of the Cross as they were at the Epiphany. The Roman connection was further strengthened by "planting" Pilate's Wife at a comparatively early point in the story, by making her see Jesus at the Feast of Tabernacles; and by causing the processions of Pilate and Jesus to meet at the gates of Jerusalem on Palm Sunday; thus leading up to the Jewish-Roman clash at the Trial and providing the machinery for the little scene which ties up the Pilate family with the Resurrection story.

A few other "identifications" supply the "tie-rods" for individual plays and episodes, the most important being that of Mary Magdalen with Mary of Bethany and with the unnamed "Woman who was a Sinner" of Luke VII.

This identification is, of course, traditional, and is sanctioned by the authority of St. Augustine of Hippo and Pope Gregory the Great. The two episodes making up Play III, *A Certain Nobleman*, were linked by making the Nobleman in question a guest at the Marriage in Cana. Similarly, the Bishop of Ripon's engaging identification of Mary of Cleophas with the second "disciple" in the Emmaus story locked up that incident with the tale of Calvary. The number of persons who flit, unheralded and unpursued, through the pages of the Gospel is enormous; and every legitimate opportunity was taken of tightening up the dramatic construction and avoiding the unnecessary multiplication of characters.

As regards the parables and the sayings, it was needful to distribute these as evenly as possible over the plays dealing with the Ministry and to provide a suitable context for each. This would not necessarily be always the original context. There is, however, no reason to suppose that each story was told on one occasion only. On the contrary, it seems most likely that they were repeated over and over again—sometimes in identical words, sometimes with variations. (Thus the parables of the Great Supper and the Marriage of the King's Son have every appearance of being the same story, varied to suit the occasion; the parables of the Talents and the Pounds offer a similar "doublet", as do the similes of the Improvident Builder and the Improvident King.) We need not imagine that the appearance of the same story in different contexts argues any inaccuracy or contradiction, or that the version of one Evangelist is more authentic than that of another. The teacher who thought of such a story as that of the Good Samaritan or the Prodigal Son would be foolish indeed to confine it to a single audience. He would repeat it over and over, till his disciples knew it by heart in all its variations.[7] So also with the "sayings". Indeed, the lapidary form in which these teachings have come down to us suggests powerfully that here we have "set pieces" of teaching with which the transmitters of the oral tradition were verbally and intimately familiar.

With the discourses and public disputations, the case is different. Most of these, such as the great passage about the Bread of Heaven, the dispute at the Feast of Tabernacles, and the long discourse and prayer after the Last Supper, we owe to St. John, and their style is so unlike that of the parables and sayings that some people have found it hard to believe that they were spoken by the

---

[7] Compare the methods of another Oriental teacher, the Sadhu Sundar Singh: "The Sadhu's mind is an overflowing reservoir of anecdote, illustration, epigram, and parable, but he never makes the slightest effort to avoid repetition; in fact he appears to delight in it. 'We do not,' he says, 'refuse to give bread to hungry people because we have already given bread to others.' Hence we have constantly found the same material occurring in more than one of the written or printed authorities we have used. 'My mouth,' he says, 'has no copyright'; and many sayings that we had noted down from his own lips we afterwards discovered to be already in print. In most cases the versions differ extraordinarily little, but we have always felt free to correct or supplement one version by another at our own discretion." Streeter and Appasamy: *The Sadhu*.

same person, and that St. John did not invent them out of his own meditations. But the difficulty is more apparent than real. It must be remembered that, of the four Evangels, St. John's is the only one that claims to be the direct report of an eye-witness. And to any one accustomed to the imaginative handling of documents, the internal evidence bears out this claim. The Synoptists, on the whole, report the "set pieces"; it is St. John who reports the words and actions of the individual, unrepeated occasion, retrieving them from that storehouse of trained memory which, among people not made forgetful by too much pen and ink, replaces the filed records and the stenographer's note-book. It is, generally speaking, John who knows the time of year, the time of day, where people sat, and how they got from one place to another. It is John who remembers, not only what Jesus said, but what the other people said to Him, who can reproduce the cut-and-thrust of controversy, and the development of an argument. It is John who faithfully reproduces the emphasis and repetition of a teacher trying to get a new idea across to a rather unintelligent and inattentive audience. It is he again who has caught the characteristic tricks of manner and delivery — the curious outflanking movement of the dialectic, capturing outpost after outpost by apparently irrelevant questions, and then suddenly pouncing upon the main position from the rear, and the ἀμὴν ἀμὴν λέγω ὑμιν ("indeed and indeed I tell you") which ushers in the most important statements.[8]

Indeed, when John is the authority for any scene, or when John's account is at hand to supplement those of the Synoptists, the playwright's task is easy. Either the dialogue is all there — vivid and personal on both sides — or the part of the interlocutor can be readily reconstructed from the replies given. And it is frequently John who supplies the reason and meaning of actions and speeches that in the Synoptists appear unexplained and disconnected. Thus, after the Feeding of the Five Thousand, there seems to be no very good reason why Jesus should have withdrawn Himself and sent the disciples across the lake by themselves; but John supplies the missing motive, and also the answer to one or two other practical questions, e.g. how the disciples were able to see Jesus coming across the water (it was near Passover, therefore the moon was full), and how some of "the multitudes" turned up next day at Capernaum (they followed as soon as the boats had put across from Tiberias to fetch them). It is John who gives us that dramatic moment when Pilate, suddenly deciding not to ratify the sentence of the Sanhedrim without enquiry, disconcerts the priestly party with the formal invitation to state their case ("What accusation bring ye against this man?"), thus leading up to the question, "Art thou the King of the Jews?" which, in the Synoptists, is launched without preliminary and without any explanation of how so fantastic an idea could

[8] The same trick of speech, but reduced to a single "amen", is found in all the Synoptists; John certainly did not invent it, though his version is more picturesque and individual. We also have the rather unexpected appearance in Matt. XI. 27 of a sentence so exactly in John's style that it might have come direct from one of the Johannine discourses.

ever have entered Pilate's head.[9] It is John who knows that, at the Last Supper, he and Judas were seated so close to Jesus as to permit of whispered conversation and the handing of the sop; John also, and John only, who knows about the interrogation before Annas, thus clearing up the where and how of Peter's denial, and explaining how it was that the Lord could "turn and look upon Peter" as He was led through the courtyard of the High Priest's house to His trial before the Sanhedrim.[10]

All through, in fact, the Gospel of St. John reads like the narrative of an eye-witness filling up the gaps in matter already published, correcting occasional errors, and adding material which previous writers either had not remembered or did not know about. Usually, he passes briefly over events that were already adequately dealt with and stories which everybody knew by heart; sometimes he omits them altogether: the Birth-story, for example, the Temptation, the Parables, and the words of the Eucharistic Institution. There is no reason to suppose that a thing is unauthentic because he does not mention it, or, on the other hand, because nobody else mentions it. In modern memoirs written by real people about another real person we should expect just that sort of diversity which we find in the Gospels. If it surprises us there, it is perhaps because we have fallen out of the habit of looking on Jesus and His disciples as *really* real people.

The playwright, in any case, is not concerned, like the textual critic, to establish one version of a story as the older, purer, or sole authoritative version. He does not want to select and reject, but to harmonise. Where two versions are really incompatible (as in St. Mark's and St. John's dates for the Cleansing of the Temple)[11] he must, of course, choose one or the other. But

---

[9] For a more detailed discussion of this point, see Frank Morison: *Who Moved the Stone?*

[10] Mark and Matthew place Peter's denial during and after the trial before *Caiaphas* (in the Sanhedrim). Then they both start off again to mention a fresh "consultation," at the end of which Jesus is condemned, bound, and taken away. That is, they both seem to know that there were in fact two enquiries, though they do not say why. John straightens out this confusion and gets the events into their right order, besides explaining the simultaneous existence in Jerusalem of two "High Priests"—Annas (High Priest "Emeritus," appointed by the Jews in the ordinary way and deposed by Rome), and Caiaphas (the "collaborating" ecclesiastic set up by Rome in his place). His narrative is perfectly lucid, though it may not seem so at first sight, owing to his confusing habit of communicating vital information in a parenthesis (John XVIII. 44—cf. the style of John VI. 22–23, XI. 2 and XVIII. 13–14).

[11] "St. John is right about it," says Archbishop Temple (*Readings in St. John's Gospel*, Vol. I, p. 42). He gives sufficient reasons why St. Mark should have omitted the story of the Raising of Lazarus, and substituted the 'Temple' incident as "the occasion for the intervention of the High Priests and the Sadduccees" (*ibid.*, p. 175). And he points out, rightly, that though Mark has a consistent *scheme*, he has no consistent chronology, and that (except for the narratives of the Passion) "we do not have to choose between two incompatible chronologies, for the Johannine chronology is the only one that we have" (*ibid.*, I, xi). I have followed St. John for an additional—for a playwright's—reason, which is that, somehow or other, the "feel" of the episode is right for the beginning of the Ministry and wrong for the end of it. I can only express this in the crudest and most humanistic way by saying that between the Jesus who casts out the money-changers and the Jesus who laments over Jerusalem some kind of development is felt to have taken place: He is recognisably an older man.

what he really likes is to take three or four accounts of the same incident, differing in detail, and to dovetail all these details so that the combined narrative presents a more convincing and dramatic picture than any of the accounts taken separately. And in doing this, he is often surprised to find how many apparent contradictions turn out not to be contradictory at all, but merely supplementary. Take, for example, the various accounts of the Resurrection appearances at the Sepulchre. The divergences appear very great on first sight; and much ink and acrimony have been expended on proving that certain of the stories are not "original" or "authentic", but are accretions grafted upon the firsthand reports by the pious imagination of Christians. Well, it may be so. But the fact remains that *all* of them, without exception, can be made to fall into a place in a single orderly and coherent narrative without the smallest contradiction or difficulty, and without any suppression, invention, or manipulation, beyond a trifling effort to *imagine* the natural behaviour of a bunch of startled people running about in the dawnlight between Jerusalem and the Garden.

For the purpose of these plays, then, I have treated all four Evangelists as equally "witnesses of truth", combining wherever I could, preserving as much as I might, and, where a choice was necessary, making dramatic propriety the criterion rather than the textual prestige of Codex Aleph or Bezae or the austerity of the hypothetical Q. Nor have I hesitated to conform to a beloved tradition if it added picturesque variety and did no harm: my Magi remain three and remain kings; they keep their fairytale names, and Balthazar is black but comely, as all good children know he should be. The haunted legend of the cry that went over the sea at Christ's death lent itself readily to the imagery of Pilate's Wife's Dream. All the Stations of the Cross are there, except the Third Fall, which would have involved more repetition than the dramatic form could well carry.[12] Apart from a few such traditions, hallowed by Christian piety and custom, the only sources used have been the Canonical Scriptures, together with a few details from Josephus and other historians to build up the general background.

I did not embark on the reading of a great mass of exegetical literature, fearing that a multitude of counsellors might only bring confusion of mind. I must, however, acknowledge my debt to Archbishop Temple's *Readings in St. John's Gospel* and Sir Edward Hoskyns' *The Fourth Gospel,* as also to R. A. Edwards' *The Upper Room,* from which I have unscrupulously lifted several happy turns of translation. And for the whole handling of the Trial Scenes I have to thank Frank Morison's *Who Moved the Stone?* — an inspired little work which clears up as though by magic everything which may appear puzzling in that curiously legal piece of illegality. Ronald Gurner's *We Crucify!* was helpful, too, in its imaginative treatment of the whole situation from the point of view of the

---

[12] St. Veronica, however, has been deprived of her miracle, which (all other considerations apart) would have struck a note out of key with the rest of the dramatic handling, besides distracting attention from the central action and the central character.

Sanhedrim. In addition, of course, there remain many fragments of interpretation and exegesis left in the memory from desultory reading and half-forgotten sermons, which defy all attempts at identification or acknowledgment.

It seems to me, as it will doubtless seem to many readers, that I set out upon this adventure with a very slender equipment, both natural and acquired.

> There comes a galley laden
> Unto the highest board,
> She bears a noble burden,
> The Father's eterne Word.
>
> She saileth on in silence
> Her freight of value vast,
> With charity for mainsail,
> The Holy Ghost for mast—

What are a detective-novelist and a crew of "West-End" actors doing in *that* galley? And what right have they to suppose that they can be trusted to bring such a ship as that to port? Let us be frank about this.

To make an *adequate* dramatic presentation of the life of God Incarnate would require literally superhuman genius, in playwright and actors alike. We are none of us, I think, under any illusions about our ability to do what the greatest artists who ever lived would admit to be beyond their powers. Nevertheless, when a story is great enough, any honest craftsman may succeed in producing something not altogether unworthy, because the greatness is in the story, and does not need to borrow anything from the craftsman; it is enough that he should faithfully serve the work.

But the craftsman must be honest, and must know what work he is serving. I am a writer and I know my trade; and I say that this story is a very great story indeed, and deserves to be taken seriously. I say further (and here I know what I am saying and mean exactly what I say) that in these days it is seldom taken seriously. It is often taken, and treated, with a gingerly solemnity: but that is what honest writers call frivolous treatment.

Not Herod, not Caiaphas, not Pilate, not Judas ever contrived to fasten upon Jesus Christ the reproach of insipidity; that final indignity was left for pious hands to inflict. To make of His story something that could neither startle, nor shock, nor terrify, nor excite, nor inspire a living soul is to crucify the Son of God afresh and put Him to an open shame. And if anybody imagines that its conventional presentation has of late been all that it should be, let him stop the next stranger in the street and ask what effect it has had on *him.* Or let him look at the world to which this Gospel has been preached for close on twenty centuries: *Si calvarium, si sepulchrum requiris, circumspice.* Let me tell you, good Christian people, an honest writer would be ashamed to treat a nursery tale as you have treated the greatest drama in history: and this in virtue, not of his faith, but of his calling.

You have forgotten, perhaps, that it is, first and foremost, a story—a true story, the turning-point of history, "the only thing that has ever really happened". If so, the humblest in our kind may venture to put you in mind of it—we the playwright and the players—because it is our craft to tell stories, and that is the only craft we know. We have done what we could; may the Master Craftsman amend all.

The text of the plays is given here exactly as it was broadcast, except that I have amended a verbal slip or two, and restored some passages which were omitted for lack of time, together with a few words that were censored for no better reason than that they were not of British origin.

The "Notes" prefixed to each play are those which I wrote at the time and handed in to the producer with the scripts. They are reprinted here—unedited—chiefly as a matter of technical interest to playwrights who have to cope with the peculiar problems of writing dramas for radio.

The Signature-tune used throughout the cycle was taken from Ravel's *Introduction and Allegro for Harp and Strings* (Record H.M.V. No. C. 1662).

The Hymns in Plays 5 and 9 were set to traditional airs.

The Soldiers' Song in Play 10 and Mary Magdalen's Song in Play 11 were composed by Benjamin Britten.

Finally, therefore, *Deo gratias.* And perhaps I may add for all of us the naive ejaculation of the mediaeval scribe who wrote at the conclusion of a somewhat lengthy and exacting piece of work:

> *Finis, finis, finis,*
> *Ludendo dicit!*

DOROTHY L. SAYERS.

KINGS IN JUDAEA

CHARACTERS

The EVANGELIST.
HEROD THE GREAT, King of Jewry.
ELPIS, Queen to Herod.
EPHRAIM, a Gentleman of Herod's Bedchamber.
PROCLUS, a Roman Officer in Herod's Bodyguard.
A SLAVE-BOY, Page in Herod's Household.
The COURT PHYSICIAN.
The HIGH PRIEST.
ZORASTES, the Chief Astrologer.
A SECRETARY.
DARIUS, a Captain in Herod's Army.
MATTHIAS, a fanatical Rabbi.
CASPAR, an aged Chaldaean ⎫ The Three
MELCHIOR, a Greek Warrior ⎬ Wise
BALTHAZAR, a young Ethiopian ⎭ Kings.
MARY, Mother of Jesus.
JOSEPH, Husband to Mary.
A SHEPHERD.
SHEPHERD'S WIFE
ZILLAH, their Daughter, a Child of Nine.
A MESSENGER.
An ANGEL.
LORDS, LADIES, SLAVES, ATTENDANTS, AND CROWD.

NOTES

EPHRAIM—He is, I imagine, about 60, and has spent the last forty-five years of his life in the whole-time occupation of trying to keep his head on his shoulders, in a court where yesterday's favourite is apt to be butchered overnight without warning, and where everybody is engaged in plotting against everybody else. He has a peevish, bleating voice like an agitated goat, and a little thin beard, and an expression of permanent anxiety. The experience of a lifetime has failed to teach him that the best way to handle Herod is to stand up to him.

PROCLUS is only 28; but a hard life and a habit of discipline make him seem more mature. He is a Roman, who has taken service in Judaea as a captain of Herod's personal bodyguard. (Later, under Archelaus, he will become part of the Roman military machine, and we shall meet him again.) In his feelings he is Roman through and through, with the contempt of the European for the Oriental, and of the metropolitan for the provincial. He is not in the least afraid of Herod, and therefore gets on with him very well.

THE SLAVE BOY, who is about 13, is the usual pampered nuisance of an Oriental court. He is probably some kind of Greek or Levantine—pretty, pert, and thoroughly spoilt.

THE MAGI—Following tradition (though not the Bible) the Magi are represented as kings, symbolising the three races of mankind, the children of Shem, Ham, and Japhet (Asia, Africa, Europe).

CASPAR (the Asiatic) is an old man, learned, mild, and dignified, and a little withdrawn and aloof. His wisdom is the wisdom of the intellect.

MELCHIOR (the European) is a man in the prime of life. His interest is chiefly in practical matters; if he consults the stars, it is to learn how to guide his actions. His wisdom is the wisdom of the bodily senses.

BALTHAZAR (the African) is a young man. He has the temperament of the mystic, and his interest is in the relationship of man to men and of men to God. His wisdom is the wisdom of the heart.

The parts of the KINGS are stylised so as to bring out this three-fold structure, and the acting should be patterned accordingly. The "Kingdom" they come to announce is a kingdom not of this earth, and I have tried to indicate this by giving them a kind of fairytale atmosphere (in their dreams, etc.), to contrast with the very practical and earthly quality of Herod's kingship.

HEROD is the most elaborate character in this little play and it is important that we should get the right idea about him. We must forget the traditional picture of a semi-lunatic monster, "out-heroding Herod" and "raging on the pageant and in the street." This man was not called "Herod the Great" for nothing. He is 70 years old, and already dying of an agonising disease, but he is the wreck of a very great man. Everything he says about himself is

35

true. He *did* keep Judaea at peace for thirty years after it had been torn to pieces by religious factions, and he *did* leave it prosperous; he was betrayed by every one he loved, and his nephews *did* try to poison him. He was a brilliant soldier and politician, and, as far as the country was concerned, no more cruel and unenlightened than other Eastern princes of his time. But his private life was one long horror of jealousy, suspicion, and bloodshed. He never got over the death of Mariamne, whom he had loved passionately, and had executed in a frenzy of personal jealousy (unfounded) and of political suspicion (perfectly well founded). Nor could he ever get over the knowledge that the strict Jews despised him for being an Edomite (a descendant of Esau) and not a true Israelite of the House of Jacob. He sat lightly to the Jewish religion, allowing pagan temples in his outlying provinces; though he built the great Temple of Jerusalem and enriched it magnificently. The Roman Eagle which he put up there infuriated the Pharisees, because it suggested that the Jewish religion was subordinate to the Roman State. Stories are told of Herod's personal courage and of his sense of humour. He was crafty, false, and suspicious, and had a vile temper; but he was a genius in his way. Caesar knew that Herod was the one man who could be trusted to keep Judaea in order; and Herod knew that if order was not kept, Judaea would be deprived of her last vestiges of independence. On the death of Herod this did in fact happen, and Judaea was put under the direct control of a Roman governor. Herod was, in fact, very much in the position of an Indian Maharajah, exercising sovereignty within the British Raj—(like many of them, he introduced a good deal of European culture into his province, and sent his grandsons to college in Rome, as they send theirs to Oxford). Thus his being "troubled" by the threat of a Jewish Messiah, and steps he took to suppress the menace were, from the political point of view, perfectly well justified.

ELPIS—She is Herod's eighth wife—a young woman married to an old man—and exercising the functions of a professional soother.

ZORASTES—There was no room to give this poor soothsayer any characteristics beyond a terrified anxiety not to give offence, and a general disposition to hand the baby to someone else.

HIGH PRIEST—He is Herod's puppet and, like the Vicar of Bray, is determined to keep his job whatever happens. (He did not succeed, for Herod sacked him over the affair of the Golden Eagle.) His office gives him a little more dignity than Ephraim or Zorastes, and he says his bit without stammering.

DOCTOR—His concern for his own neck is tempered by the authority that any physician has over his patient. I intend him to be quite honest, and not to have taken any part in poisoning Herod. (He only has two lines—but these are to be spoken firmly.)

SHEPHERD'S WIFE—Presents no difficulty—a nice, kind, bustling, motherly person. Country accent.

ZILLAH—About 9 years old. An ordinary nice child, intelligent and helpful in the house. She takes the Christ-child quite simply and naturally, as just the new baby.

JOSEPH—About 50—an artisan of a good class; a little sententious and given to quoting the Scriptures—he is the kind of man who reads his Bible regularly. He has a slight provincial accent, but less marked than that of the SHEPHERD'S WIFE.

MARY—She must be played with dignity and sincerity, and with perfect simplicity. Her voice is sweet, but not sugary; and there must be no trace of any kind of affectation. A very slight touch of accent—perhaps a faint shadow of Irish quality—would be of assistance in keeping her in her "station of life"; but if so, Joseph's accent must be in keeping (and later on, we must not get the anomaly of a Jesus speaking in a different accent from His mother).

ANGEL—A *male* angel, please!—the voice stylised to give dream-effect (avoiding the dismal wail considered appropriate to stage-ghosts in *Richard III*)—a quality vaguely suggestive of woodwind.

NOTE: *Crowd-effects and Matthias's Speech in Scene III*

I have suggested some things for the crowd to shout, because it is generally better to do this than leave it to the taste and fancy of the actors. But I leave it entirely to the Producer to decide how much of all this to put in, or how much of Matthias's speech to make audible. The speech is there, partly, of course, to explain why the Eagle gave such offence, but chiefly as an excuse for damping down the crowd-noises so that HEROD'S remarks can be heard.

The crash of stones on a marble floor will be a nuisance, I'm afraid. It is extremely inconsiderate of the 1st century not to have provided glazed windows for the purpose of being broken by missiles; I have done my best by offering Etruscan vases and a brass lamp as sacrificial victims.

Chronology

It will be seen that I have used the conventional "Twelve Days of Christmas" chronology. Actually, of course, the visit of the Magi, with the subsequent Flight into Egypt and Massacre of the Innocents, cannot have followed so quickly upon the Nativity. But since considerations of time and space did not permit me to include the Presentation among the episodes of this Cycle, the shorter time-scheme made for swifter action and better dramatic compression.

Note on Accent and Dialect

This whole question presented great difficulties. For complete realism, all the Galilean characters, *including Jesus,* ought to speak with a strong local dialect, and the Jerusalem contingent with another, while the Romans would have to be distinguished according to whether they were speaking Latin to one another or struggling to express themselves to the local inhabitants in bad Aramaic (or possibly in colloquial Greek).

It was felt that to land ourselves with a Jesus and Disciples consistently speaking broad Scots, Welsh, Irish, Yorkshire, Somerset, or Mummerzet would be trying to the listener, make difficulties in the casting, and possibly arouse a certain resentment among local patriots whose particular form of speech had not been chosen.

We decided that Jesus and His Mother should speak Standard English, but that the "multitudes" should be allowed to "speak rough", though without any attempt at discriminating between the dialects in various parts of Palestine. The question then arose: should the Disciples also speak Standard English (in which case they might, by contrast with the Crowd, sound rather like a Universities' Mission to the East End); or should Jesus have a monopoly of refined speech, at the risk of appearing among His Disciples and the Crowd like a B.B.C. Announcer lecturing to the W.E.A.? The expedient adopted was to "step up" the Disciples a little from the "multitudes", and also to step them up among themselves—John and Judas, for example, speaking Standard English, Peter being kept rougher (in preparation for his recognition as a Galilean peasant by the High Priest's people), and Matthew being given a Cockney twang to distinguish the "townee" petty official from the country fishermen. The Romans also were left with only their "class" distinctions of speech, since the perpetual use of a foreign accent might have proved irritating to the listener and hampering to the actor.

SCENE I (JERUSALEM)

THE EVANGELIST: The beginning of the Gospel of Jesus Christ, the Son of God. . . . Now, when Jesus was born in Bethlehem of Judaea in the days of Herod the King, behold there came wise men from the east to Jerusalem. . . .

(The rattle of dice and the sound of a lute)

EPHRAIM: Four, six, two. . . . Oh, stop strumming, you idle monkey! . . . Your throw, Captain.

PROCLUS *(throwing dice)*: Five, three, six.

EPHRAIM: You win, Proclus. . . . What was all that noise in the street last night? Right under the palace windows—disgraceful!

PROCLUS: A bunch of fools who'd got hold of some rumour or other. *(Throws dice)* Aha! Three sixes. Beat that if you can, my Lord Ephraim.

EPHRAIM: You have all the luck. . . . Rumour? What about?

PROCLUS: Oh, nothing. Just an excuse for rioting.

BOY: They're saying in the market-place that Judaea is to have a new king.

PROCLUS: Eh? Now then, my lad, none of that.

EPHRAIM: You've no business to repeat such a thing. It's treason.

BOY: 'Twasn't me. Those strangers who arrived yesterday told the door-keeper that—

PROCLUS: You heard what I said.

BOY *(pertly)*: You needn't shout. I've got ears.

EPHRAIM: So's a donkey. Long ones, with fur on them. They get that way with listening to gossip.

BOY: Well, have it your own way. But all Jerusalem's talking about it. *(He strums again.)*

PROCLUS: That's quite enough. You hop it, my lad, and take that confounded musical-box of yours with you.

EPHRAIM: Stay in the ante-chamber, and when the strangers present themselves, show them in.

BOY: Oh, all right.

EPHRAIM: And if I catch you talking treason again, I'll have you whipped. There's no king here but King Herod. You understand?

BOY: God save King Herod!

PROCLUS: And no emperor but Augustus Caesar. Get that?

BOY: Hail Caesar!

PROCLUS: That's right. Now clear out.

EPHRAIM: And shut the door after you.

(Exit BOY, slamming door)

Jackanapes! . . . *(confidentially)* I say, Captain Proclus, I don't like this at all. The King's a very sick man, and when he dies there's going to be trouble about the succession. I'm more or less backing Prince Archelaus. You're a Roman. What do you think? Will the Emperor support his claim?

PROCLUS: No idea. Soldiers have no politics.

EPHRAIM: One must look after one's own interests, you know. I hope to goodness there won't be a civil war.

PROCLUS: Not if Caesar knows it, there won't.

EPHRAIM: Herod's been a strong ruler in his time; but between you and me, he can't last out the year.

PROCLUS: That's bad.

EPHRAIM: These things leak out and cause a lot of unrest. Some firebrand might get up and start a movement for Jewish independence.

PROCLUS: They'd better not try.

EPHRAIM: You know that seven thousand Pharisees have refused to swear allegiance to Caesar, and have got the King's brother on their side—and they say there's a big conspiracy afoot and that (in a hoarse whisper) Prince Antipater is heavily implicated.

PROCLUS: Antipater? King Herod's favourite son?

EPHRAIM: S'sh! We're sitting on the edge of a volcano. These rumours are a bad sign. Jerusalem's full of riff-raff come up to register under the new census; the least thing might set a match to the fire. Only last week there was a story going round about angels appearing at Bethlehem, and proclaiming a new Messiah.

PROCLUS: It was only some country bumpkins. Potty, as like as not. Who are these strangers the boy was chattering about? Anybody that matters?

EPHRAIM: Heaven knows. Foreign princelings of some kind, with outlandish names. One of them's a Nubian, I think—at any rate, he's as black as a coal. They say they are astrologers, and have brought the King a complimentary message from the stars.

PROCLUS: Then he may see them: Herod has a weakness for fortunetellers.

EPHRAIM: He says he *will* see them. As a matter of fact, they're about due now. I only wish somebody would tell *my* fortune. But these magicians are so unreliable.

BOY (off): This way, my lords. Follow me, my lords. (He throws open the door and announces shrilly) King Caspar, King Melchior, and King Balthazar, desiring audience of King Herod.

EPHRAIM: Good day, my lords. Pray be seated. Boy, go and inform His Majesty that these lords have arrived. . . . I trust, sirs, that the King will be able to receive you; but you know that he is an old man, and has been ill for many weeks.

CASPAR: We are very sorry to hear it.

EPHRAIM: You *will* be careful not to say anything that may vex him.

MELCHIOR: He will be glad of our embassy. We are the messengers of great good fortune.

BALTHAZAR: To him and to his son, the heir of Judaea, the great and mighty king that is to be.

PROCLUS: That's very interesting. Which son?

EPHRAIM: Captain Proclus! Please, not so loud.... You see, gentlemen, the political situation is a little complicated. If you are fortune-tellers, perhaps you could give me a hint—

CASPAR: We are not fortune-tellers.

VOICES (off): Make way for King Herod!

EPHRAIM: Only a hint—

PROCLUS: Be quiet, you fool; he's coming.

EPHRAIM: One must look after one's interests—

VOICE (at door): King Herod!

PROCLUS (in stentorian tones): King Herod!

(Enter KING HEROD THE GREAT, with QUEEN ELPIS, the HIGH PRIEST, the COURT PHYSICIAN, the CHIEF ASTROLOGER, LORDS, LADIES, and ATTENDANTS)

ALL: God Save King Herod!

HEROD (in a voice ragged with pain and exhaustion): Set me down carefully. If you shake me, your bones will pay for it.

EPHRAIM: Here, slaves, here.... Will it please your Majesty to lie on this couch?

HEROD: In my chair—in my chair of state. Fool and traitor, what would you make of me? I am King Herod still.

EPHRAIM: And for many a long year, please God.

HEROD: You are a hypocrite. You think and hope I am dying. You are in league with my traitor sons, who would snatch at my sceptre before my carcase is cold. Don't deny it. I have seen you, licking the hand of Archelaus, fawning at the heels of Antipater—plotting, plotting—nothing but plots and treachery. (His voice dies away into a groan)

EPHRAIM: Alas! Why should your Majesty think so? We are all your most devoted, loving, faithful subjects.

HEROD: So every traitor says. You had best be careful, my lord Ephraim.

EPHRAIM: I am the King's dog. May the plague light on me if ever one disloyal word or thought—

HEROD: Bah!

ELPIS: Oh, sir; when my royal husband is in this mood it is better not to cross him. His sickness makes him impatient—but it will pass.

HEROD: Doctor, give me something to ease this pain. Though I daresay you are in league with my heirs to poison me.

PHYSICIAN: Heaven forbid, Sir.

HEROD: Heaven, or somebody, will know how to deal with you if you play tricks with me.... Now then! Who are these foreign princes, and what do they seek at the hand of Herod, King of Jewry?

CASPAR: O King, live for ever! I am Caspar, King of Chaldaea.

MELCHIOR: I am Melchior, King of Pamphylia.

BALTHAZAR: I am Balthazar, King of Ethiopia.

HEROD (with the utmost graciousness: it is like a different man speaking): Royal brothers, you are all most heartily welcome to my Queen and me.

CASPAR: We are Magi, humble searchers after the hidden Wisdom.

ELPIS: My lord and I are the more honoured by your visit. We love the company of good and learned men.

MELCHIOR: To you, King Herod, and to the whole realm of Judaea, we bring glad tidings from the High Lords of Heaven.

BALTHAZAR: Glory and dominion to the uttermost ends of the world, and the promise of an everlasting sceptre.

HEROD: That is good tidings indeed.

MELCHIOR: Therefore, O King, in the name of the most High God, we pray you to grant us our heart's desire.

HEROD: Ask what you will. Our royal bounty and favour are open to you.

CASPAR: Show us, we beg you, the noble child himself.

HEROD: Child? What child?

MELCHIOR: Show us him that is born King of the Jews.

BALTHAZAR: We have seen his star in the east, and have come to pay homage to him.

HEROD (in a dangerous tone): Sirs, I do not understand you.

CASPAR: Do not deny us; we have journeyed many miles for this.

MELCHIOR: We know that the boy is born. Nine months long the hosts of heaven were troubled. Fiery Mars glowed like gold in a furnace, and Saturn's leaden cheek grew pale. Jove himself, the imperial star, was smitten and afflicted between the sun and moon in the constellation of the Virgin.

BALTHAZAR: While yet it lay beneath the horizon, we felt the coming of the Star, and marvelled what this might be. And in our books, we read how the truth should be made known in Judaea, and in the House of the Lion, which is the House of Judah.

HEROD: Judah!

EPHRAIM (in an agitated whisper): You have touched him nearly. He is an Idumaean. He is not of Judah's line. I beseech you, my lords—

HEROD: What are you muttering there? Proceed, sirs, proceed.

CASPAR: Then we took horse and rode across the desert. And as we sat by night beside the waters of Araba, we saw the rising of the Star. Between the midnight and the day it stood, burning upon the cusp of the First House, lord of the ascendant.

MELCHIOR: And all the rulers of the firmament were gathered to do it honour. Never were such conjunctions seen in the horoscope of any earthly potentate.

BALTHAZAR: Then we knew that the hour had come, when he that should establish the kingdom was born a prince in Israel.

HEROD: Have a care, you little lords. Who sent you hither to mock me?

ELPIS: Indeed, sirs, you do not know what you are saying.

HEROD: I think there's treason here. Who sent you?

CASPAR: Herod, Herod—

HEROD: I say, who sent you? Answer me, or I will have your ancient and lying tongue torn out by the roots.

CASPAR: Our commission is from the gods, and from the God of gods.

HEROD: Villains and mountebanks! You shall be racked, impaled, crucified.

ELPIS: } Herod, my lord, dear husband, have patience.

EPHRAIM: } I warned you not to vex him.

PHYSICIAN: } Pray, sir, control yourself. You will be ill.

HEROD: Leave me alone, you fools. *(He struggles for breath, and resumes silkily)* Noble kings, learned Magi, I beg you to forgive me. You took me by surprise. You see what I am—an old man stricken with disease. No son has been born to my Queen Elpis and me. Sons I have, but they are all grown men, with sons of their own. Is it a grandson of mine, that shall sit upon my throne and rule an empire?

MELCHIOR: My lord, we do not know. But it is written in the heavens that he that is born shall be both priest and king.

HEROD: Priest and king? *Priest?* Are you sure?

BALTHAZAR: So it is written.

HEROD: This is serious. You do not know the history of this kingdom. For many years it was torn by wars and rebellions, till Augustus Caesar took it under the protection of Rome. Under his imperial mandate, I assumed the crown; for thirty years I have kept the peace, by force and policy. It has not been easy. There have been continual revolts against the Roman order—all made, do you understand, in the name of religion.

HIGH PRIEST: Pardon me, your Majesty. Not with our approval.

HEROD: As the High Priest says, not with the approval of the official priesthood, who know better. Religion has been the pretext for political ambition. It was I, Herod, that broke the power of the Hasmoneans. *They* were the priestly house. *They* claimed to sit upon this throne, and rule as priests and kings. They were traitors to Rome and to me, and I slew them. I slew my own sons for treason. I slew my queen, my first queen Mariamne, whom I loved—my queen and my sons, whom I loved. . . .

CASPAR: Sir, do not distress yourself and us—

HEROD: They were traitors. Their children are traitors to this day. Conspiring against me. Conspiring against Rome. Looking always for the warrior Messiah that shall lead them to victory, and independence. But there is no security in independence. The only safety for this country lies in playing her part within the great new order of Imperial Rome.

MECHOIR: My lord, it is written in the stars that the man born to be king shall rule in Rome.

(Murmurs)

HEROD: In Rome also? What do you say to that, Captain Proclus?

PROCLUS: Nothing. I am a soldier. It is my business not to say, but to do. If Caeser wants deeds, Caesar will command.

HEROD: Mark that, sirs. You prophesy, Herod reasons, but Caesar will command.

EPHRAIM *(tentatively):* My lord, if your Majesty's dog may presume to speak, may not these learned kings have made some error in their calculations? After all, we have no confirmation. Your Majesty's court magicians have issued no official prophecy in connection with this—er—alleged astral appearance.

HEROD: That is true. *(With instant suspicion)* And why not? Are they in the plot as well? Here, you, Zorastes—what are you doing there? I see you, skulking behind the skirts of the High Priest. Have you nothing to say about this? Hey? Come out, my lord Chief Astrologer, come out and speak the truth. Who has bribed you to hide things from Herod?

ZORASTES: No one, my lord.

HEROD *(with savage mockery):* No one, of course. No one. Stand up, man. Look at him now, white as a sheet, and his knees knocking together. Tell me, you dog, have you seen the star these wise men talk about?

ZORASTES: The star? Oh, yes, yes, my lord. A very bright star indeed. Quite remarkable.

HEROD: And what do you make of it?

ZORASTES: O King, live for ever! The favour of the King's face is brighter than the stars. *(Disconcerted by a snarl from* HEROD, *he goes on hurriedly)* Doubtless, my lord, a most happy conjunction of fortunate planets of ever-blessed augury for Jerusalem and for the high, mighty, and resplendent house of—

HEROD: I've heard all that before. You have read the Jewish prophecies?

ZORASTES: Yes, magnificence.

HEROD: Where do they say that the Messiah of the Jews will be born?

ZORASTES: Sir, it is said—that is, it appears most probable—the High Priest could tell you better than I.

HEROD: Out with it then, High Priest, where will the Christ be born?

HIGH PRIEST: Presumably, my lord, in Bethlehem of Judaea; for so it is written in the Book of the Prophet Micah; "Thou, Bethlehem, though thou be little among the thousands of Judah, yet out of thee shall he come forth that is to be ruler of Israel".

HEROD: Bethlehem, eh? Then, my wise princes, you will not have far to go. Though I doubt if you will find much when you get there. A very squalid little village. It is not usual for kings to be born in such a collection of mud walls and sheep-cotes. Boy, tell the groom of the stables to prepare horses for these gentlemen and set them on the road to Bethlehem.

BOY: Immediately, magificence.

HEROD: And now, withdraw, all of you. I would speak with these royal astrologers in private. And hark'ee—keep your mouths shut.

ALL: We are the King's slaves. God save your Majesty.

BOY *(with a malicious consciousness that he can be infuriating with perfect impunity):* We are Caesar's slaves. Hail Caesar!

ALL *(dutifully):* Hail Caesar!

HEROD: Shut the doors.

(Doors shut)

(Rapidly and smoothly) Gentlemen, you see how I am placed. Men call me tyrant and autocrat, but I am not my own master. The grip of Rome is on Judaea, and I cannot openly countenance revolt. But if it please Heaven to raise up a leader in Israel, then I am ready, heart and soul, to strike a blow for Jewish independence. May I trust you?

CASPAR: It is no part of our commission to betray the counsels of kings.

HEROD: It is well. Now, tell me: when exactly did this royal star appear?

BALTHAZAR: Twelve days ago we beheld its light in the east.

HEROD: Twelve days. *(musingly)* In the House of the Lion—the Lion of Judah—the House of David. It may be so. Bethlehem is called the City of David—did you know that? And the Scriptures speak of Bethlehem. Priest and king. Have you calculated his horoscope? What sort of man will this be that is born to be King of the Jews?

MELCHIOR: Prouder than Caesar, more humble than his slave; his kingdom shall stretch from the sun's setting to the sun's rising, higher than the heavens, deeper than the grave, and narrow as the human heart.

CASPAR: He shall offer sacrifice in Jerusalem, and have his temples in Rome and in Byzantium, and he himself shall be both sacrifice and priest.

HEROD: You speak mysteries. Tell me this; will he be a warrior king?

BALTHAZAR: The greatest of warriors; yet he shall be called the Prince of Peace. He will be victor and victim in all his wars, and will make his triumph in defeat. And when wars are over, he will rule his people in love.

HEROD: You cannot rule men by love. When you find your king, tell him so. Only three things will govern a people—fear and greed and the promise of security. Do I not know it? Have I not loved? I have been a stern ruler—dreaded and hated,—yet my country is prosperous and her borders at peace. But wherever I loved, I found treachery—wife, children, brother—all of them, all of them. Love is a traitor; it has betrayed me; it betrays all kings; it will betray your Christ. Give him that message from Herod, King of Jewry.

CASPAR: Sir, when we have found the Christ—

HEROD: True; I had forgotten. When you find him, return and let me know. We must work quickly and cunningly. The patriotic party only need a leader, and a name—some name that will unite instead of divide them. They will not support *me,* because I am not of Jacob's house; but if I myself go and swear allegiance to this royal child, then they will all fall into line behind me. But first we must make certain of the boy. May I rely on you to bring me news at once?

CASPAR: These intrigues are no affair of ours. Yet to whatever end a man is born, to that end he shall come at last, no matter how dark and devious the way. We are all the instruments of destiny, and Herod himself but a tool in the hand of God.

HEROD: If it be my privilege to restore the kingdom to Israel, then blessed is the House of Herod. . . . You will do me this favour, and guide me to the young king's feet?

MELCHIOR: The high gods permitting, we will certainly do so.

HEROD: I thank you from my heart. For your visit, your good news, and the great opportunity shown me, Herod is grateful. . . . Forgive me; I find it difficult to move. Do me the favour to strike upon that gong.

(Gong struck)

Remember, no word of this to my people, if you value your young king's safety.

BALTHAZAR: We will be silent.

(Enter BOY)

BOY: Your Majesty desires?

HEROD: The Princes are leaving immediately for Bethlehem. See them to their horses. And send me my secretary. Farewell, sirs. Heaven speed your quest. I hope you may not find it a wild-goose chase.

CASPAR: ⎫
MELCHIOR: ⎬ Farewell. May Herod's name be written in the book of life.
BALTHAZAR: ⎭

(Doors shut)

HEROD: Fools! May their own prophecies choke them! But there is danger — very grave danger. No matter. Old as he is, Herod will ride out this storm too. Let me think. To seize the child — that's the first step. To kill him straight away — that's the simplest. But if only we can implicate all the rebels — tempt them to show their hand — then strike, and clear out the whole hornet's nest at once — Yes! that is the way. That is Herod's way. . . . But we must see that no garbled accounts reach Rome. We must write —

SECRETARY: Your Majesty needs a secretary?

HEROD: Yes. Take your pen. I will dictate: "To the Divine Emperor, Caesar Augustus, from Herod, King of Jewry, greeting. . . ."

SCENE II (BETHLEHEM)

SEQUENCE I (A SHEPHERD'S COTTAGE)

THE EVANGELIST: When the wise men had heard King Herod, they departed; and lo! the star, which they saw in the east, went before them, till it came and stood over where the young child was.

SHEPHERD'S WIFE: Zillah, Zillah! Have you laid the table?

ZILLAH: Yes, Mother.

WIFE: Then run and tell Father Joseph supper's ready. You'll find him out at the back. And have a look up the road to see if your Dad's coming.

ZILLAH: Yes, Mother. (She runs out, calling) Father Joseph, Father Joseph!

WIFE: Now, Mother Mary, let me take the Baby and lay him in the cradle while you have your bit of supper. Come along, lovey, aren't you a beautiful boy, then? There! Now you go off to sleep like a good boy. But he's always wonderful good, ain't he? Never cries hardly at all. Happiest baby as ever I see.

MARY: He is happy in your kind home. But when he was born, he wept.

WIFE: Ah! they all do that, and can you blame them, poor little things, seeing what a cruel hard world it is they come into? Never mind. We all has our ups and downs. Here's your good man. Come along, Father Joseph. Here's a nice dish of broiled meat for you. I'm sure you need it, working so late, too. I wonder you could see what you were doing.

JOSEPH: It's a grand night. That great white star do shine well-nigh as bright as the moon—right over the house, seemingly. I've mended the fence.

WIFE: Isn't it a real bit of luck for us, you being such a fine carpenter? And so kind, doing all these jobs about the place.

JOSEPH: Well, that's the least I can do, when you've been so generous and shared your home with us.

WIFE: Well, that was the least we could do. We couldn't leave you in that old stable over in the inn. We'd never a-slept easy in our beds, knowing there was a mother and baby without no proper roof to their heads—especially after what Dad told us about seein' them there angels, and the little boy bein' the blessed Messiah and all. . . . There, Mother Mary, you take and eat that. It'll do you good. . . . D'you think it's really true? About him bein' the promised Saviour as is to bring back the Kingdom to Israel?

MARY: I know it is true.

WIFE: How proud you must feel. Don't it seem strange, now, when you look at him and think about it?

MARY: Sometimes—very strange. I feel as though I were holding the whole world in my arms—the sky and the sea and the green earth, and all the seraphim. And then, again, everything becomes quite simple and familiar, and I know that he is just my own dear son. If he grew up to be wiser than Moses, holier than Aaron, or more splendid than Solomon, that would still be true. He will always be my baby, my sweet Jesus, whom I love—nothing can ever change that.

WIFE: No more it can't; and the queen on her throne can't say no different. When all's said and done, children are a great blessing. What's gone with Zillah, I wonder? I hope she ain't run off too far. There might be wolves about. Hark!

ZILLAH (running in from outside): Oh, Mother! Mother!

WIFE: What's up now?

JOSEPH: Hallo, my lass! What's the matter?

ZILLAH: They're coming here! They're coming here! Dad's bringing them!

WIFE: Who're coming, for goodness' sake?

ZILLAH: Kings—three great kings! riding horseback. They're coming to see the Baby.

WIFE: Kings? Don't talk so soft! Kings, indeed!

ZILLAH: But they *are*. They've got crowns on their heads and rings on their fingers, and servants carrying torches. And they asked Dad, is this where the Baby is? And he said, Yes, and I was to run ahead and say they were coming.

JOSEPH: She's quite right. I can see them from the window. Just turning the corner by the palm-trees.

WIFE: Bless me! and supper not cleared away and everything upside down. Here, Mother, let me take your plate. That's better. Zillah, look in the dresser drawer and find a clean bib for Baby Jesus.

ZILLAH: Here you are, Mum.... One of the kings is a very old gentleman with a long beard and a beautiful scarlet cloak, and the second's all in glittering armour—ooh! and the third's a black man with big gold rings in his ears and the jewels in his turban twinkling like the stars—and his horse is as white as milk, with silver bells on the bridle.

WIFE: Fancy! and all to do honour to our Baby.

JOSEPH: Take heart, Mary. It's all coming true as the Prophet said: The nations shall come to thy light, and kings to the brightness of thy rising.

MARY: Give me my son into my arms.

WIFE: To be sure. He'll set on your knee so brave as a king on his golden throne. Look at him now, the precious lamb.... Mercy me, here they are.

CASPAR (at door): Is this the house?

SHEPHERD (at door): Ay, sirs, this is the house. Pray go in, and ye'll find the Child Jesus wi' his mother.

WIFE: Come in, my lords, come in. Please mind your heads. I fear 'tis but a poor, lowly place.

CASPAR: No place is too lowly to kneel in. There is more holiness here than in King Herod's Temple.

MELCHIOR: More beauty here than in King Herod's palace.

BALTHAZAR: More charity here than in King Herod's heart.

CASPAR: O lady clear as the sun, fair as the moon, the nations of the earth salute your son, the Man born to be King. Hail, Jesus, King of the Jews!

MELCHIOR: Hail, Jesus, King of the World!

BALTHAZAR: Hail, Jesus, King of Heaven!

CASPAR: ⎫
MELCHIOR: ⎬   All hail!
BALTHAZAR: ⎭

MARY: God bless you, wise old man; and you, tall warrior; and you, dark traveller from desert lands. You come in a strange way, and with a strange message. But that God sent you I am sure, for you and His angels speak with one voice. "King of the Jews"—why, yes; they told me my son should be the Messiah of Israel. "King of the World"—that is a very great title; yet when he was born, they proclaimed tidings of joy to all nations. "King of Heaven"—I don't quite understand that; and yet indeed they said that he should be called the Son of God. You are great and learned men, and I am a very simple woman. What can I say to you, till the time comes when my son can answer for himself?

CASPAR: Alas! the more we know, the less we understand life. Doubts make us afraid to act, and much learning dries the heart. And the riddle that torments the world is this: Shall Wisdom and Love live together at last, when the promised Kingdom comes?

MELCHIOR: We are rulers, and we see that what men need most is good government, with freedom and order. But order puts fetters on freedom, and freedom rebels against order, so that love and power are always at war together. And the riddle that torments the world is this: Shall Power and Love dwell together at last, when the promised Kingdom comes?

BALTHAZAR: I speak for a sorrowful people—for the ignorant and the poor. We rise up to labour and lie down to sleep, and night is only a pause between one burden and another. Fear is our daily companion—the fear of want, the fear of war, the fear of cruel death, and of still more cruel life. But all this we could bear if we knew that we did not suffer in vain; that God was beside us in the struggle, sharing the miseries of His own world. For the riddle that torments the world is this: Shall Sorrow and Love be reconciled at last, when the promised Kingdom comes?

MARY: These are very difficult questions—but with me, you see, it is like this. When the Angel's message came to me, the Lord put a song into my heart. I suddenly saw that wealth and cleverness were nothing to God—no one is too unimportant to be His friend. That was the thought that came to me, because of the thing that happened to *me*. I am quite humbly born, yet the Power of God came upon me; very foolish and unlearned, yet the Word of God was spoken to me; and I was in deep distress, when my Baby was born and filled my life with love. So I know very well that Wisdom and Power and Sorrow *can* live together with Love; and for me, the Child in my arms is the answer to all the riddles.

CASPAR: You have spoken a wise word, Mary. Blessed are you among women, and blessed is Jesus your son. Caspar, King of Chaldaea, salutes the King of the Jews with a gift of frankincense.

MELCHIOR: O Mary, you have spoken a word of power. Blessed are you among women, and blessed is Jesus your son. Melchior, King of Pamphylia, salutes the King of the World with a gift of gold.

BALTHAZAR: You have spoken a loving word, Mary, Mother of God. Blessed are you among women, and blessed is Jesus your son. Balthazar, King of Ethiopia, salutes the King of Heaven with a gift of myrrh and spices.

ZILLAH: Oh, look at the great gold crown! Look at the censer all shining with rubies and diamonds, and the blue smoke curling up. How sweet it smells—and the myrrh and aloes, the sweet cloves and the cinnamon. Isn't it lovely? And all for our little Jesus! Let's see which of his presents he likes best. Come, Baby, smile at the pretty crown.

WIFE: Oh, what a solemn, old-fashioned look he gives it.

ZILLAH: He's laughing at the censer—

WIFE: He likes the tinkling of the silver chains.

JOSEPH: He has stretched out his little hand and grasped the bundle of myrrh.

WIFE: Well, there now! You never can tell what they'll take a fancy to.

MARY: Do they not embalm the dead with myrrh? See, now, you sorrowful king, my son has taken your sorrows for his own.

JOSEPH: Myrrh is for love also; as Solomon writes in his Song: A bundle of myrrh is my beloved unto me.

MARY: My lords, we are very grateful to you for all your gifts. And as for the words you have said, be sure that I shall keep all these things and ponder them in my heart.

SEQUENCE 2 (THE TENT OF THE THREE KINGS)

CASPAR: Well, royal brothers! The Star has led us by unexpected ways.

MELCHIOR: The treasures we chose for a king's palace serve now as play-things for a baby. And what became of all our fine compliments and prophetic speeches?

BALTHAZAR: I think we forgot our wisdom, and could only ask questions like school-boys.

CASPAR: All man's learning is ignorance and all man's treasures are toys. But you, Balthazar, you found a strange new word to speak, "Hail, King of Heaven", and again, "Mary, Mother of God". What put it into your heart to say that?

BALTHAZAR: Do not ask me; I spoke like a man in a dream. For I looked at the Child. And all about him lay the shadow of death, and all within him was the light of life; and I knew that I stood in the presence of the Mortal-Immortal, which is the last secret of the universe.

CASPAR: You are the wisest of us three, Balthazar. But come—let us sleep, to be ready for our journey tomorrow. Bid our musicians play softly in the outer tent.

MELCHIOR: Music there! Let the flute and the harp sound sweetly together.

(Music. It fades and swells again. Then the VOICE *of the* ANGEL *speaks through the music)*

ANGEL: Caspar! Melchior! Balthazar!

CASPAR *(in his sleep):* Who calls?

ANGEL: The warning of a dream, in a horror of great darkness.

MELCHIOR *(in his sleep):* What is it? Oh, what is it?

ANGEL: A sword in the path on the road to Jerusalem.

BALTHAZAR *(in his sleep):* How can I come to you? Where shall I find you?

ANGEL: By the tall tree on the hill.

(Music fades)

BALTHAZAR: Call again! I am coming. . . .

(Music ceases)

(waking) O me, it is gone! . . . Caspar!

CASPAR: Is that you, Melchior?

MELCHIOR: I thought it was you cried out.

BALTHAZAR: I had a dream.

CASPAR: And so had I.

MELCHIOR: And I.

CASPAR: I dreamed I was going by night to Jerusalem, but the wind blew out my lantern. So I reached up to heaven and plucked down the Star to serve for a candle. And behold! a great darkness. And I fell—down—down—and woke to the sound of a voice calling my name.

MELCHIOR: I too was going up to Jerusalem, when suddenly the earth gaped open before me. So I drew my sword, and crossed the chasm, walking on the narrow blade. But when I was over, I found the point of the sword plunged in the heart of Mary, and in my ears was the desolate cry of a child.

BALTHAZAR: I also was going up to Jerusalem, by a deep valley between mountain forests. And I heard the voice of Mary calling: "Come back, come back! My child is lost in the hills." And I searched long among the thorns, for I knew that I never could reach the city until I had found the Christ.

CASPAR: Brothers, I cannot think that these are idle dreams.

MELCHIOR: I believe that if we return to Jerusalem we shall find a sword in the path.

CASPAR: We have looked into the heart of Herod, and seen only a horror of great darkness.

MELCHIOR: To be plain with you, I deeply distrust his intentions.

BALTHAZAR: Do as you will, my brothers. But I will not return to Jerusalem.

CASPAR: Then we are all agreed. Ho, there, strike the tents. Make ready our horses. . . . We will return to our own country another way.

SCENE III (JERUSALEM)

THE EVANGELIST: Then Herod, when he saw that he was mocked of the wise men, was exceeding wroth. . . .

PROCLUS: Your move, my Lord Ephraim.

EPHRAIM: I beg your pardon, Captain. There! . . . For Heaven's sake, boy, stop strumming. How often am I to tell you? It's not seemly, with the King at the point of death in the very next room.

BOY: It won't hurt him. He's too far gone to hear.

EPHRAIM: I don't care. It gets on my nerves.

PROCLUS: I huff you, my lord.

EPHRAIM: Tut, tut, tut. How did I come to overlook that?

PROCLUS: Your mind's not on the game tonight.

EPHRAIM: I was listening. . . . *Will* you stop making that noise? . . .

(BOY stops strumming with a final defiant twang)

Hark! Don't you hear shouts in the distance?

(Noise of CROWD running outside)

BOY: I think something's happening up near the Temple. Everybody's running that way.

EPHRAIM: Oh, dear! Oh, dear! We live in troubled times. Captain Proclus, if there's going to be a disturbance—

PROCLUS: Somebody at the door. Yes? Who are you and what do you want?

MESSENGER: A letter, to be delivered into the hand of King Herod.

PROCLUS: He's ill. You can't see him. Better leave it with me.

MESSENGER: My orders were: into the King's own hand. But they're saying in the street King Herod's dead.

EPHRAIM *(nervously)*: They've no right to say any such thing. The King is not dead. Certainly not. He's not very well, that's all. You'd better sit down and wait.

(Uproar in the street)

God of Abraham, what's that?

BOY *(excitedly)*: Oh, I say! it's a riot or something . . . there's a big crowd up by the Temple . . . they've got torches . . . they're coming this way . . . the street's simply swarming. . . .

(Hubbub increases)

PROCLUS: What are they shouting?

BOY: I can't hear. . . . Now the High Priest has come out of his house. . . . He took one look and went in again, double quick. . . . Here they come. . . . I can see them now. . . .

EPHRAIM: You'll be out of the window in a moment.

BOY: They're carrying something ... they're holding it up ... something big and shining ... Oh! oh! oh! ... they've torn down the Eagle!

PROCLUS: They've done *what*?

BOY: The Eagle! the gold Eagle from over the Temple gate ... they've pulled it down!

PROCLUS: Pulled down the Roman Eagle? ... Get out ... let me look....

EPHRAIM *(whimpering)*: That disastrous Eagle ... it ought never to have been put there ... it offends pious people.... All these fierce young men....

CROWD *(surging nearer)*: Down with the Eagles! ... Jewry for the Jews! The King's dead — long live Archelaus! Long live Antipater! ... Up the true Religion! ... Down with tyranny! ... Down with Rome.... Fire the palace, etc.

SLAVES *(rushing in)*: Help! help! the city's in arms.

PROCLUS: Slaves! What are you doing here? Have you left the King alone!

SLAVE: The King's unconscious.... I think he's dead....

EPHRAIM: Oh, heavens, we shall all be murdered!

CROWD *(under the window. Cries of)*: Freedom! ... Independence! ... A free Jewry! ... Down with the graven images.... Tear down the false gods.... Blasphemy.... Sacrilege.... Down with Caesar! ... Throw off the yoke of the Empire! ... Jewry for ever.... A Messiah! a Messiah! ... Stones, stones, stones! ... etc. *(Mingled with counter-cries of)*: Hail Caesar! ... Down with the rebels! ... Down with the Priests! ... Treason.... Stone the traitors! ... etc.

(Noise of fighting)

EPHRAIM: O, Captain Proclus — can't you do something?

PROCLUS: Hey, there, you Jewish dogs —

(Several sharp crashes. Cries from the SLAVES)

EPHRAIM: Come away! They're throwing stones!

(Another crash, followed by a sound of breaking crockery)

Ow! the Etruscan vases!

(And another)

There goes the lamp! Ow!

PROCLUS: In the name of the King —

CROWD: The King's dead!

(Cheers and laughter)

PROCLUS: In the name of the Emperor —

CROWD *(rather less confidently)*: Down with the Emperor!

VOICE: Run back to Rome, little soldier!

(Laughter)

VOICE *(off)*: Peace, there. Hear me speak!

CROWD: Matthias! Hear Matthias! Silence for the Rabbi Matthias! Shove him up on the rostrum.

MATTHIAS: People of Israel! Servants of the true religion! *("Hear, hear!")* You see this idolatrous image *(Groans)*, this odious symbol of a pagan power *(Hisses)* impiously set up over the sacred doors of the Temple *("Shame! Jewry for the Jews!")*, in defiance of the law which forbids graven images. Are you not ashamed to have let it stand there so long? . . . Are you Jews? . . . are you believers? . . . are you men? . . . What are you afraid of? . . .

(Mumbling from the CROWD; the noise quietens down a little, so that we can hear, loudly and suddenly in the room itself, the voice of HEROD)

HEROD: Stand back from the window!

EPHRAIM: The King! *(in an awed whisper)* Alive and walking! . . . Oh, sir! you will not show yourself . . . they'll attack you. . . .

(CROWD noises continue)

HEROD: Silence, fool! Fetch candles! . . . Proclus!

PROCLUS: Sir?

HEROD: Run to the fortress. Turn out the guard.

(PROCLUS clatters out)

Here, boy!

BOY: Yes, sir!

HEROD: Candles, you slaves, candles! Hold them up to my face!

MATTHIAS: Take courage, Israel! We will endure this oppression no longer! *(Cheers)* Lift up your hearts. *(Cheers)* The tyrant Herod is dead!

(Tremendous cheers and cries as before)

HEROD *(in a fearful voice, dominating the uproar)*: How now, rebels! Do you know me? Do you know Herod?

(Deathly silence, in which you could hear a pin drop)

(Icily, and with alarming irony) I see you do. I am obliged to you for the funeral oration. To be sure, it is a little premature, but Herod will not forget. *(With a sudden roar)* Stop where you are, fellow! *(quietly)* If anybody tries to leave while I am speaking, I will have him broken on the wheel. I observe that somebody has been carried away by his enthusiasm for the Imperial emblem. That Eagle is not intended for private use as a garden ornament. However, Caesar shall be informed of your devotion. No doubt he will be delighted. Next time you wish to hold these public demonstrations of loyalty, will you kindly do so at a more convenient

hour; you have disturbed my rest and roused all these worthy citizens from their beds.

(Sound of quick marching)

There, you see! the Guard is coming to see what all the noise is about.

*(*CROWD *utters murmurs of alarm: "Look out! The soldiers! Run! run!" etc.)*

I think you had better be getting home.

(Confused shuffling)

Hey, there! Is that Captain Darius?

CAPTAIN: Yes, sir.

HEROD: Get hold of those four men with the Eagle—and that fellow in green—and the gentleman with the hammer—and the two rabbis who are trying to sneak down off the rostrum. Then go to the High Priest's house and put him under arrest. Let the other imbeciles go.

CAPTAIN: Very good, sir.

HEROD: And report back to me with Proclus.

CAPTAIN: Very good, sir.... Go on, lads, you've got your orders. Move along there. Off with you!

*(*CROWD *is moved off, with scuffling and noise dying away)*

HEROD: Very pretty indeed. The High Priest will answer for this behaviour. Give me a chair. And some wine.

EPHRAIM *(bleating):* Yes, magnificence. At once, magnificence. Oh, my lord, we were so afraid—we thought you were—that is, we thought—are you sure you are not hurt—

HEROD: Stop gibbering, man. Here, slaves, pick up the lamp and sweep up all this mess. Who's that fellow in the corner?

EPHRAIM: That? Oh, he came with a letter. Yes. So he did. *(Giggling feebly)* I'd forgotten all about him.

HEROD: A letter, from whom?

MESSENGER: From the noble King of Chaldaea; for your Majesty's own hand.

HEROD: From Caspar of Chaldaea? Give it to me.

EPHRAIM: Shall I read it to your Majesty?

HEROD: No!

(Pause, while he opens and reads the letter)

Ten thousand plagues smite them! Leprosy seize their flesh! Listen to this piece of insolence:

(reading)

"We have seen; we have heard; we have worshipped. But we may not return as we had promised, for the command of the Most High stands in our way. Farewell."

Is that a way for one king to write to another?

EPHRAIM (warmly): Abominable. I don't know what it means. But it's abominable.

HEROD (grimly): It means trouble. Worse trouble. Insurrection. Civil war.

(EPHRAIM utters a protesting squeak)

But I will defeat them yet. I *will* have order in Judaea. I'll spread a net that their Messiah shall not slip through. Proclus!

PROCLUS: Here, sir, with Captain Darius, to report everything quiet, sir.

HEROD: Good. Here's another order. Take a band of my Thracians. Go to Bethlehem. Search out every male child in the cradle—

PROCLUS: Children, sir?

HEROD: From twelve days old—No. I don't trust them. No. Take *all* the male children from two years old and under and put the lot to death. All of them. The whole brood of adders. Do you hear? Let none escape. Kill them all.

PROCLUS: Sir, I am a soldier, not a butcher.

HEROD: You will obey orders.

PROCLUS: I won't, and that's flat. I am a Roman, and Romans do not kill children. Send one of your own barbarians.

HEROD: Insolent. You are a soldier in my pay.

PROCLUS: Excuse me, sir. I am in your service, but I am still a Roman born. You have the right to dismiss me. But if you imprison or execute me, I think there will be trouble.

HEROD: Proclus, you are a fool, but an honest fool. Captain Darius!

CAPTAIN: Sir.

HEROD: You heard the order.

CAPTAIN: Yes, sir.

HEROD: Carry it out, immediately.

CAPTAIN: Very good, sir.

(The CAPTAIN stamps out)

PROCLUS: Am I to go back to Rome, if you please?

HEROD: No, you mean well. But which is worse? To kill a score or so of peasant children or to plunge a whole kingdom into war? The Jews cry out for a Messiah. Shall I tell you Messiah's name? Fire and sword. Fire and sword. I will not have it. This country shall have peace. While Herod lives, there shall be but one king in Jewry.

VOICE (without): Squad, 'shun! . . . right turn! . . . quick march!

(The troops march out)

HEROD: I am sick. Carry me in.

PROCLUS: So that is the end of the new Messiah.

THE EVANGELIST: But the angel of the Lord appeared to Joseph in a dream, saying, Arise and take the young child and his mother, and flee into Egypt; for Herod will seek the young child to destroy him.

And when he arose, he took the young child and his mother by night, and departed into Egypt, and was there until the death of Herod.

THE KING'S HERALD

CHARACTERS

The EVANGELIST.
The DRIVER of an Ox-cart.
A FATHER.
A MOTHER.
MIRIAM ⎫
ISAAC ⎬ their Children.
HANNAH.
JOHN THE BAPTIST.
JUDAS ISCARIOT.
JOHN BAR-ZEBEDEE ("John Evangelist") ⎫ Disciples of
JAMES BAR-ZEBEDEE ⎪ John the
ANDREW BAR-JONAH ⎬ Baptist, and
SIMON BAR-JONAH ("Simon Peter") ⎭ later of Jesus.
BARUCH THE ZEALOT.
JESUS.
1st LEVITE.
2nd LEVITE.
3rd LEVITE.
1st CANDIDATE for Baptism.
2nd CANDIDATE.
1st JEW.
2nd JEW.
3rd JEW.
An ARMY SERGEANT.
CROWD.

NOTES

THE DRIVER—An ordinary peasant—shrewd, suspicious and commonplace.

FATHER AND MOTHER—Superior working people.

MIRIAM—A pert, rather waspish child of about 7.

ISAAC—About 5—a nice little boy—not pious or sentimental, though good.

HANNAH—I think she is about 40—a respectable married woman, rather more refined than the Father and Mother, but not much—cheerful and chatty.

JOHN BAPTIST—He is about 31; his voice is harsh and strong and not very flexible—suited to the open air and not the pulpit; his preaching rapid, rough, emphatic; his manner abrupt and authoritative. In his moments of ecstasy he is like an eagle; in his moments of awed humility he is a tamed eagle—but always an eagle, and when his voice is subdued, it turns to hoarseness, not to sweetness. He has no humour, no patience, and a one-track mind.

JESUS is a complete contrast to his cousin. This play does not cover the full range of his voice or character (the great fire and the great gentleness are still to come). But he has the sort of voice that can do anything, with the range and flexibility that John lacks. When he describes the temptation, he can act it with his voice and make the disciples see what he is talking about. His authority is innate and not acquired—consequently he can afford a sense of humour. He is 30 years old.

JOHN EVANGELIST—He is not more than 25—eager, sensitive, impulsive, with an intelligent brain and an intelligent heart. His headlong devotion to Jesus is partly a human feeling, but it is not mere *schwärmerei*, but an instinctive apprehension of something divine and different which at present he doesn't understand with his intellect but only with his heart. His excitability makes him seem very young and a little ridiculous. He has (as James says) a genuine and beautiful humility. He speaks with a little impulsive stammer—not as though he could not find, or could not pronounce, the word, but as though his tongue tripped over its own eagerness.

JAMES is a little older than John, and accustomed to stand up for him and protect him from other people. James and John are socially rather above Andrew and Simon—their father Zebedee keeps servants and is a fisherman in a fairly big way; and they know people in the High Priest's household.

SIMON (PETER) is impulsive, but not in John's way. He is sturdy, opinionated, self-confident. He is always sure he is right (and will be very much surprised if he is ever proved to be wrong). In fact he has insight and a good deal of intelligence; but he will learn humility only very slowly and after many bitter failures. He is 28.

ANDREW (perhaps from having lived too much with Peter) is inclined to be cautious and sceptical. His whole attitude is summarised in the recorded saying: "Here are five loaves and two small fishes—but what are they among so many?" He is matter-of-fact, inclined to see the difficulties of any project, to envisage "the Kingdom" in terms of politics, and to be chary of hoping for miracles. A kind, dependable person, with no imagination whatever.

JUDAS—He is infinitely the most intelligent of all the disciples, and has the boldness and drive that belong to a really imaginative brain. He can see the political possibilities of the Kingdom—but also, he can see at once (as none of the others can) the meaning of sin and repentance and the fearful paradox by which all human good is corrupted as soon as it comes to power. He is as yet only beginning to see it—but presently he will see it plainly, and be the only disciple to grasp the necessity of the crucifixion. And seeing it, as he does, only with his intellect and not with his heart, he will fall into a deeper corruption than any of the others are capable of. He has the greatest possibilities of them all for good, and therefore for evil. He is an opportunist; and he is determined that when the Kingdom comes, he shall have the chief hand in the business. He will not follow John to Jesus—when he comes, it will be because he thinks the moment has come for him to take matters in hand. He is in his thirties, and his voice is agreeable enough, but of rather cold quality.

SCENE I (JORDAN)

THE EVANGELIST: Now when Jesus was thirty years old Herod Antipas was Tetrarch of Galilee. And in those days came John the Baptist, preaching in the Wilderness of Judaea, and saying:

VOICE OF JOHN BAPTIST *(distant and fading out):* Repent ye, for the Kingdom of Heaven is at hand.... Repent.... Repent.... Repent....

(Sounds of an ox-cart being driven along)

DRIVER: T'ch, t'ch! git up there!

(Crack of whip)

FATHER: Oy, mate!

DRIVER: Hullo!

FATHER: Can you give us a lift over the ford?

DRIVER: Ay, for sure.

(Cartwheels creak to a stand)

MOTHER: That's very kind of you.... Now, children....

FATHER: In you get.

MOTHER: Take care, Miriam. Mind the wheel.

DRIVER: Woa! stand still there, can't you?

ISAAC: We're goin' to see the Prophet wash people in the river. Mummy says he's got a—

MOTHER: Move up, dear; make room for your father.

DRIVER: All right, there?

FATHER: All right.

DRIVER: T'ck, t'ck! git up!

FATHER: Nice pair of oxen you've got.

(Cart moves on)

ISAAC *(in a rapturous sing-song):* We're goin' to see the Prophet! We're goin' to see the Prophet! We're goin'—

MOTHER: Sit still, Isaac darling.

DRIVER: What Prophet, sonny?

FATHER: This man John there's all the fuss about. He's been preaching in the desert yon side the river.

DRIVER: Oh, *him! (with meaning)* Ah!

FATHER: What d'you mean, "Oh, him!"

MIRIAM *(rapidly):* He goes about in a camel-hair shirt and a leather belt an' doesn't have nothing to eat only locusts and wild honey, doesn't he, mummy?

DRIVER: There's worse things than locusts, well fried.

MIRIAM: He's going to baptise a lot of people in the river. He dips them under the water and washes their sins away.

63

DRIVER: Huh!

ISAAC: An' the sins go swimmin' away down the river—like—like—like little black wriggly-wiggly tadpoles.

MIRIAM: No, they don't, silly. You can't *see* sins, can you, mummy?

ISAAC: Yes, you can.

MIRIAM: No, you can't.

ISAAC: Can.

MIRIAM: Can't.

FATHER: Now then, you two.

ISAAC: You can, can't you, mummy?

MOTHER: No, dear. Sins aren't like tadpoles. They're nasty little black, wriggling *thoughts* in your mind.

MIRIAM: Told you so, told you so, told you—

MOTHER: Hush, dear; don't tease.

DRIVER: Hi-oop! git along. Hup!

(Whip. Cart splashes into the ford)

MIRIAM: We're crossing Jordan, just like Joshua and the Ark.

ISAAC: Crossing Jordan, crossing Jordan, crossing Jordan—

MOTHER: Sit still, dear.

FATHER: What have you got against the man?

DRIVER: I don't hold with all this preachifying. Be good and you will be happy and the Lord will provide and all the rest of it. Let Him provide decent wages, that's what I say, and I'll be happy enough.

FATHER: There's a lot in that. But this man John's making a great to-do. Seems he's announcing that the Messiah is coming to free Israel and bring in the promised kingdom, with good wages for everybody, and no more of these cruel Roman taxes.

DRIVER: That's politics, that is. Take my advice and keep off it. These here prophets and Messiahs mostly lands up in gaol. . . . Hu! hu! Come up, then!

(Whip)

MIRIAM: Oh look at all the people on the bank!

(Cart comes up out of the water and stops. Buzz of CROWD)

FATHER: Well, here we are. Out you get.

MOTHER: Carefully now, children.

DRIVER: All right, ma'am. I'll hand out the little 'un.

MOTHER: Jump, Isaac. What a big boy! There.

FATHER: Thank you kindly, mate.

DRIVER: You're welcome. . . . T'ck, t'ck! . . . Git up there! . . .

(Cart moves off)

(calling back) Good luck! And steer clear of politics.

MOTHER: Oh, dear, how hot it is! Keep close to Mother, children.

FATHER: Here's a nice tree with a bit of shade. . . . Excuse me, ma'am, do you mind if we sit down along of you?

HANNAH: Not at all.

MOTHER: Shall we see all right from here?

HANNAH: Oh, yes. There's a big crowd gone along the road to meet the prophet. But they're bound to come down to the ford for the baptisms. . . . Have you come over Jordan?

FATHER: Yes. The missus was dead keen to see this John the Baptist. Have you heard him preach?

HANNAH: Not yet, but I want to. You see, I knew him as a boy.

MOTHER: Did you really?

HANNAH: Yes. His parents lived quite near my old home, up in the hill-country, you know. There was rather a strange story about them.

MOTHER: Oh, do tell us the story.

CHILDREN: Story! story!

HANNAH: Well, John's father, Zacharias, was a priest—such a dear, pious old man, and so was his wife. I remember them quite well. Of course, that was thirty years ago, in old King Herod's day.

FATHER: Ah! he was a great lad, was old King Herod. In his time Judaea was still a kingdom. His son isn't a patch on him.

MOTHER: Hush, dear, be careful.

MIRIAM: Do go on with the story.

HANNAH: Well, Zacharias and his wife hadn't any children. They'd hoped and prayed and waited a very long time, till at last they'd made up their minds God wasn't going to send them any. But one day, when Zacharias was offering incense in the Temple, suddenly he looked up and saw an angel—

MIRIAM: Where?

HANNAH: Standing at the right-hand side of the altar. And the angel—

ISAAC: What was the angel like?

HANNAH: Like a very tall, handsome young man in beautiful glittering robes. He said—

ISAAC: What was the angel's name?

HANNAH: It was the Angel Gabriel.

MIRIAM: Wasn't Zacharias awfully excited?

HANNAH: He was rather frightened. But the angel said: "Don't be afraid; I've got good news for you. God is going to give you a son. He will be a very holy prophet, and you must call him John." And what do you think Zacharias said?

MIRIAM: I should think he said, "Hurray!"

HANNAH: I'm afraid he said, "I don't believe it."

CHILDREN (shocked): Oh!

HANNAH: He said, "We've waited all this time till we're quite old people, and we haven't had a baby. And I can't believe it now unless you give me a sign."

MIRIAM: What's a sign?

HANNAH: Something special, to show that if the angel said a thing it was true. So the angel said, "Very well, if you *won't* believe me, I *will* give you a sign. You shall be dumb and not able to speak till your son is born." And Zacharias was struck dumb that very minute, and couldn't speak a word to any one.

ISAAC: *Poor* Zacharias!

HANNAH: And, sure enough, all in good time Elizabeth *did* have a baby, and all the aunts and uncles said it ought to be called Zacharias after its father. But Elizabeth said, "No; I want him to be called John." And they said, "Why? There have never been any Johns in our family." So they went and asked Zacharias. And he wrote down on a bit of paper, "His name is John." And then, all of a sudden, he found he could speak all right again.

MIRIAM: I'm glad he remembered what the angel told him. John's a *much* nicer name than Zacharias.

HANNAH (to the FATHER and MOTHER): So of course the child grew up with a very strong sense of dedication. He was fifteen when I last saw him. A great, tall, bony lad, and as wild as a hawk.

FATHER: A bit touched would you say?

MIRIAM: Look at all these people coming along the road!

HANNAH: That must be him arriving. . . . No—I wouldn't say John was touched; only a bit queer. He went about a lot with a cousin of his, a carpenter's son from Nazareth. Jesus bar-Joseph was his name, and I always thought he was the more remarkable boy of the two. I often wonder what became of him.

FATHER (inattentively): Um, yes—those bright lads very often don't come to anything. . . . Dear me! half Jerusalem seem to have turned out.

MOTHER: There's quite a little party of Pharisees—

FATHER: They don't often put themselves out for wandering preachers.

HANNAH: And three or four learned Scribes. (With a certain pride) John is attracting quite a lot of attention.

MOTHER: There's two Levites coming this way.

FATHER: So there are—the Temple Police—that may mean trouble.

MOTHER: Oh, look!—this must be him—Can you see, children?—There! —isn't that John—that very tall man with long black hair?

HANNAH: Yes—that's John all right. Just as I remember him, striding about over the hills and chanting prophecies out of Isaiah. He hasn't changed one bit.

(CROWD *quite close now*)

VOICE OF CROWD: (A) Come along . . . pick a good place. . . . All right, all right, don't shove like that. . . . Is he going to preach again? . . . Yes, of course he is. . . . Well, don't go too far away. . . . He's got a good voice. . . .

Get down close where we can see. . . . Now, then, mister. . . . Mind out, there. . . . It's quite all right, thank you, etc.

(B) What's he mean about the Kingdom coming? . . . I think he's a bit cracked if you ask me. . . . I wonder the government doesn't stop this kind of thing—seditious, I call it. . . . There was a fellow in old King Herod's time who raised a rebellion. . . . These scares all blow over in time. . . . Well, don't get mixed up in anything. . . .

(C) He is inspired . . . the hand of the Lord is upon him. . . . What the people need is a leader. . . . The Messiah—the hope of Israel. . . . How long, O Lord, how long? . . .

JUDAS *(Businesslike and a little important):* Will you please leave room for people going down to the ford? . . . All those who wish to receive baptism please come close to the water. . . . Excuse me, good man—could you sit a little further back? The prophet will speak from under this tree.

FATHER: Certainly. . . . Are you a disciple of his?

JUDAS: Yes. I come from Kerioth. I've followed his preaching all up and down the wilderness. His mission will change the face of the world. . . . All over on this side, please. Hush! here he is.

JOHN BAPTIST: Men and women of Israel! Once more, once more I call you to repent. And quickly. For God's Kingdom is coming as the Prophets foretold. Not in some distant future. Not a year or a week hence. Not to-morrow, but *now.*

CROWD: Blessed be the God of Israel!

JOHN BAPTIST: Are you ready for it? You know very well you are not. For years you have been saying, "Some day, some day the tide will turn. Some day, some day the Kingdom will be restored. Some day, some day Messiah will come, and all will be well with Israel." But your hour is upon you—Messiah is at your very gate—and what will he find when he comes?

CROWD: Have mercy, O God! O God, spare Thy people.

JOHN BAPTIST: I see a worldly priesthood, a worldly ruler, a worldly people—a nation of shopkeepers and petty bureaucrats, their hearts fixed on cash and credit, and deaf and blind to righteousness. Sackcloth and ashes! Sackcloth and ashes! The Kingdom is at hand and you are not prepared. *Now, now* repent of your sins and the sins of the whole nation. *Now* let God wash away your guilt in the clear waters of Jordan. Wash and be clean, that you may be fit for the task that is laid upon you—for the great and terrible day of the Lord is at hand.

CROWD: Lord, have mercy upon us!

JOHN BAPTIST: Have you come prepared to do this? Are you here because you are sorry for your sins? Or only out of curiosity? I wonder. Some of you, I see, are Pharisees. Religious men, keepers of the Law, patterns of respectable piety, what are *you* doing here? *(With sudden violence)* Hypocrites, humbugs, brood of vipers! Who warned *you* to flee from the vengeance to come?

CROWD (*indignant murmurs*): "Well, I never . . . insolence . . . upon my word,"
etc. (*mingled with*) "That's right . . . give it 'em hot . . . confounded lot of
prigs" . . . (*and*) "Have mercy on us all . . . We are all sinners", etc.

JOHN BAPTIST: Yes, I know what you will say: "*We* need no repentance.
We keep the Law. We are the privileged children of Abraham. God will
look after *us*, whatever happens." Don't flatter yourselves. God doesn't
depend on you. He can find His children everywhere. He could raise
them out of these desert stones—which are no harder than your hearts.
You too will be lost if you don't repent and do better. Messiah is coming
like a woodman with his axe, and all the rotten trees, all the barren
trees, will be cut down at the roots and thrown into the fire. All of them.
All of them.

CROWD: Have pity! Spare us, good Lord!

VOICE: If keeping the Law won't save us, what are we to do?

JOHN BAPTIST (*more gently*): Be generous. Do more than the Law demands.
You, there, with the good coat—you don't need a cloak as well. Give it to
the naked beggar beside you. And you with the picnic-basket—how about
sharing it with some of these poor children? (*His voice rising harshly again*)
Renounce the world—weep, wail and beat your breasts—and await the
Kingdom in fear and trembling.

(*Groans from the* CROWD)

IST LEVITE: You seem pretty sure of yourself. Who do you think you are?
The Messiah?

JOHN BAPTIST: I am not the Messiah. I am sent to proclaim his coming.

2ND LEVITE: Are you Elijah come again?

JOHN BAPTIST (*curtly*): No, I am not.

3RD LEVITE: Or the Prophet foretold in the Scriptures?

JOHN BAPTIST: No.

IST LEVITE: Then who *do* you pretend to be?

JOHN BAPTIST: Nothing. I am nobody. Only a voice crying in the desert.

2ND LEVITE: The Elders at Jerusalem demand to know by whose authority
you baptise.

JOHN BAPTIST: I am the herald of God's Kingdom. I baptise—but only with
the water of repentance. There is a far greater man coming soon. I shan't be
worthy so much as to tie his shoelaces. He will baptise you with spirit and
with fire.

CROWD: Where is he? Show us the Messiah! Show us the Christ!

JOHN BAPTIST: Christ will come among you like a man thrashing corn. He
will gather the grain and burn the chaff. There will be a great purging of
Israel.

CROWD: We have sinned . . . we have sinned . . . Have mercy.

JOHN BAPTIST: Make ready to meet him. Draw near—confess your sins and
be baptised in Jordan.

(General movement. A Hymn is sung)

MOTHER: What a strange man he is.

FATHER *(critically):* He's a good preacher. I don't know that I like him speaking that way to those worthy Pharisees.

JUDAS: John doesn't care what he says to anybody.

MIRIAM: Look at all the people getting into the river!

CROWD: Blessed be the name of the Lord! Blessed be God!

JOHN BAPTIST: What is your name?

IST CANDIDATE: Tobias. I am a collector of Imperial taxes.

CROWD: Blessed be God for Tobias!

JOHN BAPTIST: I baptise you, Tobias, with the baptism of the Kingdom. Keep your accounts honestly, and don't take any rakeoff for yourself. . . . What is your name?

2ND CANDIDATE: Ezra. I am a soldier.

CROWD: Blessed be God for Ezra!

JOHN BAPTIST: I baptise you, Ezra, with the baptism of the Kingdom. Do your duty soberly. Don't be violent or quarrelsome, and don't grumble about your pay. . . . What's your name?

(Murmur of baptisms continues)

IST LEVITE: I shall report to the Elders that the movement may be dangerous.

2ND LEVITE: Obviously a political move. Better keep an eye on it.

3RD LEVITE: We don't want any trouble with Rome.

IST LEVITE *(as they move off):* Certainly not. Most inadvisable. If you ask me . . .

JUDAS: This is a wonderful day! The biggest number of penitents we've ever had. Excuse me, I must go and help to keep order.

BARUCH: One moment, young man. You're one of John's disciples?

JUDAS: I am.

BARUCH: Does he mean business? Or is this just another call to religion?

JUDAS: I don't understand you.

BARUCH: I think you do.

JUDAS: Well, perhaps I do. You belong to the party of the Zealots?

BARUCH: I belong to the party that wants a free Israel. Is that plain enough?

JUDAS: Yes. . . . Come and see me privately. My name is Judas—Judas Iscariot.

BARUCH: Judas Iscariot, I shall remember.

MOTHER: Dear me! *that's* an interesting-looking young man.

HANNAH: Which?

MOTHER: Just taking off his coat. Look—next to the stout woman in blue.

HANNAH: Where? I can't see. . . . Oh! . . . with the short gold beard, do you mean?

MOTHER: Yes, and the rather remarkable eyes.

HANNAH: Well, I do believe.... Fancy that.... Yes, it must be ... it's John's cousin I was telling you about.

FATHER: The carpenter's son?

HANNAH: Yes, Jesus bar-Joseph. Well now, isn't that strange? I must try and catch him when all this is over.

FATHER: I think he's the last of the candidates.

JOHN BAPTIST: ...Rebecca, with the baptism of the Kingdom. Be modest and diligent, and bring up your children in the love of God.... What is your— *You* here, Jesus? *You* come to *me* for baptism? But that's the wrong way about. It is I that should come to you.

JESUS: Do as I ask you now, John. It's right to begin this way, like everybody else.

JOHN BAPTIST: If you say so, Cousin.

CROWD: Blessed be God for Jesus!

JOHN BAPTIST: I baptise you, Jesus, with the baptism of water unto the Kingdom.

(Thunder)

FATHER: Hullo!

MOTHER: Was that thunder?

HANNAH: I hope we shan't have a storm.

ISAAC: That was God talking.

HANNAH: Bless the boy!

ISAAC: I saw a big white flash come down from Heaven.

MOTHER: Only summer lightning, dear.

ISAAC: P'raps it was an angel.

MIRIAM: You big silly. You're always 'magining things.

HANNAH: He may be right. I think Jesus bar-Joseph often saw the angels.

ISAAC: Told you so.

MOTHER: Well, dear, we don't know. And it's rude to say, "told you so".

HANNAH: He's coming up this way. He *looks* rather as though he was seeing visions. *(Calling out):* Jesus! Jesus bar-Joseph! Do you remember me?

JESUS: Hannah! Yes, of course I remember you. Are you well?

HANNAH: Very well. And very glad to see you and John again. How are Joseph and Mary these days?

JESUS: Joseph ben-Heli rests in Abraham's bosom.

(HANNAH makes a sympathetic noise)

My Mother is well, and often thinks of you.

HANNAH: How kind of her. Please give her my love.

JESUS: I will indeed.

JOHN BAPTIST *(arriving a little breathless):* Cousin, Cousin Jesus—

JESUS: One moment, John. Look! You haven't forgotten Hannah the daughter of Levi ben-Issachar.

JOHN BAPTIST: God's blessing upon you, Hannah, and on all who seek the Kingdom of God.

ISAAC: I say, Jesus bar-Joseph!

JESUS: Well, young man. What can I do for you?

ISAAC: I want to know something.

MOTHER: Isaac! You mustn't bother people. *(apologetically)* Children do ask such dreadful questions.

JESUS: I like children's questions. What is it?

ISAAC: Was that big noise thunder? Because *I* think it was God talking to you.

MIRIAM: 'Twasn't.

ISAAC: Did you see an angel?

JESUS: I saw Heaven opened, and the Spirit of God coming down to me like a dove. And a voice spoke to me saying, "This is My beloved Son in whom I am well pleased".

ISAAC *(awed):* Oh!... *(triumphantly)* There, Miriam, I told you—*(He catches himself up)*... I didn't say it, did I? Not really and truly *say* it. I shut my mouth up quite tight—m'm—like that. Didn't I?

JESUS *(laughing):* You resisted temptation like a man.

ISAAC *(cheerfully):* Next time I'll just think it and not say it.

JESUS: Oh, no. An ugly thought is as bad as an ugly word.

MIRIAM: Father says, "Keep the Law and speak no evil". But if you don't say the same as you think, it isn't telling the truth.

JESUS: No. But you see, if you always think good thoughts you won't want to say naughty things. Then you won't have to bother about keeping the Law, because your own loving thoughts will keep it for you.

MOTHER: Children, you mustn't worry people like this.

FATHER: Those two would argue the hindleg off a donkey.

HANNAH: Jesus, won't you come home and have supper with us?

JESUS: I wish I could. I must go away for a little into the desert to be alone with God.

JOHN BAPTIST: Cousin, before you go, I must speak to you.

FATHER: Yes—and we must be moving along. Everybody's gone, and it's getting late.

HANNAH: Well, good-bye then. Perhaps when you come back we shall see you.

JESUS: Yes, indeed you will see me again. Good-bye for the present.

(The FAMILY PARTY *move on, calling "Good-bye, John, Good-bye, Jesus")*

JOHN BAPTIST: The child heard and saw. *I* heard and saw. You are the promised Messiah.... We always knew it—and yet I swear to you that I knew nothing about it at all.... You are my cousin and my friend... we played together, talked together... we spoke of the Kingdom of God.... And the word came to me: "One day you will see the Spirit of God light down upon a living man—and that is the man that shall baptise the world with fire." . . . And when I saw it, the hair of my flesh stood up. . . . What does it mean? . . . I have known you all these years and now I see that I never knew you. . . . Tell me, Jesus, Son of Mary, who and what is the Messiah, the Christ of God?

JESUS: When you baptised me with the water of repentance—

JOHN BAPTIST: Being utterly unworthy to kiss your feet, my mother's cousin's son—

JESUS: I felt the shoulders of God stoop under the weight of man's sin. And I knew—

JOHN BAPTIST: What did you know—you whom the voice called Son of God?

JESUS: I knew what it meant to be the Son of Man.

SCENE II (BETHABARA)

SEQUENCE I (THE TENT OF JOHN THE BAPTIST)

THE EVANGELIST: Then was Jesus led up by the Spirit into the wilderness to be tempted of the devil. And when he had fasted forty days and forty nights, he came into Bethabara beyond Jordan, where John was baptising.

ANDREW: I say, Judas?

JUDAS: Well, Andrew?

ANDREW: How many did we baptise yesterday?

JUDAS: Twenty-three men, fourteen women and ten children. Forty-seven in all.

JOHN EVANGELIST: I call that very encouraging. Especially the women and children.

ANDREW: My dear John bar-Zebedee! You can't run a campaign on women and children.

JUDAS: You're wrong, Andrew. The women and children are very important. Women talk, and bring other women. Then their husbands come to see that they don't get into mischief.

(Laughter)

Besides, when the wife's converted too, the man doesn't have to face continual rows and nagging at home. If it wasn't for his wife, your brother Simon would be with us now.

ANDREW: That's true enough.

JUDAS: You can't expect a man to take risks for a cause if his wife's always at him to put the interests of the family first.

JAMES: There speaks the practical Judas.

JUDAS: Well, somebody must be practical.

JOHN EVANGELIST: Besides, if once a woman makes up her mind to a thing—

JUDAS: Nothing will stop her. True.

ANDREW: In fact, she behaves just like John bar-Zebedee. If *he* sees a thing he wants he makes a bee-line for it, charges up to it like a bull at a gate—

JUDAS: And then comes over all bashful and tongue-tied and leaves somebody else to do the work.

JOHN EVANGELIST: I d-d-don't.

JUDAS: D-d-d-don't you?

JOHN EVANGELIST: I know I get excited. But you don't understand. If a thing means a tremendous lot to one and one goes after it—and then, suddenly, unbelievably, it's *there,* within reach—one's almost afraid to touch it, for fear it shouldn't be there after all. It isn't that I want somebody else to do the work. It's just that—*(He gives it up)* I can't explain.

JAMES: Never mind them, John. You have the rare gift of humility—and that's more than can be said of you, Judas, or of most of us.

ANDREW: That's right, James bar-Zebedee. Stick up for your brother.

JAMES: What's more, if it comes to taking risks, you'll find my brother in the front line.

ANDREW: It may very well come to that. Just between ourselves I wish John Baptist would be a bit more cautious. . . . Where is he, by the way?

JUDAS: He went out alone about the sixth hour.

ANDREW: Oh, I see. Well, his attacks on Herod are attracting attention.

JAMES: Herod! it's time somebody did speak plainly about Herod. A fine ruler he makes for the Jewish nation! Weak, cruel, self-indulgent—and letting that gang of women lead him by the nose—

JUDAS: Herod's easily influenced. But that's rather to our advantage. If Herod himself could be brought to repentance and baptism—

ANDREW: Now is that likely?

JUDAS: He respects John Baptist and listens to him. He knows he's an honest man and a true prophet.

ANDREW: Yes, Judas, I dare say. But it's his wife you've got to reckon with. Herodias will never forgive John Baptist for the things he's said about her, and she's out for his blood.

JUDAS: Herod wouldn't let it go as far as that. And his conversion would make a tremendous impression.

JOHN EVANGELIST: John Baptist doesn't think twice about making an impression. He's out to rebuke sin, and he wouldn't care who it was.

JUDAS: I know. That's why he's such a grand leader. And that's why I say, Take the risk: it's worth it.

ANDREW: He intends to take it. He never seemed to value his own life. But just lately he has grown more reckless than ever—almost as though—

JOHN EVANGELIST: As though he saw the end of his mission in sight. I know. I have seen the change in him, these forty days; and so has James.

JAMES: His flesh is wasted—the fire of God consumes his very soul. Something happened that week we were away. What was it, Judas?

JUDAS: I don't know. He had been superb that day, and we had made a great many converts. When he had almost finished baptising there was a thunderclap. He looked up—and something came into his face as though he had felt the hand of God laid on his shoulder. That look has been there ever since.

JOHN EVANGELIST: Yes. James and I noticed it the minute we got back. I tried to ask him about it . . . but when it came to the point I c-c-couldn't find the words.

JUDAS: So you just st-st-stood and st-st-stuttered at him.

JOHN EVANGELIST: I was afraid. He looked at me as though he didn't see me.

JAMES: Shut up. He's just coming in. . . . Ah! welcome back, John Baptist! . . . Why—what has happened?

JOHN EVANGELIST: You have brought good news?

JOHN BAPTIST: Jesus has returned. He is here.

ANDREW: Jesus? What Jesus?

JUDAS: Jesus bar-Joseph your cousin?

JOHN BAPTIST: My cousin after the flesh; my Lord after the Spirit.

JUDAS: Whom you baptised in Jordan forty days since?

JAMES: Forty days since!

JOHN BAPTIST: All these forty days he has been in the wilderness. And I waited and wondered and taught the people. To-day, while I was preaching, he came walking by the river, and I saw the Spirit of God shine through the tabernacle of his flesh like the Shekinah of glory that rested upon the tabernacle of the Ark. And I cried to the people saying, "This, this is he of whom I spoke—the greater one than I, that should come after me". And they stared at me and him, but they could not see what I saw. And how could I blame them? For I have known him all these years and still I did not know him. . . . So I hurried back here, thinking that you my disciples would see and understand. . . . And as I went, I felt his presence close behind me—following hard upon me, and yet leading me on. For wherever I go he is behind me and before me, as he was before me from the beginning.

ANDREW: I don't understand you, John Baptist.

JOHN BAPTIST: Bring out the roll of the Scriptures. . . . Read what Isaiah says about the redeemer of Israel.

ANDREW: You are the best scholar, John bar-Zebedee.

JOHN EVANGELIST: Where shall I begin?

JOHN BAPTIST: "He is despised and rejected of men; a man of sorrows and acquainted with grief"—begin from there.

JOHN EVANGELIST (a little surprised): Oh! . . . "Surely he hath borne our griefs, and carried our sorrows: yet we did esteem him stricken, smitten of God and afflicted." . . . John, is this a prophecy of the Messiah? I always thought it spoke of the sufferings of our nation.

JOHN BAPTIST: All Israel is in Israel's Messiah. Read on.

JOHN EVANGELIST: "He was wounded for our transgressions, he was bruised for our iniquities; the chastisement of our peace was upon him; and with his stripes we are healed."

JUDAS: John Baptist, I begin to see.

JOHN BAPTIST: To see what, Judas?

JUDAS: Why your call is to baptism and repentance. Why the false peace of heart must be broken and its complacency chastised. . . . I had imagined something different . . . but now—but now—Yes; it is bigger and stranger than that. . . . I am sorry I interrupted.

JOHN EVANGELIST: "He is brought as a lamb to the slaughter, and as a sheep before her shearers is dumb"—

JOHN BAPTIST (suddenly): Look!

ALL: What?—Where?—

JOHN BAPTIST: There walks the Lamb of God, carrying away the sins of the world.

JAMES: Who is it?

ANDREW: The sun is in my eyes.

JUDAS: I recognise him. It is Jesus bar-Joseph.

JAMES: He is coming to us.

ANDREW: No, he is passing on.

JAMES: He looked this way, but he didn't see us.

JUDAS: John bar-Zebedee, what are you trembling for?

JOHN EVANGELIST: He looked at me.

JUDAS: If this is the Messiah of Israel—

ANDREW: What do you want us to do, John Baptist?

JAMES: Are we to follow him or stay with you?

JOHN EVANGELIST: *I* have no choice. I don't know what you have seen, John Baptist, and I can't understand half you say. But he looked at me. I must see and speak to him. I must follow and find him, or never know peace again. . . . Don't think I'm ungrateful. I don't want to desert you. But I must go. I must. It's something I can't explain. You do understand, don't you? Let me go, John Baptist! Let me go.

JOHN BAPTIST: Go quickly, John bar-Zebedee. Never mind me.

JAMES: He's off. . . . Run after him, Andrew. He'll stammer and get mixed up and not be able to explain himself.

ANDREW: Won't you—?

JAMES: A friend is less embarrassing than a brother. I'll stay. . . . Come back and report.

ANDREW: All right. . . . (He hurries off, calling) John! John! Wait a moment. . . .

JOHN BAPTIST (his voice fading into the background): "He shall see of the travail of his soul and shall be satisfied . . . he shall be satisfied. . . ."

SEQUENCE 2 (ON THE ROAD)

ANDREW *(running):* Hi, John!

JOHN EVANGELIST: Come on, quick.

ANDREW *(panting):* Where's the hurry? . . . Here, let me get my breath. . . .

JOHN EVANGELIST: The world might come to an end before we found him.

ANDREW *(good-humouredly):* Well, it might: but it's not very likely. He can't have got far.

JOHN EVANGELIST: He disappeared behind the olive-trees.

ANDREW: Yes. Well, take it easy. You'll kill yourself, running like that in all this heat.

JOHN EVANGELIST: Suppose, when we turned the corner, he wasn't there

ANDREW *(placidly):* I shan't suppose anything of the sort. . . . There! what did I tell you? Here we are at the corner, and there is Jesus bar-Joseph.

JOHN EVANGELIST: Yes. Yes. It's all right.

ANDREW: What are you stopping for?

JOHN EVANGELIST: Nothing. I mean, he's there and it's all right.

ANDREW: What's come over you?

JOHN EVANGELIST: Let's follow and keep him in sight.

ANDREW: You are the most extraordinary person—up in the air one minute and down the next. . . . I don't know what to make of you. Why can't you—?

JOHN EVANGELIST: He's heard us.

ANDREW: He's waiting for us. . . . Go on, John.

JOHN EVANGELIST: *You* speak to him.

JESUS: What are you looking for? Do you want me?

ANDREW: Rabbi, we are disciples of John the Baptist. You passed our tent just now and he told us—Well, anyway, we wanted very much to speak to you. So we ran after you. My name's Andrew, by the way, Andrew bar-Jonah.

JESUS: You are very welcome, Andrew.

ANDREW: And this is John bar-Zebedee. He was the one who was so terribly keen to come, and I came with him. . . . Say something, John. . . . *(apologetically)* He ran very fast and he's out of breath.

JESUS: What do you want of me, John bar-Zebedee?

JOHN EVANGELIST: You called me, and I came.

ANDREW: We don't want to bother you now, if it isn't convenient, but if you would tell us where you live—

JESUS: Quite near here. Come and see.

ANDREW: Now?

JESUS: Yes. We will all go together.

ANDREW: Wake up, John.

JOHN EVANGELIST: I feel as though I were dreaming.

JESUS: Follow me.

SEQUENCE 3 (THE LODGING OF JESUS)

THE EVANGELIST: So they came and saw where he dwelt, and abode with him that day, for it was about the tenth hour. And Andrew went to seek his brother Simon.

JOHN EVANGELIST: Andrew's been gone a long time. I do hope he'll get Simon to come.

JESUS: He'll come. Don't worry. . . . Look, on the shelf beside you there are bread and wine and a dish of dried figs.

JOHN EVANGELIST: Shall I put them on the table? . . . Of course, Simon's a married man. It complicates matters.

JESUS: The road to the kingdom is narrow and steep, and it's not everybody who can travel by it. It means giving up everything that may stand in the way—wife, father, mother and all that one has. I won't disguise that.

JOHN EVANGELIST: But it's the road to happiness for our people?

JESUS: The Kingdom of God is like—what shall I say?—it's like a well-to-do merchant, living an easy, comfortable life. And then one day he sees a pearl so rich and beautiful that he feels he can't live without it. So he sells up everything he has, and buys that pearl for his own.

JOHN EVANGELIST: My father's brother was a merchant and he was just like that. He never made any money, because he couldn't bear to part with his beautiful things. But he was a very happy person all his life. . . . Did you know my father's brother?

JESUS: I know human nature. . . . You are like your uncle, aren't you?

JOHN EVANGELIST: You know everything. You read my heart like an open book.

JESUS: I read in it that we shall be friends.

JOHN EVANGELIST: Oh, Master! . . . I wouldn't dare to call myself that. Your servant, your disciple, yes—

JESUS: But I want my disciples to be my friends. Will you, John bar-Zebedee?

JOHN EVANGELIST: How can you ask? You know I ask nothing better than to love you and follow you to the death.

JESUS (gravely): Thank you.

JOHN EVANGELIST: I don't know why I used that gloomy expression. I always talk extravagantly when I'm excited. But indeed I would gladly lay down my life for you.

JESUS: And I for you. That's what friendship means. . . . Listen! Here's Andrew coming back.

JOHN EVANGELIST: And I hear Simon's voice.

ANDREW (bursting in triumphantly): Here he is, Master. I've brought him. I said, "Simon, we've found the Messiah, and you've simply got to come." There was a bit of an argument, but here he is.

SIMON: Good evening, sir.

JESUS: So you're Simon. That means "one who hears and obeys". It sounds a very appropriate name—

(Andrew laughs)

or, no, perhaps not.

SIMON: I don't know about that. My wife argued one way, and Andrew argued the other. And in the end I said "Here", I said, "I'm not going to be argued about over my head. I'm going to see for myself," I said, and that's all about it.

JESUS *(amused):* I see.

ANDREW: Simon's always very independent. And frightfully positive about everything.

JESUS: Ah, yes. A rugged nature. Well, Simon, one of these days we'll find a new name for you. You shall be called Peter, the Rock. How would that suit you?

SIMON *(sturdily):* You're making fun of me. Never mind. Show me how the kingdom's to be won for Israel, and I'll set about earning the name.

JESUS: I shall not forget. . . . Sit down and have supper with us.

SIMON: Thank you very much. . . . Mind you, I'm as keen as anybody to see Judaea restored to her rights. I've listened to John Baptist, and it's what I call good, religious talk. But it can't stop at talk. And—excuse my blunt way of putting it—there've been so many people starting movements and claiming to be the Messiah, but it never came to anything.

ANDREW: They all broke against the power of Rome. And see here, Master, we've got to face the fact that it's a pretty big thing for a handful of common folk to set themselves up against the Empire. Simon and I are just fishermen, and so are the sons of Zebedee, though they've had a bit more education than we have. John Baptist's got a good following, and I'm sure a lot of them would be ready to follow you—

JOHN EVANGELIST: Surely you have only to speak, and the whole world would follow you.

JESUS: I can offer you no proof. I can only say, Here I am; believe in me.

SIMON: The moment I set eyes on you, I could see you were one to be trusted. But the people will look for a leader who can improve their living conditions. That's all they think of, poor souls, and you can't blame them. And the priests—

ANDREW: The priests! They won't touch politics. They're hand in glove with the government, I'm afraid,—and if the Angel Gabriel himself was to come flying straight down out of Heaven, they'd have him arrested by the Temple Police, for causing a disturbance.

SIMON: It's Rome that's the obstacle, first and last. They don't mean Judaea to be independent, and they'll listen to nothing except armed force.

JESUS: Children, children—you don't know with whose voice you are speaking. Appetite, superstition and force: none of these can bring in the Kingdom.

It is God's Kingdom we are looking for. Listen, and try to understand. When I came to John for baptism, and heard God call me His son, I went into the desert to fast and pray. And when after forty days I came out from the presence of God, I realised that I was very hungry; and in the same moment I knew that I was not alone.

JOHN EVANGELIST: Were you visited by an angel?

ANDREW: John Baptist often sees visions when he has fasted.

JESUS: Something spoke in me that was not myself, and said: "Why go hungry? If you are the Son of God—if indeed you are the Son of God— you have only to command, and these desert stones will be turned into bread." And I knew it was true. I *had* only to command.

ANDREW: But that would be a miracle.

JESUS: There are more difficult miracles than that. . . . Don't look so alarmed; the bread you are eating came from the baker. . . . But miracles mustn't be used for one's self—only for other people.

JOHN EVANGELIST: How *about* other people? Feed God's people, and they will praise His name.

SIMON: Yes, we are taught to love God for His mercies.

JESUS: For Himself first, as we love our friends—not for what He can give us. It's easy to feed the body and starve the soul. It says in the Scriptures: "Man doth not live by bread alone but by every word of God." I spoke the words, and the temptation was gone, with no more than a shudder of the flesh. . . . But that Other was still with me. We stood together on the topmost pinnacle of the Temple, looking down into the streets of Jerusalem.

ANDREW: Do you mean you were really there?

JESUS: We seemed to be really there. And the self that was not myself said to me: "If you are the Son of God—if indeed you are the Son of God—throw yourself down. You can't be killed; doesn't it say in the Scriptures that God's angels will hold you up and keep you from harm?" . . . And far below, I could see the priests and the worshippers assembling for the evening sacrifice. And the whisper came again: "Prove to them what you are. Prove it. Are you quite sure of yourself, Son of God? Prove it to yourself."

JOHN EVANGELIST *(softly)*: Dear Master, have *you* felt that? The doubt that shakes a man's reason? The fear that the blessed truth may be a lie after all?

JESUS: I said to that Other: "It is written, Thou shalt not put God to the proof. He must be trusted as a father and a friend." And the terror in the mind passed away.

ANDREW: Was that the end?

JESUS: Not yet. He took me up into a very high mountain and showed me the whole world unrolled at my feet like a map:—Byzantium and Jerusalem; with all the cities of the Mediterranean—Tyre, Sidon, Caesarea, and beyond them Athens and Rome, and far away to Carthage—city upon city, with all their power and glory. And he said, "Son of God, I will give you all

these for your own, if you will serve me and do homage for them to me."
Then I knew him for what he was, and I spoke his name: "You are Satan
the destroyer. Away with you. For it is written, Thou shalt serve the Lord
thy God and do homage to Him alone." When he saw that I knew him, he
fled.... And God sent His angels to strengthen me, because that assault
had been sharp, and laid against the very citadel of the soul.

(Slight pause)

SIMON: Master, if I understand you right, there's no way by which a man may
win power and not become corrupted. But if it's as you say, how is the
Kingdom to be restored?

JESUS: I will tell you what the Kingdom is like. You've watched your wife
making bread. She takes a little piece of yeast and stirs it into a mass of
dough. Then she sets it aside and the buried yeast begins to work in silence
and unseen, till the heavy lump rises and swells and becomes light and
ready for baking. That is how the Kingdom will come.

ANDREW: Like that?

JESUS: Just like that.... Are you disappointed?

ANDREW: I thought it would come with armies and banners, and a big
procession riding into Jerusalem.

JESUS: You may yet see the Messiah riding into Jerusalem.

SIMON: We rather expected signs and wonders and that sort of thing.

JESUS: You *will* see signs and wonders. But you won't believe because you
have seen wonders; you will see the wonders because you have believed.

ANDREW *(pursuing his own line of thought)*: We looked for a great uprising of
the people. But I see that the people must be taught to know God before
they are fit to enjoy God's kingdom.

SIMON: The people? But *we* are the people—and we don't know the first thing
about anything. God's word says we should be a holy people—but you
couldn't call Andrew and John and me "holy". We're just plain, ordinary men.

JOHN EVANGELIST: Master, what is holiness? Is it just to keep the Commandments and say the right prayers, and do the right things, and pay the proper
dues, as the priests tell us? Or is it something quite different? The preaching
of John Baptist has troubled our hearts, and the great prophets have
terrified us with their thunderings against sin. We are disheartened, because
nothing we do seems to be any good, and the righteous God is so great and
terrible and far away. How can we rise so far above ourselves? What sort of
heroic thing is holiness?

JESUS: The priests are right, and the prophets are right too. I haven't come to
take away the Law, but to show you how to keep it. This is holiness—to
love, and be ruled by love; for love can do no wrong.

JOHN EVANGELIST: As simple as all that?

JESUS: So simple that a child can understand it. So simple that only children
really *can* understand it.

ANDREW: But what has all this to do with the coming of the Kingdom?

JESUS: It *is* the Kingdom. Wherever there is love, there is the Kingdom of God.

(Another short pause)

SIMON: Master, that's a strange, new idea. And yet, come to think of it, it's what the Bible has been telling us all along. . . .

ANDREW: We'd like to turn it over a bit in our minds.

JOHN EVANGELIST: I don't need to think. It's the truth. But I must go and tell my brother.

JESUS: You are fishermen. Where is your home? By the lake of Galilee?

SIMON: Yes, Master, in Bethsaida.

JESUS: Go back now to John the Baptist. When he no longer needs you, you will see me again in Galilee.

SCENE III (AENON)

THE EVANGELIST: The day following, Jesus goeth forth into Galilee and findeth Philip and Nathanael and saith unto them, "Follow me". And Jesus and his disciples came into the land of Judaea and there he baptised. And John the Baptist also was baptising at that time in Aenon near to Salim.

JOHN BAPTIST: ... and so I bid you repent and be baptised.

1ST JEW: Excuse me, but I'm not clear about this business of baptism. There's the ordinary purification appointed by the Law—and now here's your special mission—

2ND JEW: Yes—and see here, you're not the only one. There's a man going about in Galilee—a man called—what's the name again?

3RD JEW: Jesus bar-Joseph—you remember—he was with you at Bethabara, and you said he was coming to baptise with fire—

2ND JEW: But he baptises with water, same as you—

1ST JEW: He doesn't baptise at all. His disciples do the baptising.

2ND JEW: It's the same thing. A lot of your converts have gone over to him. It's all very confusing, and I want to know what I'm expected to do.

3RD JEW: Yes. Are you the one, or is he the one, and is his baptism better than yours, or what?

JOHN BAPTIST: No man can do more than the task that God has set him. I take you to witness that I never said *I* was the Messiah. I am only sent on ahead to prepare you for his coming—haven't I always told you so?

1ST JEW: That's true—you did.

JOHN BAPTIST: You know how it is at a wedding. The best man comes to church first and receives the bride. But he's only there to see that everything's ready. When the bridegroom comes, nobody bothers any more about the best man. He's just the bridegroom's friend—happy in his happiness and glad to fade into the background and leave the chief place to him. And I am happy now, because the bridegroom of Israel is here. From now on people will turn more and more to him and less and less to me. That is right—that is as it should be. For I am nothing—he is everything. . . . Judas!

JUDAS: Yes, John?

JOHN BAPTIST: Who are those people coming down the road?

JUDAS: They look like soldiers.

JOHN BAPTIST: I thought so. . . . Go home now, good people. You had better not be found here with me.

(CROWD *disperses*)

JAMES: Andrew, what does he mean?

ANDREW: I don't know, James. But I'm afraid I can guess. . . . John Baptist!

JOHN BAPTIST: Herod's men are coming to arrest me.

ANDREW: You have spoken too openly about him.

JOHN BAPTIST: I could not speak otherwise. . . . Did you hear what that man said?

JOHN EVANGELIST: We all heard. Jesus is in Galilee.

JOHN BAPTIST: Go home to Bethsaida and wait for him there.—Andrew and James and John—Simon is there already.

JAMES: But how about you?

JOHN BAPTIST: Never mind me.

(*Sound of* SOLDIERS *approaching*)

ANDREW: We can't all desert you.

JUDAS: I have no home in Galilee. I will go with John Baptist.

JOHN BAPTIST: Judas, are you sure? it will be dangerous.

JUDAS: I'm not afraid. Herod's only bluffing. He will put you in prison to please his wife—and release you to please himself. . . . There will be great opportunities in Tiberias. . . . Leave it to me. I've established certain contacts. . . .

VOICE: Squad, halt! . . . Hey, there, fellows! By order of Herod, Tetrarch of Galilee—

JOHN BAPTIST: I am the man you want, sergeant. I am John the Baptist.

THE EVANGELIST: And Jesus, walking by the sea of Galilee, saw Simon and Andrew his brother casting their nets into the sea; for they were fishermen. And he saith unto them:

THE VOICE OF JESUS: Follow me.

THE EVANGELIST: And going on from thence, he saw the other two brethren, James bar-Zebedee and John his brother, in a boat with their father, mending their nets. And he called them:

THE VOICE OF JESUS: Follow me.

THE EVANGELIST: And they immediately left the ship and their father, and followed him.

A CERTAIN NOBLEMAN.

CHARACTERS

The EVANGELIST.
The BRIDEGROOM of Cana.
The BRIDE.
SUSANNAH, Mother to the Bridegroom.
REBECCA, Friend to Susannah.
The STEWARD (the "Ruler of the Feast").
REUBEN ⎫ Servants in the
ISSACHAR ⎬ Bridegroom's
A MAIDSERVANT ⎭ House.
The RABBI SOLOMON.
BENJAMIN BEN-HADAD, "a certain Nobleman".
DORCAS ⎫
A GROOM ⎬ Servants to Benjamin.
MARY, the Mother of Jesus.
JESUS.
ANDREW BAR-JONAH.
SIMON BAR-JONAH ("Simon Peter").
JAMES BAR-ZEBEDEE.
JOHN BAR-ZEBEDEE.
A LEVITE.
1st ELDER.
2nd ELDER ("Shadrach").
3rd ELDER.
WEDDING-GUESTS, AND CROWD.

NOTES

STEWARD—According to Hoskyns, the "Ruler of the Feast" was the Head-Servant, and not the toast-master elected to order the drinking. The Steward should thus be given the speech and behaviour of an upper servant in a middle-class house.

REUBEN; ISSACHAR—Can be given any sort of accent or manner of speech that sufficiently distinguishes them from their masters. They are not "slaves" in any degrading sense, but either "hired servants" or bondsmen "born in the house". Of the two, Reuben is rather superior and better-spoken.

SUSANNAH—A pleasant, friendly, hospitable woman of middle age and a middle station in life—such as might properly be a fairly intimate friend of the carpenter's family in Nazareth. The "feast" is not a very grand one as things go—a comfortable party of not very rich people (since seven extra guests run them short of wine and cutlery), proud to be able to invite a local magnate to their table, reasonably pious in a routine way, and with a warm welcome for everybody.

MARY is now about 48 years old. I have accepted Dr. Temple's suggestion that she "was apparently in some position of responsibility (at the wedding), as her concern about the wine and her instructions to the servants show". Her attitude to Jesus and his to her are always the great stumbling-block of this scene. I have linked this up with the episode of the Finding of Christ in the Temple, so as to show the human mother faced with the reality of what her Son's personality and vocation mean in practice. It seems pretty clear from Luke IV. 22 that Jesus had not previously performed miracles at home, so that this was presumably Mary's first encounter with His divine power, and she is both saddened and gladdened by it.

REBECCA—In every sense a busybody—the indispensable woman with whom everybody would be happy to dispense. A shrill and gabbling voice, an excellent heart, an inquisitive nose, and no tact at all.

BENJAMIN BEN-HADAD—Not a very great nobleman—a local magnate, something like a country squire. A most excellent man, full of family affection, kindly with servants, sitting loosely to his religion, but as good as gold. (I imagine that he is about 60 years old, and that his son is the youngest-born of a family of daughters, and therefore immensely precious to him.)

JESUS—He, too, is facing the division between his home life and his mission as Son of God and Son of Man, and the sterner side of him is, on the whole, uppermost, though on arriving at the party and while telling his parable, he is easy and gentle. His rebuke to his Mother must sound like a firm reminder, but the tone must not be harsh or querulous. In the Temple he is really indignant. To the disciples in Scene II he is gentle and cheerful again, but firm once more when proposing his test of faith to Benjamin.

DISCIPLES—There is nothing to add to their characters as sketched in the second play. The manner of John Evangelist to Mary is intended to prepare for a sort of intimacy which eventually leads up to the scene at the Crucifixion, when he "took her to his own home".

THE BRIDEGROOM and THE WEDDING-GUESTS present no special characteristics.

THE BRIDE, in an Eastern country, would not be expected to be anything but shy and rather silent before her new husband.

THE RABBI SOLOMON—The best kind of pious, aged man of religion—not too old to welcome new men and new ideas.

1ST and 3RD TEMPLE ELDERS—The nastiest type of ecclesiastic—impervious to new ideas and resentful of new men; time-serving, truckling to the government, and all set to bring about crucifixions.

2ND ELDER (SHADRACH)—A rather more intelligent type—disliking the scandals of the Temple traffic, and able to appreciate the quality of the "new man", and to treat his claims with some caution. Sardonic in voice and manner.

DORCAS—A young woman, deeply devoted to her master's family.

THE GROOM—Snobbish and insolent—the sort of servant who has no respect for people who walk the road in peasant costume.

SCENE I (CANA IN GALILEE)

THE EVANGELIST: After Jesus was baptised of John the Baptist, he called his first disciples: Philip and Nathanael, Andrew bar-Jonah and Simon his brother, and James and John, the sons of Zebedee. And there was a marriage at Cana in Galilee, and the Mother of Jesus was there; so Jesus and his disciples were invited to the wedding.

(Bustle of preparation—clinking of crockery and servants running about)

STEWARD: Twelve, fourteen, sixteen napkins—here you are. . . . Reuben, this garland's coming down. Put a tack in it. . . . And trim that smoky lamp. . . . Where are the water-pots for the purifying?

REUBEN: Just inside the door. I thought six'd be enough.

STEWARD: Right. See that there are plenty of clean towels. . . . Issachar, lay cushions in the alcove for the musicians. . . . Hurry up!

SUSANNAH: Steward! Steward! How are you getting on?

STEWARD: Just ready, ma'am. I hope everything's to your liking.

SUSANNAH: Yes, indeed. You've all done wonders. . . . Oh, dear! what a business it is getting a son married! . . . Yes, child, what is it?

MAIDSERVANT: Your bracelets, ma'am.

SUSANNAH: Oh, thank you. . . . I shall be forgetting my head next. . . . I hope everything's all right in the kitchen. *(Calling)* Mary! Mary dear! Time's getting on.

MARY *(arriving breathless):* We can dish up any minute now. But oh, Susannah! Here's a message just arrived from my son. He's coming—

SUSANNAH: Oh, I'm *so* glad we weren't too late to catch him!

MARY: And he's bringing six friends.

STEWARD *(taken aback):* Seven more places?

MARY: I'm so sorry. Just as you'd got everything arranged so nicely.

SUSANNAH: We only thought of it at the last minute—hearing he was in the neighbourhood.

STEWARD: Never mind, ma'am. We'll squeeze them in somehow. . . . Reuben! Move those tables up closer and set another here . . . and two more couches. . . . Issachar! run up on the roof and keep watch for the bridal party.

MARY: I do think it all looks beautiful. The flowers are really lovely.

REUBEN: We'll need another table-cloth. And some more cups.

SUSANNAH: I don't believe we've got any more in the house.

MARY: I'll run and borrow some from next door.

SUSANNAH: Indeed, Mary dear, you'll do no such thing. You've been on your feet all day.

MARY: But I'm enjoying it, Susannah. When the son of an old friend gets married—

SUSANNAH: Yes, yes—but you must rest a little before the guests arrive. One of the servants can go. Or, look! here's Rebecca. She loves running errands. . . . Rebecca!

REBECCA *(voluble and emphatic):* Yes, dear? . . . Oh, Mary, *there* you are! What's this I hear? Your son Jesus is coming?

MARY: Yes, and we wondered if you—

REBECCA *(drowning her words):* But how exciting! I haven't seen him for ages, and now I hear he's set up as a prophet or preacher or something, and making quite a stir. They tell me the young people are mad about him. I suppose he's quite given up the carpentering business? Oh, well, no doubt his cousins can manage. But you must miss him very much at home.

MARY: We do miss him, of course. But we couldn't expect to hold him back when he is called to do God's work.

REBECCA: Oh, no, dear! though I *must* say I do hope he'll be careful and keep out of trouble. I think I ought to warn you that people are beginning to say rather dangerous things. Suggesting that Jesus might be the Messiah, and all that—quite ridiculous, of course, to people who know him, but it's really not *safe* these days, and if you could just drop him a hint—

MARY: Jesus must do as he thinks right, Rebecca.

REBECCA: Naturally, dear; and I'm sure I'm the last person to interfere. But for his own sake he *ought* to contradict these rumours. I'm only trying to be helpful—

SUSANNAH *(breaking in firmly):* You're always so kind. *Do* you think you could run across to Simeon's wife and ask her to lend us some extra cups and table-linen? Jesus is bringing six friends, and we're rather short.

REBECCA: Of *course* I will, dear. The Simeons are always *most* obliging. In fact, they said only yesterday—

ISSACHAR: Madam! Madam! the bridegroom and the bride are at hand! I can see their torches far off, coming down the road from Capernaum.

REBECCA: Oh, I must fly! . . . I'll be back in no time. *(As she goes)* And do think over what I've said.

SUSANNAH: They'll be here in ten minutes. Let's sit down while we can. . . . Mary, now that Rebecca isn't here—How much does Jesus really know about—you know—the things you told me? The angels at his birth, and the prophecies, and the visit of the wise kings, and—and—everything?

MARY: When he was a child, we told him nothing. We waited upon God's good time. But when he was twelve years old, we went up to Jerusalem, as usual, for the Passover. And somehow or other, when the caravan started back, he got left behind—we thought he was with Zacharias and Elizabeth and they thought he was with us. So my husband and I went back to look for him, and after a long, anxious search we found him in the Temple, sitting at the feet of the Elders, listening to them and asking them questions. They were amazed to find how quick and intelligent he was, and what a lot he knew. And I said, "Jesus dear—it's not kind to behave like this. Your father and I were dreadfully worried; we couldn't think where you'd got to." And he looked at me quite astonished, and said, "But why? This is my Father's house—surely you know I should be here."

SUSANNAH: Yes, but Mary—

MARY: I couldn't find a thing to say—it was like a sword going through my heart. Oh, Susannah! it's glorious to have a son born to great things; but there are moments when one realises that—that he doesn't belong to one—and those moments are bitter.... He came home with us ... and then I showed him the wise king's gifts—the gold, the frankincense, and the myrrh—and told him all I knew.... He said nothing—for eighteen years he said nothing, but was tender and obedient as any son could be. And I watched and waited, knowing that the time would come when his heavenly Father would call him away from me.

(Music in the distance)

Hark! the guests are approaching.

SUSANNAH: They are only at the top of the street. Tell me quickly.

MARY: *Your* son is coming home with his bride. Mine has left me, for an end that no one can foresee.... Ten weeks ago he came to me and said, "Mother, I must be about my Father's business." He spoke gently—but my mind went back to that day in the Temple, and I knew.... He left the house next day.

SUSANNAH: Oh, Mary, that was hard.

MARY: I am his mother and I know him. Under all his gentleness there is a purpose harder than steel.... Don't look so troubled. I am very happy. And tonight I shall see my son.

(Music at the door)

SUSANNAH: God bless you, Mary.... There! I must go and receive the guests.

(Noise of arrival. Cries of "God bless the marriage", "Welcome home!" "Welcome to the bride!" etc. Laughter and music)

THE BRIDEGROOM: Mother, I have brought my bride to ask your blessing.

SUSANNAH: She is welcome to my heart. Heaven keep you both, my son and daughter, and make your marriage happy and fruitful. Would your dear father had lived to see this day.... Welcome to you all! Come in! the marriage feast is ready. *(Clapping her hands)* Quick now! Water and towels for the company! ... Welcome, my Lord Benjamin! Welcome, good Rabbi Solomon! Ebenezer, Raphael, Simeon, we are very glad to see you. David and Sarah, how kind of you to come! ... Moses ben-Ezra and Ruth dear, how are you? Isn't this a joyful day? ... Ah! and here is a face I'm glad to see—Jesus bar-Joseph, you are very welcome.

JESUS: Peace and blessing light on your house, Susannah, and on your son and daughter.

SUSANNAH: And are these your friends? We are delighted to see them all. I've

put you together at one table. You will find your dear Mother there. She
has been such a help to me....Jacob....Dorcas and Abigail...*(her
hospitable voice trails away into the confusion of greetings).*

STEWARD: Excuse me, sir, this way if you please.... Reuben, another cushion here.... Issachar, run to the kitchen and tell them to start serving.... Yes,
ma'am—your party is over here.... Reuben, wine to the upper table.... Oh,
my lord Benjamin, pray come up higher—the master requests you will sit
at his right hand.

BENJAMIN: Eh? oh! with pleasure. Certainly.

MARY: Jesus, my dear! How good to see you.

JESUS: God bless you, Mother.... You must know my friends—Philip and
Nathanael, Andrew bar-Jonah and his brother Simon....James bar-
Zebedee— and this is John.

MARY: So you managed to get here in time?

JESUS: We fell in with the wedding-party on the road from Capernaum, and
travelled along merrily together.

MARY: And what have you all been doing?

JOHN: Jesus has been telling the good news of the Kingdom. We have listened
and marvelled.... Oh, Lady, I cannot tell you how wonderful these days
have seemed. It is as though everything one said and did, every stone, every
flower and the blessed light itself had a new meaning. You must be the
happiest woman in the world. I'm sure we are the happiest men. But
everybody feels that happiness—the sick and the poor, and the women
with their little children—

JAMES: Look out, John!—There!

JOHN: Oh, I *am* sorry—how clumsy of me. I hope it didn't go on your dress.

MARY: No, no—Reuben, bring a cloth—a little spilt wine—it is nothing—

*(The bustle and JOHN'S incoherent apologies fade into the buzz of general
conversation, which carries us, as it were, through the room to the Upper
Table)*

CONVERSATION: Such a pretty wedding.... Try this lamb stuffed with
olives ... The handsomest couple I ever saw.... Wine to these gentlemen.... I should say they'd be very comfortably off.... Pass the figs....
But my mule cast a shoe, so I had to get a lift from the Ezras.... A really
lovely present—a silver bowl and five changes of raiment.... Oh, that's
the prophet from Nazareth—From Nazareth? Good heavens! ...

BENJAMIN: Well, my dear boy, this is a great day. Such a pleasure to see you
happily married. Tell me now—have you taken a peep at your bride?

THE BRIDEGROOM: Well, sir, not officially. She has not yet raised her
veil.

BENJAMIN: Ah! but unofficially, perhaps you don't need me to tell you what
a lucky dog you are. Eh, my dear?

THE BRIDE: My Lord Benjamin is far too kind.

THE BRIDEGROOM: Steward—wine to the Lord Benjamin!... We are sorry not to see your son here today.

BENJAMIN: He was coming—but he didn't seem quite the thing this evening, so his mother kept him at home.

THE BRIDE: We're sorry to hear that.

BENJAMIN: Oh, I don't suppose it's anything much. Touch of fever or something.... Hullo! I see you've got one of my humble neighbours here—Simon, the fisherman—very worthy fellow, lives on my estate—how'd he come here, Susannah?

SUSANNAH: I think he came with Jesus bar-Joseph—the prophet from Nazareth, you know. That tall man with the golden beard.

BENJAMIN: Prophet, eh? Didn't know prophets ever came to parties. That sort mostly live on bread and water, like that sour-faced fanatical fellow, what's-his-name, John Baptist, whom Herod clapped into gaol the other day. How did you come to rope in a prophet?

SUSANNAH: The mother of Jesus is a very old friend of mine.

BENJAMIN: Oh, I see. That's different. He certainly doesn't look fanatical, and he seems to eat and drink like a human being.

RABBI: The young man has the face of one who lives close to God.

BENJAMIN: I beg your pardon, Rabbi Solomon. Forgive a worldly old man's careless way of talking.... This is a very decent wine you've given us, my boy.

SUSANNAH: I'm glad you like it. Because you must now propose the health of the young people.

BENJAMIN: Who, me?

SUSANNAH: Of course. As an old friend of my new daughter—and the most important man in the company.

BENJAMIN: My dear Susannah....

THE BRIDEGROOM: Steward! The Lord Benjamin is going to make a speech.

STEWARD: Pray silence for the Lord Benjamin ben-Hadad.

(Applause and silence)

BENJAMIN: My dear young friends—and my dear old friend Susannah *(applause)*—I don't pretend to be a great speaker. I am much better fitted to do justice to the excellence of your hospitality than to the solemnity of the occasion. *(Laughter)* But I speak from long and fortunate experience when I say that a good wife and a happy home are the greatest blessings a man can enjoy. *(Applause)* Knowing both bride and bridegroom as I do, I feel confident that their friends have chosen most happily for them both *(Applause)*, and I wish them as much joy in each other and in their family as I have experienced in my own home. *(Applause)* I can't say more. Here's to the Bridegroom and his Bride. The God of Abraham bless them!

ALL: The Bridegroom and his Bride!

(Prolonged applause)

BENJAMIN: Phew! that's over. Now let the musicians give us a tune.
(Music—suggesting the passing of some little time—as it ends, the voice of the
BRIDEGROOM *emerges in the middle of a conversation)*

THE BRIDEGROOM: Of course, Rabbi Solomon. If you would really like to hear him.

RABBI: I should indeed, if my Lord Benjamin is agreeable.

BENJAMIN: Yes, yes, by all means. I only hope he won't rant and shout and go on at us about our sins. I like to have my dinner in peace. Still, I've no doubt, if we've got a prophet, the guests would like to hear him.

THE BRIDEGROOM: I really think they would. Will you speak, Rabbi? Steward!

STEWARD *(raps the table. Silence)*: The Rabbi Solomon desires to speak.

RABBI: My dear friends—we are gathered here on a most blessed occasion. It is right that we should celebrate it with feasting and laughter, for God is a kind Father and loves that His children should enjoy all His good gifts. But we must never forget that the hope of Israel looks forward to the redemption of God's people and the coming of His righteous Kingdom. I am told that we have among us a prophet of that Kingdom, and I think we should turn for a moment from our pleasure to listen to his message *(murmur of interest)*. Jesus of Nazareth—will you favour the request of an old man—too old, I fear, to see the Kingdom with his mortal eyes—and tell us, as God has inspired you, what that Kingdom is and how soon we may look for its coming?

JESUS: The Kingdom of Heaven is within you, and only the Father knows the day or the hour of its coming. For this is how it is with the Kingdom of Heaven: it is like ten bridesmaids going to a wedding. Five of them were careful, sensible girls, but the other five were rather empty-headed. They all set out together for the bride's house, wearing their best clothes and taking their lamps to join in the torchlight procession. The careless ones filled their lamps and trusted to luck, but the sensible ones each took the trouble to carry a little pitcher of oil as well. Now it happened that the bridegroom was delayed on the way and arrived very late, so that the bridal party grew tired and sleepy waiting for him—and in fact, they all dozed off. But at midnight they heard voices crying in the street: "The bridegroom's coming! Go out now to meet him!" Then all the bridesmaids got up quickly and began to trim their lamps. And the happy-go-lucky ones said to the others: "Oh dear! our lamps have burnt out. Do lend us some of your oil." But the careful bridesmaids said: "We can't do that; there wouldn't be enough to go round. You had better run to the oil-merchant's and buy some, and then there will be enough for everybody." But while the girls were knocking up the oil-merchant, the bridegroom arrived. All the people who were ready joined the procession, and away they went to the house—and as soon as they were in, the doors were shut and the wedding-feast began. And presently the poor silly bridesmaids came hurrying along and knocked at the door crying "Let us in! let us in!" But the bridegroom said, "I don't know you. It's too late now." Indeed and indeed I tell you: be always on the watch—for at any moment late or soon, the Son of Man may come.

(Pause. Somebody murmurs "Thank you"—there is a sort of hesitation and the conversation begins again)

GUESTS: Hardly what I expected.... Didn't tell us much, did he?... the Kingdom.... The Son of Man—that's the bridegroom.... Christ is the bridegroom of his people—like the Song of Solomon ... those foolish bridesmaids—exactly like you, Rachel—oh, *Mother!*... It made me rather uncomfortable....

SUSANNAH: Well, my Lord Benjamin! That was nice and short, wasn't it? And he didn't shout, or denounce anybody, or anything. Just a simple story.

BENJAMIN: I don't know—I don't know. It's a fact—one ought to think more about religion and all that.... "Too late"—that's an ugly thought—what do you say, Rabbi Solomon?

RABBI *(deeply moved):* "Too late"—I am eighty years old, and I thought "too late"—too late now to behold the Kingdom—but the Bridegroom came at midnight.

(Music)

REUBEN: Issachar! Issachar! They want more wine at the upper table.

ISSACHAR: It's all very well to say, "More wine"—but I've drained the last skin dry.

REUBEN *(horrified):* No more wine! Holy prophets! What are we to do now!

ISSACHAR: Say so, I suppose.

REUBEN: Say so! and put the whole house to shame?—We shall be flogged for this.

ISSACHAR: It isn't our fault. It was all these extra guests.... You should have managed more economically....

REUBEN: You should have left a better margin....

ISSACHAR: The master did the ordering himself. I'd nothing to do with it. Well, it's no good arguing about whose fault it was.

REUBEN: No wine! what a disgrace!...

MARY: Reuben.... What's this? Did you say there was no more wine?

REUBEN: It's a fact, Madam Mary. And they're calling for it at the upper table.

MARY: Oh, dear! what *can* we do?

ISSACHAR *(sourly):* Run round to the merchant, I should think—like the young ladies the gentleman was telling us about.

MARY: But it's too late for that—

REUBEN: "Too late"—there you are!

STEWARD *(in an angry shout):* Reuben! Issachar! Wine to the upper table!

REUBEN *(desperately):* Coming, sir, coming.

MARY: This is dreadful. Wait a moment. My son will think of a way—Jesus! *(more urgently)* Jesus!

JESUS: Well, Mother?

MARY: They have no wine. *(Silence)* Do you hear, my son? They have no wine. We must do something to help them. Quickly. I want you to think—

JESUS: Woman, why do you trouble me? What am I to you?

MARY *(taken aback):* My son! *(recollecting herself)* Oh, no. I am sorry. *(With a kind of tender self-reproach)* You have done my bidding too long. That time is over.

JESUS: *My* time has not yet come.

ANDREW *(in a whisper):* John, what does he mean?

JOHN: I don't know, Andrew.

MARY: The cups stand empty, the songs are silent, the laughter is stilled; the Bride and Bridegroom are come to the marriage—but they have no wine.

JOHN *(softly):* Lady, we must abide the time. Fix your eyes on the Master's face.

MARY: Reuben, Issachar!

SERVANTS: Madam!

MARY: Whatever he tells you to do—do it.

JESUS *(in the voice of a somnambulist):* The six great water-pots there—fill them up with water.

REUBEN: With water?

MARY: Quickly.

SIMON: John—what is the matter? Why do you look like that?

JOHN: There is power all about us, like the stir that goes before the rising of a great wind.

REUBEN: All six pots are filled to the brim with water.

JESUS: Draw out now, and carry it to the steward.

REUBEN: The water, sir? . . . very well. . . . Issachar, what madness is this?

ISSACHAR: Do as he says. . . .

(He drops his pitcher with a strangled shriek)

God of Abraham!

REUBEN: This is not water.

ISSACHAR: It is wine. . . . What or whom have we let into the house?

REUBEN: What demon? What angel?—

JESUS *(sharply and sternly):* Do your service, and say nothing.

STEWARD *(in an angry shout):* Wine, you lazy slaves—wine!—Why the delay? And what's the matter with you?

REUBEN *(quaveringly):* I am sorry, sir. We dropped the pitcher. . . .

STEWARD: Careless dogs!—Let me taste the wine.

ISSACHAR: Yes, sir.

JOHN: Lady—what ails you? Look up. Speak to him.

MARY: Oh, I have rocked him in my arms—and now the power of God is upon him. When the angel told me that I should bear a son, I praised God, and sang aloud, "For He fills the hungry with good things—" and I asked, not knowing what I asked, but He gave more. O Jesus, son of the Blessed—

JESUS: Dear Mother.

(A sudden burst of laughter from the upper table)

THE BRIDEGROOM: Here's our wine at last. What was the trouble, Steward? Opening a new wineskin, eh? Is it a good one?

STEWARD: Well, sir—most gentlemen serve their best wine first, and later on, when people have drunk well and are less particular, they bring up a second-best. But you have kept the best wine until now.

(More laughter, conversation, and a burst of music)

SCENE II (CAPERNAUM)

SEQUENCE I (THE NOBLEMAN'S HOUSE)

THE EVANGELIST: And there was a certain nobleman, whose son was sick at Capernaum. . . .

BENJAMIN: The letter is not quite ready. Sit down on the porch while I finish it.

ISSACHAR: Thank you, my Lord Benjamin. . . . My mistress will be sorry to hear that the young gentleman is no better.

BENJAMIN: He is dying, Issachar. The doctors say there is no hope. And he is my only son.

ISSACHAR: The hand of the Lord is heavy upon your house.

BENJAMIN: He gives, and He takes away.

ISSACHAR: Blessed be His name.

BENJAMIN *(with a heavy sigh):* Amen.

(Short pause, while BENJAMIN'S *pen squeaks over the parchment)*

What is this extraordinary story you have been telling them in the kitchen about the Prophet, Jesus of Nazareth?

ISSACHAR: It is true, my lord. As the God of our fathers liveth, every word is true.

BENJAMIN: Very strange. . . . Did the Prophet put anything into the water-pots?

ISSACHAR: First and last, my lord, he never went near them. Nor did he touch the water, or pronounce any magical words. He said only, "Fill", and then "Draw out".

BENJAMIN: Whoever this man Jesus is, he is not a magician. Those gentry always use long words and obscure speech, full of the names of demons. But this man spoke as simply as a child. And he is good. I've never been very religious, but I've knocked about the world a bit, and I know men. Whatever strange power he has, it is of God.

ISSACHAR: Yes, my lord. . . . They are saying in Jerusalem—

BENJAMIN: Is he known in Jerusalem?

ISSACHAR: He went up to the Passover feast last week—and they are saying there that he is the Messiah of Israel.

BENJAMIN: The Messiah of Israel?—Why? Did he do any mighty works there?

ISSACHAR: No, my lord. But I can tell you all about it, for I was there myself. My mistress Susannah had gone up to Jerusalem with my young master and mistress and all the household. And on the second day I was standing in the outer court of the Temple. Listen—this was how it happened.

> (Music: and fade in Temple sounds in background, while ISSACHAR makes his running commentary)

You know what that court is like—more like a fair than anything else— with people selling pigeons and lambs for the sacrifice—and a wicked price they charge, too—and the pilgrims going up and down all mixed up with the goats and oxen—

> (Appropriate noises of CROWD and ANIMALS)

> (CROWD conversation for the above): "Make way there . . . mind yourselves. . . . What? five shekels for that miserable animal? . . . That's my price, take it or leave it. . . . My veil! clumsy brute! . . . Sheer robbery. . . . I gave you fifteen drachmas. . . . There you are, madam— who's next? . . . Fetch me another bag of silver. . . . Is that the best rate you can give me? . . . Seven shekels and no more. . . . I'll take nine. . . . Eight, and it's a bargain. . . . You're a thief! . . . Now then, sir! . . . Keep order there! . . . etc., etc., mixed up with animal cries and the sound of chinking money)

Well, anyway, I'd just finished chaffering for a couple of doves when I noticed a bit of a disturbance, and there was a bunch of young men standing at the top of the steps leading down from the Inner Court, and at the head of them stood Jesus of Nazareth—and my word! He had a scroll of the Law in one hand, and in the other a scourge of whipcord, like a cat-o'-nine-tails—and if it hadn't been for his golden hair, just for the moment you'd have taken him for his cousin John the Baptist. And then he spoke—and everybody stopped to listen—

THE VOICE OF JESUS: Children of Israel! Chosen of the Lord!—Is this the House of God and are you His people? Chaffering, cheating, quarrelling in the very courts of the Lord. Take heed to yourselves—for what says the Prophet Malachi? "The Lord whom ye seek shall suddenly come to His

Temple. He shall purify the sons of Levi, and purge them as gold and silver; and they shall offer unto the Lord offerings in righteousness." So speaks the prophet—"offering in righteousness"—but what sort of offerings are these? Out of my sight, robbers, and liars every one of you. I will not bear you in my Father's house.

ISSACHAR: And he fell upon them with his whip—and drove them out helter-skelter. And he threw down the tables of the hucksters and the money-changers and flung the silver all over the floor.

(*Background noises:* "My money!... my pigeons ... help!.... alas!.... I'm undone—my silver! my gold! my merchandise.... Oh Lord, oh Lord! a thousand shekels of silver"—*Flutter of wings, trampling, etc. and cries of* "Serve the scoundrels right! It's a disgrace!")

The Temple police tried to interfere. But they were stopped by the Elders. I heard what they said, for they were standing close beside me.

LEVITE: But, sir, it is a scandal. Surely you won't allow it.

1ST ELDER: Leave it alone. There might be a riot. The people have no love for the merchants.

2ND ELDER: Can you blame them? I have told you this market should be regulated and the prices controlled.

3RD ELDER: I dare say. But this fellow is dangerous. He will set himself up as a popular leader, and then there'll be trouble.

1ST ELDER: There may be more to it than that. You heard what he said: "The Lord whom ye seek shall suddenly come to His Temple".

2ND ELDER: What of it?

1ST ELDER: That is a prophecy of the Messiah. And I shouldn't wonder if this Jesus were to set up a claim to be the Christ.

3RD ELDER: Do you think so? That would never do.

2ND ELDER: And supposing he *were* the Messiah?

1ST ELDER: He? the Messiah?—you're joking.... But it means we had better go carefully.

3RD ELDER: Well, we must do *something*. What do you propose?

1ST ELDER: Go, one of you Levites, and fetch him here.... We will ask him to give us a sign; and if he can't give one, we will have him locked up as a charlatan and an agitator.

2ND ELDER: And what if he does give you a sign?

1ST ELDER: In that case, my dear Shadrach, we will leave him to you, and you can acknowledge him as the Messiah—at your own risk.

LEVITE: I gave him your message, but he will not come. He said—

3RD ELDER: Well?

LEVITE: He said you could come to him.

3RD ELDER: What insolence!

1ST ELDER: What did I tell you? This is all part of the game. Shadrach, what are you doing?

2ND ELDER: I will go and speak to him. . . . I think you had better come with me.

ISSACHAR: So he stood there under the porch, smiling a little now, and drawing the cords of the whip through his fingers. The Elder Shadrach addressed him first?

2ND ELDER (*mildly*): Sir, what is the meaning of this disturbance?

JESUS: You are an Elder of Israel, and you ask me that? It is written in God's word, "My house shall be called the house of prayer"—but you have made it a den of thieves.

3RD ELDER: And what business is it of yours?

SIMON (*suddenly and loudly*): The zeal of the Lord has performed it, as it is written, "The zeal of thine house hath devoured me!"

ANDREW: Simon, be quiet.

1ST ELDER: If you take it on yourself to do this kind of thing, will you give us a sign of your authority?

JESUS: Yes; I will give you a sign. Destroy this Temple of God, and in three days I will raise it up.

1ST ELDER: Destroy the Temple?

3RD ELDER: Six and forty years it took to build it—and you say you will raise it up again in three days?

JESUS: You heard what I said, and all these men are my witnesses. Will you now give me leave to pass?

1ST ELDER: Oh, let the man go.

3RD ELDER: It's no good arguing with him.

1ST ELDER: He must be beside himself.

2ND ELDER: A very quick-witted man. You asked for a sign, and he has not refused. He has only proposed impossible conditions. If anybody has been made to look foolish, it is not Jesus of Nazareth. You will have to handle him carefully—for he is both bold and clever.

1ST ELDER: He is the more dangerous. . . . The service is beginning. I shall report this matter to the High Priest.

ISSACHAR: So they went away. But Jesus went down into the city, and a great crowd followed him, and hung upon his words, while he preached the good news of the Kingdom.

BENJAMIN: A strange man—and a strange story. . . . See, Issachar—here is the letter, and here is something for your pains.

ISSACHAR: My lord is very generous. I hope there may soon be better news to send.

BENJAMIN: It is as God wills. . . . Good-day to you. . . . Stay! where is the Prophet now?

ISSACHAR: We left Jerusalem before him; but I heard that he was expected back today in Cana.

BENJAMIN: I must try to see more of him. . . . Farewell.

ISSACHAR: Farewell, my lord, and thank you.

BENJAMIN *(alone):* Signs and wonders, tales and prophecies—the world is full of new things. And my son is dying—and what is all that to me? Have pity, O God, on an old and lonely man. *(clapping his hands)* Dorcas! Dorcas!

DORCAS: My lord?

BENJAMIN: Has the doctor been? Is the boy any better?—No; don't tell me. You are crying—that means the worst.

DORCAS *(weeping):* Oh, my lord—they say it is only a matter of hours.

BENJAMIN: O merciful God that didst restore the widow's son by the hand of thy Prophet Elijah—*(with a sudden change of tone)* Dorcas!

DORCAS *(surprised):* My lord!

BENJAMIN: Run to the stable—Call for horses. One for me and a saddlehorse with a groom to lead him—Hurry, girl, hurry!

(DORCAS runs out, crying "Horses! horses for my lord!")

It's only a chance—I can but try. . . . *(Calling off)* Hey, you there! bring me my boots. . . . If I can persuade him. . . . Gold? houses? servants? . . . Fool that I am—that sort of man doesn't take bribes. . . . God forgive me for the thought . . . Dorcas, my cloak! Are the horses coming? . . . Quickly, quickly— that will do. . . . No, no—neither purse nor sword—nothing. . . . Oh, my son, my son! . . . There, I am ready. . . . My stirrup, Eleazar!

DORCAS: My lord, where are you going?

BENJAMIN: Cana—Jerusalem—anywhere—to look for Jesus of Nazareth.

(Horses gallop off and fade out)

Sequence 2 (On the Road)

THE EVANGELIST: So Jesus came again into Cana of Galilee, where he made the water wine.

JAMES: It's no use arguing, Andrew. We've given our word to see this thing through, and we shall manage somehow.

ANDREW: My dear James, it's all very well for you and John. Your father's well off. But Simon and I have only ourselves to depend on, and Simon's got a wife and family.

SIMON: Don't bring me into it. My wife and I have talked the matter out, and she quite agrees. I dare say we'll be able to do a bit of fishing now and again. And, after all, we don't need much. A little bread and oil and a handful of dates and olives—

ANDREW: How about clothes? *They* don't grow on trees—and I must have a new pair of sandals.

JAMES: Really, Andrew! I never knew such a man for making difficulties. Cheer up! It'll be all right when the Kingdom comes.

ANDREW: Yes, but when's it coming? If we have to tramp about Galilee for years—Stop laughing, James!

JAMES: Well, you look so cross.

ANDREW *(shortly):* It's hot and I'm tired. And I'm worried. None of you people can think five minutes ahead—

SIMON: Don't let John see you looking like that.

ANDREW: Oh, John! He trots along there with his head in the clouds, chattering to the Master and taking no notice of anything. We might all starve as far as he's concerned. John, indeed!

JAMES: Here, you leave my brother alone.

ANDREW: All right, all right—but you and your brother—

JESUS: Children, children! What are you quarrelling about?

ANDREW *(sulkily):* Money.

JESUS: You must make up your minds, you know. Nobody can serve two masters, and you can't serve God and your own interests at the same time.

ANDREW: I'm only worried about how we're going to manage. We must eat to live—and our bodies have to be clothed.

JESUS: But you mustn't worry. There's more in life than eating and drinking, and the body is worth more than clothing. Live like the birds, from day to day—they neither sow nor reap nor hoard up food for the winter, yet God feeds them all the same. And these wild flowers—think how they grow. They don't spin, they don't weave—yet I tell you Solomon in all his glory was never so splendidly arrayed. And if God takes care of these little plants, which flower for a day and are food for cattle tomorrow—do you think He will not take care of you who mean more to Him than the flowers? You have so little faith. Don't plan ahead, like worldly people—let the future look after itself. And don't meet trouble half-way.

ANDREW: I am sorry—but . . .

JESUS: Take all your troubles to God. Ask, and it shall be given to you; seek, and you will find; knock, and all doors will be opened to you. If one of your sons were to ask you for bread, would you give him a stone? If he asked you for fish to eat, would you give him a snake? What do you say, Simon?

(Sound of hoofs drawing nearer)

SIMON: No, Master. I'm always ready to give my boys anything that's good for them.

JESUS: Then if you, who are sinful men, know how to give good things to your children, how much more will your Heavenly Father deal kindly and lovingly with you.

JOHN: Master, take care! These horsemen are in a hurry. They'll run us down.

GROOM *(reining up right on top of them):* Hey, there, you peasants! We're looking for a man called Jesus of Nazareth.

JESUS: I am Jesus of Nazareth.

GROOM: Oh, are you? Well, you're wanted. *(Calling)* Here you are, my lord, this is him!

BENJAMIN *(arriving and dismounting):* Thank Heaven!—Oh, sir, I have been hunting for you everywhere. You may remember me—Benjamin ben-Hadad from Capernaum—we met at Cana. I sought you there, but they said you hadn't yet come—so I set out for Jerusalem.... Pray God I am still in time.

JESUS: What do you want of me?

BENJAMIN: My son, sir—my only son—he is sick, dying. He may be dead already. Sir, I beseech you to come down with me to Capernaum and heal him if he is still alive ... a matter of hours the doctor said—it is now the seventh hour—half a day lost already!—I have brought a horse—mount and ride, and we may still do it.

JESUS: What made you come to me?

BENJAMIN: You are a Prophet—you have power. I heard what you did in Cana—the servants told me how you made the water wine ... only lay your hand on my son—your touch will do him good ... Oh, come quickly—I implore you not to waste time.... What can I say?—I know I've never been particularly pious or thought much about religion, but if only you can save my boy, I'll do anything—anything! ... I'll serve God truly—I'll try to be a better man—I'll listen to all you say and believe from my heart—

JESUS: You are all alike. Unless you see miracles, you will believe nothing.

BENJAMIN *(desperately):* Oh! I don't know what I'm saying.... Never mind me.... Sir, come down before my child dies.

(Pause)

JESUS: Go your way home.

*(*BENJAMIN *is ready to utter a cry of protest)*

Your son shall live.

BENJAMIN *(thrown off his balance):* But you—but you—

JOHN *(in an anguished whisper):* O dear God, let him only believe it!

JESUS: I tell you, he shall live.

BENJAMIN *(after a pause during which he gazes anxiously into the eyes which challenge his, and with a sigh of relief):* I believe you.

JESUS: As you have believed, so it will be. Go in peace.

BENJAMIN: Thank you. God bless you. Eleazar—my horse.

GROOM: Won't the Prophet come, my lord? Shall we bring him by force.

BENJAMIN: No. no—it's all right. He says it will be all right. We can go home.

(The horses start off at a quiet trot—Fade them out and fade in again)

GROOM: Look ahead, my lord.

BENJAMIN: Eh, what? ... I was asleep in the saddle.... Why, it's long past daybreak.... Where are we?

GROOM: Just coming down into Capernaum.

BENJAMIN: How sweet the morning air is! It's good to be home again.

GROOM (dubiously): I hope so, my lord.

BENJAMIN: What do you mean, you hope so?

GROOM: There's a bunch of people coming up the road. I think—yes, it is—it's Dorcas and some of the servants. . . . Oh, my lord, I beg you—prepare yourself—If the news should be bad—if it should be the worst—

BENJAMIN: Be quiet, Eleazar! He said, "As you believe. . . . " and I do believe, and so must you. He *said* it would be all right. . . . Look! they're waving to us. . . . They're shouting something. . . . I can't hear. . . .

(He whips up his tired horse)

GROOM: Here comes Dorcas, running like a hare.

BENJAMIN: Good girl!

DORCAS (calling and panting as she runs up): My lord, my lord!

BENJAMIN (reining in his horse): Well, now, my lass! What news?—He is alive?

DORCAS (gasping the words out): Praise God, my lord! alive and better. He will recover!

BENJAMIN: My boy will live.

DORCAS: O thank God, my lord, thank God!

BENJAMIN: Thank God, indeed. . . . Take it easy, child—get your breath. . . . When did he take a turn for the better?

DORCAS (more quietly): We all thought he was gone. He was so weak, and parched with fever . . . the mistress bathed his head—it was like fire . . . he had been rambling, but towards evening he seemed to have no strength left—he was sinking fast, and I said to my lady, "If only his father were here!" His breathing seemed to grow fainter and fainter, and I thought it had stopped, and I threw my apron over my head. And then my lady said, in a funny, quick voice: "Dorcas, see here!"—and I laid my hand on his, and it was all of a cool sweat, and he was asleep and breathing like a child. . . . (She bursts into tears)

BENJAMIN: What time was this?

DORCAS: Yesterday, at the seventh hour.

BENJAMIN: At the seventh hour, Eleazar. Will you believe now? At the seventh hour he told me, "Your son shall live"—and I believed him and it was so. Hear me, Jesus of Nazareth, wherever you are!—Whether you are prophet, angel or Christ I cannot tell, but I call all these to witness that your word is the living truth.

THE EVANGELIST: And Jesus came to Cana and thence to Capernaum. And at even, when the sun was set, they brought unto him all that were diseased, or possessed with devils; and he laid his hands upon them and healed them all.

THE HEIRS TO THE KINGDOM

CHARACTERS

The EVANGELIST.
JESUS.
PHILIP.
ANDREW BAR-JONAH.
SIMON BAR-JONAH ("Simon Peter")
JAMES BAR-ZEBEDEE.
JOHN BAR-ZEBEDEE.
NATHANAEL BARTHOLOMEW.
MATTHEW, the Tax-Collector.
JUDAS ISCARIOT.

} Disciples of Jesus.

PROCLUS, a Roman Centurion.
SOSIUS, an old Soldier, friend of Proclus.
An INNKEEPER.
CAIAPHAS, High Priest of Israel.
BARUCH THE ZEALOT.
The HERODIAN.
1st ELDER.
2nd ELDER ("Shadrack").
3rd ELDER.
NICODEMUS.
The RABBI SOLOMON.
A DISCIPLE of John Baptist.
CROWD.

NOTES

THE PLAY

The general tone of this play is rather sombre and ominous. It *has* got structure, but this may not be very clear in the reading, and needs to be emphasized in production.

The friends and foes of the Kingdom are now definitely ranging themselves in opposite camps.

On the one side stand the Jewish and Roman authorities, quarrelling bitterly among themselves, and united only in antagonism to Jesus.

On the other side are the forces of the Kingdom: (1) the Disciples, awestruck, excited, and enthusiastic, but already showing perilous signs of weakness and lack of understanding; (2) the Jewish people, fearfully unprepared for their great opportunity. Into this camp comes Judas; the man of brilliant gifts and intellect, bringing just the qualities which the other disciples lack, but foredoomed by those very qualities to play the traitor. On John the Baptist, the greatest prophet of the Old Order, falls first the shadow of doubt and finally the reality of disaster. Both the true disciples and the false disciple are his bequest to the New Order.

The light burns clear in John Evangelist and his fellows; but many of the Children of the Kingdom will be cast into outer darkness—the Gentile (Proclus) and the publican (Matthew) will take their seats at the King's Feast. There is a sense everywhere of disquiet and the breaking-up of old things; and this sense is focused in Jesus himself, and flows out, as it were, from him.

THE CHARACTERS

PHILIP—An ingenuous young man—with the accent rather on the "young"—of an engaging and puppy-like simplicity. He bounces out at Matthew with a sort of school-boy rudeness, and bounces back penitently. Later on, at the Last Supper, he will blurt out the simple and colossal demand, "Lord, show us the Father and then we shall be satisfied"—to receive the most staggering reply ever heard by human ears. But at present he is only suffering from the awareness of having made an ass of himself.

SIMON (PETER)—The character in the Gospels is astonishingly consistent. His life is a succession of vivid moments—sometimes of flashing insight and sometimes of blinding failure. Things "come over him all of a sudden", and when this happens, it is sometimes as though he did not know what he was saying. The story he tells about the Miraculous Draught is one of those moments. It was just an astonishing catch of fish—and suddenly it came over him that he was a very ordinary sinful man faced with something so beautiful as to be quite unbearable. (The other two great moments like this are the Transfiguration, when he "wist not what to say" and babbled sheer nonsense, and the confession, "Thou art . . . the Son of the living God",

when he spoke, not as "flesh and blood", but with the voice of revelation.)
When he is not inspired, he can plunge impulsively into the worst blunders
and suffer heavy rebuke—(I have given a little instance of this in the scene
with Proclus to prepare for the coming great rebukes—e.g., the "get
behind me, Peter", the "if I wash thee not" and "thou shalt deny me
thrice"). The actor should bear these other episodes in mind when telling
the story about the fish.

MATTHEW—He is as vulgar a little commercial Jew as ever walked Whitechapel,
and I should play him with a frank Cockney accent.[1] (If any of the other
disciples are slipping into rafeened speech, Matthew will kill them stone-dead;
they have been warned.) He has oily black hair and rapacious little hands,
and though his common little soul has been converted as thoroughly as
that of any Salvation Army penitent, his common little wits are in full
working order. He has been swept off his feet by a heavenly kindness and
beauty of mind which had never dawned, even as a possibility, on his
sordid experience. He has no opinion of himself—he never had—but he is
expanding and revelling in the sheer ecstasy of not being trodden upon. He
has gleefully thrown away all his worldly goods—but, all the same, his
professional instincts are shocked by financial stupidity and appealed to by
financial astuteness. He thinks the Parable of the Unjust Steward is a
frightfully funny story. He gives the account of his own conversion with
the utmost sincerity and without any sort of self-consciousness. He is
having a wonderful time and Jesus is wonderful, and he wants everybody
to know it. Jesus likes Matthew very much.

JOHN has nothing very special in this play except his little account of the
Raising of the Widow's Son. *He must not tell it sentimentally.* The emotional
dots which punctuate his narrative are not sobs of pathos over the poor
widow, but the horror of the numinous—"the dead boy sat up—and
spoke". One feels that it was touch-and-go whether everybody was going
to scream or go mad—when the boy was put in his mother's arms, and that
broke the tension and they all praised God. It wants a sort of breathless
voice, like a loud whisper. Judas restores the conversation to the earthly
and practicable by the grim reminder: "You're right. There *will* be trouble."

JUDAS—When we last saw Judas, he was beginning to catch a glimpse of what
John Baptist's call to repentance really meant. He has learnt a good deal in
those months of exile at Machaerus. He has lost his air as of a competent
undergraduate organising a mission service; he has matured into a very
intelligent young man indeed. He can answer Jesus in his own allusive and
parabolic style, and can understand without explanations. Let the actor get
out of his head any notion that Judas is insincere. He is passionately sincere.
He means to be faithful—and he will be faithful—to the light which he sees

---

[1] Not a Jewish accent—as though the others were not Jews—but just plain townee
and common.

so brilliantly. What he sees is the true light—only he does not see it directly, but only its reflection in the mirror of his own brain; and in the end that mirror will twist and distort the reflection and send it dancing away over the bog like a will o' the wisp. He has all the gifts—both the practical and imaginative; and his calculating friend the Zealot is quite right in saying that he will fall, like Adam, by the sin of spiritual pride. He could have been the greatest in the Kingdom of Heaven, but he will be the worst—the worst that is the corruption of the best.

JESUS "knew all men", and knows well enough the knife-edge of risk that Judas represents. It is the risk that has to be taken, because the Kingdom must always reckon with such men as Judas, who can be the greatest saints or the greatest sinners. The great intellect must be let in, whatever its dangers. There is no need to suppose that Jesus, with his human mind, foresees certainly or in detail what Judas will do to him. What he does know certainly is that his Father's will must be fulfilled, if not this way, then that way. But he also knows intuitively that Judas is, as it were, the key that will open the door, either on to the way of triumph or on to the way of tragedy. The Parable of the Draw-net sums up the general bearings of this first scene—and we leave Jesus taking up the history of Joshua, to whom Judas has compared him.

The third scene, with its comparison of the Old Law and the New, picks up the remarks at the end of Scene I about the "treasure new and old". At the end we get the warning about the houses built on rock and sand—and then immediately the scene with Proclus, in which the faith of the Gentile is contrasted with the failure of the children of the Kingdom. (The draw-net is at work.) The silly remarks of the crowd lead to the sharp attack on them (about John the Baptist) and the great woes, delivered with a passion of disappointment that really frightens the people; and the fierce passion melts away into a great pity. (The news of John's murder finishes the play with a sort of hammer-blow.)

PROCLUS—Our old friend of the First Play. He is now 58, and might have retired twenty years ago, but the tremendous demands on the Roman Army during the early campaigns of Tiberius kept many men in the service long beyond their time; Proclus served as a veteran all through the German wars, and is still going strong, as regionary centurion in Galilee. His long experience in Judaea has given him the kind of understanding and tact in dealing with Jewish religious prejudices that an Anglo-Indian veteran might apply to Hindu regulations about caste and sacred cows. He knows and respects a holy man when he sees him, as the same Anglo-Indian might feel genuine veneration for the piety and power of a great Yogi or Mahatma. He knows, too, that in his own religion certain persons—such as the Vestals—have to observe sacred taboos, and would quite naturally expect something of the same sort to apply to a Jewish prophet. Also, he has a dim idea that people who work miracles may be gods in disguise—not that this leads him to any definite theological conclusions about Jesus, for nobody seriously expects Olympus to burst out into anything of that sort in the modern days, in spite of the peculiar things said to happen in the Mystery-cults; still, the line between gods and men is not very clearly drawn for Proclus. In fact his religious opinions are confused, but his feelings are in the right place. After the Crucifixion, he will say, "Truly, this man was son of God"—and the empty tomb, if he ever hears about it, will perhaps not surprise him very much.

SOSIUS—He is more commonplace. If he were a soldier stationed in India, he would probably lump Maharajah, Brahmin, and coolie together as a bunch of niggers. He has, of course, a proper Roman respect for the government, but (like any other retired soldier) is critical of government officials. He knows all about the miracles in Jerusalem, but is not more impressed by them than Sergeant Thomas Atkins might be by the remarkable exploits of witch-doctors and Hindu jugglers. These things happen—you can't explain 'em—but of course one should keep one's eye on people claiming to be Gautamas or anything funny, because they might start something. He gets twinges at times in his game leg, which make him all the more disposed to irritation with things and people in general.

BARUCH THE ZEALOT—"The Zealots rejected the opportunist fatalism of the conservative Pharisees; God, they declared, would help only those that helped themselves, and it was the duty of every Jew to fight for national independence. The party developed into a powerful secret organisation which waged an unrelenting campaign of assassination and terrorism, directed as much against the loyal Jews, whom they regarded as traitors to the national cause, as against the Roman government." (A. H. M. Jones) —This man's intervention will produce a curious reaction from Judas, who (after the Entry into Jerusalem) will betray Jesus for fear lest he should succumb to the temptation of becoming Baruch's sort of Messiah. Baruch, who in fact desires nothing better than a demonstration against Rome, is ready enough to betray the conservative Jews who fancy they are making a tool of him; he in turn will try to make a tool of Judas, but that tool will turn in his hand and betray him also. Finally, Baruch will try to make a tool of Jesus; when that happens, Judas will betray both of them and himself too.

THE HERODIAN—This gentleman explains his party's views clearly enough. He will turn up again in the matter of the tribute-money.

THE ELDERS—We know all about them from the Third Play.

CAIAPHAS is the complete ecclesiastical politician—a plausible and nasty piece of work.

SCENE I (GALILEE)

THE EVANGELIST: Now after Jesus had healed many sick people, he went out one day and saw a tax-collector called Matthew sitting at the receipt of custom. And he said unto him, "Follow me"; and he left all, rose up, and followed him. And Jesus was in Galilee with his disciples.

PHILIP (*concluding a long tale of woe*): . . . so the merchant said, "That's right, isn't it?" and I said, "That's right"—but when I got home and reckoned it out I was six drachmas short.

ANDREW: Six drachmas! Well, really, Philip!

PHILIP: I'm very sorry, everybody.

SIMON: I daresay you are. But here's me and Andrew and the Zebedees working all night with the nets to get a living for the lot of us—and then you go and let yourself be swindled by the first cheating salesman you meet in the bazaar—

PHILIP: I told you I'm sorry. Master, I am very sorry. But it sounded all right when he worked it out.

MATTHEW: Fact is, Philip my boy, you've been had for a sucker. Let him ring the changes on you proper. You ought to keep your eyes skinned, you did really. If I was to tell you the dodges these fellows have up their sleeves, you'd be surprised.

PHILIP: Very likely, Matthew. But never having been a tax-collector, I haven't your advantages.

JOHN: Oh, Philip! That's not kind.

MATTHEW: I'm not denying I've pulled off some pretty shady deals in my time. Took my rake-off on everything that went through me 'ands. That's how I made my pile. I'm not sticking up for myself. But it's not right to let a twister get away with it like that. It isn't fair to your friends.

JOHN: Does it really matter? The Master says we oughtn't to bother about money. Didn't you, Master? Let the poor sinner have it, if it'll do him any good.

MATTHEW: All right, all right. Let him have it. But let him see you know all about him. Tell him, "Friend, you've cheated me, but I make you a present of the poor trash for the love of God"—then he might feel ashamed of himself. But if you behave plain silly, that only hardens his heart. It's innocents like you put temptations in a man's way. God forgive me, I ought to know. . . . What do you say, Master?

JESUS: Listen. I will tell you a story. There was once a rich man, who had a steward, and one day he got to know that this man had been playing ducks and drakes with the estate. So he sent for him and said: "I'm very sorry to hear this about you. I'm afraid I shall have to dismiss you. Bring me all the books, because I want to go through them." The steward was very much upset, and said to himself: "What am I to do now? I've lost my job. I'm no good at working on the land, and I'd be ashamed to live on charity. But

109

I've got an idea, that will make plenty of people glad to take me in and give me a new situation." So he sent for all the people who owed money to his employer and he said to the first: "How much do you owe my lord?" And the man said, "A hundred measures of oil". "Look here," said the steward, "I'm a friend of yours and I don't want to be hard on you—let's call it fifty." (MATTHEW *lets slip an unregenerate chuckle.*) And to the next debtor he said, "What ought we to get from you?" And the man said, "A hundred bushels of wheat". So the steward said, "That's rather stiff—make out your return for eighty bushels and I'll give you a receipt in full".

(MATTHEW *chuckles again*)

JOHN: But didn't the employer find out?

MATTHEW: You bet—after the chap had got his new job.

JESUS: Oh, yes, he found out eventually, and next time he met the steward he said (*menacingly*): "Fellow, you're a thorough scoundrel—(*with a change of tone*) but I do admire your thoroughness!"

MATTHEW (*slapping his thigh*): Ha, ha, ha! Good man!

JESUS: Worldly people, you see, use far more wisdom about their trifling affairs than unworldly people do about the affairs of God. They give their minds to what they are doing. And I say to you, Learn from them. Learn how to deal with the world and make friends with worldly people, so that when everything earthly fails you may know the way to their hearts. The man who is reliable in little things is reliable in great things too—and if you can't handle the goods of this world, how can you be trusted to handle the true treasures of Heaven?

PHILIP: Master, that's rather hard to understand. But I do see I'd no right to be so stupid. I'm sorry I spoke as I did to Matthew. Perhaps he'd better be our treasurer, till I've learnt a bit more worldly wisdom.

MATTHEW: No, no, not me. Please, Master, don't let it be me. I've put money out of my mind, and I'd rather not have the handling of it. I was brought up bad, you see—and I've repented; but if I was to feel the silver in my fingers again, I wouldn't answer for myself. Don't try me too hard, Lord, don't now. I'm only a beginner.

JESUS: God deals gently with beginners. He will not bear heavily on a split cane or smother a smouldering fire.

(*Knock*)

John, see who that is at the door.

JUDAS (*as the door is opened to him*): Excuse me, does Jesus of Nazareth live here? . . . Why, hullo, John bar-Zebedee!

JOHN: Judas! Where did you spring from? It's grand to see you. Come in. . . . Andrew! Simon! look who's here! . . .

(*Exclamations of surprise*)

Master, this is Judas Iscariot. He was with us when we were all disciples of John the Baptist, and he followed John when he went to prison.

JUDAS: Hail, honoured Rabbi.

JESUS: Judas Iscariot. . . . You are welcome for the love of my cousin John.

JUDAS: He sends greetings to you and to all. . . . Andrew, Simon—how good it is to be back!—Where's James?

JOHN: On the roof with Nathanael—I'll call them down . . . *(calling)* James! James! Here's Judas come to see us!

(Cry of "Coming" from overhead)

SIMON: Sit down, Judas, and tell us all the news. . . . This is Philip, by the way, and this is Matthew. . . . Your feet are dusty, I'll get you some water.

JUDAS: Thank you, Simon—Ah! here comes James! How are you, my lad?

JAMES: All the better for seeing you again. Nathanael, you've heard us talk about Judas—well, here he is as large as life. . . . I say, Judas—have you left John Baptist? He—he's all right, I hope?

JUDAS: If an eagle in a cage can be said to be all right. He is still a prisoner—in the Fortress of Machaerus.

JOHN: That grim and fearful place by the Dead Sea? Oh, Judas!

JUDAS: He is safer there. Out of sight, out of mind—and so long as the Queen forgets him, his life will be spared. Herod isn't unfriendly, and makes his captivity as tolerable as anything can be in that horrible salt desert. His friends are allowed to come and go, and news reaches us from time to time. We have heard much of your teaching, Rabbi Jesus, and of the wonderful works that you have done in Galilee, and we have marvelled. But John is restless. Day by day he looks out from his prison window over league upon league of white and barren salt. And he says, "It is well, it is well—but Herod rules in Galilee, and the hand of Caesar is over all. When will the Lord turn and visit His people? When will the long spears go up to Jerusalem?" And he sent me and two others to look for you and to ask what you mean to do.

JESUS: You shall see and hear all you will, and take back your report.

JUDAS: Concerning me, John sent you a special message. Shall I recite it?

JESUS: What does he say?

JUDAS: He says this: "Cousin and Master—I commend my pupil to you, who has been like a son to me. For I have taught him all I can"—these are John's words, you understand, and not mine—"I have taught him all I can, and I think that many things that are dark to my sight are clear to his. And I would not have him eat out his heart in the wilderness, where I remain, a prisoner of hope." That is John's message.

JESUS: Are you of one mind with him?

JUDAS: Master, I have loved John and honoured his teaching. But always he has pointed to one that should come after him; and now he stands as Moses stood on the summit of Pisgah and looked upon the new kingdom where he might never set foot. But it was Joshua that led Israel into Canaan, and are you not Joshua? For Joshua and Jesus mean the same thing; and so God's angel knew well when he named you before you were born. And I think that the new land will be very unlike the old, and the road towards it is a hidden way, and nothing will be as we supposed.

JESUS: There was a man called Nicodemus, a member of the Sanhedrim, who came to me secretly one night, asking about these things. And I told him: "Unless a man is born anew, he cannot see the Kingdom of God." But he did not understand. And I told him again. "Unless a man is born anew by water and spirit, he cannot enter in. For the wind blows as it wills, and you hear the sound of it, but nobody knows where it comes from or where it is going—and so are all those who are born on the wind of the spirit."

JUDAS: That is what I mean. John's baptism is of water—yours, of the spirit, as he said. But what does the water know of the wind that troubles its waves?

JESUS: You have subtlety and understanding, and courage too, I think. These are great gifts. Where God has given so much, He will require great things. . . . Can you be faithful?

JUDAS: I hope so. I will tell you this; if I set my hand to the plough, I will never look back, though the furrow should run with tears and blood.

JESUS: That, I am sure, is true. Take care lest it turn out truer than you think. But if you are resolved, then come and follow me—for everything that the prophets have said about me must be fulfilled, and nothing can happen except as my Father wills.

(Pause)

Children, entertain your friend. I must be alone for a little.

(He goes out)

ANDREW: You have put him in a strange mood, Judas. When he is like that, I can make nothing of him. But you seem to understand him.

JUDAS: Andrew, you don't know what you have got hold of. The world's being turned upside-down while you sit and look on. What do you think he is—that man who has just gone out?

PHILIP: We think he is the Messiah who will restore the kingdom of Israel.

NATHANAEL: And the power of God is certainly with him. He lays his hand on the sick and cures them—and does many other wonderful things.

SIMON: I remember the very first time I realised that he wasn't like other men. He had been sitting in the boat with Andrew and me, talking about the love of God. Very sweetly indeed he spoke. We'd had a bad night with the trawls, and were feeling a bit down-hearted, but we forgot that, listening to him. And all of a sudden he said, quick and cheerful: "Lads—let down the net on this side if you want a catch". I said, "It's not much use—we toiled all night and took nothing, but we'll have a try if you like". So we did—and the weight of the fish broke the net; we had a job to get 'em aboard. And I lost my head—it seemed so queer, and I was tired, and I fell on my knees and said: "Sir, go away and leave us—I'm a sinful common man, and I can't bear it". And he laughed, and said, "Have courage; follow me and I will teach you how to catch men". . . . Of course, that's nothing to the things we've seen since: but I'll never quite get over that first moment— the sun on the sea, and the fish leaping and shining, and the shock of knowing that he wasn't—that he wasn't ordinary.

MATTHEW: Ah! makes you feel bad, he does, sometimes. Laughs and talks and eats with you—and all the time you know you're not fit to touch him. . . . I shan't forget my first sight of him neither. You don't know me, mister—well, I'll tell you, I was tax-gatherer. You know what to think about that: I can see it in your face. One of the dirty dogs that works for the government and makes his profit out of selling his countrymen. That's so, and you're dead right. . . . Well, see here. When he came down our street the other day, I don't mind telling you I'd had a pretty good morning. Patting myself on the back, I was, thinking how I'd managed to put the screw on some of those poor devils of farmers and salt away a tidy bit for a rainy day. "Matthew", I said to myself, "you're getting a warm man." And I looked up—and there he was. "Hullo!" I thought, "here's the Prophet. I suppose he'll start calling me names like the rest of 'em. Let him. Hard words break no bones." So I stared at him, and he stared at me—seemed as though his eyes were going straight through me and through me ledgers, and reading all the bits as wasn't for publication. And somehow or other he made me feel dirty. That's all. Just dirty. I started shuffling my feet. And he smiled—you know the way he smiles sometimes all of a sudden—and he says, "Follow me". I couldn't believe my ears. I tumbled out of my desk, and away he went up the street, and I went after him. I could hear people laughing—and somebody spat at me—but I didn't seem to care.

JOHN: It wasn't any of us, Matthew.

MATTHEW: I know that. . . . When he got to my house, he stopped and waited for me. I said, "Will you come in?" And he said, "Yes, please". And I said, "I'd ask you to dine with us, but you mightn't like our company". And he said, "Why not?" And I said, "Look here, this isn't a fit place for you to come to. You know how I get my living." And he said, "Yes, I know. It doesn't matter." And the way he said it, I felt more ashamed than if he'd started telling me off. So he came in and sat down, and all these lads came with him. And nobody seemed surprised, only me.

ANDREW: We gave up being surprised some time ago.

PHILIP: Some of the Pharisees were rather surprised. Remember that bunch at the door as we came out? "Really, my good man, your Master should know better than to hob-nob with all this riff-raff."

MATTHEW: Yes—and he turned on 'em sharp: "Healthy men don't need the doctor," says he, "but the sick do. I've no message for respectable people—

only for sinners. Go away", he says, "and read your Bibles till you know what that means: I will have mercy and not sacrifice." And I said to him, "Master, I'm coming with you". And he said, "Come along"—and I walked straight out of the house, and here I am.

JUDAS: What happened to all your belongings?

MATTHEW: I never gave 'em a thought—not for a week. Then my brother hunted me up and asked me what I thought I was doing. "Sell the whole lot up", I said, "or do what you like. I've done with it." . . . And I'm having a wonderful time—hearing him talk and seeing the good he does. Remember that poor chap by the pool of Bethesda? Paralysed thirty-eight years, he was. Lay there all the time on a mattress. "Stand up", says the Master: and he stood straight up on his feet. Jesus said, "Pick up your mattress and go home". And he slung the mattress over his shoulder and off he went. And, oh dear, that started something, that did.

JUDAS: Why?

SIMON: The Elders didn't like it, because it was the Sabbath, and they made out it was breaking the Law to carry a mattress on the Sabbath Day.

MATTHEW: Would you believe anybody could be so paltry? Last Sabbath we were going through a field, and we were feeling a bit hungry, so we rubbed out a few ears of corn in our hands and ate them. And up comes a couple of these precious prigs, pulling a long face. "Don't you know it's against the Law to prepare a meal on the Sabbath?"—Prepare a meal, I ask you!—And the Master says, "The Sabbath was made for man, and not man for the Sabbath. Therefore," he said, "the Son of Man is lord even of the Sabbath."

JUDAS: He said "the Son of Man"? That's a direct claim to the title of the Messiah. What did they say to that?

JAMES: Nothing. But they went away muttering. There's certainly going to be trouble.

JOHN: The people will be on his side. They won't forget what happened at Nain. If you had seen that, Judas! . . . (He tells his story with some difficulty, re-living the terrifying effect it had on him). . . . A poor boy's funeral, and his widowed mother crying her eyes out. Jesus said, "Don't cry, Mother" . . . and he touched the bier, and the bearers stood still. . . . "Get up, my lad", he said . . . and the dead boy sat up—and spoke. . . . Judas, it was terrifying. . . . He put the boy in his mother's arms . . . and the people cried out, "A prophet! a prophet! God has visited His people!"

JUDAS: You're right; there will be trouble.

JAMES: I'm glad you're here, Judas. You're clever and you can see ahead. And I believe you understand the Master better than any of us.

PHILIP: Yes—do join us. . . . Have you a head for figures, by the way?

ANDREW: Judas has a good head for everything.

JUDAS: Thanks, Andrew, for your kind testimonial. I can add two and two and make four of them.

PHILIP: Then you can take over the accounts. I got swindled by an oil-merchant today, and lost six drachmas, so I'm not very popular. Even the Master read me a lecture on the necessity of worldly wisdom. So I shall hand over the bag to you with pleasure. . . . What's the matter, John? What are you looking for?

JOHN: The candlesticks. . . . I hear the Master's foot on the stairs. He usually reads to us from the Scriptures for a little before supper. . . . You'll stay, won't you, Judas? . . . Here's a taper, Andrew. Can you get me a light from the fire?

JESUS *(entering)*: Are you ready, children?

JOHN: Yes, Master. . . . Judas may listen too, mayn't he? . . . From which book will you read to-night?

JESUS: I will read the story of Joshua. . . . But first, there's something I want to say to you about the Kingdom of Heaven. It is like a trawling-net cast into the sea, which sweeps up creatures of every kind, good and bad together. And when it is full, the fishers draw it to the shore, and then they sit down and sort out the good fish and pack them into baskets—but everything useless or poisonous they throw away. And that is how God's judgment works in the world. For when the time comes, the angels will gather up the good and will cast out the evil into the destruction of fire; and there will be wailing and bitter anger. Do you understand what I am saying?

SIMON: Yes, Master. We understand that very well.

JESUS: God's judgments are written in history. And so every student, when he reads the Scriptures to find out what they can tell him about the Kingdom of Heaven, must learn to interpret the present by the past. For he is like a householder, visiting his shelves and cupboards, and bringing out of them treasures both new and old. . . . Now give me the scroll. . . .

SCENE II (JERUSALEM)

SEQUENCE I (THE COURTYARD OF AN INN)

THE EVANGELIST: And his fame went throughout all Syria. And there followed him great multitudes of people from Galilee, and from Decapolis, and from Jerusalem, and from Judaea, and from beyond Jordan. But the Pharisees took counsel with the Herodians against him, how they might destroy him.

PROCLUS: Landlord!

INNKEEPER: Sir?

PROCLUS: A flask of wine and some bread and cheese.

INNKEEPER: Yes, sir. . . . Drawer, wine for the noble Centurion. . . . Where will you have it, sir?

PROCLUS: Out here—the bench under the fig-tree.

INNKEEPER: Where the other gentleman is sitting, sir?

PROCLUS: Yes. I don't suppose he'll object. . . . Excuse me, sir, do you mind if I—Sosius, by the gods!

SOSIUS: Proclus! Well, well!

PROCLUS: We haven't met since the last German war.

SOSIUS: How are you, after all these years?

PROCLUS: Pretty well, for a veteran of fifty-eight. And you?

SOSIUS: Well enough—except for my stiff leg. They invalided me out after that wound I got at Münster. So you're still in the Army? I imagined you'd retired years ago.

PROCLUS: Not me! No. I pleaded good health and good service, and they kept me on. Sent me down into the country to keep order and train auxiliaries. Nice little place I've got there, too. Near Capernaum. One-horse sort of a town, but very pleasant.

SOSIUS: What are you doing in Jerusalem?

PROCLUS: Just brought up a draft. They seem to be expecting some sort of trouble.

SOSIUS: They're always expecting trouble. . . . Here's health! . . . Pilate got the wind up properly over that uproar about the dedication ceremony.

PROCLUS: I thought the Emperor settled that.

SOSIUS: So he did. But he backed up Herod, and told Pilate to respect Jewish feelings and dedicate his shields at Caesarea. Since then, Herod and the Governor haven't been on speaking terms. It's a bad thing when the Imperial and the local authorities can't pull together.

PROCLUS: I wouldn't put anything past Herod Antipas. He's an oily, foxy brute. Not like his father. I served ten years with old King Herod. Fearful old barbarian, of course, but a thundering good ruler, and perfectly loyal to Rome.

SOSIUS: It needs a thundering good ruler to keep these Jews in hand.

PROCLUS: Oh, they're not so bad. You only need a bit of tact. Pilate never had any tact, that's his trouble. Sound enough man, but he's all tied up with red tape and the importance of being Governor of Judaea. These Jews are very honest people if you take 'em the right way. I get on like a house a-fire with the Elders at home. They invited me to subscribe to build 'em a synagogue; which I did, and they were as pleased as punch.

SOSIUS: Very likely. But you try inviting them to build you a temple, and see what they say. You may oblige their Jehovah, but they won't oblige your Jove. That's their idea of religious toleration. Even among themselves they quarrel like cats. There was a tumult only the other day about some prophet or other. They're holding an indignation meeting about it this afternoon—the Elders and the Pharisees—and a bunch of the Herodian party have lined up with them too. Only thing their confounded sects ever agree about is in hounding down some unfortunate person without a party label. This prophet—Here, I say, I think the man comes from your part of the country. Jesus-bar-Something—bar-Joseph—what do you know about him?

PROCLUS: Not very much. He's a carpenter's son from Nazareth, and they say he's a miracle-worker. I've only seen him once, but I liked the look of him. A good man, I thought, with something godlike in his face. When Apollo the All-Healer took human shape, he might have looked like that.

SOSIUS: Apollo the Healer? Well, he's healed a good many people in Jerusalem. But apparently he picked on an unlucky day or something, and the strict Jews took offence. However, it's just as well he's fallen out with the Jewish authorities, because some people have been trying to run him for a national leader, and Pilate got worried about it. But he'll get no backing for a rebellion if he goes on being so broad-minded. He's got quite a following of young men among the lower classes—fishermen and tax-collectors, and that sort. But they don't cut much ice. Are you staying in Jerusalem?

PROCLUS: No. I've handed over my men and I've got to get back. My wife's expecting me.

SOSIUS: All well at home?

PROCLUS: Very well, thanks. . . . Except my batman, who's laid up with some confounded disease the doctors don't understand. A good man, too. I'd be very sorry to lose him.

SOSIUS (lightly): You'd better get your Jewish Apollo to work a miracle.

PROCLUS (seriously): I've a very good mind to try. But I don't know whether a Jewish healer would do anything for a Roman. I might ask my local Elders to approach him. But I don't know how he'd take it.

SOSIUS: Well, dash it, you built 'em a synagogue—they owe you something. . . . Hullo! what's this old party want?

IST ELDER: Excuse me, sir. Do you happen to know whether the Sanhedrim are meeting in the old Gazzith or in the new hall?

SOSIUS: I couldn't say, good Pharisee. But I've seen a number of Elders going into the High Priest's house.

IST ELDER: Oh, thank you. Perhaps the meeting is being held there.

2ND ELDER: Very likely. It isn't a formal council.

IST ELDER: I'm obliged to you, sir. Good day. . . . Dear me, now we've come right out of our way. We're very late already.

2ND ELDER: We can take the short cut through the Temple court.

SEQUENCE 2 (THE HIGH PRIEST'S HOUSE)

IST ELDER (He is the same IST ELDER who took part in the Temple Scene of the Third Play, and he is concluding a speech): . . . and I think the meeting will agree that this kind of thing must be stopped (murmurs of agreement). We need not argue about the man's alleged miraculous powers. He may be a charlatan. He may be a sorcerer. But he has deliberately encouraged a lot of foolish people to fancy that he is the Messiah, and to fan a flame of revolt which may provoke reprisals by Rome. We want no such exhibitions of fanatical and unregulated zeal. *(Applause)*

BARUCH: My Lord High Priest! I object strongly to the Reverend Elder's last expression, which seems intended to be offensive to the party of the Zealots to which I belong. Zeal for our religion and for our chosen races should know no limits, and I am horrified that anybody should wish to suppress it on the ground that we have to appease the heathen empire of Rome. My complaint against Jesus bar-Joseph is that, so far from showing zeal for the restoration of the Jewish kingdom, he insults religious leaders, openly flouts the Law of Moses, and consorts with Gentiles and Samaritans and the contemptible tax-gatherers who bleed our people to death in the interests of Rome. *("Hear! hear!")*

A VOICE: He preaches the coming of the Kingdom.

BARUCH: But he interprets it in some sort of far-fetched mystical sense of which nobody can make head or tail. What he is preaching is simply himself, and a fanatical devotion to his own person. If he sets up anything, it will be an idolatrous cult of Jesus. Do you want to see temples dedicated to Jesus bar-Joseph? Is a Divine Carpenter any improvement upon a Divine Caesar? *(Angry murmurs)* Didn't we have enough of such blasphemous nonsense in the days of Herod the Great?

HERODIAN: Sir! sir!—My Lord Caiaphas, this is intolerable! As a Herodian I must protest against these abominable aspersions cast on the ancestor of our Royal House. King Herod the Great never permitted idolatry within the boundaries of Jewry.

VOICE: How about Syria?

HERODIAN: If the Syrian heathens in their blindness chose to erect temples to Herod, that was their own affair. When by quarrelling among ourselves we broke up the power of the Herodian house, we sold ourselves into bondage to Rome—and I say that only by again uniting ourselves under the rule of a Herodian can we have the slightest hope of restoring independence. Sectarian movements only split up the national effort. Jewry will not march to victory under the leadership of a Nazarene carpenter, but only under the banners of the House of Herod.

IST ELDER: According to prophecy, the Messiah of the Jews will be born of the royal House of David, and not of the line of Herod, who was an Edomite and a usurper.

(Protest and applause)

SHADRACH: The man Jesus has anticipated you there. He says he *is* of the House of David.

(Angry buzz)

3RD ELDER: Aren't we rather straying from the point? Nobody is suggesting that we ought to countenance Jesus of Nazareth. The question is, how to get rid of him, without causing a popular uproar that would provoke interference by Rome. The Governor will not support us in punishing a purely ecclesiastical offence. But if the man were to make some sort of statement which could be interpreted as defiance of the Emperor—

BARUCH: The Emperor! Do you mean that we should degrade ourselves by appealing to the authority of Rome?

(Interruptions and confusion)

CAIAPHAS: Elders of Jerusalem—

(Silence)

VOICE: The High Priest! Silence for the High Priest!

CAIAPHAS: I understand the suggestion is that we should play off Jesus and Rome against one another—make use of Rome, in fact, to pull our chestnuts out of the fire. That seems to me a thoroughly diplomatic scheme for spoiling the Egyptians.

(Laughter)

Consequently, we should try to entangle this man in his talk, and get him to make publicly some claim to the Messiahship which might look like a signal for a national rising—or alternatively, provoke him into instigating a breach of the Roman Law, such as a refusal to pay the Imperial taxes or what not. Is that what you had in mind?

3RD ELDER: My Lord High Priest has precisely interpreted my meaning.

CAIAPHAS: In that case, we may proceed to—I see that the Elder Shadrach has something to say. Yes?

SHADRACH: I've only this to say. Jesus of Nazareth is no fool, and it won't be so easy to entangle him. Also, we are under the disadvantage that we none of us really know what this movement is aimed at. We all agree that we disapprove of it, but that's about the only thing we do agree about. Jesus has united the people and disunited us—and whether his claims to inspiration are true or not, I think he is an opponent to be reckoned with.

BARUCH: What the elder Shadrach says is very wise. May I also make a suggestion? If we could disunite his disciples, and at the same time obtain inside information about his plans, we might break up this movement from within.

CAIAPHAS: A very sensible scheme, good Zealot. Have you any practical steps to propose?

BARUCH: I know a man who might be useful to us. A former follower of John the Baptist, who has been seen about with Jesus these last few weeks. I made contact with him some time ago, and found him keen, daring, and zealous for Israel.

CAIAPHAS: Is he susceptible to threats? or bribes?

BARUCH: Not in the ordinary way. No. He has a subtle mind and would see through any crude efforts to corrupt him. But, he may be led into deceiving himself with specious arguments. That is the weakness of all clever people. Intellectual dishonesty springing from intellectual pride—the sin by which Adam fell.

CHORUS OF APPROVING VOICES: Very true, very true.

NICODEMUS (*suddenly and loudly*): And do you think this proposal is honest?

CAIAPHAS: Brother Nicodemus—that is a very uncalled-for remark. Let the wicked fall into their own pit.... I take it, the meeting approves the suggestion that this gentleman should open up negotiations with—what is the young man's name, by the way?

BARUCH: Judas Iscariot.

CAIAPHAS: With Judas Iscariot.

(Murmurs of approval, on which the scene fades out)

SCENE III (GALILEE)

THE EVANGELIST: And Jesus called unto him his disciples; and of them he chose twelve, that they should be always with him, whom also he named his apostles: Simon bar-Jonah and Andrew his brother; James and John the sons of Zebedee; Philip, and Nathanael, James and Jude the sons of Alphaeus, and Simon the Canaanite; Thomas surnamed Didymus, and Matthew the tax-gatherer; and Judas Iscariot, which also betrayed him.

(Slight pause)

And he taught the multitudes, saying:

JESUS: Never think that I have come to destroy the Law. I am here to show you how to keep it. For the old Law says: "Thou shalt do no murder", and lays down how murderers are to be punished. But *I* say "Never hate anybody"—for hatred is what leads to murder—it *is* murder; when you hate your fellow-man there is murder in your heart. And the old Law said: "If you take an oath, you must keep it." But *I* say, "Think truth and speak truth, and then there will be no need to insult God with oaths." And the old Law said: "Revenge must be kept within limits: an eye for an eye, a tooth for a tooth and no more." But *I* say, "Take no revenge at all. If a man hits you once, let him hit you again if he feels like it; if he is mean to you, take pains to be generous to him; if he makes demands upon you, give him double what he asks, and so coax out the bitterness from his heart." And the old Law said: "Love your friends and hate your enemies." But *I* say: "Anybody can do that. Give up this bargaining attitude altogether. Love even your enemies, do them all the good you can, and when they treat you badly, pray for them. Be like your Father in Heaven, who sends His rain to water the earth for all men, good and evil alike." Behave to every man as you would like him to behave to you—for this is the way to keep the Law and fulfill all the teaching of the prophets.

CROWD: Ah, Rabbi! what beautiful teaching that is!... Go on talking, dear Master.... We could listen to you all day.... Tell us more, good Rabbi! It does us good to listen to you!

JESUS: Yes, but it's no use calling me Master if you don't do what I tell you. Plenty of people will come to me in the last day, crying, "Lord, Lord, in your Name we have taught and healed and done this and that"—and I shall have to say to them: "Go away, I don't know you—you have never belonged to the Kingdom." The man who not only listens, but *does* the things I say is like a wise man who built his house on a rock, and the rain fell and the winds blew, and the waves beat on the house but could not shake it, because it was founded upon the rock. But the man who only listens and does nothing about it is like a foolish man who built his house upon sand; and the rain fell and the wind blew and the waves beat on it and washed it away—and the ruin of that house was great.

JOHN: Thank you, Master, for the warning; God helping us, we will try to build our house upon the rock.... Will you teach any more to-day?

JESUS: No, not now. We will go down to Capernaum.

SIMON: That's all for today, good people! Go home now, and Jesus will talk to you again tomorrow....

CROWD: Well! I've never heard anybody preach like that.... Not a bit like the Scribes—they tell you "Moses said this" or "Isaiah said that", but this man says "*I* tell you", as though he was just as important as Moses.... What did he mean about coming to *him* in the last day? The way he talks you'd think he was God almighty.... He makes you see what the Law *means*—if we didn't sin we shouldn't need any Law, same as he says.... Goes about with some funny people, doesn't he?... He's not my idea of a holy man—now John Baptist, *he* didn't go to dinner-parties; *he* lived on locusts.... John? he was a mad sort of fellow.... It's the most wonderful preaching I ever heard—I must hear him again.... Come on! they're all following him—let's see if we can pick up anything else....

ANDREW: Oh, Master—here's a deputation from the Elders at Capernaum—will you speak to them? They seem very anxious.... It's that nice old Rabbi Solomon, who came to the wedding at Cana.

JESUS: Yes, of course.... Honoured Rabbi, how can I serve you?

RABBI: God be gracious to you, Jesus bar-Joseph. We have come on behalf of this good friend of ours—Proclus, the Roman Centurion, who lives near us. His servant—an excellent man—is desperately ill, and he thinks that if you would come and lay your hands on the poor fellow—

SIMON: The Master lay hands on a heathen! On a Roman soldier! My good sir, you must be out of your mind. Every Roman is an enemy to Israel—

JESUS: Oh, Simon! Don't you ever listen to a word I say? I said: "Love your enemies".

RABBI (*eagerly*): But, indeed, Proclus isn't an enemy! He is a heathen, of course, but *most* friendly—very fond of the Jewish people, and very kind to us. He even built us a new synagogue. And he's so distressed about this servant of his, who has been with him a very long time—

JESUS: I will come and see him.

RABBI: You will? That is very good of you. You hear that, Proclus? Jesus says he will come and visit the poor sick fellow—It's quite close—only about half a mile—

PROCLUS: Just a moment, just a moment, sir. I'm deeply grateful to these good Elders and to you. But I don't expect you to come to my house. We Romans quite understand about prophets and dedicated people. We know their persons are sacred and mustn't be polluted by touching anything that isn't ceremonially clean. And, of course, we're unclean to you. Besides, in my house you'd see all sorts of things that you couldn't approve of—statues of the Emperor and of our gods and so on. It really wouldn't be fitting for you to come, and I don't ask it.

JESUS: Then what do you ask, Proclus? Don't you want your servant healed?

PROCLUS: Yes, indeed I do. But surely you don't need to see him. You've only to say the word, and he'll be cured.

JESUS: What makes you believe that?

PROCLUS: Sir, I have only to look at you. I know authority when I see it. I've been a soldier all my life. I've had to obey my colonel, and my men have had to obey me. I say to the corporal, "Come here", and he comes, and to another man, "Go there", and he goes; or I tell my batman, "Do this", and he does it. And I know very well that when *you* command, you are obeyed.

JESUS (*vehemently*): Do you hear that, all of you? It is amazing. Nowhere have I met faith like this—not in the length and breadth of Israel. And I tell you that many shall come from the east and from the west and sit down with Abraham and Isaac and Jacob in the kingdom of our Father, while the rightful heirs to the kingdom are cast out into the darkness to gnash their teeth and howl. . . . Go your way, Centurion, and as you have believed, so it will be.

PROCLUS: Thank you very much, sir. (*He clanks off*)

JUDAS: Master, the disciples who came with me from John the Baptist want to go back to him now; and they ask what message they are to take him from you.

JESUS: Very well, Judas. Are they here?

JUDAS: Yes, Master—here they are.

JESUS: Now, my lads, what was it John Baptist told you to ask?

DISCIPLE: He asked: "Are you really he whose coming the prophets foretold? Or must we look for yet another?"

JESUS: Yes. Well now, go back and tell John how you have seen the prophecies fulfilled—how the blind see and the lame walk, the lepers are healed, and the deaf hear and the dead are raised to life—

DISCIPLE: That is a miracle indeed.

JESUS: —and the good news of the Kingdom is announced to the poor. Don't forget to say that.

DISCIPLE: Perhaps that is more wonderful still.

JESUS: Perhaps it is. Happy is the man who has no doubts about me.

DISCIPLE: We will deliver your message. Good-bye, Jesus bar-Joseph.

JESUS: Good-bye. . . . Now, all you people, listen to me. Those men are going to John the Baptist. Today you all come running after me. A little time ago you were all running after him. Have you forgotten him? Herod has put him in prison. That was rather a shock, wasn't it? When you went after John, what did you expect to see? A reed, blown this way and that by every wind of opinion? But John wasn't like that. What did you expect to see? A man dressed in gorgeous clothes? Oh, no! you must go to the king's palace if you want to see that sort of person. But what *did* you really expect to see? A prophet?—Yes indeed, and far more than a prophet—the very messenger of God. Indeed and indeed I tell you, that of all men born there has never been any one greater than John the Baptist. Yet the humblest of those who enter the Kingdom is a greater man than he. All the Prophets and all the Law pointed forward to the coming of John. And ever since he came, the Kingdom of Heaven is here. It stands among you—it is here for you to seize and possess, and resolute men may take it by assault.

But you—your great moment has come—and what are you doing? You are like silly children running about in the streets. Your playmates say to you, "Why won't you take part in our game? We have played you a jig, but you won't dance. We have played at being mourners, but you won't join in." When John came, he fasted from food and drink, and you said he was a madman. The Son of Man comes eating and drinking like other people, and you complain that he is gluttonous and a drunkard and keeps bad company. Nothing pleases you. But all God's children are wise in their own way.

But woe to you, Chorazin! woe to you, Bethsaida! For if the mighty works that have been done in you had been done in heathen Tyre and Sidon they would long ago have repented in sackcloth and ashes! And woe to you, Capernaum—for if the wicked city of Sodom had seen what you have seen, God would not have needed to destroy it. But it will be more tolerable for Tyre and Sidon and Sodom in the day of judgment than for you!

CROWD: Alas! alas! what shall we do? What shall we do to be saved?

JESUS *(The fire of anger has gone out of him, and left only pity)*: Come to me, all you who are weary and heavy laden, and I will give you rest. Take my yoke upon you and learn from me; for I am gentle and humble of heart and you shall find rest for your souls. For my yoke is easy and my burden is light.

EVANGELIST: Now, when King Herod was keeping his birthday, the daughter of Herodias danced before them and so pleased Herod that he promised with an oath to give her whatever she asked. And she, being prompted by her mother, said: "Give me, I pray you, John Baptist's head on a platter." And Herod was sorry; but he had to perform his oath. So he sent and had John beheaded in prison, and his head was put in a great dish and given to the damsel and she brought it to her mother. And his disciples buried the body, and came and told Jesus.

THE BREAD OF HEAVEN

CHARACTERS

The EVANGELIST.
JESUS.
BARUCH THE ZEALOT.
BARUCH'S WIFE.
JUDAS ISCARIOT.
PHILIP.
ANDREW BAR-JONAH.
SIMON BAR-JONAH ("Simon Peter")
JAMES BAR-ZEBEDEE.
JOHN BAR-ZEBEDEE.
NATHANAEL.
THOMAS DIDYMUS.
MATTHEW, the Tax-Collector.
1st JEW.
2nd JEW.
3rd JEW.
CROWD.

} Disciples of Jesus.

THE PLAY

This play, for a change, contains a certain amount of action. If it is found too long, Scene II may be omitted bodily. In this and the following scene, the CROWD has been stylized, so that the omission of Scene II might throw Scene III out of key; in that case, the CROWD part in Scene III may be slightly expanded and treated more naturalistically.

[I hope you won't think the hoodwinking of the crowd by a change of headgear too like a "thriller" episode. It seemed to emerge, somehow, from the text of Matthew, Mark, and John together. The Synoptists say that Jesus "constrained His disciples . . . to go before Him to the other side while He sent the multitudes away". But why? *He* was the person the multitudes wanted, and commonsense would suggest His leaving the disciples to maintain good order and discipline while He "went apart". If He could disperse the crowds by merely telling them to go home, what was the point in sending the disciples ahead? Simply in order that He might stage a perfectly unnecessary display of miraculous water-walking? That would be most unlike Him — He *never* did superfluous miracles for fun.

St. John has got it right as usual. He says, almost in so many words, that Jesus gave the crowds the slip: "He departed" (John VI. 15) because they wanted to seize Him and make Him king. The people obviously followed the disciples down to the shore, since John says (VI. 22) that they "saw that Jesus went not with His disciples into the boat" — and how could they have seen that, unless they were there at the time? (John lumps all this in, retrospectively, in a paragraph about "the day following", but that's only John's involved way of writing; they couldn't have "seen" *on the day following* that somebody hadn't been in a boat which had put off the night before. What he evidently means is that they had followed the disciples to the shore, seen *then* that Jesus wasn't with them and that there was no other boat, so that "on the day following" they had to wait for the ferry to come over from Tiberias before they could cross themselves.)

Allowing for John's "flash-back" methods, the thing is perfectly clear. The people went down to the shore; they saw the disciples into the boat, and *only then realised* that Jesus wasn't with them. Therefore, something had previously led them to suppose that He *was* with them, or they wouldn't have followed the disciples at all — they didn't want to make kings of *them*. The boat presumably put off a little way, and then hung about, waiting for Jesus to turn up. But He didn't come — no doubt because the crowds were still on the shore — so, seeing that it was getting dark, and a nasty storm coming, the disciples gave it up as a bad job and started to cross (VI. 17). Then, when the crowds had gone (either to hunt for Jesus or to take shelter), Jesus came to the shore, observed that the oarsmen had got into difficulties, and followed them across the Lake. Taken like that, it all makes perfect sense.

The only question is: *Why* did the crowds imagine that Jesus had gone down to the boat with the disciples? Presumably they mistook somebody else for Him—at any rate, that is the suggestion I have made, and the headshawl provides a "machinery" for their mistake....

John's dates and places are always suggestive and helpful. For instance, he mentions that the Passover was nigh (VI. 4). Consequently, during the crossing, a good gibbous moon would be struggling with the storm, so that the disciples could see Jesus coming across the Lake without any of the supernatural aureoles and fireworks which one usually sees in paintings of this episode. The "fourth watch of the night" (3 a.m.) seems a bit late for all this, but they had had to pull a good three miles against the wind with a heavily laden boat, so no doubt it's quite reasonable; the moon would be still up, any way.

I find that when Mark and John are available they usually make sense, either separately or together; John doesn't always bother much if he is telling something that had already been written about—he just mentions the episode and hurries on. Even so, he often provides some missing link—*e.g.,* the *reason* why, at that point, Jesus appealed to Peter for his confession of faith. The Synoptists introduce it quite casually and abruptly. But John links it to the fact that, after the "Bread of Heaven" speech, followers had begun to drift away....

You will notice that I have translated and glossed the Beatitudes rather freely. I wanted to get rid of the "reward and punishment" notion that has got attached to them. They are surely a description of the sort of people who *do* belong to the Kingdom and *are* (not in the chronological sense "will hereafter be") blessed. I've even got rid of the word "blessed"—not because it isn't really a better word than "happy", but because it is popularly connected with the idea of God arbitrarily bestowing favours. Besides, nobody today thinks much in terms of "blessedness"—it's a churchy sort of thing; what people look for is "happiness", and though "happiness" is a poor, thin, pagan kind of word, it means more to them. I believe "single-hearted" is an accepted rendering of $\kappa\alpha\theta\alpha\rho\text{o}i\ \tau\tilde{\eta}\ \kappa\alpha\rho\delta i\alpha\ (\kappa\alpha\theta\alpha\rho\acute{o}\varsigma$ = unmixed), and it is a much wider and profounder word in English than "pure", which has got narrowed down to an almost technical connotation which in the context is positively misleading....

For the sake of dramatic compression I have cut out all reference to the Four Thousand and transferred Peter's confession from Caesarea Philippi to Capernaum, making it follow directly on the argument with the Jews, to which it clearly belongs logically, if not geographically, as John makes plain.

From letters written to Dr. Welch.]

Warning to the Record Library! The "Sea" of Galilee is an inland fresh-water lake, and the boat was a rowing-boat. Do not vex the Producer (who has troubles enough already) with the offer of "Schooner in a Storm—Sail-Flap and Shroud-Whistling Effects", or "Atlantic Rollers Breaking on Cornish Coast", or even that sweetly-pretty thing with the Seagulls, which we know so intimately. "Squall on Lake Windermere" is nearer the mark; but you may have plenty of wind and waves, because it says so.

Song in Scene IV—I don't think it's necessary to expend research on a Hebrew tune for this psalm. Any old, strong, ancient hymn-tune will do, to which the oars can keep time.

THE CHARACTERS

JESUS—The theme of the play centres round a sort of suggestion that the threefold temptation of the Devil is here repeated, and forced each time to a refusal and a challenge. There is a refusal to exploit (1) popularity from material benefits (healing and feeding), (2) signs and wonders (walking on the sea), (3) offers of worldly power (the kingship offered and rejected). All this is met by the deliberate and almost violent challenge about the living bread, which affronts everything that the common man could desire or religious tradition hold sacred. This brings the desertion of the idle curious or the timid, the searching-out of the weak and strong elements among the disciples, and the certainty that salvation will have to come by the way of the cross. Scene II (if retained) and Scene IV should be played with a kind of gaiety; Scene III with a kind of determination to force both the crowd and disciples to a point of crisis; Scene V is the crisis; the first part should be played with unflinching determination, and reiterated emphasis on the main point (in John VI the same phrases are repeated over and over, as though to drive home the idea); the second part (with Peter) is played with passion. The Beatitudes in Scene I (being "flash-back" technique) may be a little stylized in treatment.

BARUCH THE ZEALOT—Pure politician. His speeches may be cut a little if necessary—but they have their topical appeal. Baruch sees Jesus as the Nazi party may have seen Hitler—the Heaven-sent spell-binder, rather mad but a valuable political tool in the right hands.

JUDAS—In this play at last defines himself. He has got the right idea, and holds it with passion and sincerity. But his intellectual pride, his jealousy, and a fundamental lack of generosity make him a ready ground for the sowing of seeds of suspicion. He can trust nobody but himself. He has grasped in the abstract the idea of purgation by suffering—he sees it; but will anybody else see it? Does Jesus really understand what it means? He proclaims that Jesus is incorruptible—but suppose Baruch is right after all! "I would kill him with my hands"—if he were to let down my idea of him; that is the key-speech. And the next things that happen don't look too good. The popularity ("if there's a popular man in Judaea today", yes, indeed!) and the reckless appeal to the herd-instincts of the Five Thousand, followed (so inevitably) by the offer of a kingdom. Jesus has refused; that's good—but does he mean it? What is he doing there on the other side of the Lake? is something sinister going on?—Then the scene with the Jews and with

Peter—splendid, splendid! Judas is satisfied; but why should the blessing be pronounced on Peter? why should the confidence be given to John? Why not these marks of favour for Judas, who really understands? (But he does not, of course, understand the thing that Peter and John understand—Peter by unconscious inspiration and John by a sort of instinct—that the personality they are dealing with is something more than human.) Judas, without knowing it, also sees Jesus as a kind of tool—a person intended to carry out his, Judas's, idea of the way of salvation; and if Jesus shows any signs of shrinking from that way, he, Judas, will force him into it (with as much determination as certain religious elements forced France into defeat for her own good). I have not shown Judas doing any work of healing; I think he would probably stick to the preaching side of the job.

BARUCH'S WIFE—She isn't allowed into her husband's political intrigues (no place for women), but she knows his point of view. Her only excuse for intruding on the play is that she provides the slight relief of a female voice. But she has this much "feminine intuition"—that she divines instantly that Judas is subconsciously jealous of Philip's miracle.

PHILIP—He continues to be a "nice boy", quite unaffected and humble about himself. He knows he is not particularly bright, and admires Judas, who is so clever and preaches so well. Astonishing that he, the stupid one, should be allowed to work a miracle. It is all very surprising and exhausting. Not being of nervous or introspective temperament, Philip has a healthy animal knack of doing what is required of him and then folding up and sleeping it off. He can be relied on to behave amiably, say thank you nicely, and go to bed when he is told, like a well-brought-up schoolboy.

SIMON PETER—Here he has two of his great moments, each followed by the usual collapse. One moment, the other world seems real and this world nothing: he can walk on the water; he can see the face of God. Then he loses hold of it, thinks of himself—and it's all gone, and there's only a blunt fisherman, familiar, grumbling, abrupt, and inclined to treat his Master as a sharp-tongued vigorous nursemaid might treat a wayward infant prince.

THOMAS—An excellent man—faithful enough in any physical danger (as we learn later) but cursed with a pessimistic temperament and constitutionally averse from making any sort of fool of himself.

MATTHEW—Nothing new about him, except a certain talent for organisation (possibly he has had to deal with queues and crowds before) and the townsman's strong objection to damp discomfort, and rocking boats. He is the kind of optimist who goes over the top singing "I don't want to die", and "Ain't it a lovely war?"

OTHER DISCIPLES—Nothing new.

THE JEWS—Not Priests or Pharisees, but ordinary citizens, delighted to gape after marvels and get anything good that's going, so long as it leads to no difficulties or dangers; but constitutionally conservative and prosaic.

SCENE I (GALILEE)

THE EVANGELIST: Then Jesus called his twelve apostles together and gave them power to cast out devils and to cure diseases. And he sent them out, two by two, to preach the Kingdom of God and to heal the sick. And he said unto them:—

THE VOICE OF JESUS: Take nothing with you for your journey—no money, no food, no extra clothing—just a stick to help you along, that's all. When you come to a town or village, ask for hospitality from some decent man, and stay in his house till you leave the place. Don't gad about accepting invitations from all and sundry. If people won't take you in or listen to your teaching, shake off the dust of the place from your feet and leave it to God's judgment. And don't be afraid of anybody—God, who looks after the sparrows, will look after you. Remember, you won't be on your own: whoever receives you, receives me; and whoever receives me, receives God, who sent me.

THE EVANGELIST: And they departed, and went through the towns, preaching the gospel and healing everywhere.

BARUCH: Well, Judas, that is a wonderful story. Most interesting and impressive. You talk as well as you preach. Wife! our guest has nothing to drink.

JUDAS: No more, kind hostess, thank-you.

BARUCH: One cup only. You must need it after your day's work, Philip?

PHILIP: What? I beg your pardon.

JUDAS: Philip's half asleep.

PHILIP: No, I'm quite awake.

BARUCH: He hasn't said a word all evening.

WIFE: Poor boy, he looks tired to death. A bowl of warm milk, that's what he wants, and then off to bed.

PHILIP: Thank-you. I should like some milk.

WIFE: Of course you would. Here you are—drink it up like a good lad. . . . Are you sure you're feeling all right?

PHILIP (rousing himself): Yes, indeed. I'm perfectly well. Please don't bother about me.

JUDAS: Philip has had rather an exciting day. He has performed his first work of healing. They brought us a poor woman, possessed with a spirit of madness—

BARUCH: You know her, my dear. Poor crazy Esther.

WIFE: Crazy Esther! And you cured her? But how marvellous! I wish I had seen that! I thought she was quite incurable.

BARUCH: So did everybody.

WIFE: How did you do it? A young lad like you.

PHILIP: I don't know. I mean, I didn't do it. Jesus our Master did it.

JUDAS: Philip was only God's instrument—as we all are.

PHILIP: I suppose it was God. I know it was Jesus.

WIFE: But do tell me about it.

PHILIP: The parents brought the poor creature along and said, would we please cure her?—just like that. She looked awfully mad and miserable and I was dreadfully sorry for them, but I hadn't an idea what to do.... Of course, Jesus had given us authority to heal people—but somehow I'd never thought of *me* doing it. I'd sort of imagined Judas doing it, and me looking on. I did try to catch your eye, Judas—but you were busy answering questions and didn't notice.... The parents stood and looked at me as if they expected something to happen, and I just felt an utter fool. Still, I thought I must do *something*—so I said a bit of a prayer and laid my hands on the woman. The minute I touched her, she went off into a kind of fit and started to struggle and shout—so I grabbed her by the shoulders. Whew!

JUDAS: Those maniacs have the strength of ten men.

BARUCH: Hers was a very powerful devil.

PHILIP: I'm pretty hefty, but it was all I could do to hold on to her. "I'm no good at this", I thought—and then it passed through my head, "Not in my own power", and I called out, "In the name of Jesus Messiah!" And all at once—you'll never believe it—

WIFE: Yes, yes—go on.

PHILIP: I felt hands close over my hands. Pressing them down. Like iron. I never dreamed that hands could be so strong. They held me and they held the woman. I felt her shoulder bones under my fingers.... And then I realized that the hands were *my* hands. *I* was exerting that tremendous grip. The poor girl yelled and writhed and bit me—and I suddenly heard myself speaking, loud and quick, like somebody giving an order ... but it wasn't my voice at all, and I don't even know what I said.

JUDAS: You said, "Devil, be quiet and come out of her!" ... You startled me. You spoke so like the Master.

PHILIP: It wasn't my voice. It was his.

JUDAS: When Philip spoke, the woman stopped struggling. She stood quite still and began to cry. Then she suddenly seemed to realise that there was a crowd of people staring at her. She said, "Oh, Mother, what's happened? Please take me away." She was quite gentle, and as sane as you or I.

WIFE: Well I never! Fancy that! How amazing! ... You must have felt proud of yourself.

PHILIP: I felt absolutely done. My knees shook and the sweat poured off me, and every bone in me ached like fury. As if all my inside had been sucked out of me.... Judas was marvellous. He got between me and the crowd and preached a splendid sermon, while I sat on the ground and sorted myself out.... Judas! when the Master heals people, do you think he feels like this?

JUDAS: He could scarcely heal twenty and thirty in a day if he did. His power is native to him.

PHILIP: But it costs him something, all the same. Remember that time at

Tiberias? We were pushing through a terrific crowd when he stopped dead and asked, "Who touched me?" Simon—you know his funny, rough, familiar way—Simon said, "Come, Master. We're being squashed to death in this mob, and you want to know who touched you!" But he insisted: "Somebody caught hold of me." And it turned out that a poor sick creature had snatched at the hem of his garment and been healed. When we asked him how he knew, he said, "I felt power go out of me". I didn't know what he meant, but I know now all right. . . . Yes. . . . But it's not quite the same. He felt the power go. I felt it come *and* go. . . . I wish I knew what to make of it.

JUDAS: It will probably come easier to you next time.

PHILIP: Yes—I'll be expecting it. I'll just keep quiet and let it happen—so that it only has to *come* through and not to *push* through, if you see what I mean. I should think it was me being so frightened that made it difficult—shouldn't you?

JUDAS: Very likely. But look here, wouldn't it be a good idea to take things quietly now? You're getting all worked up.

BARUCH: You've had a terrific experience, and you mustn't exhaust yourself, or you won't be fit for anything to-morrow. It's taken a lot out of you, you know.

PHILIP: You mean, it's time I went to bed. Yes, I expect you're right. . . . I am awfully tired. . . . Good-night, everybody. . . . And thank you *very* much for asking us to stay and being so kind to us.

BARUCH: You are very welcome. Wife, show our guest to his room.

JUDAS: Good-night, Philip. I'll be up in half an hour—and I want to find you asleep!

PHILIP (*calling back*): Good-night, Judas!

BARUCH: Well, Judas Iscariot. Now that your young miracle-worker has gone to bed—

JUDAS: You think the time has come for a little political discussion. I thought you were waiting for something like that.

BARUCH: You recognised me then? I wasn't sure.

JUDAS: Oh, yes. You are Baruch the Zealot. We last met twelve months ago, when John Baptist was baptising at the Lower Ford. You wanted to know whether he was ready to preach revolution, and whether, if he did—

BARUCH: Whether, if he did, we could count on your enthusiasm. At that time you were zealous in the cause. I have been hoping to meet you again, and when I saw you and Philip this morning, I seemed to recognise the finger of God.

JUDAS: It's safe enough to recognise the finger of God in *any* event. It's harder to be sure which way it's pointing. I told you then, I couldn't answer for John Baptist's intentions.

BARUCH: John the Baptist is dead. This man Jesus seems to be a different proposition.

JUDAS: Very different.

BARUCH: Tell me frankly, what is he?

JUDAS: According to the people, the Messiah of Israel. According to himself, the Messiah of Israel.

BARUCH: And according to you?

JUDAS: According to me—the Messiah of Israel; if Israel knows her own salvation.

BARUCH: Very well. Let us agree that he is the Messiah of Israel. But what sort of man is Israel's Messiah? Politician, madman, inspired prophet, religious genius? How does one handle Jesus of Nazareth?

JUDAS: He is not the sort to be handled by anybody.

BARUCH: Tush, man! Everybody has a weak point somewhere. . . . Let's stop fencing with words and put the cards on the table. . . . The man has power, that's a certainty. But unless some one handles his business for him, he'll come to a worse end than John the Baptist. The Priests and Pharisees—Heaven confound their lick-spittle, time-serving hypocrisy—will break him like a straw if he does anything to make trouble with Rome. They're only waiting for the first little slip. One word of rebellion, one hint of a national movement, one demonstration against the Emperor, and crack! down comes the trap—Church and State join hands to put an end to Israel's Messiah. And then what becomes of your salvation?

JUDAS: There is no salvation for Israel, unless—

BARUCH: Unless! Unless! I've heard that word so often. No salvation *unless* — you know what I say to that.

JUDAS: Go on. Say it.

BARUCH: *Unless*—when the moment comes, there's a popular rising, well timed, with an organisation and armed force behind it. That means *our* force and *our* organisation. The party is ready, as you know. All we need is a figurehead, a leader, a spell-binder to fire the imagination of the masses and make them fall in to march behind the party. . . . Brains aren't enough. You've got to appeal to the emotions—stir these peasants out of their slave mentality and give 'em something to fight and die for.

JUDAS: To die for—yes. That's the right word, Baruch. . . . I once thought as you do, that Israel should ride the royal way to triumph. But now I think we were wrong. Since I have sat at the feet of Jesus, I know why John came preaching repentance. The way to salvation is through suffering and death.

BARUCH: But I agree with you there. The people must learn to dare and suffer. But Caesar preaches another kind of salvation—prosperity, security, the world-wide peace of Rome. "Order and safety"—that is their motto. A single benevolent despotism over the whole earth—and the Lion of Judah tamed and patient, munching his ration of government fodder like a fat ox in a stall. And so they dope the masses with propaganda, while we that have heart and spirit to fight are kept quarrelling among ourselves—Pharisee against Sadducee, Galilean against Samaritan, House of David against House of Herod—till we are disarmed one by one and corrupted away from within. The rot has gone far, Judas, the rot has gone far.

JUDAS: So far that it is now too late to resist. Israel must pass through the fire, and judgment must burn away her iniquity. You talk of salvation—but all the time you are trying to escape it—like a sick man shrinking from the surgeon's knife. This is the meaning of the Gospel—that all must be endured, and the cup of humiliation drunk to the very dregs. Only when we are stripped naked—when we have reached the nethermost pit of desolation—then, only then, can the white flower of happiness, the blessedness of God's salvation, blossom out of the dust of our corruption.

BARUCH: That is a Gospel of good news indeed! Is this the doctrine of your Messiah?

JUDAS: You don't understand.... Nobody understands him.... On the day that he chose out twelve of us to be his close companions, he led us up into a mountain, away from all the people. He prayed there all night, and in the morning he called us about him and spoke to us.... The mists were not yet off the hill-tops; it was cool with a little breeze, and so quiet. There was a spring bubbling out of the rock, and he sat beside it, and the rising sun was on his face. If only I could make you see him. If only you could hear his voice as we heard it then, speaking about happiness, and the blessed Kingdom of God. I hear it now ... it will be in my ears till I die....

THE VOICE OF JESUS: ... Listen, and I will tell you who are the happy people whom God has blessed.

Happy are the poor, for nothing stands between them and the Kingdom. Happy are the sorrowful, for their souls are made strong through suffering. Happy are the humble, for they receive the whole world as a gift. Happy are they who long for holiness as a man longs for food, for they shall enjoy God's plenty. Happy are the merciful, for they are mercifully judged. Happy are they who establish peace, for they share God's very nature. Happy are the single-hearted, for they see God.

And think yourselves happy when people hate and shun you, when they insult and revile and persecute you for the Son of Man's sake. When that happens to you, you may laugh and dance for joy. It is a sign that you are right with God, for all true prophets are persecuted, and God will be your reward.

But unhappy are the rich! They have had their share of good things already and have nothing more to look for. Unhappy are the well-fed and self-satisfied! There is an emptiness in their souls that nothing can fill. Unhappy are the frivolous and mocking hearts! The time will come when they will mourn and weep and not know where to turn for comfort. And think yourselves unhappy when you are popular and applauded by all—for only false prophets are popular.

You are the salt of the world. But if salt grows insipid and loses its sharpness nothing can bring back its savour. It is only fit for the rubbish-heap.

You are the light of the world. Stand up then and shine, that men may see your well-doing and give glory to your Father in Heaven. . . .

JUDAS: . . . so he laid our burden upon us—sorrow and humility and torment and shame, and poverty and peace of heart. God's salvation. And we were filled with a strange happiness. Then he blessed us. And we bathed our faces in the running stream and so came down from the mountain.

BARUCH: You make me feel as though I had been there. . . . Well, if I ever doubted the man's power, I doubt it no longer. He has done something to you that I wouldn't have believed possible. . . . I only hope, for your sake, that Jesus will give heed to his own sermons.

JUDAS: What do you mean?

BARUCH: "Only false prophets are popular." . . . If there's a popular man in Judaea to-day, I should say it was Jesus of Nazareth. It needs very great integrity to stand being made the idol of the people.

JUDAS: I have no fear of him. He is incorruptible.

BARUCH: So you think. And so he thinks, no doubt. But we have seen many prophets of late. They start well—then they get a following, success goes to their heads, and before you know where you are the man who was too unworldly even to earn his own living is accepting presents from rich old ladies, setting up fashionable religious cults, and creeping up the back stairs into politics.

JUDAS: You don't know Jesus.

BARUCH: He is a man. Every man has his pride—or his pet vanity. Just now it's all holy poverty and the world well lost—but on the day you see Jesus Carpenter ride into Jerusalem with palms waving and the people yelling Hosanna—remember, I told you so.

JUDAS (passionately): If I thought you were right, I would kill him with my hands while he was still uncorrupted.

BARUCH: Nonsense, nonsense! These madmen of genius are made for us to use. Let's him have the hosannas—but let's see to it that there's an army to march in while the going's good. Otherwise—one more opportunity for Caesar to clap down the extinguisher on what's left of Jewish liberty.

JUDAS: That is not the right way. I tell you I'll have nothing to do with it.

BARUCH: There's no hurry. Think it over. Sleep on it. . . . Ah, here's my wife. My dear, you are just in time to bid good-night to Judas.

WIFE: Good-night. May God's angels watch over you. Go quietly, I think your friend is asleep.

JUDAS: Good-night. Baruch, good-night. I shall not change my mind.

BARUCH: Good-night.

(Door shut)

Well—what do you think of that pair?

WIFE: The boy is charming.

BARUCH: An honest simpleton. And Judas?

WIFE: I think he is jealous of his friend without knowing it.

BARUCH: I shouldn't wonder. Judas is a clever fool. I know where to have him, if we want to get rid of Jesus.

WIFE: Baruch—must Jesus be got rid of? Such power as his must surely be of God.

BARUCH: So is the power of fire. But it has to be harnessed. This Jesus might set the world ablaze. What a tool, what a tool he would be in the right hands! A hammer against Caiaphas—a sword in the heart of Caesar. If only we could get hold of him. . . . But I have a horrible feeling—

WIFE: Yes?

BARUCH: That he may be incorruptible after all.

SCENE II (TIBERIAS)

THE EVANGELIST: When the twelve apostles had returned from their travels, they told Jesus all that they had done, and what they had taught. And the multitudes thronged about them, and there was so much coming and going that they had no leisure so much as to eat.

> (*The following introductory passage strongly stylised: confused background of the* CRY OF THE WORLD, *with little islands of dialogue rising out of it and sinking back into the sea of supplication. The producer to select as required*)

THE CRY OF THE WORLD: Lord, have mercy upon us. Christ, have mercy upon us. Lord, have mercy upon us. Son of David, have mercy upon us. We are blind, we are sick, we are unhappy. Open our eyes, teach us, save us, O Lord. What shall we do to be saved? My child is sick. My daughter is dying. We are ignorant, we are poor. Teach us and heal us, O Lord. Jesus Messiah, Jesus our Master, Jesus our Physician, Jesus our help. Hear us, look on us, have pity.

A. Unclean! unclean! a leper and unclean! Jesus, have mercy! JESUS: I will; you are clean. A. Blessed be the name of Jesus!

B. My son is possessed. THE LUNATIC (*shrieking*): Ah, ah! ah! let be, Jesus, let be! Legions of devils, burning, burning, burning. Don't touch me! Ah! JESUS: Hold your peace and come out! THE LUNATIC: Ah-h-h! (*a long sobbing cry*) B. Glory be to God! Jesus, O Jesus!

C. Blind! blind! pity the blind! Jesus, kind Jesus, give sight to the blind. JESUS: Receive your sight. C. Oh, the sun! I see the sun!

D. I am sick, I am deaf, I am paralysed! DISCIPLES: In the name of Jesus of Nazareth! D. We are mad, we are miserable. DISCIPLES: In the name of

Jesus of Nazareth. D. We are lame, we are helpless, deaf, dumb, blind, diseased. DISCIPLES: In the name of Jesus of Nazareth.

E. Alas! alas! my father is dying. My little sister is dead. Widowed, bereft, orphaned—dying and dead, dying and dead. JESUS: They are not dead, but sleeping. Arise, stand up alive! E. Alive—alive—alive—Glory to the living God! O blessed Jesus!

JAMES: There's a mother here with a sick child. Where's Philip?

JUDAS: Worn out and asleep. Philip!

JAMES: No, don't wake him. I can manage.

NATHANAEL: John! can you come and deal with this lunatic? I can't do anything with him.

JOHN: I'm coming.

ANDREW: There's a deputation of elders asking to see the Master.

SIMON: They must wait. He's gone down the village to a fever-stricken family.

THOMAS: Can somebody come at once to a dying woman?

JUDAS: Here's a lame man hobbled six miles on crutches.

JAMES: Here's a stretcher-case brought all the way from Bethsaida.

ANDREW: There's a man here wants Jesus—but he says Matthew will do.

MATTHEW: Right you are—coming in half a minute.

THOMAS: Here, let me go; you've had nothing to eat.

MATTHEW: It's all right, Thomas. I know who it is.

JUDAS: There's an old woman here with a bad leg.

NATHANAEL: Oh, I can't *bear* to see any more bad legs!—where is she?

CROWD (*pressing in upon the house*): We are here, we are here, we are waiting. Waiting upon the Lord. We are sick, we are blind, we are unclean. Heal us. Help us. Lord, have mercy upon us. My son is mad. My father is ill. My mother is dying. Where is Jesus? Bring us to Jesus! Have pity upon the poor.

ANDREW: Here's John back again.

JOHN: Let me sit down.

ANDREW: What's the matter?

JOHN (*almost in tears*): Nothing, but I'm so *tired.*

SIMON: Look here, we can't go on like this. It's more than flesh and blood can stand. We can't eat, we can't sleep—

MATTHEW: How can we turn all these poor folk away?

JOHN: Jesus refuses nobody.

ANDREW: I don't know what he's made of. He can go on and on—

SIMON: He drives us too hard.

JAMES: He drives himself harder.

JUDAS: John, you're wanted.

JAMES: John can't go.

JOHN: Yes, I can.

JAMES: Brother, indeed you must spare yourself.

JOHN: There is too much misery in the world.

JUDAS: "Hungry and thirsty, their soul fainted in them"—Let the body faint and the soul sicken—but God drives us, and the work must go on.

CROWD (outside): Jesus! Jesus! Jesus of Nazareth! Touch me! speak to me!

SIMON: The Master has come back.

JESUS (outside): Daughter, you are healed. Go home now, and live better.... Stand up, old man, and give thanks to God.... Open your eyes, and as you have believed, you shall see.... Mother, give me the child....

CROWD: Blessed be God! Blessed is Jesus the Prophet of God! How can we thank you, blessed of the Lord?

JESUS: Love one another, keep the commandments, and pray for the coming of the Kingdom. That is the best way to give God thanks.... Go to your homes now. Go in peace. And the spirit of our Father be with you all.

CROWD: Amen!

JESUS (entering briskly): Fishers of men—you have toiled hard to-day. The nets have been full—to breaking-point, perhaps?... My poor children! John, you look ready to drop. Give me your hand. I see I must finish up by healing my own disciples. Andrew has a headache, I fancy; Philip seems to have given up altogether and James doesn't seem too happy, either. Simon!

SIMON: Yes, Master?

JESUS: Something about you tells me that you have been grumbling. And has nobody had any dinner?

JOHN: M-m-master, there were such a lot of people, and we were very tired. I expect if we had more f-f-faith it would come easier. But you weren't here, and we rather let it g-get on top of us. But we're quite ready to go on as long as you want us to.

JESUS: No, you shall not go on. We will go right away by ourselves into a quiet place up in the hills and rest. I don't want to drive you too hard, Simon.

SIMON: Master, I did grumble, and I'm very sorry.

JESUS: Did you? Well now, listen. There was a man with two sons, and he told them to go and work on his allotment. And one of them said, cheerfully, "Yes, rather, Dad". But he met some friends and forgot all about it and never did a stroke. The other son said: "No, I won't go. I hate digging." But afterwards thought, "Oh well, I suppose I'd better," and went off grumbling and did as he was told. Now which of those two did the will of his father?... It doesn't need an answer, does it?... Put something to eat in your baskets, and somebody wake up Philip. We'll take a boat and go across the Lake to Bethsaida and spend the night in the mountains. And the Lord God of Israel shall give rest unto His people.

SCENE III (NEAR BETHSAIDA IN THE TRANSJORDAN)

THE EVANGELIST: So they departed into a desert place by ship privately. But the people saw them departing and recognized Jesus, and they ran after him. And when Jesus came out next day from the place where they had been resting, he saw the crowds, and was sorry for them, because they were like sheep without a shepherd. And he taught them and healed those that were sick.

CROWD: Jesus, son of pity, speak to us, comfort us. We are hungry, we are thirsty, we are weary. The day is so long. The night is at hand. Call us, feed us, Shepherd of Israel.

ANDREW: Master, it's getting on towards evening, and the people have got nothing to eat.

JOHN: The children are crying. We don't know what to do with them.

JUDAS: Hadn't we better tell them to go away and buy some food?

JESUS: There's no need for them to go. Give them some of your own food.

SIMON: But that's ridiculous. We haven't enough for all this crowd. Why, there must be three or four thousand of them.

THOMAS: Nearer five thousand, if you ask me.

JESUS: Then you must go and buy some. You go, Philip. Ask Judas for the money.

PHILIP: We'd need two hundred pennyworth of bread at least. And even then they'd only get a snack apiece.

JUDAS: Two hundred pence! You might as well ask for two hundred pounds! Really we can't.

JESUS: Well, how much food have you got? Go and see.

PHILIP: Master, I've been to see, and there's scarcely anything left. Look!

ANDREW: We've got five barley loaves and two dried fish—rather small ones. But what's the good of them among all this lot?

JESUS: Well, we must do the best and trust to God. Tell the people to sit down—over there, on that smooth slope of green grass.... What's the matter now, Thomas Didymus?

THOMAS (bluntly): It seems a bit silly, that's all. But just as you like, of course.

JESUS: Thomas, we could do with a little more faith and rather fewer objections.

MATTHEW: Here, come on, Thomas. Why don't you do as he says? Argue anybody's head off, you would, and don't you know he's always right?

THOMAS: I don't like looking a fool.

MATTHEW: What's it matter what *you* look like? Let's get on with it.

ANDREW: What are we to say to them?

JAMES: Better put a bold face on it.... Now, you people! The Rabbi knows you've come a long way and you must be tired and hungry. We didn't expect such a large party and we can't invite you to a banquet— only some bread and fish. But our Master makes you welcome to what we've got.

(Murmurs of approval)

Will you all please sit down over there?

MATTHEW: Here! not all in a bunch like that! Make a nice row here of fifty or so. That's right. Now another row behind — see! . . . Move up a bit, missus — this your youngster? Well, catch hold of him. . . . That's famous!

(Confusion and some laughter)

DISCIPLES: Another row here. . . . No, a little further back. . . . Sit a bit closer . . . . Four, six, eight. . . . We can get a hundred in between these two rocks. . . .

JOHN: Master — the people are ready. Shall we serve to them now?

JESUS: Children of Israel. To-day you are my guests, and the guests of my Father's Kingdom.

MAN IN CROWD: Thank-you, good Rabbi. Blessed are they that shall eat bread in the Kingdom of God.

JOHN: Master, will you bless the bread?

JESUS: Father of all goodness, we thank Thee for Thy gifts. Blessed be this bread and meat unto our bodies, as Thy word to our souls. Amen.

DISCIPLES: Amen.

JESUS: Take the food, and distribute it to the people, that every one may eat and be filled.

DISCIPLES: Eat and be filled . . . eat and be filled . . . eat and be filled.

CROWD: Thanks be to God! Blessings on the name of the Prophet. . . .

(Keep this going while THE EVANGELIST *speaks)*

THE EVANGELIST: And they did all eat and were filled. And they took up of the fragments that remained twelve baskets full.

CROWD: A prophet! A prophet! Blessed be Jesus the Prophet! A miracle! The Kingdom is come among us! — A land flowing with milk and honey! — Blessings on the name of Jesus! Blessed be the Prophet of God! Follow the Prophet who feeds his people! A prophet in Israel! Follow him! follow him! Hail to the Prophet Jesus!

A VOICE: A Messiah! a Messiah!

CROWD: Jesus Messiah! Jesus Messiah!

VOICE: Follow him and make him King!

CROWD: A king! a king for Israel! Jesus King! Jesus King! a Jewish king for the Jewish people! a king!

(Tumult and a stampede)

JESUS: Be quiet, you foolish people!

(His voice is drowned in the uproar)

CROWD: You shall be our king! We want no other leader! The kingdom! The kingdom! Jesus shall be king!

JUDAS: What will you do now, Master?

JESUS: Go down quickly. Take the boat. Cross the lake. See that you get there before they do. I will slip away from them and join you later. . . .

SIMON: Take off that blue head shawl, Master. It marks you out.

JAMES: Give it to me—

SIMON: You put it on, James. You're about his height—

CROWD: After them! follow them! That's him in the blue shawl!—Catch him! seize him! Carry him to Jerusalem! a Messiah! a Messiah!

(The chase fades out)

SCENE IV (LAKE OF GALILEE)

(The noise of water and the creak of oars in the rowlocks. Wind violent)

SIMON: Pull harder, boys—there's a nasty storm coming up. Look at those black clouds driving across the moon.

JOHN: It'll be a dirty night—I hope the Master got away safely.

JUDAS: I hope he did. And I only hope—never mind!

ANDREW: What, Judas?

JUDAS: I only wondered. Was he getting rid of the people—or of us? They may be making him king now.

SIMON: What, without us? He wouldn't let us down like that. If there are any crowns going, we shall be there.

PHILIP: Sitting on thrones, judging the twelve tribes of Israel. He said so.

JUDAS: Did he indeed?

JAMES: One day when we were arguing about the Kingdom. But I think he was making fun of us. Anyway, he wouldn't go and do anything behind our backs.

JUDAS: Are you quite sure?

JAMES: Of course I'm sure. What a beastly idea.

JOHN: I don't think Jesus wants to be made a king. Not that sort of king, anyway.

JUDAS: No? well, he was rather asking for it, wasn't he? All those people, and a miracle like that! What did he expect?

JOHN: The people don't understand.

THOMAS: Do any of us understand?

JOHN *(vaguely)*: When I held the bread in my hands—so little—and yet enough and to spare for all that multitude—God's plenty, multiplying itself in my hands—I don't know! It was as though we had touched the very source of all life—as though—

(Storm increases)

SIMON: John! John! don't dream! Keep her head to the waves!

ANDREW: Whereabouts are we?

SIMON: Not more than three miles out, with this wind. Put your backs into it!

PHILIP: It's a filthy night.

ANDREW: Look out! there's a squall coming.

(Crash of waves breaking over the boat)

All right, there?

JAMES: We've shipped a lot of water.

MATTHEW: I don't like this. Give me the dry land every time.

JOHN: Poor Matthew! Here, take this bowl and bale out.

MATTHEW: Oh, well—we can only die once. They that go down to the sea in ships see the wonders of the Lord—yes, I don't think. It's all very well for you chaps, you're used to it, but if ever I—*(with a yell of very real terror)* Ow! ow! look there!

ANDREW: What is it?

MATTHEW: There! there! something coming along—walking on the tops of the waves—

JUDAS: Nonsense!

JAMES: I can't see anything.

MATTHEW: Wait for the moon—there! O there! look! it's a spirit or something!

DISCIPLES: Heaven defend us! It's a demon! an angel! the ghost of a drowned man! How fast it comes! it's catching us up!

SIMON: Row for your lives!

MATTHEW *(rapidly)*: God forgive me, God forgive me. I've been a great sinner—

PHILIP: If only the Master were here!

JAMES: Speak to it, somebody.

SIMON: In the name of God, what are you? Who's there?

JESUS: I AM.

JAMES: It spoke Hebrew.

SIMON: It spoke the great name of God.

JESUS: Don't be afraid. It is I.

JOHN: It is the Master.

SIMON: Is it really you, Lord? Don't go! Wait for me.

JESUS: Come then, Simon.

SIMON: Yes, yes, I'm coming.

ANDREW: Simon—what are you about? Stay in the boat. You're mad.

SIMON: Let me go!

ANDREW: Trim the boat. Take care. Hold her! Back her! Catch him, somebody.

JAMES: He's gone. . . . He's walking on the water. . . .

PHILIP: The waves bear him up. . . .

JOHN: His eyes are on the Master—O great and merciful God! . . .

THOMAS: He's looking back at us—he's waving to us. . . .

DISCIPLES *(together)*: He's gone under.

SIMON: Help, help! I am drowning. Help, Lord!

JESUS *(quite close)*: Hold on. I am here. I've got you. Why did you lose faith all of a sudden?

SIMON: I was afraid—the wind and the waves—I looked back—

JESUS: You were all right till you stopped to think about yourself. Into the boat with you!

ANDREW: Pull him in, boys! . . . Look out there!

(Wind and waves)

JESUS: Well, children? Is there room in the boat for me?

DISCIPLES: Yes, Master. Yes, of course.

JESUS: You're not afraid of me, are you?

JOHN: Master, when you are here we are afraid of nothing. . . . Shift over, Matthew. . . . Dear Master—

JESUS: Peace be unto you.

(The wind drops instantly)

SIMON: The storm is over.

JESUS: Row on now, for we are nearly at the land.

ANDREW: Give way, boys!

> SONG: All they that to the sea go down
> The wonders of our God behold,
> At His command the winds arise
> With storm and angry billows rolled.
>
> When in distress on Him they call
> He stills the raging of the sea,
> And brings them glad of heart unto
> The haven where they long to be.

SCENE V (CAPERNAUM)

THE EVANGELIST: The day following, the people on the other side of the lake, who had seen the disciples go away in the only boat, searched everywhere for Jesus. So when they found he was not there, they too crossed the lake (fresh boats having now arrived), and went to look for him in Capernaum. And they found him teaching near the Synagogue.

IST JEW: There he is!

2ND JEW: We mustn't lose him this time. Rabbi! rabbi!

JESUS: Well?

1ST JEW: We have been hunting for you everywhere. How did you manage to get over here? There wasn't a boat on that side.

JESUS: Does it matter how I got here?

3RD JEW: Oh, not at all, not at all, but—

2ND JEW: We felt sure you had performed another of your most holy and blessed miracles.

1ST JEW: It does us so much good to contemplate all these wonderful works!

JESUS: I don't think you came to look for me because of the miracles. You came because you ate the loaves and fishes, and expected favours to come. How hard you work for earthly food, which is consumed and perishes! Work to win the food which builds up body and soul to everlasting life.

3RD JEW: Yes, but how?

2ND JEW: What *is* God's work?

JESUS: God's work is simply this: to trust in the Son of Man, who comes to you by God's authority.

3RD JEW: Who do you mean? Yourself? But *where* is your authority? Show us a sign, so that we may know for certain who you are.

1ST JEW *(a man of extremely literal mind)*: Or do you mean that the loaves and the fishes were a sign? But they didn't come from Heaven. They came out of a basket.

3RD JEW: Our ancestors ate manna in the desert. That was the sign Moses gave. And that really did come down from Heaven—it says so in the Bible.

JESUS: Indeed and indeed I tell you, it was not Moses who gave the bread. But my Father gives you the true bread from Heaven; for he that comes to you from Heaven is the bread of God, that gives life to the world.

1ST JEW: Then give us that bread, so that we shall never be hungry again.

JESUS: I am the bread of life. The man who comes to me shall never know hunger, and he that believes in me shall never thirst again. I have come to do the will of my Father, and it is this: that he who believes in me shall have everlasting life, and I will raise him up from death in the last day.

1ST JEW: What does the man mean?

2ND JEW: How can *he* be the bread from heaven?

3RD JEW: Raise us from the dead at the last day? What's he talking about? Who is this man anyway?

1ST JEW: It's only Jesus, the carpenter of Nazareth.

2ND JEW: Yes, of course, we know all about him and where he comes from.

1ST JEW: We know his people. He's the son of Mary and Joseph ben-Heli. What's all this nonsense about coming down from Heaven?

JESUS: You needn't whisper among yourselves like that. I tell you again. I am the bread of life. Your forefathers ate manna in the wilderness, and they died nevertheless; but eat of the bread that comes down from Heaven, and you shall live and not die. Indeed and indeed I tell you: I am that living bread. The bread I shall give you is my very flesh that is given for the life of the world.

1ST JEW: This is madness! How can the man give us his flesh to eat?

2ND JEW: I don't know what he's talking about.

JESUS: Indeed and indeed I tell you—Unless you eat the flesh of the Son of Man and drink his blood, you have no life in you. For my flesh is meat indeed and my blood is drink indeed. As the living Father has sent me and I live by Him, so the man that eats of me shall live by me.

1ST JEW: This is blasphemy, or worse! it is forbidden by the Law to taste blood.

2ND JEW: I call it very heathenish talk.

3RD JEW: The man's an idolater—if he isn't raving.

2ND JEW: Come away; have nothing to do with him.

3RD JEW: Certainly not. I only came out of curiosity.

1ST JEW: I don't think this sort of thing ought to be allowed to go on. . . .

(They drift away muttering)

ANDREW: Master, they are not taking this at all well. You will lose your following if you say such extraordinary things.

THOMAS: I must say it's very hard to understand. Can you make it out, Judas?

JUDAS: I have seen a great danger come and go. But whether he is preaching God's kingdom, or merely preaching himself—

JESUS: At any rate, Judas, it does not look like being a popular doctrine. The crowd is drifting away. Comfort yourself with the reflection that they are not likely to crown me king today.

JUDAS: No. You have challenged them. So far, so good.

JOHN: Master—when you said you would give your body for the life of the world—what did you mean?

JESUS: I will tell you presently. . . . Thomas, are you still in difficulties? Is it because I spoke of coming down from Heaven? What would you say if you saw the Son of Man go back to the Heaven from which he came? Or is it the words about the flesh that you find so hard? Without the spirit, the flesh is nothing, for it is the spirit that gives life to the flesh. The words I speak to you are spirit and life. . . . But some of you do not trust me.

MATTHEW: We trust you all right. But you've given offence to a good many people. Some of them have gone, and they won't come back.

JESUS: True enough. And how about you, my children? Do you, too, want to go away?

SIMON: Lord, to whom could we go? *You* have the words of eternal life.

JESUS: Do you think so? Tell me—all these people—who do they say that I am?

JAMES: Well, some of them say you're John the Baptist come again.

ANDREW: Some think you are Elijah—or one of the other great prophets.

JESUS: But who do *you* say that I am?

DISCIPLES: You are our master—our teacher—

SIMON: You are the Christ of Israel—*(with a change of tone)* you are the Son of the living God!

JESUS: Blessed are you, Simon bar-Jonah, for you did not say that of yourself. That word was not spoken by flesh and blood; it was God that spoke by your mouth.

SIMON *(bewildered)*: I don't know why I said it. It—just came to me.

JESUS: I told you once that I would give you a new name. Now you have earned it. You shall no longer be called Simon, but Peter, which means the Rock. You are Peter, and upon that rock I will build my church, and the gates of hell shall not prevail against it. And I will give you the keys of the Kingdom of Heaven. You shall bind men to God and that bond shall hold fast in Heaven. You shall set men free on earth to walk in the liberty of Heaven.

But tell nobody what you have said, nor even that I am the Christ. For the enemy is strong, and the way hard—and I think, indeed, that I must go through sorrow and shame, and tread the sharp road to the gallows to win my people back to life from the power of the grave.

SIMON: What? What are you talking about? The gallows? How can you say such things? It can't happen. It shan't happen. Never! never! Master, put that horrible idea out of your mind.

JESUS: Simon—are you tempting me? Is this the old fight with the devil all over again? Stand out of my sight, Satan! for your speech is no longer of God, but of men. . . . If any man wants to follow me, he must walk the way of suffering with me. If he clings to life, he will lose it, but if he is ready to lose his life, he will save it. Indeed and indeed I tell you—there are some of you standing here that shall not taste death till they see the Kingdom of God come with power. . . . John, come and pray with me. I need your faith.

JOHN: Yes, Lord. . . . Only you must teach me what to pray for.

(Brief pause)

SIMON: Heaven forgive me, what have I done? He called me Peter—he called me Satan—I don't know where I am.

PHILIP *(distressed)*: What's happened to everything? It was all so wonderful, and now—it's all going wrong.

THOMAS: Do you understand it, then, Judas?

JUDAS: I understand. But does any one of you?

JAMES: John, I think, understands.

THE EVANGELIST: This is the testimony of John the Beloved Disciple: In the beginning was the Word, and the Word was with God, and the Word was God. In him was life, and the life was the light of men. And the Word was made flesh, and dwelt among us.

THE FEAST OF TABERNACLES

CHARACTERS

The EVANGELIST.
JESUS.
JUDAS ISCARIOT.
JAMES BAR-ZEBEDEE.
JOHN BAR-ZEBEDEE. } Disciples of
MATTHEW the Tax-Collector. } Jesus.
PHILIP.
THOMAS DIDYMUS.
SIMON PETER.
JOSEPH. } Kinsmen to
SIMEON. } Jesus.
CAIAPHAS, High Priest of Israel.
ANNAS, father-in-law to Caiaphas.
NICODEMUS.
SIMON the PHARISEE. } Members of the Sanhedrim.
An ELDER.
CLAUDIA PROCULA, wife to Pontius Pilate, the Governor.
REBECCA. } attendants on
A FREEDMAN. } Claudia.
A SECRETARY ("Hezekiah").
A HECKLER (mouthpiece of the Priests and Pharisees).
The CAPTAIN OF THE TEMPLE GUARD ("Captain Elihu").
EUNICE, a Syro-Phoenician, masseuse at the Public Baths.
Ist JEW.
2nd JEW.
3rd JEW.
4th JEW.
A JEWESS.
A SERGEANT OF THE TEMPLE GUARD.
Ist LEVITE.
2nd LEVITE.
Ist ROMAN SOLDIER.
2nd ROMAN SOLDIER.
Ist ZEALOT.
2nd ZEALOT.
CROWD.

NOTES

THE PLAY

This play is presented in two main parts (marked as "Scene I; Scene II"), each of which is composed of a set of short sequences leading up to a revelation of Christ's Godhead which closes that part. I think that the Interval Music should occur only between Scenes I and II, some other device being used to separate the various sequences of each scene, so that the continuity of each main part is preserved.

THE CHARACTERS

JESUS — The only aspect of Jesus which is at all new in this play is that it shows him as a dialectician, seizing points in an argument, and ramming them home. With his kinsmen in Scene I, Seq. 2, he is aloof and cold; and there is already a touch of the grim determination that will drive him up to Jerusalem, six months later, to face death. *Challenge* is, perhaps, the dominant note to strike. In the Samaritan village (Sc. I, Seq. 4) he is more sad than angry — the spirit of violence has affected even John — and the Parable of the Unmerciful Servant is offered gravely and uncompromisingly as a parable of judgment. But after Peter and Matthew have shown some effort to understand, he is more gentle with these bewildered people, and the name "sons of thunder" is addressed to the downcast James and John with a sort of grave playfulness — a "you're a nice pair, aren't you?" touch about it. The "Our Father" is given in a tone which shows that forgiveness is complete and a right relation completely re-established.

In Scene II, Seq. I, the effect we want to get is that Jesus is "teaching" in the sense that he is carrying on some kind of exegesis and argument with a group of Scribes and Pharisees, and interrupts this from time to time to pick up and answer the observations of the lookers-on. (This seems to be what St. John means by saying that "Jesus cried as he taught".) The appeal "Listen to me, listen to me *now*" — is a pick-up from the presence and conversation of the LEVITES, which suggest a threat to his life.

In the last scene (Sc. II, Seq. 4) he begins with great exaltation on the "water" and "light" speeches; then, when the HECKLER starts, cracks back at him stroke after stroke, as though to force the issue up to the great challenge.

JOSEPH and SIMEON — Commentators differ a little as to whether these "brethren" really "did not believe" in Jesus, or whether they did not believe in the right way. I have therefore made one of them take one point of view and one the other.

SIMEON does not genuinely believe at all; he is inclined to think that Jesus is a rather disreputable member of the family who ought to curb his

151

extravagances and conform to the decencies of Jewish domestic life— submission to parents, keeping up appearances, etc.

JOSEPH, on the other hand, believes in the Messianic claim, and wants a public demonstration and the formation of a properly-constituted political group to exploit the situation.

JUDAS is beginning to get on other people's nerves—and his own. He is becoming obsessed by the feeling that nothing will ever go right unless he is helping to pull the strings. He has rejected Baruch's proposals and told him that Jesus is incorruptible, but he keeps on fidgeting in his mind— things are going on in the background; kinsmen are exerting undesirable influence in the foreground; the other disciples are so stupid; Jesus is taking the right line, but will he stick to it without assistance? He stoutly asserts his Master's integrity before Caiaphas—but lets slip that he has been watching Jesus put to the test; he is walking, not by faith, but by proof. His outburst to Caiaphas about Rome is perfectly sincere; but his conception of the whole thing remains narrowly national. Above all, there is this feeling that everything has to be managed by himself; without realising it, he is slipping into Baruch's attitude and trying to make Jesus a political pawn, on the other side of the game.

JOHN—For the first time we see that John's enthusiasm can be tinged with a touch of fiery temper. It peeps out in the scene with the kinsmen, and bursts out in the Samaritan village. It is not personal, and is only excited by fierce indignation when anybody insults the beloved Master. But it blows over and leaves no trace, because he has the humility that can take rebuke. Consequently, he is not astonished that Jesus should have forgiven him and James so completely as to make them witnesses of the Transfiguration. And though, at the time, he was filled with fear and wonder, it does not seem to him a thing out of nature. He can sleep after it, and it has not altered his relations with Jesus, only deepened them. He might almost, one feels, have lost touch with earth and been wholly absorbed into the glory, but for the human love of his brother that kept him still a little earthbound.

JAMES, on the other hand, only as it were enters Heaven clinging to John's hand. James links John to earth; John links James to Heaven. All his life, James has had to look after John—protect him from ridicule, leap to his defence against criticism; in childhood, he must always have been running after little brother when he got too venturesome—and if John were to be snatched straight into Heaven, James would go too, to make sure he was all right. (The two brothers seem never to have been separated except at the Crucifixion—at that point John must really have asserted himself; or perhaps James had to stay and look after their mother Salome.)

SIMON PETER—His link with this world is the solid earth itself—the ground and the sky and the plants. He is the Rock, with its feet in the earth and its head in the clouds; and he has the simultaneous double vision of both worlds at once. He must play the Transfiguration scene with a kind of strong, earthy poetry.

MATTHEW — Nothing special to add about him. His faith is of the implicit and unquestioning kind. Nor has he the smallest intention of allowing himself to be stampeded by Judas out of what he considers proper behaviour.

CAIAPHAS — As before; a smooth and supple politician, and completely unscrupulous. The timid decency of Nicodemus and the passionate insults of Judas slide off him like water off a duck's back. He sneers even at his own momentary loss of control. One feels that he keeps a sinister little dossier, in which the names of disaffected or rash persons are carefully noted down for future reference. One remembers that in the Trial he will — having failed to get his witnesses to agree — deliberately strain the Law by putting the Prisoner under the Great Oath, so as to convict him out of his own mouth, and will stage a beautiful little dramatic act of garment-rending in the most effective manner. His *one* moment of sincerity is when he pays homage to the politician's household god of "expediency". This repeats Herod's argument at the end of Play I, but with a difference; Herod was passionate and patriotic; Caiaphas is ice-cold, and egotistical — he is a much nastier piece of work than Herod.

ANNAS — A rather sour and querulous old gentleman, peevishly aware that the world in general is going to the dogs, and with a high opinion of his son-in-law.

NICODEMUS — The decent man with sufficient courage to state his opinions, but not the temperament that embraces martyrdom for them.

SIMON THE PHARISEE — This gentleman once condescended so far as to offer a little patronage to a travelling Nazarene Preacher, and received a shock from which he has never recovered. To-day, he would, I think, be church-warden in a church in Kensington. He is particular about the people he mixes with — especially emotional females "described as actresses".

HECKLER — Just heckles, loudly and offensively.

CAPTAIN OF THE GUARD, and LEVITES — These men are Jews, and under the orders of Caiaphas. I don't know how they are to be distinguished from the ROMAN SOLDIERS, except that they lack that curt and confident note of unshakable discipline which we associate with Rome, and that they have, of course, no touch of the Roman contempt for the people they have to deal with. They are really just a police-force.

CLAUDIA PROCULA — The very best of patrician lady — sure enough of her own position to talk with unaffected interest and simplicity to bath-attendants and her own servants. (Pilate married rather above himself; the daughter of the Claudians is out of the top drawer.) Clear, cool, gentle-woman's voice. She is about 35.

EUNICE — I imagine her in the middle twenties, with a little girl of about eight or nine. I don't know what language she and Claudia would speak together; but for the purposes of the play, we will suppose that Claudia uses Latin, and that therefore Eunice can be given a little foreign accent, to distinguish her from both the Jews and the Romans. She is quick and vivacious in her Greek way—a suggestion of French in the accent might convey the corresponding effect to the listener.

SCENE I (ALTERNATELY IN JERUSALEM, AND ON THE WAY UP FROM NAZARETH)

Sequence 1 (Jerusalem: The High Priest's House)

THE EVANGELIST: After these things, Jesus walked in Galilee, for he would not walk in Jewry, because the Jews sought to kill him. Now the Jews' Feast of Tabernacles was at hand. . . .

SECRETARY: Will there be anything more, most Venerable?

CAIAPHAS: No—the preparations for the Feast seem to be well in hand. . . . No, wait—one more thing. Call in the Captain of the Temple Guard.

SECRETARY *(at the door)*: Captain Elihu, you are wanted by the High Priest.

CAIAPHAS: Ah, yes, Captain. This man, Jesus of Nazareth. You know him by sight?

CAPTAIN: Yes, my lord.

CAIAPHAS: I understand he is now in Nazareth. But he may try to come up to the Feast. If so, I want him stopped before he enters the city. Set a watch on the road, will you, and detain him?

CAPTAIN: Very good. On what charge?

CAIAPHAS: Blasphemy, sorcery, sedition—anything you like. I don't want to have to arrest him in the middle of the Feast. There would probably be a riot. Catch him before he has time to work up public sympathy or make inflammatory speeches. . . . By the way, didn't I see a carriage standing before the Governor's house? Is Pilate in Jerusalem?

SECRETARY: I think it's only his wife, come up on some business or other.

CAIAPHAS: That would be just as bad. We can't afford a disturbance. All right, Captain—you know what you have to do.

CAPTAIN: The High Priest's orders shall be obeyed.

Sequence 2 (Nazareth)

THE EVANGELIST: And when the time of the Feast drew near, the brethren of Jesus came unto him where he abode in Galilee. . . .

JUDAS *(to somebody outside)*: If you'll wait just a moment, I'll find out if he can see you.

(He comes in, shutting the door rather sharply)

John, where's Jesus?

JOHN: Upstairs with his Mother. Who wants him?

JUDAS: Those relations of his are here again. Joseph and Simeon.

JOHN: Very well, Judas, I'll tell him. *(He goes out, calling softly)* Master!

JUDAS: They want to know if we're going up to the Feast with them. Are we, Matthew?

MATTHEW: Shouldn't think so. Too big a risk. It's a great pity. I like the Feast of Tabernacles. The harvest thanksgiving, and all the little tents built of green boughs, and everybody camping out in them. And the Temple services — the pouring of the water, and the great gold candlesticks lit up in the Women's Court. Pretty, I call it.

JUDAS: Yes, yes. But for heaven's sake don't encourage Jesus to go.

MATTHEW: Who, me? That's a nice way to talk. It's not for me to tell the Master what he's to do. Besides, I tell you it's too dangerous.

JUDAS: So it is. But not in the way you mean.

MATTHEW: In what way?

JUDAS: Never mind. I can't explain all that.

MATTHEW: See here, Judas. I know you're a lot cleverer than what we are. But I do wish you wouldn't always try to *run* everybody.

JUDAS: You needn't take it like that.

MATTHEW: The Master can manage his own affairs, see? I mayn't understand a lot about it, but I do understand that much. We just gotter trust him. And anything he says is right.... That's the way I look at it.... Hadn't we better let these people in? It's not our house, you know. Looks a bit funny, leaving 'em there in the porch.

JUDAS: As you like.

MATTHEW (*opening the door*): Morning, gentlemen. Come in, won't you? John bar-Zebedee's gone to look for the Rabbi.

JOSEPH: } Good morning, Matthew ben–Levi.
SIMEON: }

JOSEPH (*a little offended*): I hope we are not unwelcome.

MATTHEW: Not at all. Not at all. Of course we try not to disturb the Master if he's at his prayers or anything. But naturally, any relation of his — Ah! here he is.

JESUS: Peace be unto you, Joseph and Simeon.

SIMEON: We came to ask whether you had changed your mind about coming up with us to the Feast.

JESUS: No, Simeon. I have not changed my mind.

JOSEPH: Now do be reasonable. You really ought to show yourself in Judaea.

JESUS: I left Judaea because my life was threatened.

SIMEON: What else can you expect, if you hide away in a corner of Galilee? Naturally, the authorities think you are hatching conspiracies. People who have nothing to conceal go about openly. If you are seen at the Feast, as a pious, respectable Jew, under the protection of your own family —

JESUS: Last time you offered me the protection of my family, you were anxious that I should come home and stay there.

JOSEPH: That was when the people were saying you were out of your mind. Your Mother was anxious about you. We were all very much worried.

SIMEON: And you behaved very ungratefully. You refused to see us; and we heard that you had spoken very unkindly. You said your disciples were more to you than your family.

JESUS: No, Simeon. I said that everyone who did the will of my Father in Heaven was brother and sister and mother to me. Everybody who will hear God's word and do it—like these disciples of mine. They have faith in me, but you have none.

JOSEPH: I have a great deal of faith in you. I believe in your great mission, and your wonderful gifts. But I agree with Simeon that you should come up to Jerusalem, and assert your claims openly. You are trying the faith of your followers rather high. Show your works and your teaching to the world, and they will have more confidence in you.

JOHN: You've no right to talk like that. We have p-p-perfect confidence in the Master.

MATTHEW: That's right.

JOHN: It's m-m-monstrous to suggest—

JUDAS: That'll do, John. Keep your temper.

JOSEPH: Well, we needn't argue about that. But we're setting out for the Feast tomorrow, and for the last time, Jesus, we beg you to change your mind and travel with us to Jerusalem.

JESUS: I cannot go with you, Joseph. It is not the right time.

JOSEPH: What time could be better? It's a great occasion, and you would draw a great audience.

SIMEON: And we should be there to support you.

JESUS: All times are right for you. The world is your friend. But it hates me, because I bear witness against its evil ways. Do you go up to the Feast tomorrow. But for me the time is not yet fully come.

JOSEPH: Jesus, I'm only speaking for your own good. Do think again.

SIMEON: It's no use wasting words. We'd better be getting on.... Goodbye.... I think you are asking for trouble.

(They go out and bang the door)

JUDAS: Well, that's that. Master, I am glad you made that decision.

MATTHEW: So'm I. Not but what I like the Feast of Tabernacles. But it ain't safe, dear Master, really—not safe for you, I mean.

JESUS: You're not afraid for yourself?

MATTHEW: Me? They wouldn't bother about me. I wasn't thinking of that.

JESUS: That's good. Because we are going up to Jerusalem.

JUDAS: } We are?
MATTHEW: }

JESUS: Yes. But not with them. And not yet.

MATTHEW: How, then?

JESUS: Quietly. By ourselves. And without making any public announcement.... Children, do you understand? We are—*expected* in Jerusalem, and we have to make sure that we get there.... Say nothing to anybody, but be ready to start when I tell you.

JOHN: Master, when will that be?

JESUS: When God appoints the time.

SEQUENCE 3 (JERUSALEM–THE PUBLIC BATHS)

THE EVANGELIST: Now at this time, Pontius Pilate was Governor of Judaea....

ATTENDANT: Was the bath to your ladyship's liking?

CLAUDIA: Yes, thank you.

ATTENDANT: You are not too hot?

CLAUDIA: Not at all.

ATTENDANT: Will you have your massage now?

CLAUDIA: Yes, please.

ATTENDANT: Your ladyship's usual attendant is ill, I am sorry to say. But we have a new woman—a Syro-Phoenician—who is very good. All the ladies like her.

CLAUDIA: That will do quite well. As long as she has good hands.

ATTENDANT: I am sure you will be pleased with her, madam.... Eunice!... Come here, girl, and do your very best. It is the Governor's wife, the Lady Claudia Procula.

EUNICE: I will try to satisfy your ladyship.

CLAUDIA: I'm not hard to please. You have a nice cheerful face; I like that. There's a little pain here in my shoulder. See if your fingers can charm it away.

EUNICE: Yes, madam.

CLAUDIA: Where do you come from?

EUNICE: I live near Sidon, madam. My husband was a bath-attendant there. But he died a year ago. So I came to Jerusalem, thinking to get a little more money, as I have a small daughter to keep.

CLAUDIA: You are young to have lost your husband. Your little girl must be a great comfort to you.

EUNICE: She is now, madam. But she used to be my greatest grief. She never was quite normal, and had fits, poor little soul. People said she was possessed. But last spring she was healed by a most wonderful miracle.

CLAUDIA: Indeed! To what god or goddess did you pray?

EUNICE: To all of them, madam. I had prayed many years in vain.

CLAUDIA: Who wrought the miracle, then?

EUNICE: Madam, a Jewish prophet.

CLAUDIA: A Jewish prophet! And you a Greek! I thought the Jews would have nothing to do with the Greeks.

EUNICE: I thought so too. But this man had a great reputation, and I was determined to try, if ever I got the chance. So one day—but I am wearying your ladyship.

CLAUDIA: No, no—go on.

EUNICE: One day he passed through our town, and I ran after him, calling for help. His disciples tried to drive me away. But I was desperate, and pushed my way through to him, crying "Sir, sir, have pity on me!" They said, "Send her away, Master—she keeps on pestering us". And he looked at me and never said a word. So I fell at his feet and implored him to heal my child. Then he spoke, rather sternly: "I am not sent to you, but only to the sons of Israel". "Oh, sir," I said, "do please help me." But he answered, "It is not right to take the children's bread and throw it to the dogs".

CLAUDIA: Oh, cruel!

EUNICE: That's what the Jews call us—heathen dogs. But his voice wasn't cruel. He looked at me with a sort of challenge. I thought "I must say the right thing—quick!" So I said, "That's true, sir. But the dogs eat the crumbs that fall from the children's table." Oh, madam! You should have seen how his face lit up! "Well done!" he said, "your faith and your wit have saved your daughter. Go home now—she is healed." So I ran to the house, and there she was—as fit and bonny as a child could be.

CLAUDIA: How wonderful!—I should like to see this prophet.

EUNICE: Madam, the Jews' Feast of Tabernacles begins tomorrow. They say he's expected. It lasts eight days, and on one of them he's pretty sure to be preaching in the Temple.

CLAUDIA: I will make enquiries. What is the prophet's name?

EUNICE: They call him Jesus of Nazareth.

SEQUENCE 4 (SAMARIA)

THE EVANGELIST: When the time came that Jesus should go up to Jerusalem, he sent messengers ahead, and they went and entered into a village of Samaria, to make ready for him. Now the Jews and the Samaritans were always at enmity between themselves.

JAMES: Oh, dear! I shall be glad to get to my bed tonight.

JOHN: Cheer up, James. It's not half a mile to the village. Look! here come Philip and Matthew to say that everything's ready for us.

THOMAS: They're running. And waving their arms. I think something's gone wrong.

JAMES: You always expect the worst, Thomas Didymus.

THOMAS: What else can you expect of Samaritans?

MATTHEW: ⎫
PHILIP: ⎬ Master! Master!

JESUS: What is the matter, children?

MATTHEW: They won't have us in the village—

PHILIP: They saw we were going up to Jerusalem—

MATTHEW: They called us a pack of filthy Jews—

PHILIP: They said you were a vile Jewish heretic—And they set the dogs on us!

JOHN (incoherent): Brutes and b-b-beasts! How d-d-dare they?

JAMES: Insolent savages!

THOMAS *(gloomily)*: I knew Samaritans were no good.

JESUS: Never mind, we will go to another village.

JAMES: Those people ought to be punished.

JOHN: To speak like that of the Master!

JAMES: Master, shall we call down fire from Heaven—

JOHN: And burn their d-d-disgusting village to the ground?

JESUS: James, John—I am ashamed of you.

JOHN: But, Master—

JESUS: You do not know what spirit you are of. The Son of Man has not come to destroy men's lives, but to save them.

JOHN: I'm sorry, Master. I didn't think.

JAMES: We lost our temper. Please forgive us.

JESUS *(gravely)*: But have you forgiven these men? Forgiveness cannot help you if you cherish an unforgiving spirit. The Kingdom of Heaven is like a ruler, one of whose servants owed him a debt of a thousand talents. So he gave orders that the man was to be sold up and put in prison for debt. But he pleaded so movingly for time to pay, that the king forgave him and cancelled the debt altogether. Then this man remembered one of his fellow-servants who owed him a little sum of a hundred pence, so he went and took him by the throat, crying "I want my money back". "Have mercy," said the poor man, "give me time and I will pay you in full." But the creditor would not listen to him, and threw him into prison till he should pay the debt. Then the king sent for his servant and said: "You wicked man! I forgave you all that great debt because you asked me to. Couldn't you have pity on your fellow-servant, as I had pity on you?" And, finding no grace in the man, he handed him over to the law, to exact every penny that was due.—And so it will be with you, unless from your very hearts you forgive your brother men all the wrongs they do you.

MATTHEW: Master, does the king in that story stand for God?

JESUS: Yes, Matthew.

MATTHEW: But that's terrible. We couldn't ever pay God everything we owe Him.

SIMON PETER: No—but the first man wouldn't have had to pay the king if he hadn't behaved like a brute to the other man. His debt would have been forgiven.

JESUS *(pleased; Peter has really seen the point)*: Quite right, Peter. So you see what you have to do.

SIMON PETER: Yes, Master. But suppose my brother man goes on wronging me. How often ought I to forgive him? Seven times?

JESUS: Seven times? No. Seventy times seven. Just as often as you need God's forgiveness. . . . James and John, you sons of thunder, what do you say to that?

JOHN: I think we're worse than the Samaritans, because they know no better. But we have you to teach us and still we behave badly. Tell us how to pray, Master, that the Kingdom may come to them, and to all of us.

JESUS: When you pray for the Kingdom, say this: Our Father, which art in Heaven, hallowed be Thy name. Thy kingdom come. Thy will be done in earth, as it is in Heaven. Give us this day our daily bread. And forgive us our trespasses as we forgive them that trespass against us. And lead us not into temptation, but deliver us from evil. . . .

(Fade on last sentence)

SEQUENCE 5 (JERUSALEM)

THE EVANGELIST: Then the Jews sought him at the Feast, and said, "Where is he? . . . "

CAIAPHAS: Well, Captain. Have you laid hands on Jesus bar-Joseph?

CAPTAIN: No, my lord High Priest.

CAIAPHAS: How's that?

CAPTAIN: He didn't arrive. Got the wind up, very likely. We pulled in a bunch of his friends and relatives, and questioned them. They said he had refused to come.

CAIAPHAS: Well, that saves trouble.

CAPTAIN: Are we to go on guarding the roads?

CAIAPHAS: No. The Feast has begun. He's not likely to come now.

CAPTAIN: Very good.

SEQUENCE 6 (A VILLAGE ON THE ROAD)

THE EVANGELIST: And it came to pass that he took Peter and John and James, and went up into a mountain to pray. . . .

(The following all in whispers)

SIMON PETER: James! John! Are you awake?

JAMES: Is that you, Peter? . . . Yes, I can't sleep for thinking—

PETER: Nor I. I must talk about it to somebody. But the others were round us all the evening. And *he* said we weren't to tell them.

JAMES: Speak low, or you'll wake them.

PETER: Can't we slip up on the roof a moment?

JAMES: I'm afraid of disturbing John. He's asleep on my shoulder.

JOHN: I *was* asleep—till Peter tripped over my foot.

PETER: You were asleep?

JOHN: Yes, why not? . . . Go on up, Peter. We'll come.

PETER: Where's the ladder?

JAMES: About three paces to the right. . . . You'll have to step over Thomas.

(A pause, and stealthy movement. A sleeper turns over with a snort and sigh. The following in low voices, but not whispers)

PETER: We're all right here, if we talk quietly. . . . It's rather cold.

JAMES: I have brought our cloaks. . . . Look at the stars. . . . Spread above the earth like a robe of glory.

PETER: But nothing to compare with the glory we saw today in the mountain.

JAMES: No. Tell me, Simon Peter—what did you see? Was it the same for all of us?

PETER: I was tired with the climb. . . . I watched him for a time as he stood and prayed, never speaking, never moving, with his face toward Jerusalem . . . as though he saw nothing but some strange inward vision that held him entranced. . . . I tried to pray too, but no thoughts would come. . . . It seemed to go on for ever. . . .

JOHN: As though time had stopped.

PETER: I think I lost myself a little . . . there in the silence. . . . For the next thing I knew was a great terror, as though I was drowning in it—and when I looked at his face, it was not of this earth. It was . . . it was like . . . it is a thing I dare not think of. . . .

JAMES: Don't, Peter. We saw it too.

PETER: And his garments whiter than the light—the way no fuller on earth could whiten them. . . . And those two others were with him. . . . They spoke together, but I couldn't tell what they said. . . . The glory was upon them both and I knew them for blessed Moses that talked with God in Sinai, and holy Elijah, who passed up to Heaven in light and fire. . . . And it seemed that what I saw was the reality, and the earth and the sky only a dream . . . yet I knew all the time that the sun was shining, and I could feel the rough stems of the heather between my fingers.

JAMES: I had lost touch with everything—except John's hand in mine.

JOHN: Dear James!—I felt you, but as though we were children again—do you remember?—when the great thunderbolt fell, and I was frightened.

JAMES: Oh, John—my little brother, John. It is you now that stand between me and fear.

JOHN: I was afraid too. Peter was the bravest. He spoke.

PETER: Yes—but such nonsense! I thought the vision was departing. I remember calling out: "Lord—it's good to be here. Can't we build three tabernacles for you and Moses and Elijah, and all stay like this for ever?"—so stupid—but I didn't know what I was saying. . . . I thought of the Ark in the wilderness and the glory of the Lord in the pillar of fire . . . all mixed up somehow with the Holy City and the Feast of Tabernacles. . . . And then, and then—the fire and the light were all about us . . . and the Voice . . . was it without us or within? . . . and was it a voice at all?

JOHN: It filled everything—there was nothing in the world but the voice: "This is My beloved Son, hear Him".

JAMES: And after that—nothing. Only the hills and the sky, and Jesus standing there alone.

PETER: He held out his hand, and I was afraid to touch him. . . . But he was just the same . . . as though nothing had changed in him.

JOHN: I think the change was not in him but in us. I think we had seen him for a moment as he always is.

JAMES: But why should this wonder have been shown to *us*? . . . You and I, John—we had angered him so the night before.

JOHN: Perhaps it was a sign of forgiveness. He said once—do you remember? —that there was more joy in Heaven over one who had sinned and was sorry than over ninety-and-nine good men who had never felt the need for repentance.

JAMES: Perhaps that was it. But what did he mean by the thing he said afterwards—that we were to tell nobody what we had seen—not even the rest of the Twelve—until after the Son of Man was risen from the dead?

JOHN: Oh, James, I know. That frightened me more than anything. . . . The Son of Man—that's himself—he has often called himself that. But—"risen from the dead"! He has spoken sometimes lately as though he might die before long. But that would be unbearable.

PETER: Those men in Jerusalem have threatened to kill him.

JAMES: And he is walking straight into the danger. I dare not ask him what he sees ahead. Simon Peter—you who spoke boldly when we were both afraid—can't you ask him what he means?

PETER: No—I couldn't do that. Once, when he spoke of his death, I rebuked him—and he silenced me with words I shall never forget.

JAMES: He didn't say "after I am dead"; he said, "after the Son of Man is *risen* from the dead". The Sadducees say there is no resurrection, but we are taught that the dead will rise some day. But when? At the end of the world? Is our story never to be told till God reveals all secrets?

PETER: I don't know. But he spoke as though the time were not very far off.

JOHN: Perhaps the end of the world is quite near.

(Pause)

PETER: When we came down from the mountain, it was as though the world closed in on us like a gulf. The sun was setting and there were black shadows across the plain. And there were those wretched people with the poor demoniac boy screaming and writhing—

JOHN: And he laid his hands on him and healed him. And even among those shadows there was peace.

SCENE II (JERUSALEM)

SEQUENCE I (THE HIGH PRIEST'S HOUSE)

THE EVANGELIST: And it was now about the middle of the Feast. And there were many rumours about Jesus, but the people dared not say much openly, for fear of the Jewish authorities.

ANNAS: Well, Caiaphas. This is the fourth day of the Feast, and so far there has been no trouble.

CAIAPHAS: No, Father Annas, everything has gone very well.

NICODEMUS: You didn't succeed in arresting Jesus of Nazareth?

ANNAS: Unfortunately, no; but something will have to be done about the man. He has a very bad influence. I've had several complaints from parents that their sons had gone wandering after him instead of staying dutifully at home. I don't know what's come over the young people nowadays.

ELDER: And he's got hold of a number of the women, too. I don't know what their husbands have to say about it. When respectable women get led away—

SIMON THE PHARISEE: Some of them aren't at all respectable. There's a woman called Mary of Magdala, with a very bad reputation indeed. She pushed into my house one day when Jesus was there—

NICODEMUS: *Your* house? How did Jesus of Nazareth come to be in the house of Simon the Pharisee?

SIMON: I asked the man to dinner. I wanted to see what he was like. This Mary Magdalen came in and made a scene. She wept over his feet, and kissed them, and poured perfume on them and wiped them with her hair, and behaved in the most extravagant way.

ANNAS: Good heavens!

SIMON: It was all very emotional and unpleasant.

CAIAPHAS: Did he rebuke her?

SIMON: Far from it. He had the impertinence to say that she was only doing what *I* ought to have done for a guest. That to me, if you please, from the son of a Galilean carpenter! And he crowned it all by telling the woman that her sins were forgiven.

ELDER: Well, really! who does he think he is?

CAIAPHAS: I know the woman you mean. She's a dancing-girl or something. Where is she living now?

SIMON: In Bethany, with her sister Martha and a brother called Lazarus. I think Jesus stays with them there sometimes.

CAIAPHAS: I'll have an eye kept on the house.

NICODEMUS: Isn't it true that since meeting Jesus Mary has become a reformed character?

ANNAS: That's not the point, Nicodemus. No God-fearing prophet would go about with dancing-girls. And as for forgiving them their sins—

CAIAPHAS: That, Father Annas, is the most sinister part of the business. He claims to forgive sins because he is the Son of Man. Anybody who uses *that* title is pretending to be the Messiah. And you know where *that* leads us.

ANNAS: If the people take it up, it means a clash with Rome, and that

(Noise in the street)

must be avoided at all costs. Hark! what's that noise in the street?

(Tramp of soldiers, mingled with shouts and booing)

CAIAPHAS: Soldiers! Something's happened. I did hope we should get through without a riot.

ANNAS: Put your head out, Simon. See what it's all about.

SIMON *(at the window)*: Hey, there, what's happening?

VOICE *(outside)*: They've caught Barabbas the robber!

SIMON: I'm glad to hear it. *(Pulling his head in)* It's all right, that brigand Barabbas has been arrested. They're marching him off to gaol.

CAIAPHAS: Roman justice has a long arm.

ELDER: I will say for Rome—she may be heathen, but she's certainly efficient. It's as well to keep on the right side of the Government.

CAIAPHAS: Precisely. That is why I propose to discourage Messianic claimants and disturbers of the peace. And why I am devoutly thankful—

SERVANT *(bursting in unceremoniously)*: My Lord High Priest—

CAIAPHAS: Fellow! where are your manners?

SERVANT: Jesus of Nazareth is preaching in the Temple.

CAIAPHAS: *What!!!* *(mastering himself)* It would not be becoming in the High Priest to use forcible expressions, but I should like to be an Egyptian camel-driver for just five minutes.

SIMON: It really is most provoking!

ANNAS: How on earth did he get there?

CAIAPHAS: It doesn't matter. He's got there. Well, if necessary, we must arrest him in the city and chance it. Here, fellow, take this note to the Captain of the Guard. . . .

SERVANT: Yes, my lord.

NICODEMUS: My lord Caiaphas, do you really mean to proceed to extremities against this man?

CAIAPHAS: Not at the moment, if I can avoid it. I have merely given orders that he is to be kept under surveillance. But one of these days, I fancy he will have to be—liquidated.

NICODEMUS: But to punish an innocent man for the sins and mistakes of his followers—

CAIAPHAS: Brother Nicodemus, your feelings do you honour. But if Rome is offended, our whole nation will suffer for it. Let me tell you this—and one day you may be glad to remember it—it is sometimes expedient that one man should die for the people.

SEQUENCE 2

EVANGELIST: So Jesus went up into the Temple and taught. And the Jews were astonished at him.

(Slight background buzz)

1ST MAN: You may say what you like. I call him a wonderful preacher.

WOMAN: Do be quiet. I want to hear what he says.

1ST MAN: It's all right. He's stopped to argue a point with one of the scribes.

2ND MAN: How does this man come to be expounding Scripture? He's had no theological training.

3RD MAN: I don't know where he gets his doctrine.

WOMAN: There! He heard you.

JESUS: My doctrine is not mine. It is the doctrine of Him that sent me. If you do the will of God, you will know where my teaching comes from.

2ND MAN: Who gave you your doctrine?

JESUS: He who gave Moses the Law. And Moses gave the Law to you—but you don't keep it. Why, for example, do some of you want to kill me?

3RD MAN: You're mad. Who wants to kill you?

JESUS: You are angry with me because I once healed a man on the Sabbath Day. But Moses commanded you to perform religious duties and works of mercy on the Sabbath. So why is it wrong that I should heal soul and body? You must not go by the letter, but by the spirit of the Law. . . . But as to the text you quote, good Scribe. . . .

(His voice dies away into the murmur of argument)

4TH JEW: Is this really the man they said ought to be done away with? He speaks boldly enough, and nobody interferes with him.

1ST JEW: Do you think the rulers of the Synagogue have an idea that he really is the Messiah?

2ND JEW: Nonsense, nonsense. We know all about this man and where he comes from. Nobody knows where the Christ is to come from.

4TH JEW: Yes, we do. Christ is to come from the house of David, and David's city of Bethlehem.

3RD JEW: Well, there you are! This man's a Galilean, and comes from Nazareth.

JESUS: You know me, and you know where I come from. But I have not come of myself, I come from Him that sent me, whom you do *not* know. But I know Him because I came from Him—and He that sent me is the very truth.

2ND JEW: Yes—but *where* does he come from? and who sent him?

WOMAN: Well, I believe he *is* the Messiah, all the same.

2ND MAN: That's just like a woman—believing things without an atom of proof.

IST MAN: Proof? Look at the mighty works he does! When Christ comes, could he possibly do greater miracles than this man?

IST LEVITE: Sergeant, you hear what these people are saying. Shall we arrest him now?

SERGEANT: Hold hard, my lad. Not just yet. I want to listen to him. I have never heard anything like it before.

2ND LEVITE: Makes you think, don't it? Suppose he *was* the Messiah?

SERGEANT: There, that'll do. . . . Soldiers aren't paid to think.

JESUS: Listen to me, you people, listen to me now. I am only with you for a little while, and then I must return to Him that sent me. Then you will look for me and not find me, for I am going where you cannot follow me.

3RD JEW: What's he mean? Where's he going that we can't go? Is he going out of the country to teach among the Gentiles?

2ND JEW: I don't know what he means. If you like to imagine—

IST JEW: I don't know either. All I said was—

3RD JEW: If you ask me—

(Fade out as they argue)

SEQUENCE 3 (THE HIGH PRIEST'S HOUSE)

THE EVANGELIST: On the last day, the great day of the Feast, the Officers of the Guard came to the Chief Priests and Pharisees . . .

CAIAPHAS: Now, Captain—I must have an explanation of this. I gave you clear orders yesterday. Why was Jesus not arrested?

CAPTAIN: My lord, the men refused to do it.

ANNAS: Refused?—I never heard of such a thing. It's mutiny.

CAIAPHAS: Did they offer any reason?

CAPTAIN: Well, my lord, they didn't seem to like the job. Said they'd never heard a man talk like this man. . . . I rather fancy they've got it into their heads—if you'll excuse me mentioning it—that this man might be—the Messiah.

CAIAPHAS *(thoughtfully)*: I see. . . . You don't seem very certain about it yourself, Captain. Has this imposter got hold of you, too? Surely it should be enough for you that neither I, nor any of the rulers of the Synagogue, believe in his claims.

ANNAS: It's this wretched mob, that knows nothing of the Law. There's a curse on our people.

NICODEMUS: Does our Law condemn a man without proper examination and inquiry? I don't say he's the Messiah, but he may very well be a prophet.

CAIAPHAS: Brother Nicodemus, your attitude surprises me. Anybody would think you were a Galilean. Think again. Galilee is not likely to produce a prophet at this time of day. . . . You can go now, Captain. I shall have to think this matter over.

CAPTAIN: Very good.

(He goes out and shuts the door)

ANNAS: I don't like this.

CAIAPHAS: Nor I. But we can't force an arrest with disaffected troops.

ELDER: What happened to that man Baruch the Zealot, who undertook to get hold of one of the Nazarene's disciples?

CAIAPHAS: He sent in a rather vague report to the effect that the disciple was perfectly sound, and had solemnly assured him that no political move was intended.

ELDER: H'm. I shouldn't trust Baruch too far. My information is that he has retired to the hills with a band of guerrillas, and is plotting some kind of coup. I think he's playing a double game.

CAIAPHAS: I shouldn't be surprised. In fact, I took the precaution of getting into touch with the disciple myself. Judas Iscariot is the name. I asked him to come and see me, and he's here now. Would you like to question him?

ALL: We should, very much.

CAIAPHAS: Call in the man Iscariot. . . . He made no difficulty about coming . . . . We must handle him carefully, because of course everything we say will be reported back to Jesus bar-Joseph. . . . Ah! good morning, my man. Your name is Judas Iscariot?

JUDAS: It is.

CAIAPHAS: You are a follower of Jesus of Nazareth?

JUDAS: I am.

CAIAPHAS: The Sanhedrim have been disquieted by rumours—no doubt quite unfounded—that your Master is engaged in political activities of a rather indiscreet kind, such as might provoke reprisals from the Government. We are very unwilling to believe that this is the case.

JUDAS: You may take my word for it, the story is quite untrue.

CAIAPHAS: Good. We are glad to hear it. It would be a pity that your charitable work among the—the poor, and so on—should be interfered with. But as you know, Rome does not look with favour on group activities which might have a subversive tendency.

JUDAS: I understand you. You think my Master belongs to the Nationalist party. You think he might encourage Jewry to shake off the Roman yoke. Little you know him! And how little you know of this nation! Rome is the punishment that this people must bear for their sins. Jewry is corrupt, and Rome is God's judgment on her—the Roman rod is laid on the sinner's back, and the Roman axe to the root of the rotten tree. . . . Does that gall you, my Lord Caiaphas? . . . There was a time when the Lord High Priest could give orders in Israel. Today, you must cringe to Caesar. That is the measure of your humiliation, and of your sin.

ANNAS: You are insolent.

JUDAS: For Israel, as for her Messiah, there is no salvation but in the patient enduring of all things.

ELDER: Upon my word! The disciple is as fanatical as his Master.

CAIAPHAS *(smoothly)*: It is at least an original point of view. . . . You speak of the Messiah. Is it true that your Teacher claims to be the Christ?

JUDAS: He is the Christ. But he is the Messiah, not of an earthly but of a spiritual Kingdom.

CAIAPHAS: Quite so . . . *(abruptly)* What do you know of a man called Baruch the Zealot?

JUDAS: He is a man to beware of. He would like to get hold of Jesus, and make him a tool for political ends. I know that for a certainty, for he approached me in the matter.

CAIAPHAS: Ah, thank you. . . . You think your Master would not lend himself to such an intrigue . . . ?

JUDAS: I am confident he would not. There was a moment by the Sea of Galilee when the mob tried to make him king. But he refused. And several times since he has shown himself proof against temptation.

CAIAPHAS: Very laudable, very laudable indeed. But the pitcher may go once too often to the well. The motives of successful demagogues are apt to become less lofty as they go on. If at any time he were to weaken in the spiritual purity of his intentions—

JUDAS: I should be the first to denounce him. . . . But he will not weaken.

CAIAPHAS: That is very satisfactory. We are glad to be reassured. At the same time, you might give him a hint to be careful. . . . Your own views on the subject of national regeneration are most important and interesting. I think myself that a policy of reconstruction and collaboration with Rome is in the best interests of Jewry. . . . Thank you . . . we need not detain you further. . . . Good morning. Hezekiah, show this worthy man out.

(The door is shut)

ANNAS: Caiaphas, I congratulate you.

CAIAPHAS: That man has ideas. People with ideas are always jealous of their leaders. Yes, gentlemen, I think we may say we have now got Jesus of Nazareth where we want him.

SEQUENCE 4 (BEFORE THE TEMPLE)

(CROWD noises)

IST PASSER-BY: Blessed be God! It has been a happy festival!

2ND PASSER-BY: A good harvest and a good holiday, blessed be He! . . .

IST ROMAN SOLDIER: Hey, Marcus! You on duty?

2ND SOLDIER: Just sent to picket the Temple steps, in case of trouble. Praise the gods, this confounded festival's nearly over.

1ST SOLDIER: I hate this provincial service. Too much police-work. Give me a good war any day. . . .

3RD PASSER-BY (in a secretive tone): Is that you, Bildad ben-Ishmael?

4TH PASSER-BY (louder): Who are you? And what do you want with me?

3RD PASSER-BY: Not so loud. I come from the hills with a message from Baruch the Zealot.

4TH PASSER-BY: Good. I have men and weapons. . . . Where is the place?

3RD PASSER-BY: Take care!

HECKLER: What a mob on the Temple steps!

HIS COMPANION: If Jesus of Nazareth starts to address them, be ready to shout him down.

HECKLER: I will. Have you got supporters in the crowd to back you up?

COMPANION: Trust me for that. . . .

(Noise of a horse-carriage driven slowly through the CROWD)

SERVANTS: Make way, you dogs! Make way for the Governor's wife! Room for the Lady Claudia Procula!

(Keep CROWD *noise going in background)*

CLAUDIA: Stop the carriage, Rufus! We shall see very well from here. . . . How grand the Temple looks, with the candle-light and the torchlight, and that great moon riding overhead! . . . I am glad I came, Eunice.

EUNICE: It was most gracious of your ladyship to bring me.

CLAUDIA: I do hope we shall see your Prophet.

EUNICE: Indeed, I hope so, madam.

(Burst of singing from the Temple)

CLAUDIA: Rebecca, you are a Jewess. . . . What is the meaning of this feast?

REBECCA: Madam, it is the feast of water and of light, when we give God thanks for the harvest—for the good rain that swells the corn and the blessed sun that ripens it.

EUNICE: Oh, madam, see! There is the Prophet. Just coming through the cloisters into the outer court. There! there!—do you see him?

CLAUDIA: I see him. So that is Jesus of Nazareth!

EUNICE: Madam, is it not a beautiful face?

CLAUDIA: It is a wonderful face, Eunice.

REBECCA: He is going to address the people.

CROWD: Jesus, Son of David, speak to us!

JESUS: If any man thirst, let him come to me and drink. He that believes in me, as the Scripture says—out of his heart shall spring a fountain of living water, welling up to eternal life.

CLAUDIA: Strange that a face and voice should stir one so. Oh, girls, girls! Does he not look like a son of the Immortals, standing between the golden candlesticks?

JESUS: I am the light of the world. He that follows me shall not walk in darkness, but shall have the light of life.

CROWD: Blessed is Jesus, the Prophet of Israel!

JESUS: If you continue to keep my words, then are you my disciples indeed. For then you will know the truth, and the truth shall make you free.

HECKLERS: Don't listen to him. He's a deceiver.

(Uproar)

Listen, you Nazarene prophet. We are the children of Abraham—we were never anybody's slaves.

JESUS: I know you are the seed of Abraham, but you are no true sons of his. For some of you would like to kill me, because I have told you the truth. Abraham would not have done that. Like father, like son—your actions show whose spiritual sons you are.

HECKLERS: We are true-born Israelites. We have only one Father—we are the children of God.

JESUS: If God were your Father, you would love me—for I came forth from God and am sent by God. Why do you not understand me? Because you will not listen. You are the children of the devil, and you do the devil's work.

VOICES OF THE HECKLER'S PARTY: Down with him! Kill him!

JESUS: Will you murder me? The devil was a murderer from the beginning. He hates the truth, because there is no truth in him. His lying words come of himself, for he is a liar and the father of lies. But when I tell you God's truth, you will not believe me. Why? The children of God listen to His word—but you will not hear truth because you are not God's children.

HECKLER: Do you hear this fellow? This mad Samaritan heretic? It is death to listen to such talk.

JESUS: Indeed and indeed I tell you—if a man will keep my saying, he shall never see death.

(Uproar)

HECKLER: Now we know you are a madman. Abraham is dead, and the prophets are dead—and now you say that if a man keeps your saying he shall never taste death. What monstrous claim is this? Who or what do you think you are?

JESUS: If I tell you who I am, it is not to honour myself. My honour comes from my Father—from Him whom you call your God. Your father Abraham rejoiced to see my day, and he saw it and was glad.

HECKLER: You are not yet fifty years old—and have you seen Abraham?

JESUS: Indeed and indeed I tell you—before Abraham was, I AM.

(A moment of stupor—then pandemonium breaks loose)

CROWD: Blasphemy! Blasphemy! Sacrilege! He has taken God's name in vain!

Down with the blasphemer! Away with him! Drag him down! Stone him to death! Stones! stones! stones!

(Screams from the WOMEN*)*

CLAUDIA: Oh, heavens! They will kill him! Send for the guards! Where is my freedman?

(Keep the CROWD *noise going to end of scene)*

FREEDMAN: You had better get out of this, madam. These Jewish dogs! There's going to be a riot. Coachman, whip up!

CROWD: Out of the way! Stones! Stones!

SLAVES: Get back there! Make way! Stand away from the horses! Guards! Guards!—Out of the road, you curs!

(Whips and squeals)

CLAUDIA: Stay! stay! I must interfere. We can't let that man be killed.

FREEDMAN: He's escaped, madam. He slipped away in the confusion. He is quite safe.

CLAUDIA:
EUNICE: } Thank God!
REBECCA:

(As the noise fades out, we hear the tramp of the ROMAN GUARD*)*

THE EVANGELIST: Jesus said: "Think not that I am come to send peace on earth: I came not to send peace, but a sword".

THE LIGHT AND THE LIFE

CHARACTERS

The EVANGELIST.
JESUS.
LAZARUS. ⎫ Friends
MARTHA. ⎬ of
MARY MAGDALEN. ⎭ Jesus.
JOHN BAR-ZEBEDEE.
JAMES BAR-ZEBEDEE.
SIMON PETER. ⎫ Disciples of
THOMAS DIDYMUS. ⎬ Jesus.
MATTHEW the Tax-Collector. ⎭
JUDAS ISCARIOT.
JACOB BEN-ISSACHAR, a man born blind.
ISSACHAR. ⎫ his parents.
RACHEL. ⎭
Ist ELDER. ⎫
2nd ELDER. ⎪ Members of the
3rd ELDER. ⎬ Synagogue Court.
4th ELDER. ⎭
CLERK to the Synagogue Court.
CAIAPHAS, High Priest of Israel.
JOSEPH OF ARIMATHAEA. ⎫
NICODEMUS. ⎪ Members of
SHADRACH. ⎬ the
Ist ELDER. ⎪ Sanhedrim.
2nd ELDER. ⎪
3rd ELDER. ⎭
CLERK to the Sanhedrim Court.
Ist MOURNER.
2nd MOURNER.
3rd MOURNER.
4th MOURNER.
Ist PHARISEE.
2nd PHARISEE.
RUDE VOICE.
PEASANT.
Ist ZEALOT.
2nd ZEALOT.
ARMY SERGEANT.
CAPTAIN OF CAVALRY.

NOTES

THE PLAY

In the first half of the play the atmosphere is that of the lull before the coming storm. The opening scene (House of Lazarus) is serene and almost lyrical; the scene in the Synagogue Court and that between Jacob and his parents should be played with drive and humour: the scene in the street with cheerful confidence—the note of it is: "we face ostracism and possibly death, but we don't mind; we know what we are doing, and all shall be well, and all shall be well, and all manner thing shall be well."

In the second half, the storm begins to blow up: the peaceful sojourn in the Trans-Jordan comes abruptly to an end; the disciples are uneasy about Judas, and troubled by Jesus' prophecy of his death; the outburst from Judas shows his faith already shattered beyond repair; there are hints of plotting in the background; the Raising of Lazarus is a challenge and a paean sounding over an abyss of terror and unbelief. (The "Chorus" of Jewish Mourners here should be stylised.)

The play presents two sharp contrasts: (1) That between the will to life and the will to death. Jesus, Mary, Martha, Jacob, each in their own way, accept life. Lazarus rejects it, and has to find the will to live by passing through death and finding life there. Judas also in his way represents the will to death, in his determination that Jesus shall accept sacrifice for its own sake. (2) That between trust and mistrust. On the one hand is Lazarus, whose attainment of the will to life is conditioned solely by his personal recognition of and faith in Jesus; and also the bold and simple trust of Jacob. On the other, we have the mistrustful suspicion of Judas, the half-belief of the two sisters and their Jewish friends, and the timidity of Nicodemus and Joseph of Arimathaea, who (unlike Jacob) are not prepared to defy authority for the sake of their convictions.

THE CHARACTERS

JESUS—The above notes on the play give the line of Jesus throughout. In the opening scene the quiet humanity and commonsense of his dealing with Martha and Mary is shot through with a strong mood of "God-consciousness" (in the speech about the "Word and Wisdom" playing in the world). This happens again in the scene with Jacob; Jacob says: "Suppose you were looking at the moon for the first time", and the answer is, "God looked at all He had made"—with the implication that this was part of his own experience. In the bit with the Pharisees ("the true Shepherd") there is entire serenity and confidence—"this is what I am, and you can do nothing to me except as I choose".

In the second half, the tone is changed. The challenge to Judas is uncompromising and is met with the silence of mistrust. The proclamation to Martha is met with a formal, and quite uncomprehending, assertion of conventional faith—"I am resurrection and life—do you believe it?"—"I believe that you are the Messiah"—it is faith of a sort, enough to go on with but misses the essential. Mary goes further—she believes that death cannot touch Jesus; but in its more obvious sense, that belief is going to be falsified by the unbelief of the world, and Jesus "groans within himself". They have to be shown that "resurrection and life" mean, not escape *from* death, but the passing through death to life. Only the faith of Lazarus, who has been through death, can be relied upon, and he is ready, as he promised, to "live for the Master's sake". The words: "Lazarus, come forth" are a call not only to faith but also, in a sense, to sacrifice; and that call really will be answered. But the triumph is a stern one.

LAZARUS—He is the natural melancholic—gentle, charming, but undervitalised. He is attracted to powerfully vital people, though he is, I think, a little afraid of Martha; Mary is his favourite sister. He has an affectionate nature and this saves him from egotism, though he is obviously introspective, and a little inclined to self-pity. . . . After his raising from death, he is completely changed; the few words he speaks burst from him triumphantly and with tremendous confidence.

MARTHA is not a subtle character. "House-proud" would sum her up, except that she is capable of a good, sturdy honesty about herself, when she has time to think about it. What she feels in Jesus is "the Truth", and to that touchstone she reacts by a sudden flash of insight about herself. Her religion is probably rather conventional: the tremendous phrase about "the resurrection and the life" produces only a formal declaration of belief that Jesus is the Messiah—that much she has grasped, but its theological implications are beyond her. . . . When she says that if Jesus had come earlier Lazarus would not now *be lying dead,* she is thinking only that he would have healed the bodily sickness. Yet, "even now" she knows that the prayers of Jesus are effective; she says so—but commonsense will keep breaking in—after all, Lazarus has been dead a long time, and she doesn't see what even the Messiah can do about that.

MARY is vivid with vitality. Nothing—not even repentance—can quench her spirits for long. Once she loved the wrong things, now she loves the right things; but she does both passionately—nor is she going to pretend that the old, worthless pleasures were without their glamour. What she sees in Jesus is "the Life"—the blazing light of living intensely, which shows up the tinsel and the tawdry for what it is. She is mercurial—laughing readily, enjoying readily, weeping readily; and she sits easily to the mechanism of life (one feels that if, at any time, the rations failed to arrive, she would make everybody eat boiled potatoes and find it amusing). . . . When she says: "If you had come earlier, Lazarus would not *have died*", she means, literally, that he would have repudiated the very idea of dying—he could not die with Jesus there—nobody could.

JOHN, JAMES, SIMON PETER—Nothing very special about them in this play, except that the uncomfortable feeling about Judas begins to arouse a real repugnance in John.

THOMAS—the pessimist, as usual; but sturdily devoted.

MATTHEW—again as usual, is quick to spot anything wrong on the financial side. He has been too well used to that kind of thing to feel much surprise, or repugnance. In such matters he is a realist. Experience has taught him that when you can't prove anything, the only way is to carry on as though nothing had happened, keeping your eyes open and your mouth shut.

JUDAS—I am sorry to drag him along for the sake of a single speech, but it seems important to get a reaction from him at this point. The speech itself will sound rather inexplicable: the explanation will come in the next play. Actually, he suspects (quite rightly) that the double-faced Baruch and his followers in the hills are planning a political coup with Jesus as its centre, and (quite wrongly) that Jesus is falling for it. He has been bribing Baruch's followers to give information—hence the thefts from the alms-box. He has now worked himself up into a state of mind where he is quite incapable of taking Christ's word for anything; even open announcements about the suffering and death to come sound to him like hypocrisy. He is genuinely tormented, but he is in the mood of a jealous husband, whose suspicions would only be confirmed by protestations of innocence. The only thing that can be said to him is "Do you trust me or not?"—and in reply to this he can utter no expression of confidence. From this moment, everything that happens will only confirm his suspicions, and he will go to pieces, till he commits an unspeakable crime and realises what he has done. Rather like Othello, he can only believe in innocence after he has killed it.

JACOB the Blind Man—He is about 40, and the salt of the earth. His robustness and humour send this scene with the Elders rattling along, as also the scene with his parents. He is extremely intelligent and quite properly instructed in his religion, with a strong grasp of the essentials of any situation: "One thing I do know—once I was blind, and now I see. . . . " "If God hears good people and not bad people, Jesus is good, because God hears him." . . . "You're the Messiah, and of course I trust you." Thirty years as a beggar have made him a judge of character; he is completely fearless, and when he has found a good thing, he sticks to it. He has also a real streak of poetry in him, seeing the moon "fresh as the day it was created". He has something in common with Matthew, but his humour is rougher and pawkier; he is not surprised by the grace and goodness of Jesus—he *recognises* it instantly as something which "belongs" where it should belong.

THE ELDERS—These are not the big-wigs; they are the rulers of the local synagogue—the vicar of the parish and the churchwardens, so to speak. The First Elder is presiding over the court. The Third Elder is a timid person—the others more venomous.

JACOB'S PARENTS—Through these timid, hardworking, respectable people, one feels the power of the official religious organisation. Their narrow lives are ruled by Church and Chapel—their livelihood depends on keeping on the right side of the Elders—who would buy vegetables from a man in disgrace with the Synagogue, or entrust their washing to his wife? Even a miracle cannot embolden them to defy authority. They have only one aim—to keep out of trouble, and not to give offence. They will take no responsibility for anything. Of course they have heard all about Jesus of Nazareth—but they will flatly deny it, the moment it becomes plain that Jesus is not *persona grata* with the Elders. The FATHER compensates himself for his timidity by flying into a rage at home. The MOTHER is a born whiner, and whines consistently.

NICODEMUS; JOSEPH OF ARIMATHAEA—These men are followers of Jesus in secret, and their consciences prompt them to make an effort to save him from his fate. But when it comes to the point, they too dare not face an open rupture with ecclesiastical authority. They are rich and respected members of the Sanhedrim, and the prospect of being publicly disgraced like any pauper is too much for them. But they are sincere as far as they go, and make their pleas passionately.

CAIAPHAS—Knows, of course, exactly where to have people like NICODEMUS and JOSEPH. He pins them instantly to the crucial question of the Messiahship and forces them into a position where they must either rebel or retract.

THE MOURNERS at Bethany should, I think, for choric effect, be partly men and partly women, whether or not this is correct Jewish custom. The "keening" can be used as a sort of interlude to represent the passage of time.

SCENE I (BETHANY; IN THE HOUSE OF LAZARUS)

THE EVANGELIST: Now, in the village of Bethany, nigh to Jerusalem, there dwelt a man named Lazarus, with his sisters Martha and Mary. Mary had been a great sinner, till she met Jesus; and now, when he came to visit the house, she sat at his feet and listened to his words. But Martha was cumbered with much serving. . . .

JOHN: There you are, Martha. It's working all right now.

MARTHA: Thank you, John bar-Zebedee. I wish everybody was as helpful as you are. Now I must get on with the cooking. How many to supper? The Rabbi and you and us three—that's five—

JOHN: Simon Peter and James, if they back from Jerusalem in time.

MARTHA: Seven. . . . I hope James will remember the spices.

JOHN: James won't forget. . . . Sure there's nothing more I can do?

MARTHA: No—run along now. You'll find the Rabbi in the courtyard with Mary and Lazarus. . . . *(going out)* Abigail! Hurry up with those peas. . . . *(calling from a little way off)* Oh, John!

JOHN *(nearer to the microphone)*: Yes?

MARTHA: Does the Rabbi like fig-stuffing or dates? Or shall I just do it up with raisins and a few olives?

JOHN: Oh, fig-stuffing, I think. . . . *(to himself)* Poor Martha! She does fuss so! . . . *(aloud)* Hullo, everybody! Sorry to be so late.

MARY: Come along, John, and sit down. You look hot.

JOHN: It's the kitchen fire. I was mending the spit. There wasn't much wrong with it.

MARY: Oh, dear! It would have done quite well to-morrow. We've kept some sherbet for you.

JOHN: Thank you, Mary. . . . It's lovely and cool out here. I think sunset is the pleasantest hour of all the day.

MARY: And autumn is the pleasantest season. Look at the leaves of the vine—so green with the light slanting through them—and the dappled shadows dancing on the pavement.

LAZARUS: The leaves will not be green much longer. They are beginning to fall already.

MARY: They are beautiful when they fall—red and yellow and russet-brown, crisped and curled at the edges. When the wind blows them along the ground they make a little whispering noise as though they were telling a gay secret. . . . But Lazarus is always sad in the autumn. Rabbi, tell my brother he should be merrier.

LAZARUS: In a world like this, what is there to be merry about? There is much labour and great disquiet, fear, and a little trembling laughter. The most a man can hope for is tranquility, and perhaps even that is too much to expect. I think there is a terror at the heart of God's mystery. Is it not so, Rabbi? Is not the fear of the Lord the beginning of wisdom?

JESUS *(dreamily)*: "When He established the foundations of the earth, I was with Him forming all things, and I was delighted every day, playing before Him, playing in the world and delighting myself among the sons of men."

JOHN *(a little startled—it sounds almost autobiographical)*: Master, of whom is that said?

JESUS: Of the Word and Wisdom of God.

LAZARUS: Does joy go so deep as that? To the very foundations of the world? . . . Well, I will do my best. But I am not light-hearted by nature.

MARY: No. Even as a boy you were quiet and melancholy—my grave elder brother. You tried to tame my wild spirits. If I had listened to you I should never have sinned so deeply. But there was so much—so much to enjoy. I loved the beauty of the world. I loved the lights and the laughter, the jewels and the perfumes and the gold, and the applause of the people when I danced and delighted them all, with garlands of lilies in the red braids of my hair.

LAZARUS: You are always in love with life.

MARY: I love the wrong things in the wrong way—yet it *was* love of a sort . . . until I found a better.

JESUS: Because the love was so great, the sin is all forgiven.

MARY: Kind Rabbi, you told me so, when I fell at your feet in the house of Simon the Pharisee. . . . Did you know? my companions and I came there that day to mock you. We thought you would be sour and grim, hating all beauty and treating life as an enemy. But when I saw you, I was amazed. You were the only person there that was really alive. The rest of us were going about half-dead—making the gestures of life, pretending to be real people. The life was not with us but with you—intense and shining, like the strong sun when it rises and turns the flames of our candles to pale smoke. And I wept and was ashamed, seeing myself such a thing of trash and tawdry. But when you spoke to me, I felt the flame of the sun in my heart. I came alive for the first time. And I love life all the more since I have learnt its meaning.

JESUS: That is what I am here for. I came that men should lay hold of life and possess it to the full.

LAZARUS: Rabbi, it is true. I feel it in you too—that immense vitality at which a man may warm himself as at a fire. In your presence, I think, no one could easily yield to death—not even I. Yet I am not like Mary. I hold to life only with one hand, and not with a very strong clasp. If death came to me quietly one day when you were not beside me, I should not struggle, but slip away with him in silence and be glad to go.

JESUS: Do you love me so little, Lazarus?

LAZARUS: I love you dearly. To say that I would die for you is nothing. I would almost be ready to live for you if you asked me.

JOHN: Oh, Master, hold him to that promise. Look, Lazarus, you have made your sister cry.

LAZARUS: I'm sorry. I'm afraid I'm rather a depressing companion. Pay no attention. Dry your eyes, Mary—here's Martha coming. She'll scold me if she sees you in tears.

MARTHA (arriving in a flurry): That careless girl has broken the big yellow pitcher. And something has gone wrong with the scullery door. It won't shut properly. How much longer are Peter and James going to be? The meat will be dried to a cinder. Mary, I do wish you'd take a little interest in the housekeeping. There's too much work for one pair of hands, and that Abigail's no use at all. It's all very well for men to sit about talking all day, but a woman's place is in the kitchen. Rabbi, why do you encourage Mary to leave everything to me? Don't you think it's a little unfair? Do tell her to come and help me.

JESUS: Martha dear, you are the kindest soul alive. You work so hard and you take so much trouble about everything—except, perhaps, the greatest thing of all, the thing that Mary cares about. She has chosen the better part, and you must not take it away from her.

MARTHA: Rabbi, I don't grudge Mary anything. But I still don't think it's quite fair. She was away from home long enough, goodness knows—and considering *everything,* I think the least she can do—

JESUS: Martha, can the cooking get on without you for just five minutes?

MARTHA (grudgingly): Well, I daresay it *could*—

JESUS: Then stop worrying about it for one moment and think. Sit down. Do you remember a story I told you the first time I ever came to see you?

MARTHA: The day you brought Mary back to us? About the younger son who ran away abroad to see life, and he wasted all his money and had to keep pigs? And then he was sorry and came home and his father forgave him?

JESUS: Yes, that one. Did I tell you about his elder brother?

MARTHA: No, Rabbi. It ended with the father having a feast for the one who'd come home.

JESUS: Well, the elder brother was working in the fields all this time, and when he came back, he was surprised to hear music and dancing and a party going on. So he called one of the servants, and asked, "What's happening?" And the servant said: "Your brother's come home, sir, and your father has killed the fatted calf, because he's so glad to have him back safe and sound." But the elder brother was angry, and wouldn't go in, but sat sulking outside, till his father came out and begged him to join in the merry-making. "Look here, sir," said the young man, "I've worked for you all these years, and been a good son to you, and you've never let me have so much as a roast kid to entertain my friends. And here's this brother of mine, who's squandered your money in dissipation and bad company, and you go and kill the fatted calf for him. It isn't fair." And the father said: "Son, you are with me all the time, and everything I have is yours. But it is right that we should rejoice and make merry to-day, for your brother is alive when we all thought he was dead: he was lost, and now we have found him."

MARTHA *(upset)*: Oh, Rabbi! Have I really been behaving so unkindly?

MARY *(distressed)*: No, no, never! Rabbi, indeed she hasn't. She and Lazarus have been perfect angels to me.

MARTHA: I don't know. Perhaps I *have* resented things a little bit. Down underneath, not on top. Rather pleased with myself, you know, for acting more generously than I felt. Staying at home all day, one gets a bit narrow and exacting—a bit—Yes, Rabbi—I know what you're going to say: don't say it.

JESUS: Very well, then, I won't.

MARTHA: "Self-righteous"—I can see it in your face.... Mary, my lamb, don't take on so. He's quite right—and I'm sorry. There, there! Come along in now. We won't wait for the others. If their supper's spoilt it'll be their own fault for being late.

JAMES *(arriving with Peter)*: Who says we're late? Here we are. We ran half the way—

PETER: We'd have started earlier, but the—

MARTHA: Did you bring the groceries?

JAMES: Yes, rather.... I say, Master—you know that blind man you healed yesterday?

JESUS: Yes—what about him?

PETER: The Pharisees are frightfully upset—

JAMES: They've had up the man and his parents before the Synagogue Court—

MARTHA: Come and have supper, do—you can talk afterwards—

PETER: And they're saying in the bazaar—

(They go towards the house, talking energetically)

SCENE II (JERUSALEM)

SEQUENCE I (A MEETING OF THE SYNAGOGUE COURT)

IST ELDER: Now, let's get this straight. You say you are Jacob ben-Issachar, blind from birth, and you get your living by begging?

JACOB: That's right. Blind from my birth till yesterday. Everybody knows me. I've had my pitch on the corner of the Temple steps this thirty years.

IST ELDER: Now tell us exactly what happened.

JACOB: I was sitting in my old place yesterday afternoon as usual—

2ND ELDER: Yesterday; that was the Sabbath?

JACOB: That's right. I was sitting there, and I hears a party of men come along. Might have been ten or a dozen of 'em. One of 'em puts a penny in my bowl, and says to another one: "Rabbi Jesus, why was this poor man born blind? Was it to punish some sin of his parents, or did he commit sin himself in a pre—a pre—" something or the other.

1ST ELDER: "In a previous existence?"

JACOB: That's right. Before I was born, I took him to mean. And the other gentleman answers him and says, "Neither he nor his parents are to blame. But it was ordained that the works of God should be shown in him." And then he says: "I must work the works of Him that sent me while the daylight lasts, because the night's a-coming, in which no man can work." Rather sorrowful-like, he says that. And he goes on: "So long as I am in the world, I am the light of the world."

3RD ELDER: What did he mean by that?

JACOB: How should I know? . . . Then this same gentleman—him they called "Jesus"—comes up close to me and puts something on my eyes—like clay, or summat of that—and he says: "Now go to the Pool of Siloam and wash yourself."

2ND ELDER: Nothing more?

JACOB: Not a word.

1ST ELDER: Did he say you would get your eyes opened?

JACOB: No. Nothing only what I've told you.

2ND ELDER: Then why did you go?

JACOB: I dunno. But I sort of made out by his voice there was something good coming. Voices mean a lot when you're blind. I knowed as that voice meant well by me. So off I goes to the Pool and washes careful—and when I'd got the clay all off, I found I could see. . . . Lord, mister, that was queer, that was. I'd never seen in my life, you know. At first, I didn't know what to do with myself—blundered about all over the place. But I soon learnt. Ah! it's a beautiful thing to be able to see the people and the city and the blessed sky and the trees. You sighted folk don't know how lucky you are.

1ST ELDER: Quite so, quite so. . . . This happened on the Sabbath, you say.

JACOB: That's right. And a blessed Sabbath it was for me.

2ND ELDER: A clear case of Sabbath-breaking.

1ST ELDER: This Jesus seems to go out of his way to affront all decent feeling. He could perfectly well have cured the man some other day of the week.

JACOB: The better the day, the better the deed, ain't it?

4TH ELDER: Nonsense. That's a very wicked thing to say.

2ND ELDER: All work is a sin on the Sabbath, however beneficial its effects. This man Jesus is a notorious Sabbath-breaker and a very bad man.

JACOB: Ho! is he? I wish there were a few more like him.

3RD ELDER: I must say that if the miracles are genuine . . . I don't say they are . . . but if they are, where does Jesus get his power, if not from God?

2ND ELDER: From the devil, for all I know. The man's probably a sorcerer.

1ST ELDER: Plenty of sorcerers profess to perform cures.

2ND ELDER: And half the time the thing's a fake. I shouldn't wonder if this

Jacob was a confederate. I don't believe he ever was blind at all. Has he been properly identified?

CLERK TO THE COURT: We've got his parents here, sir.

1ST ELDER: Send them in.

CLERK: Yes, sir. (at door) Here, you two, you're to come along in.

FATHER: } Very good, sir. Certainly, sir. Good day to you, gentlemen.
MOTHER: } God bless your worships.

1ST ELDER: What are their names? Give me that paper. Yes—Issachar and his wife Rachel, living in the Lower Town. Sure these are the right people?

CLERK: Oh, yes, sir. Well known to the police, sir. Quite respectable. The man hawks vegetables and the wife takes in washing.

1ST ELDER: Very well. Now. Issachar and Rachel—you see this man here. Do you know him?

ISSACHAR: Be a funny thing if we didn't, sir, when that's our own son.

RACHEL: Yes, sir, that's our boy Jacob. Born blind and never saw the sun, sir, till yesterday when his eyes was opened, glory be!

1ST ELDER: Born blind? Then how do you explain the fact that he now sees perfectly well?

ISSACHAR: Why, sir—

2ND ELDER: Take care! If you tell a lie, or if you are in a conspiracy to deceive the authorities—

RACHEL: Oh, no, sir, no! We are honest people. We know this is our son, and we know he used to be blind. But we don't know how he got his sight; we don't indeed.

1ST ELDER: Who opened his eyes? Do you know that?

ISSACHAR: No, sir.

3RD ELDER: Have you ever heard of a man called Jesus of Nazareth?

ISSACHAR: Certainly not, sir.

RACHEL: We don't know nothing about it at all.

ISSACHAR: Why don't you ask Jacob? He's of age to answer for himself, ain't he?

RACHEL: That's right, sir. Jacob'll tell you. We don't know nothing.

1ST ELDER: All right, you can go.... Now, Jacob, come back here.... I adjure you solemnly, in the great name of God, speak the truth.

JACOB: Jesus of Nazareth opened my eyes, and that is the truth before God.

1ST ELDER: It is our considered opinion that the man Jesus is an imposter. Do you question the decision of the court?

JACOB: Well, sir, all I know is, I used to be blind and now I can see.

2ND ELDER: But how do you know Jesus had anything to do with it? How did he open your eyes?

JACOB: I've told you all that already. Weren't you listening? You seem dead set on 'earing about the Rabbi Jesus. Are you thinking of becoming his disciples?

2ND ELDER: How dare you speak like that? It's contempt of court.

3RD ELDER: Look here, my good man, *you* may be a disciple of Jesus. *We* follow Moses. We know that God spoke to Moses, but as for this fellow, nobody knows who he is or where he comes from.

JACOB: Well, now, that's a queer thing, ain't it? You don't know where the man comes from—and yet he knew how to open my eyes. He's a bad man, you say. All right. Does God hear the prayers of bad people? "No," says you, "of course He don't." Does He hear the prayers of good people? "Yes," you say, "He does." Well, look'ee here. Here's a thing never heard on since the world began, that somebody should open the eyes of a man as was born blind. Nobody can't do a thing like that, only by God's help—stands to reason.

1ST ELDER: You are altogether born in sin. Have you the effrontery to preach to us? You shall be excommunicated for this.

2ND ELDER: Cast out of the synagogue.

4TH ELDER: And cut off from the congregation.

1ST ELDER: Is the court agreed about that?

2ND ELDER: Yes.

3RD ELDER: Yes. On the whole, I agree. We can't tolerate this sort of behaviour.

4TH and remaining ELDERS: The court is agreed.

1ST ELDER: Jacob ben-Issachar, pay heed, while I pronounce the sentence of excommunication. In the name of God, to whom be glory.... (fade out)

SEQUENCE 2 (JACOB'S FATHER'S HOUSE)

FATHER: Our son turned out of the synagogue! What a disgrace!

MOTHER: How shall we ever hold up our heads again?

FATHER: We've been respectable all our lives. I wonder you ain't ashamed to look us in the face.

JACOB: The wonder is that I got eyes to look with. You've forgot that, seemin'ly.

FATHER: You'd better have stayed blind till your dying day than bring this trouble on us all.

JACOB: That's a queer thing for a man to hear from his own father.

MOTHER: Why did you go and speak so impertinent to the reverend gentlemen?

FATHER: You 'adn't no call to stick up for this Jesus. Couldn't you have kept quiet and said you knew nothing, same as us?

MOTHER (tearfully): We was that careful not to give offence.

JACOB: Left it all to me, didn't you?

FATHER: We thought you could a-been trusted to 'ave more sense, at your age.... 'ere, you didn't go and say this fellow was the Messiah, did you?

JACOB: No, I didn't. I said he was a good man and God was with him, and that I'll stand by. You don't think I could stand there, knowing what he done for me, and 'ear him blackguarded by that lot?

MOTHER: Is that the way you speak of the learned Elders and Pharisees?

FATHER: I'll have no followers of Jesus in *my* house. If you ain't fit to go to synagogue, you ain't fit to stay here.

JACOB: All right, if you feel like that! I'll go and work for myself. Thank God, and thanks to Jesus of Nazareth, I *can* do a job of work now.... I *'ad* thought, it 'ud be nice to work for you, seein' you worked all your lives for me. Lookin' forward to that, I was. Never mind. Goodbye, Mother. I'm sorry things 'ave turned out like this. So long, Dad.... I suppose you won't give me your blessing before I go.

FATHER: My blessing? A father's curse is what you deserve, my lad.

MOTHER: Oh, Issachar, no! You won't curse my boy?

FATHER: Not if he gets out quick.

JACOB: Well! let's be thankful for small mercies. Good-bye again. *(going)*

MOTHER: Jacob! Jacob! If you was to go back and apologise to the Elders—

JACOB: Apologise to them? No fear.... Look here, Dad, can't you—?

FATHER: Get out!

(He slams the door on him)

JACOB: Well!... Funny world, ain't it? Turned out of 'ouse and 'ome at this time o' night.... All very well to talk about gettin' a job, but 'oo's goin' to employ a bloke what's been kicked out o' the synagogue?... Still, no use grousin'. I got my sight and I got my strength, and you never know your luck.... Lord! what a lovely thing the moon is! To think I never seen it till last night.... Beg your pardon, sir—I didn't 'ear you comin'.... Now, that's queer. If I'd been blind, same as I used to be, I'd a-heard you right enough. Excuse me, but 'ave you ever looked at the moon? Really to *look* at it, I mean? You wouldn't think anything could be as pretty as that, if you wasn't 'ardened to it, in a manner of speaking. Think what you'd feel if it come all *fresh* to you, like it does to me—fresh as the day it was created.

JESUS: "And God looked at everything He had made, and behold! it was very good."

JACOB: Here, I say! I ought to know that voice.... Sir, speak again. For God's sake, speak again.... I never set eyes on your face before—faces mean nothing to me—but you look the way you ought to look if you're the man I take you for.

JESUS: Jacob ben-Issachar—are you glad of the gift that you found in the Pool of Siloam?

JACOB: That's it! that's the voice that brought the light to me that sat in darkness. I couldn't be mistaken. You are Jesus of Nazareth. Oh, sir—

JESUS: Not so loud, Jacob.

JACOB *(in a lower tone)*: That's right. You're in danger in Jerusalem. Why did you come?

JESUS: To look for you. They said that for my sake you had been cast out of the synagogue.

JACOB: And out of my father's 'ouse. But never you fret for that, sir. I'll make shift somehow. . . .

JESUS: The foxes have holes and the birds have nests—but the Son of Man has nowhere to lay his head.—Tell me, Jacob, do you believe in the Son of Man?

JACOB: Do you mean the Messiah? Of course, I believe in his coming.

JESUS: Are you ready to trust him?

JACOB: Why yes, sir, if I knew who he was. . . . You speak as though he was here. Tell me where to find him and I'll trust him right enough.

JESUS: You have seen him already, and he is speaking to you now.

JACOB: You, sir? Indeed, I might a-known it. If ever a man came straight from God, sir it's you. Say no more, Rabbi, I trust you. I'd follow you to the world's end. You won't send me away?

JESUS: If anyone comes to *me, I* will never cast him out.

1ST PHARISEE: Dear me! A very affecting sight. And a most moving conversation.

JACOB: Who's that?

2ND PHARISEE: We are rulers of the synagogue, Jacob ben-Issachar. The lattice of this house overlooks the street very conveniently. Do you know that it is an offense to acknowledge this man as the Messiah?

JACOB: You made that pretty clear this afternoon. But you've thrown me out, and there ain't nothing more you can do to me. I'm finished with you now, and I'll go where I'm wanted.

1ST PHARISEE: Quite so. The blind go to Jesus of Nazareth by night. Most appropriate. But *we* have eyes and ears.

JESUS: As you say, it is appropriate. For wherever I go, I bring judgment. And I came into the world that the blind might see, and that the seeing might be struck blind.

2ND PHARISEE: Do you mean to insinuate that *we* are blind?

JESUS: Blindness is not a sin. If you were blind and knew it, you would not be to blame. But you are blind and you insist that you see clearly; that is your sin.

1ST PHARISEE: We will not bandy words with you. But one thing we *have* seen and noted. You have deliberately welcomed as your follower this excommunicated rascal—this black sheep who has been cast out of the fold of Israel.

JESUS: Cast out of the fold? Say rather, he came at my call. Indeed and indeed I tell you, the man who will not enter the sheepfold by the door but climbs in some other way is nothing but a thief and a robber. But he that goes in by the door is the shepherd himself. He calls his own sheep by name, and leads them out to pasture. And the sheep follow him willingly, because they know his voice. But they will not follow a stranger, for the strange voice frightens them.

1ST PHARISEE: What do you mean by that?

JESUS: I am the beloved shepherd, whom the sheep are glad to follow. I know my own, and they know me. This is the mark of the true shepherd—that he gives his life for the sheep. The false hireling cares nothing for the sheep, because they are not his own. When he sees the wolf in the distance, he runs away and leaves the flock to their fate. But I am the true shepherd, and I lay down my life for the sheep.

2ND PHARISEE: If you go on provoking the authorities I dare say they *will* take your life.

JESUS: Nobody can *take* my life. I lay it down of my own accord—and will take it again when the time comes. That is my Father's command, and the measure of His love for me. And because I am the shepherd of Israel—

1ST PHARISEE (*interrupting angrily*): The Lord God is the shepherd of Israel.

JESUS: My authority is of God. Just as my Father knows me and I know Him, so I know my sheep and am known by them. My gift to them is eternal life, and no one can snatch them out of my hand. For my Father gave them to me, and He is almighty. No one can snatch anything from the hand of God, and my Father and I are one.

SCENE III (THE TRANS-JORDAN)

THE EVANGELIST: When he had said these things, the Jews sought again to stone him. But he escaped out of their hand and departed beyond Jordan, and there abode; and many believed on him. . . .

   And presently it came to pass that Martha and Mary sent unto him saying, "Rabbi, Lazarus whom thou lovest is very ill". And when Jesus heard it, he said, "This sickness is not unto death, but for the glory of God, that the Son of God might be glorified thereby". And he went not unto Bethany, but remained where he was for two days longer.

PETER: What have you got there, John?

JOHN: Roses of Sharon. They're in bloom all over the valley.

PETER: It's a treat to see the spring again. But I've enjoyed these last few months, haven't you?

JOHN: Yes, Peter. It's been grand. So peaceful—and such a relief to be out of Jerusalem. I know it's the Holy City and all that, but you could feel hatred and hypocrisy oozing out of the very stones. And thinking all the time the Master would be arrested, or murdered.

THOMAS: I was afraid, when that message came about Lazarus, that he'd want to go up to Bethany again and run his head into danger.

PETER: So was I, Thomas; it's a blessing the illness was only a slight one.

JOHN: Ye-es. I've wondered about that, rather. Of course, the Master knows best. But Lazarus hasn't much vitality, and if he got *really* ill, I don't think he'd put up much of a fight.

PETER: If he's held his own till now, he'll probably pull through. Perhaps the Master thought he ought to make the effort.

JOHN: Perhaps that was it. Anyway, I'm thankful—selfishly thankful—that we're staying on here. No riots, no heckling, no arguments—nothing but the country people really loving him—it feels as though the Kingdom were here already.

PETER: Ay—like the Master said. "Wherever there is love, there's the Kingdom" —and maybe this is the way it's to come, just working quietly like the yeast in the dough, same as he told us.

JOHN: The Master has been happy here. Gay and serene as he was when we first knew him.

THOMAS: I'm afraid it's too good to last. . . . You weren't here last night. He talked about dying again.

JOHN: Oh, Thomas! I'd sort of hoped . . . I mean, he hasn't mentioned it lately, and after we'd got away from Jerusalem—I'd managed to forget about it—almost. . . . I can't bear it—it gives me a kind of sick feeling in my stomach . . . what did he say?

PETER: He used that horrible phrase again—"strung up on the gallows"—I saw Judas looking awfully queer.

THOMAS (finding it rather a relief to change the conversation): Look here, John, what's the matter with Judas? He's always hinting things. . . .

JOHN: What things?

THOMAS: About not taking too much for granted, and the bad effects of popularity. . . .

PETER: That's what the Master says.

THOMAS: I know. But why does Judas watch him so closely, as though he was waiting to catch him out in something? . . . And the other night I saw him talking to a very wild-looking man, like a hill-bandit, and giving him money,—in a furtive sort of way.

JOHN: Giving him money? What money? Not out of the alms-box?

PETER: Look here, Thomas, what are you trying to say? Are you accusing Judas—?

THOMAS: I'm not accusing anybody. But I thought it looked funny, that's all.

JOHN: You oughtn't to say such things, Thomas, unless—

MATTHEW (breaking in unexpectedly): I've had my doubts about Judas for some time.

PETER: Heavens, Matthew! I thought you were asleep.

MATTHEW: No—I'm not asleep. See here. I wanted cash last week for a poor family. Seemingly there wasn't none. Well, I knew we couldn't have spent all what we got for the last catch of fish. "What's gone of it?" I said. Judas looked me straight in the eye—too straight—and said he'd bestowed it on a deserving object. I know them deserving objects what you can't put a name to. . . . But there! I couldn't prove nothing, so I didn't say nothing. . . . Here's the Master coming. Don't get worrying him with it. . . . not till you're sure.

JOHN: Of course not. . . . Oh, dear! He's got Judas with him. . . .

JESUS: Well, children, we have spent a happy winter—but the time has come when we must be moving. Let us go into Judaea again.

DISCIPLES: Into Judaea?

PETER: Master, you know what happened last time. They tried to stone you. Do you really want to go back there?

JESUS: Are there not twelve hours in the day—twelve hours of daylight? By day, a man can walk without stumbling, because the sun is there. It is only at night that he stumbles, when the sun has gone and left him in the dark. . . . I have had news of our friend Lazarus.

JOHN: Is he worse?

JESUS: He has fallen asleep, and I must go and wake him.

MATTHEW: But if he's having a good sleep, he's in a fair way to mend.

JESUS: Children, Lazarus is dead.

JOHN: Oh, I am sorry. . . . Master, if only—

JESUS: If only I had gone earlier? Well, John: for your sakes I am glad I was not there, because you must learn to believe.

THOMAS: But if he's dead, it's no good going now.

JESUS: Let us go to him all the same.

PETER: Do you really want to go?

JESUS: I am going. But don't come if you would rather not.

JUDAS: Master, can't you speak plainly?

JESUS: Yes, Judas? What about?

JUDAS: About this journey. *Why* do you want to go to Judaea? To weep at the grave and console the bereft? Is that all?—Or do you mean to come out boldly—to leave this pleasant backwater and face the floodtide of events? *(passionately)*—I wish I knew what to make of you. Sometimes you speak as though you meant to dare everything and take the consequences. But which way—which way? You have made the way of the Kingdom plain to my eyes and my heart. But there is another way and another kind of kingdom—and there are things going on that I don't understand. Or perhaps I understand too well. . . . For God's sake, Master, are you honest? Or do your words say one thing and your actions another?

JESUS: I said to you once before that some of you still do not trust me. And I have said, and I tell you again, Blessed is the man that has no doubts about me. Without faith, you can do nothing; and if you believe in God, you must also believe in me. But you must trust me altogether or not at all.

(Slight pause)

When the Son of Man comes, shall he find faith in the world? *(going)*

PETER: There, now—he's gone. . . . Look here, Judas, what on earth made you go off the deep end like that? You talk as though the Master was up to some sort of funny business.

JUDAS: Why didn't he answer my questions?

PETER: What questions? I couldn't make out what you were driving at.

JUDAS: *He* understood well enough. And he wouldn't give a straight answer.

MATTHEW: Well, I don't see you had any call to come busting out with a lot of questions. Ain't he got enough to worry him—with pore Lazarus dead, and his wanting to go to Bethany, and people only waiting to throw stones at him, let alone us objecting to everything and contradicting and getting cold feet about it? We ain't even 'ad the grace to say whether we're going with him or not. A nice bunch of disciples we are, I must say—shilly-shallying about.

PETER: I only said it was dangerous for him in Judaea.

MATTHEW: That won't stop him. You ought to know that by now. He's made up his mind, and he'll go if it kills him.

PETER: That's a fact. We've got to trust him to know what's right. And after all, he came out safe before.

THOMAS: I shouldn't count on that. What I say is, he's our Master and our friend; and if he's going to be killed, let us go too, and die with him.

PETER: Of course, there's nothing else we can do.

JOHN: There's nothing else we'd want to do.

MATTHEW: There ain't nothing else *to* do. What do you say, Judas?

JUDAS: If he goes, I will go too. It's not death that I am afraid of.

SCENE IV (BETHANY)

SEQUENCE 1 (ON THE ROAD)

THE EVANGELIST: When Jesus came to Bethany he found that Lazarus had lain in the grave four days already. And many Jews had come from Jerusalem to comfort Martha and Mary concerning their brother. Then Martha, as soon as she heard that Jesus was coming, went and met him, but Mary sat still in the house....

MARTHA: O Rabbi, Rabbi! You've heard what trouble we're in.

JESUS: Yes, my dear.

MARTHA: Lazarus is dead. Oh, if only you had come earlier, you would have healed him and he wouldn't be lying there cold in his grave. Even now, I know that God will give you anything you ask.... Yet what can prayers do for one who is dead and buried?

JESUS: Take comfort, Martha; your brother shall rise again.

MARTHA: Yes, Rabbi. I know that he will rise again—in the resurrection at the last day.

JESUS: I am the resurrection and the life. They that believe in me shall live, even though they were dead, and the living that believe in me shall never die ... do you believe this?

MARTHA *(puzzled, but sticking to the thing she really does believe)*: Yes, Master, I do believe in you. I believe you are the Christ, the Son of God, sent into the world as the prophets foretold.

JESUS: So much at least you believe. Where's Mary?

MARTHA: At home. I'll run and fetch her.

SEQUENCE 2 (THE HOUSE)

(Sound of the Jews lamenting—general suggestion of an Irish wake with people keening)

MARTHA *(in a low, urgent tone)*: Mary, Mary!

MARY: What is it, Martha?

MARTHA: The Master is here, and is asking for you. Come quick! he's waiting out there on the road.

MARY: Thank God he has come at last!

MARTHA: Here's a cloak.

MARY: Thank you, dear. . . . Oh, Martha—I hope it wasn't dangerous for him to come back.

MARTHA: We'll slip away quietly.

(Keening continues)

1ST MOURNER: What has become of Mary?

2ND MOURNER: She has left the house with Martha.

3RD MOURNER: They have gone to weep at their brother's grave.

4TH MOURNER: Let us go and mingle our tears with theirs.

1ST MOURNER: Look! The two sisters are hurrying along the road.

2ND MOURNER: They have gone past the turn that leads to the cemetery.

3RD MOURNER: Shall we follow them or go back to the house?

4TH MOURNER: Follow! In their grief they may do something desperate.

MARTHA: Oh, Mary—our friends have seen and followed us.

MARY: It can't be helped now. We must hurry to the Master's feet.

1ST MOURNER: See! there is somebody waiting for them at the turn of the road.

2ND MOURNER: Who is it?

3RD MOURNER: Mary has fallen down and kissed his feet.

4TH MOURNER: It is Jesus of Nazareth.

MARY: Oh, Rabbi! Oh, dear Master! You are welcome to our sad hearts. Alas! if you had come earlier, our brother would never have died.

JESUS: Are you sure of that, Mary?

MARY: Oh, yes, I am sure. For I heard him tell you so. And indeed I believe that death itself could never abide your presence.

JESUS *(troubled)*: O my sisters! O my children! if only the world had faith enough, that would be true indeed. . . . Where have you laid Lazarus?

MARY: He lies in a cave a little way from here.

JESUS: Show me the place.

1ST MOURNER: The prophet is troubled.

2ND MOURNER: He is weeping.

3RD MOURNER: He must have loved Lazarus very much.

4TH MOURNER: He opened the eyes of the blind—couldn't he have prevented his friend from dying?

1ST MOURNER: Alas! no man is strong enough to deliver the world from death.

(Keening renewed)

SEQUENCE 3 (THE GRAVE)

MARTHA: Here is the place, dear Master. He lies in that quiet tomb, hewn out of the rock, with the great stone laid across it.

MARY: Lazarus, our brother, who had no love for life, let the burden slip from his shoulders, and now is troubled no longer.

MARTHA: He carried his life as a condemned man carries his cross. But now he has laid it down.

JESUS: If any man love me, let him take up his cross and follow me.... Roll away the stone from the tomb.

MOURNERS: Roll away the stone?

MARTHA *(horrified)*: Master ... he has been four days dead! The stench of corruption is on his flesh.

JESUS: Did I not tell you that if you believed you should see the glory of God? Roll back the stone.

MARY: Will none of you men do as the Rabbi says?... Oh, John, they are afraid.

JOHN: We will do it for you, Mary. Peter and James, come—set your hands to the stone.

1ST MOURNER: Here is a crowbar.

PETER: Lift all together.

(The stone is heaved off with a crash)

1ST MOURNER: The grave is open.

2ND MOURNER: What will he do?

3RD MOURNER: Something fearful is going to happen.

4TH MOURNER: Look! he is praying.

JESUS: Father, I thank Thee that Thou hast heard me. And I know that Thou hearest me always. But I give Thee thanks aloud, that these people that stand by may hear it and believe that Thou hast sent me.... *(loudly)* Lazarus!

1ST MOURNER: Oh, God! He is calling to the dead.

JESUS: Lazarus, come forth!

(A fearful pause)

JEWESS *(in a thin, strangled gasp)*: Listen!... Listen!... A-ah-ah!

2ND MOURNER *(in a quick babble of terror)*: Oh, look! Oh, look!... out into the daylight... blind and bound... *moving*—with its feet still fast in the grave bands!

JESUS: Unbind him. Take the cloth from his face.

3RD MOURNER: No—no! What will it look like? the face of the four-days-dead?

MARY: Oh, Martha, come and help me.... Lazarus—dear brother—speak if you can!

LAZARUS: Lord Jesus!

MARY: You are smiling—you are laughing—you are alive!

LAZARUS *(joyfully)*: Yes, I am alive!

MARTHA: Where have you been?

LAZARUS: With life.

MARY: Do you know who called you back?

LAZARUS: Life. He is here and he has never left me.

JESUS: Loose him and lead him home.

SCENE V (JERUSALEM;
A MEETING OF THE SANHEDRIM)

THE EVANGELIST: Then many of the Jews which came to Bethany and had seen what Jesus did, believed on him. But some of them went their ways to the Pharisees and told them of it. And the Chief Priests and Pharisees gathered a council together.

IST ELDER *(passionately)*: ... and here's this man wandering about the country, preaching sedition, breaking the Law, practising magic and necromancy and goodness knows what. And what are we *doing* about it? Nothing! absolutely nothing!

SHADRACH *(acidly)*: Come, come. We have held several committee meetings, and passed quite a number of resolutions.

IST ELDER: Yes! and what's the good of that?—He comes and goes as he likes, and nobody interferes. All we get is an entry in the minute-book saying that the Sanhedrim recommends having him arrested or stoned.

2ND ELDER: If the nation rallies to this miracle-worker, Rome will intervene, and take away even such miserable remnants of liberty as we have left. Will you tell us, my Lord Caiaphas, whether any active steps are being taken in the matter or not?

CAIAPHAS: Yes, they are being taken.

IST ELDER *(venomously)*: I am glad to hear it.

CAIAPHAS: But we have to have a clear case and choose the right moment.

Otherwise, Rome might intervene on the side of Jesus, and that would be disastrous.

(Murmurs of assent)

We want to have the thing so watertight that nothing—*nothing*—can intervene to save this man from the gallows.

3RD ELDER: I agree. We must go cautiously.

1ST ELDER: I don't see the need for all this caution. What is the matter with you all? Are you afraid of the man?

(Cries of "No! No!")

NICODEMUS: Yes, we *are* afraid. And we ought to be afraid. Whose power is in this man? . . . I tell you, there is fear in my very bones, lest in fighting against Jesus we are fighting against God.

(Angry cries)

JOSEPH OF ARIMATHAEA: I agree with Nicodemus. Jesus is a prophet of God— shall our names go down to history with those who persecuted the prophets? . . . I implore the Sanhedrim to think again before committing what is certainly injustice and may be the most appalling sacrilege.

CAIAPHAS: Brother Joseph, and Brother Nicodemus—do I understand that you admit the claim of Jesus of Nazareth to be the Messiah? Because that is what he does claim. He does not say he is a prophet: he says he is the Christ. If you propose to support that claim publicly, you may. Of course, there is a penalty attached. A person was excommunicated the other day for the same offence. Only a pauper, certainly—but God forbid that the Sanhedrim should be any respecter of persons—however wealthy they may be, Joseph of Arimathaea. If anybody takes the view that Jesus bar-Joseph is the promised Messiah and the King of Israel, he had better say so at once, and then we shall know where we are.

NICODEMUS *(after a pause)*: I have no wish to defy the Sanhedrim.

JOSEPH: I am only anxious that an innocent person shall not be victimised.

CAIAPHAS: The word "victim" always arouses feeling. But I said before, and I say again, that it is better to sacrifice one man, rather than the whole nation. That is not persecution: it is policy. I think we had better put the matter to the vote. The proposal is that we should proceed against Jesus of Nazareth for witchcraft and blasphemy. Will those in favour kindly signify their assent in the usual way? . . . Thank you. . . . Against. . . . Thank you.

CLERK: The proposal is carried, *nemine contradicente.* Two members abstained from voting.

THE EVANGELIST: And from that day forth they took counsel together how they should put Jesus to death.

ROYAL PROGRESS

CHARACTERS

The EVANGELIST.
BARUCH the Zealot.
LAZARUS.
JESUS.
JUDAS ISCARIOT.
JAMES BAR-ZEBEDEE.
JOHN BAR-ZEBEDEE.
PETER ("Simon bar-Jonah"). } Disciples
ANDREW BAR-JONAH. of
THOMAS DIDYMUS. Jesus.
MATTHEW the Tax-Collector.
PHILIP.
NATHANAEL.
PROCLUS, a Roman Centurion.
CAIUS PONTIUS PILATE, Governor of Judaea.
CLAUDIA PROCULA, Wife to Pilate.
FLAVIUS, Freedman to Pilate.
1st ELDER.
SHADRACH.
CAIAPHAS, the High Priest of Israel.
ANNAS, father-in-law to Caiaphas.
SERVANT to Caiaphas.
1st MAN.
2nd MAN.
3rd MAN.
4th MAN. } Guests at
1st WOMAN. Bethany.
2nd WOMAN.
3rd WOMAN.
4th WOMAN.
A MESSENGER.
SERGEANT.
FATHER.
MOTHER. } Travellers to
CHILD. Jerusalem.
PILGRIM.
A YOUNG MAN, the "Rich Young Ruler".
SADDUCEE.
1ST JEW.
2ND JEW.
LITIGANT. } Hecklers.
HERODIAN.
SCRIBE.

NOTES

THE PLAY

From the point of view of the plot-structure, this is the tie-up play which brings the Judas-Baruch story into close relation with the Caiaphas-Pilate situation. It also collects some people who will appear in the Crucifixion scenes (Pilate, Mary Magdalen, Proclus) and establishes them. From the doctrinal point of view, it chiefly presents a contrast of values between this world and the next (Dives-Lazarus parable, sheep and goats, "great refusal", request of the Zebedees).

[There is a major puzzle in this story, viz.: the mysterious readiness of the "ass's colt" for the Entry into Jerusalem. I don't believe Jesus was making a sort of stage-managed parade in order to fulfil a prophecy. I mean, I can't see Him going to somebody and saying in conspiratorial tones, "I want you to have a donkey ready for me to-morrow, so that I can make a spectacular entry into the city in order to conform with what Zachariah laid down". It wouldn't be like Him—and the fulfilment of a prophecy isn't a fulfilment if somebody does it on purpose. I think the arrangement was made, and the password devised, by somebody else, and for another reason; somebody asked for a sign and was given a sign—and the prophecy was fulfilled in a perfectly natural way, and so was *really* fulfilled. (Just as, e.g., the prophecy about where Christ should be born was fulfilled, not by Mary's deliberately going to Bethlehem in order to put things straight with the prophets, but through the perfectly ordinary machinery of a census, which *brought* her there.) In my childhood I always thought that the phrase "that it might be fulfilled which was spoken, etc." meant that Jesus and the others deliberately did things because that was what was expected of them: "He sent for a donkey"—"Why a donkey?"— "Because Zachariah said it had got to be a donkey, so that everybody could see He was fulfilling a prophecy." But as a matter of fact, nobody did see it at the time.

There's the same sort of difficulty with the passages where Jesus foretells His suffering and death. He surely can't have told the disciples all about it in detail; "it is going to happen exactly like this, and this, and then this"—as though it were a play they were to act. It must all have been much more vague and human and scattered than it appears in the text—not so precise and categorical—more like John XII. 23–26 than Matt. XV. 21. Then, when it had all happened and they thought it over, they realised that they *had* been warned, and saw it as something predestined, "fulfilling the prophecies". "These things understood not His disciples at the first, but when Jesus was glorified, *then* remembered they that these things were written of Him." . . .

From letters written to Dr. Welch.]

THE CHARACTERS

BARUCH—Straightforward—the complete man-of-action of this world. He dictates his letter with the air of a man issuing an ultimatum.

JESUS—This is a play full of changes of mood. He has faced the situation, and knows pretty well what awaits him in Jerusalem. Thus he gets moments of that curious gaiety and relaxed tension which often accompany the acceptance of the inevitable. The Dives-Lazarus parable should be told, I think, rather easily and intimately—gravely, of course, at the end, but not menacing; more a plain statement of a melancholy but indisputable truth. . . . In the short scene with Judas there is a last effort to coax open the door of mistrust—a final appeal to the man to save his own soul. Disaster is inevitable, but there is still time for Judas to refuse to be an agent in it. But Judas has barred the door with a lie, and neither warning nor prayer will now move him. . . . The scene with the donkey has the alternation of mood very clearly marked. The complaint of Judas is met by a quick challenge: "Why shouldn't they welcome me?" Let Judas, even now, make his accusation openly—but he will not. . . . The lament over Jerusalem is the lament over the inevitable—"if only you had known—but now it is too late". . . . Then comes the gay and tender little bit with the ass, and the acceptance of the fugitive triumph. . . . In the scene with the Hecklers, the mood is again relaxed, almost as though he enjoyed playing with these clumsy opponents. (There can be only one end to the hunt, but in the meantime it is exhilarating to watch the baffled hounds at a check.) The answer about the little child—that really does leave them all absolutely standing, and it is comforting to turn from them to the simple delight of the proud mothers and the innocent caresses of the children. . . . Then the Rich Young Man; it would be good to have his allegiance, even at this last moment—but he won't face it, and it's a pity, and it can't be helped. God forces nobody— not Judas, not this young man—the will of the creature is free. . . . Now the disciples are being naively priggish and absurd, clustering round like children when one of their companions has been scolded, and saying, "*We've* been good, haven't we? What do we get?" One must laugh at them—"You'll get all you want and to spare—go on, take it with both hands". Till the request of the Zebedees brings the great shadow down again. They *still* can't understand, and they are being silly and quarrelsome— but one must be gentle with them, because the time is so short.

JUDAS—In this play the whole structure of his intellectual idealism cracks and falls apart, revealing the fundamental flaws of character. It is true that, given those flaws, the whole situation is such as to mislead him. Life is like that. If one has worked one's self into a state of mind where one mistrusts everybody's motives, then circumstances will seem to conspire to give colour to one's worst suspicions. At the core of Judas are the devil's own sins of pride and unbelief, and beneath all his idealism is a rooted egotism.

NOTE that in Play 2, when he first met Jesus, he was asked: "Can you be faithful?" His answer was that he could be faithful to any undertaking of his own ("If I put my hand to the plough I will never look back"). But this is not faith in Jesus, which means childlike trust *in a Person* — and so it is understood by John, by Matthew, by the Blind Man of Play 7, and, with various fumblings and hesitations, by the other disciples, and by people like the Nobleman of Play 3, or Proclus, and the other people who obtain miracles.

In Scene I, Sequence 3, Judas' suspicions seem to be confirmed, and he at once accepts the worst construction that can be put on the matter. His egotism has the psychological effect of making him transfer his own failings to the person of whom he is suspicious: "Jesus has sold himself". (Thus the drunkard accuses his companion of being drunk, the sensualist suspects his wife's virtue, the cheat complains that everybody is trying to do him down.) ... At this moment, when distrust has made a spy and a thief of him, Jesus confronts him with the sudden question: "To whom were you talking just now?" and the lie leaps out of him instantly: "Nobody!" Having taken up this position, his pride makes it impossible for him to confess, or to offer or accept any explanation.

In the scene with Caiaphas and Annas, his first words strike the note of egotism: "I have misled you. ... I have been mistaken. ... I have been made a fool of." That is the galling thing. Then he justifies himself: "I was not really wrong — I was right all the time — it is Jesus who has deteriorated". He makes it clear that what he admired in Jesus was not really Jesus at all, but only the projection of his own ideas in another person — "*my* dreams — *my* prayers — all *I* had ever imagined". What Judas really wanted was a Jesus who would interpret Judas to the world, under his guidance and direction. (He has, in fact, been doing exactly what he condemned in Baruch — trying to make Jesus a tool for his own ends, though, of course, in a much subtler and less conscious way.) ... Then, out come all the petty, personal grievances which have hurt his pride; less intelligent people have been preferred to him; Jesus has not trusted him (again, he transfers his own failings to his victim). ... Caiaphas then makes the suggestion that soothes and flatters and restores self-esteem: Jesus may still be forced into doing what Judas thinks he ought to do — and Judas snatches eagerly at this. I doubt whether Judas starts out with any clear idea about getting Jesus put to death — he probably only wants to stop his activities. But the idea of killing is now presented to him under its most attractive form — sacrificial, idealistic, flattering to his rather morbid theories about suffering, and containing just that grain of plausibility which makes a half-truth more deadly than any lie. Also, there is in Judas' masochism something which can easily invert itself and become a kind of sadism — the worship of suffering for its own sake is not very far from a desire to inflict suffering. ... Finally, the infection of his mistrust spreads itself from Jesus to every living soul. To live *wholly* without stability is impossible; one must have something to cling to; so he suddenly demands assurance in its lowest and crudest form: things, money, a document in black and white. The self-destruction of the intellectual idealist has come its full circle.

THE OTHER DISCIPLES—Note that they and Judas are completely at cross-purposes in the donkey-scene. When Judas says, "This is the thing I have been afraid of", they think he is expressing the fear that this bold move by Jesus may bring him into danger. In Scene III, Seq. 2, though Judas is not bodily present, he has left a jealous and quarrelsome influence behind him, which has infected the others, especially Philip (the one who, in Play 5, accompanied Judas on the Apostolic mission, and is most easily influenced by him). . . . The triumphal entry into Jerusalem goes to all their heads a little; this, at last, they think, is the goods. It seems as though the ugly shadow of the Cross had lifted, and in the excitement, even John, James and Matthew have been thrown a trifle off their balance.

LAZARUS—It seemed better not to give him too much to say, for fear of making the whole thing banal. Lazarus must remember that he is in possession of an amazing secret—which is incommunicable. It is a secret both of laughter and terror, and only Jesus shares it with him. But when commanded he will try—even for the benefit of that stupid woman—to explain something of it; after all, she too has her place in the "pattern". What Lazarus has seen in death is the identity of Christ the Creator ("the Weaver") with Christ in His mystical body ("the Loom" of Creation), and the identity of both with Christ Incarnate—but there is as yet no theological language for this. . . . The following may help in interpretation: "The gods are strange to mortal eyes, and yet they are not strange. He had no faintest conception till that very hour (of death) of how they would look . . . but when he saw them he knew that he had always known them. . . . That central music in every pure experience which had always just evaded memory was now at last recovered" (C. S. Lewis: Screwtape Letters). "I felt when I first saw Him (in a vision) as if there were some old and forgotten connexion between us, as though He had said, but not in words, 'I am He, through whom you were created'. I felt something the same, only far more intensely, as I felt when I met my father again after an interval of many years. My old love came back to me; I knew I had been his before."—(The Sadhu Sundar Singh.)

THE GUESTS—Various types of foolish people. The 1ST WOMAN is the sort of person who wants a thrill at all costs; the 2ND WOMAN is the one who knows all the celebrities and has inside information about everybody. The 3RD WOMAN is one of those gushing females who make other people (including this lady's unfortunate husband, 2ND MAN) go hot and cold in public. The 4TH WOMAN is genteel and conventional. The 3RD MAN is the bore whose experiences are always more remarkable than anybody else's. The 4TH MAN is a vulgar go-getter. The 1ST MAN is quite amiable and probably hen-pecked.

MARY MAGDALEN has only a few words to say, and if necessary this little part may be omitted, if it means a special journey for her.

PROCLUS—His little scene is put in, primarily so as to get his presence in Jerusalem "planted" for the Crucifixion Play; secondarily, to give a little helpful background about the Feast and the Pilgrims, and the Roman attitude to it all. The Soldiers are his local militia whom he has been training (see Play 3), so he naturally hopes they will do themselves and him credit. The "Passover-affair" is to him just one of these peculiar Jewish bean-feasts chiefly remarkable as being apt to give rise to disturbances, and as offering opportunities for a display of spit-and-polish.

PILATE—Here he is; and here at last is Rome in person. He is bored; he is contemptuous; his mind is fixed on getting a good report from his superior, the Governor of Syria, and, with luck, a transfer to a more congenial post. As for the Jews, they are a nuisance—"Tell the lictors to flog them out of the way"—not savagely, but as a man would brush off mosquitoes. But Pilate is devoted to his wife, and would gladly oblige her in anything.

NOTE: It appears that when Pilate was appointed to Judaea he asked, and obtained, the unusual privilege of taking his wife with him. It is probably not strictly correct that she should ride in the carriage with him, but I have used this liberty to avoid awkwardness. . . . The carriage is preceded by a small troop of Cavalry, moving rather slowly, so as neither to get too far ahead of the cumbersome vehicle nor to over-run the Lictors. When Pilate wishes to pass his escort, the Captain moves the Cavalry to line the road on both sides, and the carriage goes up between the two sections. When they move on again, the Lictors and the Cavalry start off first, and the carriage falls in behind them. The Producer and Grams have my cordial sympathy—but they need not be bothered with Crowd-noises as well, because the Crowd are occupied with preserving a sulky silence, and spitting as ostentatiously as they dare into the dust.

CLAUDIA—Nothing new—except to establish beyond doubt that her relations with her husband are excellent. (NOTE: I gather that "Pontius" was the gentleman's *nomen* and "Pilate" his *cognomen*. I have therefore presented him with the *praenomen* of "Caius" for domestic use. If this is thought confusing, his wife could call him "Pontius", in the manner of an 18th-century lady addressing her husband as "Mr. Bennet"; but I would rather have their relations appear more intimate. I have endeavoured to make the thing clear by letting Claudia address him in the first place by the double name, "Caius Pontius".)

FATHER, MOTHER, PILGRIM, etc.—Pious Jews, looking forward to the Festival, and expressing the general hatred of Rome. The CHILD would be about seven.

HECKLERS—The SADDUCEE is one of those smart-alecks, and has the impertinent manner of a conceited undergraduate. The idea is that he should start out by making Jesus look foolish and so hamper him in his dealing with the serious hecklers. Unfortunately, though he is a great hand at ridiculing other people, he cannot take ridicule himself; also, his manner irritates the

Crowd from the word go, and, though they are quite willing to laugh with him about the much-married lady, they are only too ready to have the laugh turned against him. This gives the party a bad send-off. . . . The other questions all turn upon *authority:* the IST JEW'S question is designed to draw out a claim to Messiahship; the LITIGANT is tempting Jesus to set up as a legal authority; the HERODIAN, of course, wants to provoke a denial of Caesar's authority; the SCRIBE, who is the only honest questioner, yet raises the whole issue of the authority of Moses; the 2ND JEW opens up the way for a whole series of inflammatory topics, as noted in the text. . . . All this scene to be played very briskly.

THE YOUNG MAN — This Rich Young Ruler is one of those nice people who have always lived virtuously and gone to church, but have a perfectly well-founded feeling that that is not what the real saints and mystics understand by "religion". He has a hankering after some sort of a thing called "spiritual religion", which gives you lovely feelings. He would like to be at home in both worlds at once — to enjoy exalted religious emotions without disturbing his ordinary way of life. It is a shock to him to be told that real mystical experience is a catastrophic thing. (There are a good many people of this sort; they write wistful letters to the papers urging that what the nation needs is a more spiritual attitude to things — without its ever occurring to them to revise their own attitude to their investments, or to the Borough Council.) This Young Man will need a good many more shocks before he understands the Kingdom. If he lives long enough to see the Sack of Jerusalem, he may understand something.

CAIAPHAS and ANNAS — These experienced politicians can, of course, see all through and round Judas. They play on him like an organ, pulling out each stop at will. They are professionals at this kind of thing. Yet Caiaphas himself is only a tool in God's hand and all his half-truths are half-prophecies. His most ingenious lie — that the death of Jesus will be for the good of Israel — is true in a sense he does not contemplate. Upon him, though not in him, the prophecies are fulfilled.

SCENE I (FROM GALILEE TO BETHANY)

THE EVANGELIST: Now the Feast of the Passover was nigh. And Jesus set his face steadfastly to go up to Jerusalem.

SEQUENCE 1 (A CAMP IN THE HILLS)

1ST ZEALOT: Captain Baruch! The messenger has returned.

BARUCH: Bring him forward into the firelight. . . . Well, what news? Will Jesus of Nazareth come up to the Passover or not?

MESSENGER: He is coming. He will lie to-morrow night in the house of Lazarus at Bethany.

BARUCH: Good. Go and get something to eat. . . . Is there anybody here who knows how to write?

2ND ZEALOT: Yes, Captain. I can make shift with a pen.

BARUCH: Write, then: "Baruch the Zealot, to Jesus of Nazareth, the Son of David, King of Israel, greeting. I have observed you, and I know who you are. To every man opportunity comes once and not again. The Priests and Pharisees are in league to deliver you to Rome; but the people are on your side, and I have men and arms. Give me a sign, for now is the moment to strike and seize your kingdom.

"When a king comes in peace, he rides upon an ass; but when he goes to war, upon a horse. In the stable of Zimri, at the going-up into the City, is a war-horse saddled and ready. Set yourself upon him, and you shall ride into Jerusalem with a thousand spears behind you. But if you refuse, then take the ass's colt that is tied at the vineyard door, and Baruch will bide his time till a bolder Messiah come.

"Say only: *The Master has need of him,* and the beast is at your service." Have you written that?

2ND ZEALOT: Yes, Captain.

BARUCH: Have it delivered to Jesus privately, to-morrow night at Bethany. . . . Wait. The man Iscariot has been tampering with our messengers. Find me some fellow who cannot read what he carries.

SEQUENCE 2 (BETHANY: THE HOUSE OF SIMON THE LEPER)

THE EVANGELIST: And when Jesus came to Bethany, they made him a supper in the house of Simon the Leper. And Martha served; but Lazarus was one of them that sat at table with him.

(Background of general conversation)

1ST WOMAN: . . . Yes, but which is Lazarus? He's the one we came to see.

2ND WOMAN: Sitting next to our host—that quiet-looking man with dark eyes.

IST WOMAN: I don't know how anybody can bear to sit next him. It would give me the creeps.

2ND WOMAN: Hush, dear! That's his sister Mary just beyond you—the red-haired girl.

IST MAN: Lazarus and Jesus are having some kind of joke together.

IST WOMAN: Fancy laughing and joking after you've been dead and buried! It doesn't seem decent, somehow.

IST MAN: I suppose he really *was* dead?

2ND WOMAN: Oh, dear, yes! My daughter-in-law's aunt is the woman who laid him out.

(Move over to next group)

3RD WOMAN: *Do* tell me, Lazarus *(with a nervous giggle)*—I *hope* I'm not being impertinent—but what does it *feel* like to be dead?

2ND MAN: My dear! What a question to ask a man in the middle of dinner!

3RD WOMAN: Oh, but it's so *important! Please!*

LAZARUS: Master, what shall I say?

JESUS *(laughing)*: I'm sorry, Lazarus. You must do your best with it. But no State secrets.

LAZARUS *(as he speaks, the conversation dies away into an inquisitive silence)*: This life is like weaving at the back of the loom. All you see is the crossing of the threads. In *that* life you go around to the front and see the wonder of the pattern.

3RD WOMAN: What sort of pattern is it?

LAZARUS: Beautiful and terrible. And—how can I tell you?—it is *familiar.* You have known it from all eternity. For He that made it is the form of all things. Himself both the weaver and the loom.

3RD WOMAN: I see. *(She doesn't)* But what I want to know—

2ND MAN: That'll do, my dear. You are talking too much.

(Tension relaxes. Move over to next group)

3RD MAN: Some people have the most extraordinary manners.

4TH WOMAN: Yes, indeed. I made up my mind to behave *exactly* as though nothing had happened. I just said, "Well, my dears! I'm delighted to see your dear brother looking so fit."

3RD MAN: I daresay the whole thing's been exaggerated. When I had that illness last spring I was unconscious five hours and had the most extraordinary dream. I remember saying to my wife when I came to . . .

(Move over to next group)

4TH MAN: Come, Judas—a little more of the roast kid. I always say Martha's the best cook in Palestine. . . . You know, if only this miracle was properly advertised—

JUDAS: Good heavens!

4TH MAN: You could work up such a religious revival as hasn't been seen since Moses led Israel out of Egypt.... Don't you agree, Rabbi Jesus? If Lazarus was to tour the country and relate his experiences, the whole world would be converted and embrace salvation.

JESUS: Do you think so?... There was once a rich man who dressed in purple and fine linen and dined sumptuously every day. And there was also a certain beggar, diseased and wretched, who sat in the porch and lived on the scraps from his table. Nobody cared for him, but the dogs, who came and licked his sores. But after a time, the beggar died and was carried by the angels to feast with our Father Abraham. And the rich man also died, and went to the place of torment.

4TH MAN: Why, Rabbi? Because he was so rich?

JESUS: Because he was heartless.... And he looked up, and there—far, far away—he saw Abraham with the beggar sitting beside him. So he called out: "Father Abraham! I am burning in agony. Won't you send that man to bring me a drink of water?"

2ND MAN: Why should he expect a blessed soul in Heaven to run errands for him?

JESUS: He was that kind of man.... But Father Abraham said: "Son, remember, you had your good time on earth. You were top-dog and this beggar was under-dog. But in *this* life, things are different. And besides, between you and us there is a great gulf fixed, and you cannot pass over to us or we to you. It isn't allowed." So the rich man said: "Well, couldn't the beggar go to my father's house and warn my five brothers, so that they don't come into this dreadful place like me?"

3RD WOMAN: He was getting a little less selfish, then.

JESUS: Just a little. But he still thought his own family the most important people on earth.... But Father Abraham said: "Your brothers have their Bibles. All they have to do is to pay attention to what Moses and the Prophets say."—"Yes, of course," said the rich man; "but if somebody went to them from the dead, they really *would* listen." But Abraham replied: "If they will not heed Moses and the Prophets, they will never be persuaded, even though a man should rise from the dead."

(Pause. Conversation resumes)

1ST WOMAN: I don't think I like that story.

3RD WOMAN: I suppose the beggar is Lazarus. But who's the rich man? And what does it *mean?*

2ND MAN *(who has suffered enough)*: Read your Bible and do your duty. That's what it means.

3RD WOMAN: How dull!

(Move over to next group)

1ST WOMAN: Oh! What a marvellous scent all at once. What ever is it?

2ND WOMAN: It's Mary, the sister of Lazarus—she's broken the lid from a vase of perfume—

1ST WOMAN: So she has! A beautiful alabaster vase. What a shame to destroy it!

2ND WOMAN: She's pouring the perfume on the Rabbi's feet—

1ST WOMAN: How extravagant!

1ST MAN: I daresay it's not very expensive.

2ND WOMAN: How like a man! Perfume of that quality must have cost pounds and pounds.

1ST WOMAN: Now she's anointing his head, as though he were a king.

JUDAS: Madam, let me beg you not to use an expression like that.

1ST WOMAN: I beg your pardon, Judas Iscariot. I meant no harm.

JUDAS: The Rabbi has no wish at all to be treated as a royal personage. Mary is always rather excitable and demonstrative.

1ST MAN: Well, it's natural she should want to show her gratitude.

JUDAS (coldly): I see no reason for this waste. That perfume might have been sold for twenty-five pounds and the money given to the poor. That would have been far more suitable.

2ND WOMAN: I told you it was expensive—how does she come by it?

JUDAS: Mary used to be a dancing-girl.

1ST WOMAN: Oh, indeed! that explains it.

2ND WOMAN: I should have thought she'd have given up everything that reminded her of that part of her life.

JUDAS: You would think so, wouldn't you?

JESUS: Judas!

JUDAS: Master?

JESUS: Why are you so unkind? Let Mary alone. What she has done for me is a work of charity. For if she kept this perfume, it was that she might anoint me for my burial.

LAZARUS: Sister, don't let that word startle you. It is a word that you and I and he have no reason to fear.

JESUS: Indeed and indeed I tell you—wheresoever the gospel is preached, they will tell this tale of Mary, and remember the thing she has done.

SEQUENCE 3 (BETHANY: THE HOUSE OF LAZARUS)

JUDAS: Ps'st!

MESSENGER: Who's there?

JUDAS: You know very well who I am.

MESSENGER: Judas Iscariot?

JUDAS: Yes. What's your errand at the house of Lazarus?

MESSENGER: What would you give to know?

JUDAS: A piece of silver.

MESSENGER: Two pieces.

JUDAS: Two then. *(A chink of coin)*

MESSENGER: I have brought Jesus a letter.

JUDAS: From Baruch the Zealot?

MESSENGER: Of course. Who else?

JUDAS: What was in the letter?

MESSENGER: I don't know. I can't read.

(JUDAS gives an exclamation of annoyance)

... But for two pieces more, I will tell you the answer.

JUDAS: Well—here is the money. What did Jesus say?

MESSENGER: His answer was: Say to him that sent you, "To-morrow he shall have the sign he looks for."

JUDAS *(horror-stricken)*: Oh, God! ... *(to the* MESSENGER) What is Baruch doing? ... There! That is my last coin. I have no more. Speak.

MESSENGER: He is getting ready to march with a thousand spears.

JUDAS: I knew it—I knew it! Jesus has sold himself. ... Look out! Someone's coming. ... Get away quick.

JESUS: Is that you, Judas?

JUDAS: Yes, Master.

JESUS: We are waiting for you, to begin night-prayers. ... To whom were you talking just now?

JUDAS *(hastily)*: Nobody. What do you mean? ... Don't look at me like that! It's you who ought to explain—

JESUS: What?

JUDAS *(sullenly)*: Nothing.

JESUS: Nobody and nothing. ... My son—have you lost faith in me altogether?

JUDAS: I believe you are the Messiah. I have never thought otherwise. But I warn you, you are heading for disaster.

JESUS: In a sinful world, disasters are inevitable; but the man who brings them about is guilty none the less. Nothing can turn me from my appointed end. In you or upon you the prophecies must be fulfilled. Make your choice; for he that is not with me is against me. ... Come in—and pray for faith.

SCENE II (THE ROAD TO JERUSALEM)

SEQUENCE I (CAPERNAUM)

PROCLUS: 'Morning, sergeant. Got the men paraded?

SERGEANT: Yes, sir.

PROCLUS: Good. ... Kit all in order?

SERGEANT: Yes, sir.

PROCLUS: Right. ... Now, you men, you know what you have to do. You're going up to Jerusalem for this Jewish Passover-affair. The place'll be packed with pilgrims, and you're to help keep order — see there's no rioting, line the road for processions, and so on. The Governor's going to be there — show him you can be as smart and disciplined as the Guards. If anybody gets himself crimed, he's for it, or my name's not Longinus Proclus.... Here, you there! look at your legs. Ever see a guardsman with his sandals half-laced? ... *And* you. A bit more spit-and-polish on that corslet, my boy.... I want you all to behave like Guardsmen and do yourselves credit.... H'rrumph! Everything ready, sergeant?

SERGEANT: Yes, sir.

PROCLUS: Good.... Squad — Right turn.... By the left — march!

(The draft tramps off)

SEQUENCE 2 (THE MOUNT OF OLIVES)

JAMES: We're going to have grand weather for the Passover. Oh Master, doesn't Jerusalem look beautiful shining there in the sun?

JESUS: Yes, James. "The City of Zion is a fair place and the joy of the whole earth."

JOHN: If only it wasn't so full of detestable people. I like it best from a distance.

PETER: I always say there's nothing to touch this view from the Mount of Olives.

ANDREW: Look at all the pilgrims streaming along the roads.

JUDAS: Master — a merchant from the City called at the house this morning. He said the people had got news of your arrival, and were coming out to meet you.

JESUS: Well, Judas? And why shouldn't they?

JUDAS: I gathered they were planning some sort of demonstration.... A great many of your followers from the country are now in Jerusalem, and their enthusiasm has rather gone to their heads.... If you go forward, they will welcome you in triumph as the Messiah.

JESUS: "Say ye to the daughter of Zion: Behold, thy salvation cometh." ... Children, you have waited a long time to see the Messiah ride into Jerusalem.

PETER: Master, has the moment come?

JESUS: Andrew and Nathanael.

ANDREW: } Yes, Master?
NATHANAEL:

JESUS: Go into the village over against you to the house of a man called Zimri. At the vineyard door, you will find an ass's colt tied. Loose him and bring him here.... If anybody asks what you want with the colt, say only: "The Master has need of him", and he will immediately let him go.

JUDAS: Jesus, Jesus, what are you doing?

PETER: Master, this is splendid—but is it wise?

JOHN: Dear Master, you are taking a fearful risk.

JESUS: It is not a risk, John. It is a certainty; for the prophecies must be fulfilled. . . . Go now, Andrew and Nathanael. I will wait here till you come.

ANDREW: } Yes, Master.
NATHANAEL: }

PHILIP (to the other disciples): My word, this is exciting!

JUDAS: This is the thing I have been afraid of. It has haunted my dreams.

JAMES: Perhaps there's no real danger. He has so many friends among the people. His enemies will have to give way.

PETER: If they laid hands on him during the Festival there'd be a riot.

MATTHEW: Perhaps that's why he's chosen this time to do it.

JUDAS (bitterly): Oh, it has all been arranged. You may be sure of that.

PHILIP: And the Kingdom will be established after all just as we always hoped!

THOMAS: Then what was all that talk about danger and dying?

MATTHEW: 'Ere, Thomas—don't be such a wet-blanket. We're going up to Jerusalem, the Kingdom of Heaven's coming to earth, and everything's going to be fine. The Master wouldn't be doing this if it wasn't going to work out right—would he, John?

JOHN: The Master is weeping.

MATTHEW (dashed): Oh, dear!

PHILIP: Perhaps we have done something to grieve him. John, ask him what is the matter.

JOHN: Master, why do you weep?

JESUS: For my people and my country, and for Jerusalem. . . . Dear City of God, if only you had known while there was still time the things that made for your peace! But the moment is past. You cannot see them now. And the days will come when your enemies will surround and besiege you, and undermine your walls, and press in upon you from every side. They will slay your citizens, and destroy your buildings till not one stone is left upon another—because you could not recognise your salvation when you saw it. . . .

JUDAS: Rabbi, do you threaten the City with armies?

JESUS: No, Judas. But I prophesy. . . . O Jerusalem, Jerusalem! you that kill the prophets and stone the messengers of God, how often would I have gathered your children together, as a hen gathers her chickens under her wings! But you would not let me. And now your house will be left desolate; and after you have lost me, you will never see me again till you are ready to cry: "Blessed is he that comes in the name of the Lord!"

JOHN: Master, may that day come soon. . . . Perhaps they will recognise you to-day, and escape these terrible judgments.

JESUS: Let us go forth in peace, in the name of the Lord. Look, here come Andrew and Nathanael, with the ass.

ANDREW *(arriving with the donkey)*: Master, here you are. There's a great crowd at the bottom of the hill, waiting to welcome you.

NATHANAEL: They are tearing down palm-branches from the roadside and spreading their cloaks on the ground before you.

PHILIP: The mothers have brought their children. . . .

PETER: Come, Master—mount and ride.

JAMES: Is there no saddle? Lay my coat on the back of the ass.

ANDREW: And mine—

JOHN: And mine—

PHILIP *(struggling with the donkey)*: Whoa, there, steady . . . I don't think he's ever been ridden before. . . . Stand still, can't you?

JESUS: Come now, little ass, don't you know me? You too are a child of my Father's house. . . . Yes, of course. . . . There, now you're as good as gold.

JOHN: Your touch has cast out his little devil of fear.

JESUS: Lend me your back, little brother . . . so. . . . Now carry your burden bravely.

PETER: You should be a proud donkey to-day. You are carrying the Messiah.

> *(Noise of distant crowd shouting "Hosanna!" "Welcome!" "Hail, Messiah!" etc.)*

JAMES: The people are shouting and waving their palms!

PETER: Ride on, Master. "Good luck have thou with thine honour!"

ANDREW: Forward to Jerusalem!

> *(The hoofs of the donkey patter forward, and the noise of the CROWD grows louder as the little procession advances down the slope of Mount Olivet. As they join the CROWD, the DISCIPLES take up the cry: "Hosanna! Blessed is he that comes in the name of the Lord! Hosanna in the highest!")*

SEQUENCE 3 (THE VALLEY OF KEDRON)

THE EVANGELIST: And there were many people went up at that time to the Passover. . . .

> *(Confused CROWD background)*

CHILD: Daddy, Daddy, I'm tired. Are we nearly there?

FATHER: Yes, my son. We're coming up the Valley of Kedron now. Look! ahead of us on the left is the Mount of Olives. And on the right are the walls of Jerusalem.

A PILGRIM: Good morrow, neighbours! A happy Feast to you.

FATHER: And to you, good friend.

PILGRIM: It's a blessed day to me. It's five long years since I set foot in Jerusalem.

FATHER: A blessed day indeed! God send you find all your family well and happy.

CHILD: Mummy, can I have a drink? I'm so hot.

MUMMY: Yes, dear, of course. . . . Stop a minute, while I find the waterbottle.

PILGRIM: The road is long and dusty for little feet. . . . Hullo! What's that noise behind?

(Distant shouting)

FATHER: It's cavalry!

PILGRIM: It's the Governor coming up to Jerusalem.

CROWD: Look out! Look out! the soldiers!

FATHER: The accursed Romans!

PILGRIM: God smite their insolence! God break the wheels of their chariots!

FATHER: Riding rough-shod over Israel, with their heathen emblems and their damned imperial pride.

(Shouting and noise of carriages and cavalry comes nearer)

MOTHER: Out of the road, darling. Here come the lictors.

CHILD: What's lictors?

FATHER: The men with the rods and axes, running before the Governor's carriage.

PILGRIM: The scourge of Jewry.

LICTORS *(in a monotonous sing-song)*: Make way, make way, make way for the Governor!

PILGRIM: Spit in the dust as they pass, my son, like a true Israelite.

LICTORS: Clear the road, clear the road! Make way for His Excellency the Governor of Judaea!

(A troop of horsemen jingles past, followed by a carriage)

CHILD: Is that the Governor, Daddy?

FATHER: That's him. That's Pontius Pilate.

PILGRIM: And that's his lady, Claudia Procula.

FATHER: Look at the heathen woman! Sitting brazenly beside her husband, instead of coming behind him like a decent Jewish matron.

(Soldiers and carriages go rumbling and tramping past)

CHILD: Oh, I'm all over dust.

PILGRIM: May Rome and all her Empire bite the dust!—How long, O Lord, how long?

SEQUENCE 4 (IN PILATE'S CARRIAGE)

CLAUDIA: A penny for your thoughts, Caius Pontius.

PILATE: I was thinking, my dear Claudia, that the Jews are a very tiresome people, that their religious festivals are a crashing bore, and that I wish to all the gods we were back in Tyre.

CLAUDIA: Taking instructions from the Governor of Syria, and listening to his interminable reminiscences?

PILATE: He isn't a bad old stick. And anyhow, it's a civilised place, and you can get some sea-bathing.... He congratulated me on my report, and promised to recommend me for a transfer.

CLAUDIA: That's splendid.

PILATE (gloomily): Always provided nothing regrettable happens at this Feast. There's a good deal of unrest about, and I've an idea that the Zealots are preparing to make trouble. We've shut up that fellow Barabbas, but he's not the only one....

(Confused noise. Carriage and horses come to a standstill)

... Hullo! what's the matter now? Flavius, what are we stopping for?

FLAVIUS: I don't know, Pilate. There seems to be some kind of holdup.... Captain! Captain! His Excellency wants to know why we're stopping.

CAPTAIN: Very sorry, sir. Crowd ahead. Some sort of procession coming down from Mount Olivet.... Fellow on a donkey and a rabble of peasants, waving palms and things.... What's that? ... Oh! ... Man here, sir, says it's the prophet Jesus of Nazareth and his followers.

PILATE: Tell the lictors to flog them out of the way.

CLAUDIA: Oh, no, Caius! No, Please don't! It's the man I told you about. I'd like you to see him.

PILATE: If you wish it, my dear. Captain, the Lady Claudia would like to see the show. Let the carriage through to the front.

CAPTAIN: Very good, sir.... Leading section—left incline. Walk—march! ... Halt! ... Front!

(Horses clatter into position)

PILATE: Though you know, my dear, your prophet is a bit of a revolutionary.

CLAUDIA: Surely not.

CAPTAIN: Number 2 section—right incline—walk—march! ... Halt! ... Front!

PILATE: Drive on!

(Renewed clatter. Carriage goes forward. Cries of "Hosanna!" become audible. Carriage stops)

CROWD: Hosanna! hosanna! Hail, Jesus! Hail, Messiah!

PILATE: Looks harmless enough.... Not a very distinguished following, I must say.

CLAUDIA: Oh, Caius—it's pretty. Look at the little children. Aren't they sweet?

CHILDREN: Hurray! hurray! Welcome, welcome, Jesus! Hosanna!

DISCIPLES AND CROWD: Shout for the Messiah! Messiah! Hosanna to the Son of David!

PEREMPTORY VOICE FROM THE CROWD: Hey, you, Jesus! Tell your disciples to stop that row.

(Lull in the shouting)

JESUS: Not I. If these men were to hold their peace, the very stones would cry out.

CROWD *(with fresh enthusiasm)*: Hosanna! hosanna! hosanna!

(The shouts die away as the procession passes)

PILATE: That seems to be the lot. Carry on, Captain.

CAPTAIN: Sections—form troop! Walk—march!

(The carriage moves on with its escort, and is followed by the tramp of the infantry)

SCENE III (JERUSALEM)

SEQUENCE I (OUTSIDE THE TEMPLE)

THE EVANGELIST: Then the Pharisees and the Herodians sent out spies to entangle Jesus in controversy, so that they might take hold of his words, and get him into trouble with the Governor.

IST ELDER: Good-day, Brother Shadrach. Are you coming with me to the Temple?

SHADRACH: What's happening?

IST ELDER: Jesus of Nazareth is preaching. We've planted out a bunch of people in the crowd to heckle him. It ought to be amusing.

SHADRACH *(ironically)*: Very likely. I hope your hecklers have their wits about them.

IST ELDER: Oh, yes—they're smart fellows. If only we can make the man look ridiculous and lose his temper, he may be provoked into saying something definitely seditious. Then Rome can deal with him.

SHADRACH: Quite, quite. Ridicule is a two-edged weapon, you know. However!... Ah! The sermon is still proceeding, I see. We shall be in time for any fun that's going.

(Fade JESUS in as they approach)

JESUS: ...For God will not make any man virtuous by force; so the good and evil must grow together until the harvest, like the cockles among the corn. But in the last day, when the Son of Man comes in glory to judge the world, he will sort them out, as a shepherd sorts out his sheep from the goats. And to those on his right hand he will say: "Come, happy souls, inherit the kingdom of my Father. For when I was hungry and thirsty, you fed me; when I was naked, you clothed me; when I was a stranger, you took me in; when I was sick, you visited me; when I was in prison, you brought me comfort." And they will say: "But when, Lord, did we do these things for you?" And he will answer: "When you showed kindness to the humblest of my brother-men, you were showing it to me". But to those on his left hand, he will say: "You neither fed nor clothed nor sheltered me, you never helped nor visited me; for when you neglected my brother-men, you neglected me". . . . So the men that could not recognize their Lord shall go to their long punishment but the good shall enter into everlasting life.

(Buzz of appreciation)

SADDUCEE: Rabbi! can I ask a question?

JESUS: Certainly.

SADDUCEE: Could you oblige us with your views about everlasting life? I am a Sadducee.

RUDE VOICE: Then you're a cursed heretic!

(Booing and laughter)

SADDUCEE: I don't believe in the resurrection.

RUDE VOICE: Cheer up, cocky! That won't stop it happening.

SADDUCEE: I'll believe it when I see it.

RUDE VOICE: Oh, what a surprise! *(Laughter)*

SADDUCEE: I should think it would be full of surprises. . . . Rabbi—Moses laid down that if a man should die without issue, his brother should take his wife, and raise a family by her, so as to keep his brother's name alive. Well, now—there were seven brothers and the eldest died without children. So his wife was married to the second brother, and the same thing happened. And so with the third brother and the fourth—

RUDE VOICE: Try, try again! *(Laughter)*

SADDUCEE: . . . right on down to the seventh. None of them had any children. Last of all the woman died also.

RUDE VOICE: And high time too! *(Laughter)*

SADDUCEE: Isn't it going to be rather awkward in the resurrection? *(Laughter)* She belonged to all seven of them. Who gets the girl in the end?

VOICES: That's a good one! Answer that! *(Shrieks of laughter and cat-calls)*

JESUS: That is a very silly question. Do you think the resurrection will be just this world all over again? Blessed spirits neither marry nor are given in marriage—any more than the angels of God.

VOICES: Well spoken! That's right! Now then, Sadducee! Laugh that off! *(Laughter)*

JESUS: But as to the resurrection—doesn't God say in the Bible: "I am the God of Abraham, of Isaac, and of Jacob"? How can that be if they are dead for ever? God is not the God of the dead, but of the living.

VOICES: What about it, Sadducee? Come on! answer him!

SADDUCEE *(disconcerted)*: I can't split hairs about texts. I'm not a Bible critic.

RUDE VOICE: Then sit down and shut up. *(Laughter)*

1ST JEW: Rabbi—where do you get your authority for your teaching?

JESUS: I'll answer that question if you'll answer another. *(Buzz of excitement)* The mission of John the Baptist—was it from God? or was it—bogus?

1ST JEW: Well I—I don't know—I suppose—

2ND JEW: Look out: if you say "from God", he'll say "then why didn't you listen to him?"

1ST JEW *(irritably)*: I wasn't going to say that.

PEASANT: 'Ere, mister! Don't you dare say John was bogus. He was a great prophet, was John.

VOICES: That's right. So he was. . . .

JESUS: Make up your mind. We are all waiting.

RUDE VOICE: Go on! Answer the Rabbi. Take a chance on it.

1ST JEW *(sulkily)*: I can't tell you anything about John.

JESUS: Well, then, all *I* can tell *you* is—When you know about John, you'll know about me. . . . Next?

SHADRACH: I don't think much of your hecklers. He can make rings round 'em.

LITIGANT: Rabbi—since you set up to be such a Solomon *(laughter)* can you decide a lawsuit between my brother and me? He won't give me my share in the estate. I've sued him in all the courts. . . .

JESUS: My good man, who made me a judge in chancery? Steer clear of covetousness. If you and your brother weren't both so greedy, you'd have settled it out of court. . . . Any more questions?

HERODIAN *(belligerently)*: Yes. My friends and I are Herodians—true Jewish people. *(Applause)* We know you say what you think, and don't care twopence for anybody—Now, then. Is it, or is it not, lawful to pay tribute to Caesar?

CROWD: A-a-ah! *(This question is really important and they all know it)*

JESUS: You hypocrites! Are you laying a trap for me? . . . Show me the tribute-money. . . .

HERODIAN: Here's a coin. Now, what about it?

JESUS: Look at it. Whose is this image and superscription?

HERODIAN: Caesar's, of course.

JESUS: Then pay to Caesar the things that are Caesar's. But pay to God the things that are God's. You are men—and the image stamped upon *you* is the image of God. So what do you owe to Him?

SCRIBE: Rabbi, we all know that. We owe to God our whole duty and the keeping of His commandments. But which of the commandments is the most important of all?

IST PHARISEE: Good! good!—answer the learned scribe. . . .

2ND PHARISEE: How about honoring one's parents?

IST PHARISEE: How about keeping the Sabbath?

2ND PHARISEE: How about the law of blasphemy? Answer! answer!

JESUS: Hear, O Israel: Thou shalt love the Lord thy God with all thy heart and with all thy soul and with all thy mind and with all thy strength. That is the first and great commandment. And the second is very like it: Thou shalt love thy neighbour as thyself. On these two commandments hang all the Law and the Prophets.

SCRIBE: Well spoken, Rabbi. That's very true indeed. To love God with heart and soul and understanding, and one's neighbour as one's self is worth any amount of burnt offerings. And if a man were really to keep these commandments, the rest would keep themselves.

JESUS: If you understand that, my son, you are not far from the Kingdom of God. . . . Does any one else want to ask me anything?

2ND JEW: Only this, Rabbi. You talk of the Kingdom of God. When that Kingdom comes, who will be the chief person in it?

(Buzz of excitement)

IST ELDER: Good, good! that'll get him.

SHADRACH: H'm! . . . He's burst out laughing.

IST ELDER: He'll find it's nothing to laugh at. If he plumps for a priesthood, he'll offend the Herodians; if he proclaims a secular monarchy, he'll offend the Pharisees—

SHADRACH: And if he says, himself, he'll offend everybody, and be had up for sedition. . . . Do you really think he's such easy game?

JESUS: My disciples know the answer to that question—and now I will tell you . . . Mother, will you lend me your little girl for a moment? . . . Come along, dear—up on my shoulder where they can all see you. . . . Indeed and indeed I tell you, to the eager and the simple heart, the doors of the Kingdom stand open. He that will humble himself to be like this little child is greatest in the Kingdom of God *(mild sensation)*. . . . Yes, and take care what you do. The man who warps the mind of a child, or breaks its spirit, commits a fearful crime. He had better by far have a millstone hung about his neck and be drowned in the depths of the sea. . . . Thank-you, my dear. Give me a kiss, and God bless you.

WOMEN: Rabbi—Rabbi, dear Rabbi—please bless our children, too. . . . Run to the good Rabbi, dear. . . . Don't forget my little boy. . . . Rabbi, Rabbi. . . .

(Babble and confusion)

MATTHEW: 'Ere, 'old 'ard a minute. The Rabbi's busy. He can't be bothered with 'undreds and thousands of kids.

JESUS: It's all right, Matthew. Let the little children come to me—don't turn them away. They are the stuff of which the Kingdom is made. And their guardian angels look perpetually on the face of my Father in Heaven. . . . God bless you, my child, and your mother too. . . . God bless you and bring you to His Kingdom. . . .

SEQUENCE 2 (IN THE STREET)

THE EVANGELIST: And as he walked through the streets, a young man came running to him, and knelt down at his feet.

YOUNG MAN: Holy Rabbi! Holy Rabbi! what shall I do to inherit eternal life?

JESUS: Why do you call me holy? There is only one that is holy, and that is God. Don't use words like that unless you mean something by them. . . . And you know what you have to do. There are the Commandments: Do not murder, do not steal; do not tell lies, don't make love to your neighbour's wife, honour your father and mother—

YOUNG MAN: Oh, yes—I have kept the commandments from a child. But there must be more to it than that. I feel that I lack something—there's some great spiritual experience which I have missed. What can I do?

JESUS: If you really want to be perfect, there is a thing you can do. And indeed, I hope you will, because I like you very much.

YOUNG MAN: What is it, Rabbi?

JESUS: Go straight away, sell everything you possess, give all the money to the poor, and then come and follow me.

YOUNG MAN (staggered): Sell everything I have? . . . Rabbi, I don't think you realise. I'm a rich man. . . .

JESUS: You will have treasure in Heaven. . . . Will you do it? . . . These disciples of mine have done it.

YOUNG MAN: It's different for them. . . . Is there no other way?

JESUS: No other way for *you.*

YOUNG MAN: I'm sorry.

JESUS: So am I.

JOHN: Master . . . he is going. What a pity! Won't you call him back and persuade him?

JESUS: No, John. He must make his own choice. . . . How hard it is for rich people to enter the Kingdom of God! You must pity them, for they find life very difficult.

PETER: You surprise me, Master—it never occurred to me that rich people were to be pitied.

JESUS: Didn't it, Peter?

JAMES: They have so many advantages! It's easy for the rich to be clean and virtuous and honest and respectable, and contribute to charities and improve their minds and find time for church-going.

JESUS: So you think, James. But I tell you it is easier for a camel to go through the eye of a needle than for those that set store by riches to enter the Kingdom of God.

PETER: Well—if they can't be saved, who can?

JESUS: Humanly speaking, it's impossible. But everything is possible with God.

PETER: Master—we have given up everything we had—such as it was—to follow you. What will happen to us?

JESUS (gaily): Well, Peter, I can assure you that anybody who, for my sake, has given up father or mother or wife, or children or worldly goods, will get it all back a hundred-fold, even in this world. The whole of mankind will be his family, and their affairs will be his affairs—and a nice, big troublesome family he will find them. He will have a life crammed with incident—plenty of worry and persecution—and in the world to come, life everlasting.

JOHN: Dear Master—we don't mind the troubles, if only we can always be close to you.

JAMES: And when you enter into your kingdom, we shall be with you, shan't we? That's all we want. To sit on your right hand and on your left, just as we've always done.

JESUS (with a change of tone): James and John, you don't know what you are asking. Can you drink the bitter cup that I must drink, or be baptised in the deep waters of my baptism?

JOHN: Master, we are ready to do anything.

JAMES: There's nothing we wouldn't face.

JESUS: You shall indeed drink of my cup and be baptised with my baptism. But to sit on my right hand and on my left is not mine to give. It will come to those for whom it is prepared. You don't understand now—but you will.

JAMES: Yes, Lord. . . . Perhaps we oughtn't to have asked.

JOHN: There must be people more deserving than us.

THOMAS: You two Zebedees think a bit too much of yourselves.

ANDREW: The Kingdom isn't made for your special benefit.

PHILIP: Judas was saying only yesterday—By the way, what's become of Judas?

ANDREW: Dunno. I haven't set eyes on him since we entered the city.

PHILIP: Oh, well—it doesn't matter. . . . He was saying he didn't like favouritism.

JOHN (angrily): That's the sort of thing Judas would say.

JAMES: He's jealous—and so are you.

MATTHEW: All right, you two Zebedees. Keep your hair on. We all know the Master's fond of you, but you didn't ought to take things for granted.

JESUS: Children, children—this is no time for quarrelling. Listen. You've got it all wrong. In earthly kingdoms, the rulers exercise authority and have servants to wait upon them. But it mustn't be like that with you. In our kingdom, the greatest man is the one who does the greatest service to others. For the Son of Man himself comes, not as a prince, but as a servant, and to give his life for the sake of mankind.

SEQUENCE 3 (THE HIGH PRIEST'S HOUSE)

THE EVANGELIST: Then entered Satan into Judas, surnamed Iscariot, being of the number of the Twelve.

SERVANT: My Lord Caiaphas, there is a man outside asking to speak with you.

CAIAPHAS: We are very busy. Has he an appointment?

SERVANT: He says you will see him. His name is Judas Iscariot.

CAIAPHAS: Oh! . . . Yes. I will see Judas Iscariot. Send him in. . . . Well, now, Father Annas, I think this sounds rather promising.

ANNAS: Yes. It looks as though that foolish demonstration with the donkey had upset our high-minded young friend. All the better—since I gather that the heckling-party didn't go any too well this afternoon.

CAIAPHAS (curtly): It was badly managed. . . . But I fancy that the inspired Carpenter has over-played his hand. The trouble about preaching unworldliness is that one's followers may take one literally.

ANNAS: You, my dear son-in-law, will never make that mistake.

CAIAPHAS: So far as my official position permits, I am a realist. . . . Ah! here comes our friend Judas. . . . Good evening. You look fatigued. . . . Samuel, set a stool for this worthy man. . . . Thank-you. . . . Shut the door, if you please.

(Door shut)

Now, Judas, you can speak quite freely. There is nobody here but my father-in-law and myself. I fear by your face that you are in some trouble.

JUDAS: In bitter trouble. My Lord High Priest, I have misled you.

ANNAS: Not intentionally, I am sure.

JUDAS: My Lord, I am humiliated. I answered to you for his honesty. And now I find that Jesus is corrupt to the bone.

CAIAPHAS: Indeed? You horrify me.

JUDAS: I believed in his pretensions. I supported his claim. Despite all appearances, and against my better judgment, I stifled my growing suspicions. I sincerely thought he had sufficient character to resist temptation. I suppose I was a fool to trust him.

ANNAS: "Put not your trust in any child of man"—how sadly true that is!

CAIAPHAS: A trustful nature is a very beautiful thing. But in this imperfect world it suffers sad disappointments. . . . In what way has Jesus proved unworthy?

JUDAS: His hypocrisy is nauseating. He preaches God's Kingdom and the way of purification—and all the time he has been plotting to destroy the soul of Israel.

ANNAS: Dear, dear!—But perhaps you are exaggerating. Adulation has gone to his head, perhaps, and the applause of the crowd has thrown him a little off his balance—but is it anything more than a touch of harmless vanity?

JUDAS: I have evidence. Baruch the Zealot is waiting in the hills with a thousand spearmen. Last night he sent a messenger to Jesus. The answer was: "Tell Baruch I will give him the sign". To-day there was an ass ready and waiting—and a password arranged beforehand. On Baruch's ass Jesus rode into Jerusalem, in the midst of a crowd openly hailing him as Messiah.

CAIAPHAS: That sounds bad. . . . Anything more?

JUDAS: Yes. Jesus has proclaimed war against Jerusalem.

ANNAS: Great heavens! Are you sure?

JUDAS: I heard him. He said: "Because you would not accept me when I came in peace, you shall be besieged and destroyed, and not one stone left standing."

CAIAPHAS: How very reckless! . . . This shall be dealt with. . . . We are grateful to you, Iscariot, for the warning. I'm afraid this must have been a most painful shock to you.

JUDAS: It is horrible to have been so mistaken in the man. . . . And yet I swear I was *not* mistaken. God meant him for the Messiah. He *was* the Messiah, if only he had been true to himself. Indeed, my Lord Caiaphas, there was a great man lost in Jesus of Nazareth. The noblest dreams I ever dreamed, the holiest prayer my heart could utter, all my hopes, all my ideals, seemed incarnate in him. Yet he has lowered himself to the measure of little minds, eating the applause of the ignorant, and bartering his heavenly birthright for the mess of pottage which he despises even while his mouth waters at the thought of it. . . . Why would he not listen to me? I warned him again and again.

CAIAPHAS: I am sure you were his better angel.

JUDAS (*all his personal grievances suddenly boiling to the top*): I understood him. I could have kept him straight. But he never gave me his confidence. He surrounds himself with fools and toadies—callow lads like Philip, common fishermen like Thomas and Andrew, with no more imagination than a couple of their own carp, Simon Peter, whose bluffness and bad manners pass muster for originality—and of course, his bosom-friend John bar-Zebedee, who can only stutter abject admiration, gaze at the Master with the eyes of a sick dog, and lap up his lightest word as a revelation from on high.

ANNAS: Ah! when a man is a popular idol, he likes to be king of his company. His true friends don't flatter him sufficiently.

CAIAPHAS: And you were never more truly his friend than when you came here to-night. For you know the best service Jesus can do to himself and Israel?

JUDAS: What?

CAIAPHAS: To die now—while his image in men's minds is still untarnished.

Alive, he is an ordinary demagogue with all the failings of his class; dead, he is an idea—a symbol—the spirit of martyred Jewry, purged of all human dross and frailty. Nobody will remember that Jesus had any faults; they will remember only his teaching and his works of power.

JUDAS *(catching eagerly at this justification)*: True, true! You are right. That is the way. You speak to my very soul. The Son of Man must die before he can save—he said so. In his better moments, he knew it. If he has lost the will to follow his true destiny, we must make his words true in spite of himself. In us, or upon us—one way or the other, the prophecies must be fulfilled. Those were your words, your own words, Jesus of Nazareth. And so the salvation of Israel shall be accomplished.

CAIAPHAS: Spoken like a true patriot. I am so glad to have been able to set your mind at rest. Now—if you will forgive me—we must be practical. Jesus must be arrested, before Baruch's insurrection can come to a head. Do you know when it is timed to break out?

JUDAS: Not exactly. But I imagine he will seize the opportunity when so many followers of Jesus are in Jerusalem for the Feast.

CAIAPHAS: That's running things rather close. We must act quickly.

ANNAS: But carefully, Caiaphas, carefully. We don't want a riot. Especially with Pilate in Jerusalem.

CAIAPHAS: No . . . let me think. . . . Iscariot, there are two things I should like you to do—for the sake of Israel.

JUDAS: Name them.

CAIAPHAS: First—to find out if you can the moment when Baruch intends to move. And secondly: to let us know when we shall find Jesus unprotected by the people, so that we may take him without a disturbance. Will you do this? You can rely upon our gratitude.

JUDAS: I will do it. But as for relying upon your gratitude—I am past relying on anybody. I gave up all I had to follow Jesus—and now he has let me down. What security have I that you will not make a fool of me and then cast me off? Fine words about patriotism are all very well. But do you think this has cost me nothing? Did Baruch's messengers pour out secrets to me out of disinterested love of truth? I have worked and plotted to get my information—I have lied and stolen—yes! stolen from the common fund. And they are beginning to suspect me. That vulgar little tax-collector Matthew might denounce me any day and land me in gaol. And what should I say to the judge? Refer him to the Chief Priest? Bid him collect the money from the Temple Treasury? Trust in the Sanhedrim to come running to my assistance? I tell you, I trust nobody. I will believe in nothing but what I can see and handle. All men are liars—only *things* cannot lie. Make me a payment—and let it stand in your books in black and white as a witness that what I did, I did for you and for Israel.

CAIAPHAS: But of course; of course. Naturally you must have your expenses, and a suitable reward for your services. That is only right and proper. Tell me what you ask, and we shall be happy to pay you anything in reason. . . .

THE EVANGELIST: And they made their bargain with him for thirty pieces of silver.

THE NINTH PLAY

THE KING'S SUPPER

CHARACTERS

The EVANGELIST.
JESUS.
SIMON PETER.
ANDREW BAR-JONAH.
JAMES BAR-ZEBEDEE.
JOHN BAR-ZEBEDEE.
PHILIP.
NATHANAEL.
THOMAS DIDYMUS.
MATTHEW, the Tax-Collector.
JAMES BEN-ALPHAEUS ("the Less").
JUDE ("not Iscariot").
} Disciples of Jesus.

SIMON OF CANAAN.
JUDAS ISCARIOT.
CAIAPHAS, High Priest of Israel.
SECRETARY to Caiaphas ("Hezekiah").
ANNAS, father-in-law to Caiaphas.
SHADRACH, an Elder.
CAIUS PONTIUS PILATE, Governor of Judaea.
CLAUDIA PROCULA, wife to Pilate.
CAPTAIN OF THE TEMPLE GUARD ("Captain Elihu").
MALCHUS.

NOTES

The underlying note of this play is *crisis*. From first to last, there is a feeling of urgency and expectation—held up in the middle for the great, static moment of the Institution, and then hurrying on with increasing momentum, and an ever-heavier sense of impending doom, to the swift clash at the end. At no moment must any ecclesiastical associations obscure the fact that this is the greatest of all *human* tragedies (I don't mean my play—I mean the story).

This is the focal point of the whole series of plays. Consequently, it is full of echoes and reminiscences. The opening words of PETER and JOHN recall Play 7 (but there it was "roses of Sharon"—now, it is "bitter herbs"). In the same scene, JESUS reminds us of Play 2—when John first came running to find him; the DISCIPLES remind one another of their calling, of the first Apostolic mission, of the raising of Lazarus, of the Feast of Tabernacles, and of the preaching of Jesus. The dispute about "who should be the greatest" brings back the promise to Peter (Play 5); it also reminds us of the previous argument on the same subject, and the request of James and John (Play 8). The Washing of the Feet points back to the Baptism of John (Play 2), and JUDAS reminds us of his answer to Jesus about setting his hand to the plough (Play 4). At the Institution, JOHN refers back to the discourse on the Bread of Heaven (Play 5). Finally, the scene in the Garden points back to the Transfiguration (Play 6).

The Passover: for technical reasons, I have disregarded John's chronology, and assumed that the Last Supper actually was the Passover. I have supposed that the actual cooking was done in the courtyard by the women, and that the Disciples, as they passed through, brought up the dishes as they were ready.

The order of the Passover was: The first cup of wine; the bitter herbs (eaten with sauce); the unleavened bread; the second cup—at which point the eldest son had to ask the head of the household the ritual question: "What mean you by this service?" In the ordinary way, the father would reply: "This is the sacrifice of the Lord's Passover ... " after which the Passover Lamb would be eaten. Then followed the third and the fourth cups, after which the Hallel was sung. The Institution fits very well into this frame with the explanation "This is my blood of the New Covenant" taking the place of the usual ritual answer, and suggesting, by association with that answer, the "sacrificial" nature of the Eucharist, without the actual use of that controversial word.

The unleavened bread was a thin flat biscuit, apparently rather like the Jewish motze of today, and would crack like a biscuit when broken.

For the Producer's convenience, I append here a plan of the seating arrangements. It would not be very convenient for serving—but since the party presumably waited upon themselves, this would not matter, and it is much handier for conversation than the usual pictorial arrangement, with all the important people ranged along the long side of the table. I have accepted

Archbishop Temple's suggestion that Judas, as Treasurer, sat next to Jesus—he must, at any rate, have been within hand's reach to receive the sop. It will be seen that Peter, John, and Jesus are all within whispering-distance of one another, and Judas within whispering-distance of Jesus, as the text requires; and that Matthew, leaning on his left elbow, and looking across the feet of Nathanael and Philip, can easily see Judas go out. Thomas is the only person who need raise his voice at all to speak to Jesus. . . . Not that all this matters frightfully at the microphone, but it's a satisfaction to know that it's all quite reasonable, and may help to get the perspective.

THE CHARACTERS

THE DISCIPLES—At the beginning of the play they are still in the keyed-up mood of the Entry into Jerusalem. They expect to see the Kingdom established any minute; and though they are baffled and bewildered by one shock after another, they never, to the last moment, lose their rooted notion about a sudden *coup d'état* of some kind. A note of disquiet and danger is struck at the very opening, with the nervousness of the owner of the house, and the precautions taken about their arrival; and JOHN's "birthday-party feeling" underlines their sense of expectation. Being excited, like children, they rather easily get quarrelsome; there is a little breeze at the beginning between THOMAS and the ZEBEDEES; and though, in the presence of Jesus they start off full of companionable feeling and friendly reminiscence, MATTHEW's unfortunate, and quite innocent, remark induces a fit of silliness, which the rudeness of JUDAS might very soon work into real pettishness. But this bit should be played quite lightly—not "ponging" it and not on any account playing it for loud laughs. It is chaff—but with a little edge to it—and they have lost their heads just a trifle. PETER and JOHN—who are the ones who are being "got at"—don't like it; but this is less on their own account than because they feel actually that Jesus is not liking it either.

The Washing of the Feet is their first shock, and sobers them completely. From now on, they get blow after blow—each more shattering than the last:—

1. *One of you will betray me.* This is unpleasant enough—just as the Kingdom is about to materialise. Even the people who dislike Judas, or have been uneasy about him, have never suspected him of anything of that sort. Certainly, he has been bad-tempered and queer—and certainly two or three of them know that there has been something funny about the accounts. But that isn't at all the same thing—and clever people like Judas *do* say puzzling things; but you no more expect they'll go and do really frightful things than—say—in 1939 you expected the French Government to sell their country. These things just don't happen. Anyway, the Master has just handed the sop to Judas—that's a mark of favour—and whispered to him; Judas goes

out—plenty of explanations for that—and then, just as they are trying to worry out this extraordinary problem, it is driven out of their minds by shock No. 2.

2. *I am going away.* The master has the air of making an announcement. . . . He has made it—and it is simply incredible. He is going to *leave* them. Nothing about the Kingdom. He is simply going. Almost immediately. At this moment of all moments, to a place where they can't follow him. And something incomprehensible about seeing him and not seeing him. And it sounds final. He is laying down a new law for them as a parting instruction— it is past all understanding. . . . Somehow their consternation must have been allayed in the interval, but it is a very subdued company that has pulled itself together to go through with the rest of the Passover.

3. *This is my body.* Peter, James, and John have received the second blow with less bewilderment than the lower end of the table, but with much more fear. They know more than the rest. JOHN especially is becoming sensitive to something very unusual indeed. Human distress and a different sort of supernatural terror are coming over him in waves. The sacramental words are terrifying and incomprehensible—(*we* associate them with "Early-Morning-Service", and "the-beautiful-simplicity-of-the Roman [Anglican, Free Church] rite" and "having-a-good-number-of-communicants", being on the Electoral Roll of the Parish Church, and all that sort of thing—but *what* must they have sounded like against the background of the Jewish Temple sacrifices with their daily, weekly, monthly slaughters, and the Passover rites, and the blood sprinkled on the doorposts; and with the living man whom you had eaten, drunk, talked, laughed and lived with for the past two or three years sitting there beside you?). . . . JESUS tries to calm them a little—but THOMAS is impatient with this allegory about roads and lodging-houses. He wants an explanation. The explanation merely leads up to the astonishing remark that they not only know God, but have seen Him. It is firmly fixed in the Jewish mind that no man may see God and live—and if this remark is meant seriously—PHILIP (being young and impetuous) means to have this thing out. Jesus has always been hinting at things—if he can really show them the Father, let him do it and then they will be satisfied.

4. *The man who has seen me has seen God.* This—to a strict Jewish monotheist—is either an appalling blasphemy, or an appalling fact. It is not recorded how the Disciples reacted to it. Perhaps they were too dazed to take it in. From their subsequent behavior, one concludes that they did not think it blasphemy. But St. John leaves it at that—and so do we.

At any rate, in the closing scenes, we find the Disciples listening, with such composure as they may, to their Master's final instructions and his last prayer for them. From this point, we have only to deal in detail with PETER, JAMES and JOHN—except to note that PHILIP is far from suspecting his friend Judas, and hails his appearance in the garden as that of a friend.

PETER—In the opening scene, he has taken chief charge of the arrangements for the Supper—laying the table, seating, etc. All through the play, he is his usual self; headlong, impulsive, self-confident, blundering into error and then quickly humble and repentant—and then doing exactly the same thing all over again. All his instincts are generous—and he is really humble, and instantly sorry and quick to confess when he is wrong. Only nothing seems to teach him to remember beforehand that he is liable to go wrong. He is confident about the Washing—then, in a moment, he sees his mistake, rushes into the other extreme and has to be checked again. He is loud and positive that he would die, he would never disown Jesus; when swords are mentioned he rushes to the conclusion that the Kingdom is (after all) going to be conquered by force; in the garden he is prepared to do it single-handed if necessary. No warnings shake his confidence in himself; prayer is lavished on him, but he takes no notice. Only when that ghastly cock-crow comes will he really get the shock that brings him to himself. . . . But he still has the vision. Peter can always see the angels. And when he does finally know the extent of his own weakness, his real generosity and humility will save him from the despair that overtakes Judas, who has no humility, and no real generosity at all.

JOHN—The only important new thing to notice about John is the way in which his personal feelings gradually get the better of him. When the moment of trial in the Garden comes, the Beloved Disciple is of no more help than the rest. Even more than by the growing realisation of his own cruel personal loss, he is made helpless by watching the human agony of the man he loves. It is more than he can endure, and he can do nothing about it at all. He understands better than James or Peter exactly what Jesus is going through, and it plunges him into a sheer black fit of wretchedness—he is like a child in the dark. At the Transfiguration, he could reassure James—he is not really afraid of the splendour of God; but he *is* afraid at the stark depths of human misery, and now it is his turn to cling to James. . . . In the final scene, the appearance of Judas rouses the old "Son of Thunder" in him to one furious shout of anger and disgust.

JAMES—Note what is said about JOHN. James is less personally distracted than John—he can bear to speak with Peter about the things they are witnessing; and when John collapses James is there to comfort his little brother—they are children together again, as at the Transfiguration.

JESUS—He has—even more than usual—to carry this play on his shoulders. Here we have the "gentle" Jesus right through, except for a brief moment at the end.

In the first scene there is, running under all other preoccupations, his insistent consciousness of Judas. He knows (using the word in its purely human sense) that Judas intends to betray him, and *soon*. He must do two things tonight— (a) find out how much time he really has, and (b) make a final effort to save Judas from himself. (We needn't wrestle with the theology of this—that's how it works out on the human and dramatic side.) He and Jesus are playing a grim kind of game of move and counter-move to find out each other's position.

Jesus opens with a gracious gesture—he invites Judas to sit next him. Judas counters with an inquiry about where they are spending the night—so framed as to make his own suspicions plain. The ambiguous reply is designed to remind Judas of the "hour of the Son of Man", and leave *him* to interpret it by his own intentions.

At the Washing of the Feet, Jesus delivers a grave and tender warning, and is met with a flat rebuff. Judas intends to carry out his purpose at all costs. (The other disciples do not, of course, hear this exchange.) After this blow in the face, Jesus puts the cards on the table: "One of you will betray me". Judas now feels pretty sure that Jesus knows all there is to be known. At the handling of the sop, he makes the direct challenge. Jesus answers: "Yes—it is you—do it quickly"—and Judas takes the gloves right off. His answer amounts to "I know all about your political intrigues and I shall denounce you." He goes out at once.

This puts the answer to (a) past all doubt. Jesus has only a few hours at most. "It is *now.*" And from this point on, he is dominated by a desperate sense of *urgency*. The Disciples are still miles away from really understanding, though he has tried so hard to prepare them. Now they *must* be told plainly—and they are going to be terribly disappointed and bewildered. And he must try not to alarm them too much. To bring them up to the night's crisis is like coaxing frightened horses out of a burning building. So he gentles them over the great, startling statements—the New Covenant, the declaration of his Divinity, the announcement of his death, the promise of the Holy Ghost—with warning, reassurance, prayer. But they are too agitated to take it all in, and it's quite clear they are not going to stand up to the test. And, such as they are, they have got to go on and stand alone; the curtain is going up for them, and they have to be left to stumble through their parts by themselves. Poor little flock! But they have the root of the matter in them; the Spirit will come and make everything plain presently— but in the meantime it is going to be desperately hard for them.

And looming up behind it all is the personal agony. In the Upper Room, the God-consciousness and the Man-consciousness are very closely fused, with the God-consciousness often coming to the top. In the Garden, it seems as though the Man-consciousness became permanently uppermost, and I think it must be played with a very strong and real sense of the human horror at physical death, of the failure of human companionship, and of the apparent vainness of prayer; till the time comes when he looks across the bodies of the sleeping disciples to see the lanterns and torches, and the unbearable thing has to be faced—and is faced with dignity. Then come the three moments of asserted authority: the human master, with the great voice ringing out: "Put up your sword!"—the echo of the previous

Divine assertion: "I AM"; and the sudden consciousness of power: "I that could have angels at my call"—followed by the willing acceptance and surrender.

(*The Last Discourses and the Last Prayers:* I have reduced four chapters of St. John to 600 words, trying to keep in most of the best-loved and familiar passages. It more or less holds together now as a connected line of thought, and I hope its weight will be sufficient to carry it without further cutting. I have left in one or two of the repetitions with which the original abounds, so as to keep some of the feeling of stress—the reiterated effort to hammer home the salient points. I have also slightly glossed the difficult, but important, passage about the purse and sword; connecting it with the lines, "I ask not that Thou shouldst take them out of the world".)

JUDAS—For the opening scene, see what is said above under JESUS. Judas feels sure that *something* is going to happen tonight—John's innocent words confirm his suspicion as to what it is, and the ambiguous answer given by Jesus is interpreted by him to mean that the *coup* to seize the Kingdom is to be pulled off in the Garden. The certain knowledge that Jesus sees through him hardens him into a fury of pride and hatred; gentleness and graciousness only increase his resentment (here is the sharp contrast between him and Peter), and he is now almost consciously out to hurt and destroy for sheer lust of destruction. He goes to Caiaphas, and his report of what Jesus said is a subtle distortion of the facts (like a stunt journalist, he reports the words correctly, but with a false suggestion of context). But he has been impressed—after all, he is very intelligent—and a fearful doubt begins to rise in him whether he may not have been wrong about Jesus all through. Is it possible that Jesus is really being true to himself, really going the way of suffering of his own will? and does he, Judas, only figure as the detestable engineer of a quite unnecessary evil, built out of a phantasmagoria of self-deception?—This doubt hardly rises before he hastily stamps it down. His pride cannot bear it: Judas cannot be wrong—Jesus has *got* to be guilty, to vindicate Judas. Anything else would be unbearably humiliating. It would mean that Jesus was incomparably, detestably the superior of Judas, on Judas' own ground—and that is not to be thought of. But the hidden lust of cruelty, which has masqueraded under the disguise of a masochistic love of suffering, is crawling out in its own shape. Judas is beginning to enjoy the idea of holding Jesus helpless in his embrace while the guards seize him. . . . In the next play Judas will learn the truth, see himself for a ghastly moment as he really is, and know that in his heart he has always hated Jesus as the egotist hates God.

CAIAPHAS—In this play he shows himself a quick and intelligent organiser, with a ready grasp of the essential situation and a head for detail and rapid improvisation. From the "plot" point of view, his scenes are important, as making clear: (a) the hurried nature of the trial, which led to one great legal irregularity, viz.: that the prisoner was eventually condemned, not on the evidence of witnesses, but on his own oath; (b) the urgent necessity that the trial should, if possible, be in strict accordance with Jewish law, if Pilate was to ratify the sentence;[1] (c) the need for getting the execution done and over before the Sabbath; (d) the formal relations between Judaea and Rome, which make it necessary that the trial before the Sanhedrim should be for the ecclesiastical offences and not for sedition; (e) the reasons why Judas offered no evidence at the trial.

PILATE—What is said under CAIAPHAS helps to explain Pilate. There is nothing remarkable about his ratifying a Jewish sentence. He is in the position of a British magistrate in, say, Kenya. The natives are encouraged to administer their own law, and the foreign government will uphold the findings, if the trial has been properly conducted according to the native code, and if the over-riding Government code is not infringed. (Thus a native may be tried by his own laws for stealing, and the sentence will be upheld—but not if it is a question of punishing a runaway slave, since British law does not recognise slavery.) Consequently, if anything in the trial seems irregular, Pilate may re-open the case. Therefore (the circumstances being peculiar) he has to be informed that there is a case for the charge of sedition as well.

Pilate has no bias against the prisoner—if anything, he would be quite glad to see the prosecution fail, what with his general dislike and contempt of Jewish feuds, and the knowledge that Claudia will be distressed. The suggestion about sedition, however, convinces him that the man is probably better out of the way. He has got into trouble before about affronting the Jews, and he does not want to offend Caesar again. *But* he is already sufficiently interested to make it likely that he may not sign the warrant quite automatically. He may take just a little trouble to inquire whether justice is really being done.

CLAUDIA—Her reactions are of the kind called "typically feminine": (1) The natural distress at the execution of somebody she has seen and admired; (2) the ruthless drive straight through laws and regulations to the essential: good men should not be hanged; (3) impatience with foreigners and barbarians and red tape; (4) the instant reaction when it becomes a matter of her husband's interests. She submits, under the ominous sound of the name "Caesar". (But in the night, something will happen that will cause her to send Pilate that desperate note: "*Don't touch this case*—have nothing to do with it!"—and on the day of the Crucifixion, she will tell her dream.)

---

[1] Frank Morison in *Who Moved the Stone?* shows, as I think conclusively, that Caiaphas did see Pilate that night and received his promise to ratify the sentence; and that this is the key to the whole of the subsequent legal proceedings.

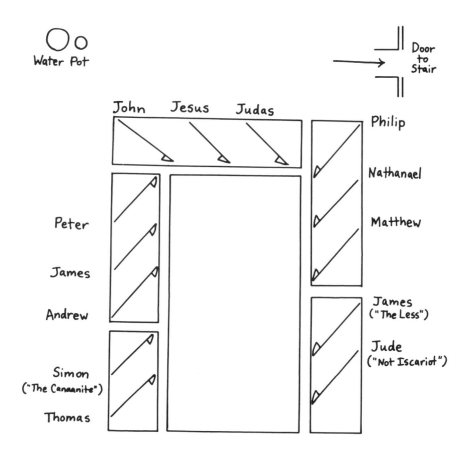

SCENE I (JERUSALEM: THE UPPER ROOM)

THE EVANGELIST: Now, on the first day of unleavened bread, when they sacrifice the Passover lamb, Jesus sent Peter and John, saying to them: "Go into the City, and there shall meet you a man carrying a pitcher of water. Follow him till he enters a house, and there say to the owner: The Rabbi saith: Where is the guest-chamber, where I shall eat the Passover with my disciples? He will show you a large upper room, furnished; there make ready." And they went, and found everything as Jesus had said, and they made ready the Passover.

PETER: I think everything's in order. What have you got there, John?

JOHN: Bitter herbs.

PETER: Set them down here with the sauce, ready to the Master's hand. How are the women getting on?

JOHN: The lamb is roasted. As soon as the others come, we can sit down.

PETER: I hope they won't be late.

JOHN: Judas and Philip are on the stairs.... Oh, Judas! has any one else arrived?

JUDAS: Andrew and James and Thomas were to start soon after us—weren't they, Philip?

PHILIP: Yes. The Master said to come in twos and threes, so as not to attract attention.

JOHN: All the better. The owner of the house is getting nervous. He's friendly enough, but he seems to imagine we're rather dangerous guests.

PETER: He's been listening to bazaar-gossip.

JUDAS: Perhaps he's not far wrong.

JOHN: He keeps asking whether we want the room for the whole Feast, or only for tonight. Do *you* know, Judas?

JUDAS: I am not favoured with instructions for anything beyond tonight. Martha asked if we were returning to sleep at Bethany. I had to tell her I didn't know.

JOHN: We'll ask the Master when he comes.... Here's somebody.

JUDAS: Your brother, I expect.... No, it isn't—it's the other James.

PETER: And the other Judas. I say, Jude, what's become of James bar-Zebedee and his party?

JUDE: We passed them on the way—going slowly. Thomas has a blister on his heel.

JOHN: Poor Thomas! Always something wrong! When he sits on his throne in the Kingdom he's sure to find lumps in the cushion.... Oh, dear! I feel frightfully sleepy and excited all at once. As if something tremendous was going to happen and I didn't know how to keep awake for it. A kind of birthday-party feeling.

PETER *(practically)*: You've had a busy day.

JUDAS: What do you imagine is going to happen tonight, that's so important?

JOHN: I don't quite know. But from the way the Master talks, I shouldn't wonder if it was the coming of the Kingdom.

JUDAS: That's very interesting.

PETER: Ah! here they all come. . . . How's the heel, Thomas? . . . Here, James bar-Zebedee, let me take those.

JAMES: Martha thought you'd need some more unleavened bread. . . . Look out! It's very brittle. Just off the griddle.

PETER: Right you are. . . . Oh, look what's here! Come along, Andrew, come along.

ANDREW: Yes, I've brought up the roast. Shall I put it on the chafing dish?

JAMES: Nathanael and Simon the Canaanite are just coming through the gate.

JOHN: Then that's everybody except Matthew.

THOMAS: He's following on with the Master. . . . I think I'll sit down. My foot's rather painful.

JAMES: You can sit there. That's John's place.

THOMAS (offended): I beg your pardon, James bar-Zebedee. All right. I'll take the lowest seat. I hope nobody will object to *that*.

JOHN: Oh, Thomas, *please!* I don't mind where I sit.

PETER: Don't let's go through all that argument again.

MATTHEW (arriving): Argument! What argument! I never knew anything like you chaps. Here we are, all set to keep the Passover like one 'appy family, and me and the Master strolling along as pleasant and peaceful as you like, watching the moon come up and 'im telling me a beautiful story, about a Samaritan what was kind to a pore wounded Jew—and fust thing we 'ear when we get in, you're 'aving an argument! . . . Stop it, can't you? 'Ere he comes.

JESUS: Peace be with you, my children.

DISCIPLES: And with you.

PETER: Everything's ready, Master. We have set this couch for you at the head of the table. . . . Is that cushion right for your elbow?

JESUS: Thank-you, Peter, that will do well.

PETER: Who will you have next you?

JESUS: I wish I could have you all, for tonight you are all specially near and dear to me. But I have only one right hand, and there I think I must still have John. He was the first of you that came to me—so he must be my eldest son, to perform the Passover rite.

JOHN: Yes, Master.

JESUS: And on my left—Well, our small community possesses at least one officer. Judas, you are our treasurer. Will you sit by me at supper?

JUDAS (a little taken aback): I? . . . With pleasure. . . . By the way, are we returning to sleep at Bethany?

JESUS: No; we will spend the night in the Garden of Gethsemane.

JUDAS (with meaning): And wait there for the coming of the Kingdom?

JESUS: For the appointed hour, Judas. . . . I have told Martha and Mary.

PHILIP: Master—can Nathanael and I come next to Judas?

JESUS: Certainly, Philip. Peter, will you take the head of the couch on John's right?

PETER: Oh, yes, rather!... Here, James—come and sit between me and Andrew.... Simon.... Thomas.... Jude and the other James.... Has Matthew got a place?

MATTHEW: Here I am, next Nathanael. I'm fine, thanks.

PETER: John, are you looking after the wine?

JOHN: I have poured the first cup. Master, pray speak the blessing.

JESUS: Blessed art Thou, O Lord God, that has created these meats to our use. Amen.

DISCIPLES: Amen.

JOHN: Here are the herbs, Master—and the sauce....

(A soft bubble of general conversation as background to the next few speeches)

ANDREW: Well, this is the third Passover we have eaten together. We've seen some wonderful things since we first met the Master. Brother, do you remember me bringing you to him?

PETER: That I do, Andrew. Aye, we've had our ups and downs. Hard times and peaceful times, one or two frightening times, and some grand, uplifting moments. There's been things we'll not forget in a hurry—hasn't there, John?

JOHN: None of it can ever be forgotten.

PHILIP *(striking in across the table)*: I'll not forget those early days—when the power first came to us to heal the poor, sick people. Nor the marvel of seeing Lazarus rise from his grave and cry aloud for joy.

NATHANAEL: I was afraid then. And afraid when they tried to stone the Master—though it was brave to hear him defy them, and pierce their hard hearts with his great words.

MATTHEW: Ah! but it's his kind, loving words as puts real 'eart in a man. Master, I can't tell you what them words done for me. It's been a grand time, every bit of it. And *this* Passover's goin' to be the best of the lot—for why? Because it's going to see the Kingdom come for all of us—ain't that right?

JESUS: The Kingdom is very near.

MATTHEW: And 'ere we sit, a-tasting of it, in a manner of speaking, beforehand. There sits the Master, like it might be in his royal palace, with his counsellors about him—John one side and Judas the other—between the 'eart and brains of the undertaking, as you might say.

JUDAS *(unpleasantly)*: I am glad to learn what is John's official capacity.

ANDREW: My brother had a position given him too. Hadn't you, *And* a title.

PETER: That'll do, Andrew.

JAMES: Keeper of the Keys, wasn't it?

ANDREW: There you are! Judge of the Supreme Court.

JUDAS: It sounds more like the Head Gaoler.

ANDREW: Judas, that's rude. . . . No, Peter was to be the foundation-stone of the Church.

NATHANAEL: High Priest then.

JAMES *(slightly shocked)*: Oh, but he's not of a priestly house. Now our father Zebedee—

PHILIP: Of course, James, of course. All right—John shall be High Priest, and Judas the Lord Treasurer.

MATTHEW: Don't I get anything? *I've been* a government official. A bad job, and a dashed bad government—still, experience counts for something.

THOMAS: Are *all* the appointments going to you people at the head of the table?

JUDE: That's right, Thomas. How about you and me and Simon here? . . .

(Babble at the lower end of the table, from which words like "Captain of the Horse", "Lords of the Council", "Secretary of State", emerge at intervals)

JOHN: What is it, Master? Does all this folly vex you?

JESUS: It troubles me, John. They understand so little, and the time is getting so short. . . . Is there water in the great pot over there?

JOHN: Yes, Master. Shall I fetch you some?

JESUS: No; sit still. . . . Help me off with my upper garment.

MATTHEW *(his voice coming out of the babble)*: 'Ere, be quiet, you chaps! The Master's got up from table. We've been talking silly and he don't like it. It was my fault. I began it.

ANDREW: No, it was me. I was boasting about Peter.

THOMAS: I was grumbling. It's a bad habit. One didn't ought to grumble— especially at Passover-time.

ANDREW: What is the Master doing? . . . Stripped to the waist and girded with a towel like a slave!

PETER: Carrying a pitcher and basin! It's not fitting. What on earth is John about?

JESUS: John, son of Zebedee—give me your feet, that I may wash them.

JOHN: Master? *(he checks his instinctive protest)* Whatever you will, Beloved.

(The splash of water into the basin)

PETER *(in a scandalised whisper)*: John! How can you let him?

JOHN: Don't, Peter.

JESUS: Simon Peter, son of Jonah—

PETER *(energetically)*: No, Lord, no! Never! Never! I wouldn't dream of letting you wash my feet.

JESUS: No, Peter? Indeed and indeed I tell you, unless I wash you, you have nothing in common with me.

PETER: Oh! . . . Oh, I didn't understand. Then wash me, Lord, wash me! Not my feet only, but also my hands and my head.

(Water)

JESUS: They who are washed already do not need to be washed again. Only their feet become travel-stained. When those are washed, they are clean altogether. Give me your feet then, James bar-Zebedee. . . .

(Water)

JAMES: Master, we all were baptised for the washing away of sin. Are we clean, then?

JESUS: You are clean. . . . Andrew bar-Jonah, let me wash your feet. . . .

(Water)

Yes, you are clean. But not all of you—not all of you. Simon of Canaan. . . .

(Water)

PETER *(in a whisper to John)*: John, why does he say that we are not all clean?

JOHN *(whispering back)*: I don't know, Peter. But when I look into my heart, I find it full of unswept, dusty corners.

JESUS: Thomas Didymus, give me your feet that I may wash them. . . . You are footsore?

THOMAS: It is nothing, Master—nothing at all.

JESUS: I will wash away the soreness with the stain. . . .

(Fade down, till we have only the sound of water and the murmur of names)

Jude. . . . James. . . . Matthew. . . . Nathanael. . . . Philip *(then bring it up again)* Judas Iscariot, give me your feet that I may wash them.

(Water)

They are fouled with the mire, my son. . . . Pray that they do not carry you into temptation.

JUDAS *(grimly)*: I have set my hand to the plough. Through mud or blood, the feet must follow.

JOHN: Dear Master, let me put away the pitcher. . . . Here is your coat. . . . Come and take your place with us again.

JESUS: Thank-you, John. . . . Listen now, my children. Do you understand what I have been doing? You call me Master and Lord—rightly, for so I am. If I, your Lord and Master, have washed your feet, like a servant, you ought also to wash one another's feet. I have given you an example, that you should behave to one another as I have behaved to you. The servant must not be prouder than his master, nor the messenger who is sent grander than the Lord who sent him. . . . I think you see what I mean—

(Murmurs of assent)

Then happy are you if you do as I say. . . . I don't say this of all of you. I know who are my chosen, and who will reject me, as the Scriptures foretold. Remember—to accept me is to accept Him that sent me; and to reject me is to reject Him too.

JOHN: Master, how sadly you speak!

JESUS: Indeed and indeed I tell you that one of you will betray me.

PETER: Betray you?

JAMES: Impossible!

MATTHEW: Who'd be mean enough to do a thing like that?

PHILIP: Betray the Master! But that's absurd.

NATHANAEL: Master, you don't mean anybody'd do it on purpose?

THOMAS: No, no, he can't mean that.

MATTHEW: We might do something silly by accident.

PETER: Yes—I'm always blurting things out. Master—is that what you meant? Is it me?

DISCIPLES: Or me? Or me?

ANDREW: Perhaps it's some other disciple—not one of us?

JESUS: It is one of the Twelve—one who has dipped his hand in the dish and eaten bread with me.... The Son of Man goes indeed, as it is written of him; but woe to that man by whom the Son of Man is betrayed! It would be better for him if he had not been born.

DISCIPLES: One of us twelve? ... Who can it be? ... Deliberate treachery? ... That's horrible.... What can he possibly mean?

(Keep this murmur going under the following conversation)

PETER *(in a low tone)*: John, for pity's sake, ask him who it is.

JOHN *(in the same tone)*: Dearest Lord, who is it?

JESUS *(in the same tone)*: I will hand him a sop from the dish. But say nothing.... *(aloud)* Judas Iscariot!

JUDAS: Master?

JESUS: Will you take the sop at my hand, my son?

JUDAS: Thank-you. *(in a low voice)* Master, am I the man?

JESUS *(in the same tone)*: Yes. What you have to do, do quickly.

JUDAS: You seem to be well informed—King of Israel.

MATTHEW *(his voice again rising out of the background)*: Well, it's all a mystery to me.... Hullo! ... Where's Judas gone?

NATHANAEL: To buy something for the Feast, I expect; or distribute alms to the poor.... What I want to know is—

MATTHEW: Hush! The Master is speaking.

JESUS *(almost to himself)*: So it is now, Son of Man, it is now.... *(aloud and urgently)* Oh, my children, listen to me. I shall not be with you much longer. Soon, very soon you will look for me in vain—for, as I once told the people, so now I tell you: I am going where you cannot come. In a little while you will see me no more—and again a little while, and then you will see me indeed, because I am going to the Father.

MATTHEW: Master, you don't mean to say you are *leaving* us!

NATHANAEL: When? How?

ANDREW: Why?

PHILIP: But how about the Kingdom?

JUDE: What's he talking about? In a little while we shan't see him. . . .

JAMES THE LESS: And then in a little while we *shall* see him. . . .

SIMON THE CANAANITE: Because he's going to the Father?

THOMAS: What is all this? "A little while"—I can't make out a word of it.

PETER: Master, we don't understand. Why do you speak of leaving us? Where are you going?

JESUS: To a place where you cannot follow me yet, though some day you will. So, before I go, I want to give you a new law to live by. Love one another. Love one another as I have loved you. That is how the world will know you for my disciples—because you love one another.

SCENE II (JERUSALEM)

SEQUENCE I (THE HIGH PRIEST'S HOUSE)

THE EVANGELIST: But Judas, when he had received the sop, immediately went out. And it was night.

JUDAS: My Lord Caiaphas, you must act instantly. He suspects me already. And he has made an assignation for tonight, at Gethsemane.

CAIAPHAS: For what time, Iscariot?

JUDAS: I do not know. But he said: "We shall wait there tonight for the coming of the appointed hour".

CAIAPHAS: Did he mention Baruch?

JUDAS: No; but what else could he have meant? *(A disturbing thought strikes him)* Unless—unless—No, that's impossible. He cannot mean to take the way of suffering. He is guilty—I know he is guilty. He must be. . . . Listen, most Venerable. When I left, supper was not half over. You can take him in the garden before his confederates join him.

CAIAPHAS: Yes. . . . I wish we could have had more notice. Tomorrow night is the Sabbath. We can't keep him in prison till next week—there'd be a riot. We've got to get the thing done before anybody realises what's happening. . . . Is it possible to get him arrested, tried, convicted, and the sentence ratified and carried out before six o'clock tomorrow evening? . . . It's quick work, but I think we can just do it. . . . Hezekiah!

SECRETARY: Most Venerable?

CAIAPHAS: Send out runners at once to all members of Sanhedrim, calling an emergency meeting—here in this house—

SECRETARY: They may not have finished supper.

CAIAPHAS *(grimly)*: Then they must eat it in haste—as Moses commanded. . . .

Say, in an hour's time. . . . What next? Witnesses. You have made a note, I think, of people with complaints against Jesus.

SECRETARY: I have it here.

CAIAPHAS: Pick out the most likely names and see that they're here before midnight. . . . Take this order to the Captain of the Temple Guard. Bid him bring — Iscariot, how many are there with Jesus?

JUDAS: Eleven men.

CAIAPHAS: Tell the Captain — enough force to overpower twelve able-bodied men — or rather more, in case we should find more than twelve. Let them wait here till they get their orders. . . . Hurry, hurry, Hezekiah!

SEQUENCE 2 (THE UPPER ROOM)

THE EVANGELIST: And while they were at supper, Jesus took bread and wine, according to the rite of the Passover. . . .

JOHN: Master, will you now bless the bread?

JESUS: Blessed art Thou, O Lord, God of the universe, who dost bring forth bread from the earth. Amen.

DISCIPLES: Amen.

JESUS: Take and eat. This is my body which is broken for you. . . . do this in remembrance of me.

(He breaks the wafer)

PETER *(whispering)*: John, what is this? His body?

JOHN *(whispering)*: He said once: "Unless you eat the flesh of the Son of Man" — Do you remember?

PETER: Yes, but I don't understand. Ask him what it means.

JOHN: I *must* ask — when I give him the cup. It's part of the Passover ritual. . . . But, oh Peter, I am afraid.

PETER: Pour the wine, and ask the question.

JOHN *(rather shakily)*: Master — will you bless the wine for the second cup?

JESUS: Blessed art Thou, O Lord, God of the universe, who dost create the fruit of the vine. Amen.

DISCIPLES: Amen.

JOHN *(summoning his resolution with the familiar words)*: What mean you by this service?

JESUS: Drink, all of you, of this. For this is my blood of the new Covenant, which is poured out for many, to release them from sin. . . . I have longed with a great longing to eat this Passover with you; for I tell you, I shall never eat it again, until it is fulfilled in the Kingdom of God. Take it, therefore, and share it among yourselves and the cup also; for I will never more drink of the fruit of the vine till the Kingdom of God is come.

JOHN: Master, these words are very strange and disturbing.

JESUS: Don't let your hearts be troubled. You believe in God — believe in me too. There are many inns on the road to my Father's house. I am going ahead to prepare the lodgings for you. You will always find me there to welcome you, so that at each stage we shall be together. Don't worry. You know where I am going, and you know the way quite well.

THOMAS: But we *don't* know where you are going, Master. So how can we know the way?

JESUS: I am the way, and the truth and the life. Nobody can come to God our Father, except by me. If you really knew me, you would know my Father too. Indeed, you do know Him now, because you have seen Him.

PHILIP: Can any one see God and live? Master, if indeed you can show us the Father, then we shall be satisfied.

JESUS: Have I been with you all this time, Philip, and still you do not recognise me? ... The man who has seen me has seen God.

SEQUENCE 3 (THE HIGH PRIEST'S HOUSE)

THE EVANGELIST: Then the High Priest called the Council together....

CAIAPHAS: That is settled, then.... Father Annas, will you take charge? Collect the witnesses, receive the prisoner, have them sent round to the Old Gazzith, and get the Court assembled. I will join you there.... Oh! and remember to send somebody along with my robes.... I must go and see Pilate, and persuade him to ratify the sentence at once, without further trial. If he takes it into his head to re-open the case, we may be held up all day. But this tale of a conspiracy will do the trick, I fancy.

SHADRACH *(nastily)*: Is Jesus to be tried by the Sanhedrim as an offender against Rome?

CAIAPHAS: No, Brother Shadrach. That would scarcely do. The charges are witchcraft, contempt of our Law, and blasphemy.

ANNAS: Are you calling this man Iscariot?

CAIAPHAS: I think not. He is a tainted witness, and would make a bad impression. Besides, our Law requires the agreement of two witnesses, and there is nobody to confirm his statements. He has served his purpose— better keep him out of it.... Now, we mustn't waste a moment.... Hezekiah, my cloak! ... I leave all the arrangements to you.

SEQUENCE 4 (THE UPPER ROOM)

JESUS: If you love me, keep my commandments. And I will pray to the Father, and He will send you a mighty helper—the Spirit of Truth, the Comforter, to be your abiding strength. The world cannot accept Him, because it does not know Him; but you know Him, and He will stay with you for ever.... Trust me. I will not leave you comfortless—I will come to you. The world will not see me, but you will see me, and know that I am alive; and in my life you shall live too.

PETER: Master, how will you show yourself to us and not to other men?

JESUS: If any one loves me and keeps my sayings, my Father and I will come to him and make our home in his heart. I tell you these things now, while I am still with you; when the Spirit, the Holy One, comes He will make you remember and understand. . . . There is so much I want to say to you, but you cannot bear it now; and there is no time, for the alien power of the prince of this world is rising up to oppose me. . . . Fear nothing. My peace I leave with you; my peace I give you; not peace as the world understands it, but the peace that is mine. For—don't forget—you and I belong together. I am the vine—you are the branches. Unless the life of the vine runs through them, the branches can bear no fruit. So, without me you can do nothing; but if your life is rooted in mine, then you may ask whatever you will, and the living power will be given you. I want you to be happy about this—I want the gladness of my presence to fill you with perpetual joy. . . . And I say once again: Love one another, as I have loved you. The greatest love that a man can show is to lay down his life for his friend. And you are my friends—I won't call you my servants, for a master doesn't take his servants into his confidence—you are my friends, with whom I have shared all the secrets of God.

JOHN: Dear Lord, we love you as a friend—and as our master, too.

JESUS: But bear in mind what I told you: the servant is not greater than his master. If the world hates you, remember that it hated me first. You will be thrown out of the synagogues and persecuted—yes, and the time will come when people will imagine that they are doing God service by killing you. In the world you will have distress and sorrow—but be of good courage: I have overcome the world.

PETER: Master, whatever happens, your words will give us strength and confidence.

JESUS: Kneel close about me now, and I will pray for you—my very dear friends—my children:—

Father, the hour is come. I have glorified Thee on the earth; I have finished the work Thou gavest me to do. Now glorify Thou me with Thine own self, with the glory I had with Thee before the world was made. I have shown Thee to these men whom Thou gavest me; Thine they were, and Thou gavest them to me, and they have kept Thy word. While I was with them, I held them safe—I have lost none of them, save only one who cast himself away; for so it had to be. And now that I must leave the world, I bring them back to Thee. Bless them and keep them, Father, that they may be one, as Thou and I are one. I do not ask that Thou shouldst keep them apart from the world—only guard them from this world's evil. For I am sending them out into the world, as Thou didst send me. And I pray, not for them alone, but for all whom they shall bring to Thee by their teaching; that they may all be one: I in them, and Thou in me—all one and all perfect together. Amen.

DISCIPLES: Amen.

(Hymn: from the Great Hallel. Fade out on this)

SEQUENCE 5 (THE GOVERNOR'S HOUSE)

PILATE *(a little testily)*: Yes, yes, my dear Caiaphas. Of course I will ratify any sentence of a local tribunal, provided it does not conflict with Imperial order and that the trial has been properly conducted according to the law of the land. But why should I have to get up at dawn to do it?

CAIAPHAS: Excellency—the quicker the better. The man has followers; if they are given time to organise, there might be a good deal of unpleasantness. And besides—this, in your ear, because, of course, it has nothing to do with the ecclesiastical offence—I have evidence that Jesus is implicated in a nationalist movement, led by one Baruch, a Zealot, and that some sort of rising is due to take place tonight.

PILATE: Indeed!

CAIAPHAS: Here are the papers to prove it.

PILATE: Thank-you. *(sardonically)* Caesar will be touched by your concern for the safety of the Roman state. I will look into the matter.

CAIAPHAS: And the sentence?

PILATE: Send me the prisoner and the report of the court proceedings, and I will sign the warrant first thing.

CAIAPHAS: I am obliged to your Excellency.

PILATE: Not at all. Good-night. . . . *(To himself)* This won't please Claudia. . . . *(Aloud)* Flavius! Get hold of the police reports about Jesus of Nazareth— and find out if anything is known about this man Baruch. . . . I don't trust Jews.

SEQUENCE 6 (THE UPPER ROOM)

(Fade in the closing lines of the Hymn from Sequence 4)

JOHN: It is over—this strange Passover night. . . . Master, you're not leaving us yet? You said we were going to Gethsemane. . . . We're going together, aren't we? You won't desert us?

JESUS: No, John, I won't desert you. But tonight, you will all desert me; it will be like what the Prophet says: "I will smite the shepherd, and the sheep shall be scattered abroad". But all will be well in the end, for when I am risen, I will call my sheep again, and walk before you, as I did of old, in Galilee.

PETER: Master, I can't have that. Even if everybody else should desert you, I never will.

JESUS: Simon Peter, Simon Peter—Satan is trying to get hold of you all, to shake you apart as a man sifts wheat. But I have prayed for you that your strength may not fail. And when you have really found your own soul, then strengthen your brothers.

PETER: But, Lord, I'm not afraid. I'll go anywhere. I'll face anything—never mind the spies and traitors. I would gladly go to prison with you. I would die for you, indeed I would.

DISCIPLES: We all would.

JESUS: Would you die for my sake, Peter? Indeed and indeed I tell you: before the cock crows, you will disown me three times over.

PETER: Disown you? Master, I would die first.

DISCIPLES: Indeed, Master, indeed. . . . We will never desert or disown you. . . . We would give our lives for you and the Kingdom.

JESUS: My poor little flock! Once again I am sending you out like sheep among the wolves. Do you remember that first mission, when I told you to take neither purse, nor wallet, nor shoes—nothing but what you stood up in?—Did you go short of anything then?

JAMES: No, Master—we always had enough.

JESUS: But this time things cannot be the same. This time I say: If you have a purse, take it, and your wallet too. And if any of you has no sword, let him sell his garment and buy one. I must go, as the prophets foretold, to the end that awaits all criminals, for everything that has to do with me is drawing to its fulfilment. But you will remain in the world, and you must learn to control the powers of this world—money, and the sword.

PETER: Do you mean we shall have to fight for the Kingdom? We have only two swords among us.

JESUS: It is enough. Come now, let us be going. . . . Say good-bye to this Upper Room. . . . Keep close beside me.

SEQUENCE 7 (THE GOVERNOR'S HOUSE)

PILATE: Claudia, I am sorry. I knew this would distress you.

CLAUDIA: But Caius, *must* you ratify the sentence? I am sure Jesus of Nazareth is a good man.

PILATE: So he may be. But he is a storm-centre. The first time you saw him, you remember, there was a riot.

CLAUDIA: He has enemies, no doubt. Most good men have. The accusation may be quite false. . . . You won't let him die if he is innocent?

PILATE: What a question for my wife to ask Pontius Pilate! Rome dispenses justice. But she respects local codes, and if this man has offended against the Jewish law—

CLAUDIA: Oh, what do these barbarians matter, with their crazy superstitions and their everlasting feuds?

PILATE: My dear, listen to me. I simply dare not have any more trouble with the Jews. I have dealt summarily with them before, as you know; and the last time, Caesar interfered. If I make him angry again—that will be the end of me.

CLAUDIA: Oh, no! No. Caius—of course you must not offend Caesar! He is . . . Caesar.

SCENE III

SEQUENCE I (THE GARDEN OF GETHSEMANE)

THE EVANGELIST: Then Jesus went forth with his disciples over the brook Kedron, unto a place called Gethsemane. . . .

JESUS: Peter and James and John—are the others asleep?

JAMES: I think so, Master.

JESUS: Come with me. I need you.

PETER: Yes, Lord.

JESUS: Let me feel you beside me. . . . I have loved you. . . . Oh, children, this moment is bitter—how can the flesh bear it? . . . Out of the deep, O Lord, out of the deep . . . the deep waters . . . all thy waves have gone over me. . . . It is the waiting that is so hard. . . .

JOHN: Oh, my dear, my dear.

JESUS: My soul is full of sorrow—it is like the horror of death. Stay here a little and watch with me, while I go and pray. . . .

PETER: We three together again, as we were before in the mountain.

JAMES: What shall we see tonight?

JOHN: I have wept so much that my eyes can see nothing.

JESUS (a little way off): Abba, Father—all things are possible with Thee. If it be possible, let this cup pass from me. . . . If it be possible—nevertheless, not as I will, but as Thou wilt.

JAMES: How earnestly he prays.

PETER: As though in a torment that grinds him, soul and body.

JAMES: The sweat shines on his forehead—I have seen it so on the face of men stretched upon the rack.

PETER: It falls to the heavy earth like drops of blood.

JAMES: Such prayer cannot go unanswered.

PETER: There is no answer—no light—no vision: only the dark agony of the mortal flesh.

JOHN: Oh, I can't bear it. (Like a child) James, hold me tight—I'm frightened of the dark—

JAMES: Be still, little brother; be still. . . .

(Fade on the last words and pause)

JESUS: Children! . . . They are asleep already. . . . Wake up, my sons.

JOHN (still half asleep): Yes, love, yes. . . .

JAMES *(half asleep)*: Who called?

PETER *(struggling awake)*: Dear Lord, forgive us.... I think we had wept ourselves to sleep.

JESUS: Could you not watch with me one hour?

JAMES: Oh, we are ashamed—

JOHN: How could we fail you so?

PETER: We meant to keep awake.

JESUS: The spirit, indeed, is willing, but the flesh is weak. Do I not know it? But watch and pray, lest you fail in the moment of trial.... *(going away)*

JOHN: How long have we slept?

JAMES: It is near midnight. The shadow has shortened under the olive-trees.

JESUS *(a little way off)*: O Abba Father—if it be possible ...

PETER: The same words again....

JAMES: More and more urgently.

JOHN: As though they would break through the barriers of time and space.... Peter! is the earth going? Is the vision here?

PETER: I see one beside him—one of the shining ones—holding and strengthening him—

JAMES: But the light is like shining darkness, and his face stern and pitiful—

JOHN: It is Azrael, angel of death—oh, my heart, my heart—

JAMES: Let us pray too.

PETER: I can think of no words to say.

JESUS: Father, if this cup may not pass from me except I drink it, Thy will be done.

JOHN: Pray as he prays. Pray as he taught us—"Our Father"—

PETER: ⎫
        ⎬ Our Father, which art in Heaven....
JAMES: ⎭

SEQUENCE 2 (THE HIGH PRIEST'S HOUSE)

ANNAS: Now, I think, we can proceed. Captain Elihu!

CAPTAIN: Reverend Sir?

ANNAS: Make the arrest now. Iscariot here will guide you to the place.... That garden is dark with trees.... Make sure you get hold of the right man.

JUDAS: Trust me. Captain, watch what I do. There will be twelve men there. I shall go up to one of them, saying "Hail, Master". Then I will grip him by the arms—so—and kiss him. That is your man. Hold him fast.

CAPTAIN: Very good.... Now then, you men—come on!

(The party moves off, not with the steady tramp of the Roman guard—for these are only Jewish policemen—but in a more irregular manner)

SEQUENCE 3 (THE GARDEN)

THE EVANGELIST: And the third time Jesus came to his disciples, and found them sleeping, for their eyes were heavy with sorrow . . .

JESUS: They are worn out. God help you, my poor boys. What use to wake you again?

JOHN (*stirring in his sleep and half rousing himself*): Jesus, Jesus—

JESUS: Sleep on now and take your rest; for the hour is at hand, and the Son of Man is betrayed into the hands of wicked men. . . . (*With a change of tone*) No. Up with you, quick! They are upon us! Here comes the traitor. Look!

JAMES: Lights in the garden!

JOHN: A band of men with lanterns and torches—

PETER: And weapons! Hey, there, you lads! Andrew! Thomas! stand by!

DISCIPLES (*rushing forward*): Who's there? What's up? Where's the Master?

JESUS: Steady, children.

(Noise of men approaching)

PETER: Stand round the Master. . . . Don't let them see him!

JAMES: Who's that at the head of them?

PHILIP: It's all right—it's all right—it's Judas!

JOHN: Judas!—You filthy traitor!

JESUS: Friend, what are you doing here?

JUDAS: Hail, Master!

JESUS: Judas—will you betray the Son of Man with a kiss?

CAPTAIN: Are you Jesus of Nazareth?

JESUS: I AM.

(Confusion, and a squawk of superstitious terror from the SOLDIERS)

CAPTAIN: Who are you that answer with the name of God?

JESUS: Whom are you looking for?

CAPTAIN: Jesus of Nazareth.

JESUS: I tell you, I am he. If you want me, let these men go their way.

PETER: D'you think we'll stand for that! Come on, lads! Out swords and make a fight for it!

(Clash of weapons and a yell)

JESUS (*dominating the uproar*): Peter! put up your sword! . . . They that take the sword perish by the sword. I do not want you killed. I that might have at my call more than twelve legions of angels—but the cup that my Father gives me to drink—shall I not drink it? . . . Is anybody hurt? Captain, I am sorry for this.

VOICE: Malchus is wounded.

MALCHUS (*growling*): He's cut my ear half off.

JESUS: Come here, friend. . . . Let go my hands a moment. . . . There—it is nothing. It is healed. . . . Why have you come out with swords and pikes, to seize me as though I were a robber? Every day I sat teaching in the Temple, and you laid no hand on me. . . . But this is your hour and the power of the lords of darkness. . . .

THE EVANGELIST: Then all the disciples forsook him, and fled.

THE TENTH PLAY

THE PRINCES OF THIS WORLD

CHARACTERS

The EVANGELIST.
JESUS.
SIMON PETER. ⎫ Disciples of
JOHN BAR-ZEBEDEE. ⎬ Jesus.
JUDAS ISCARIOT. ⎭
THE PORTRESS at the High Priest's House.
CAIAPHAS, High Priest of Israel.
ANNAS, father-in-law to Caiaphas.
HEZEKIAH, secretary to Caiaphas.
SHADRACH. ⎫
1st ELDER. ⎪
2nd ELDER. ⎪
3rd ELDER. ⎬ Members of
4th ELDER. ⎪ Sanhedrim.
NICODEMUS. ⎪
JOSEPH OF ARIMATHAEA. ⎭
CAPTAIN. ⎫
1st GUARD. ⎪ Levites, members of the
2nd GUARD. ⎬ Temple Guard.
3rd GUARD. ⎪
4th GUARD. ⎭
BARUCH the ZEALOT.
1st WITNESS.
2nd WITNESS.
3rd WITNESS.
CAIUS PONTIUS PILATE, Governor of Judaea.
FLAVIUS, freedman to Pilate.
MARCUS, clerk to Pilate.
A SLAVE in Pilate's house.
A CENTURION ("Marcellus"). ⎫
A SERGEANT. ⎪
1st SOLDIER. ⎬ Roman
2nd SOLDIER. ⎪ Soldiers.
3rd SOLDIER. ⎪
4th SOLDIER. ⎭
HEROD ANTIPAS, Tetrarch of Galilee.
TECHELLES, a Greek slave, secretary to Herod.
A CHEER-LEADER, mouthpiece of the Priests and Elders.
CROWD.

NOTES

The general movement of this play is straightforward enough. It presents two peculiar difficulties which cannot be eliminated.

(1) The central Character is required by the text to obtain his effects by "keeping on saying nothing". This is very good business in a stageplay, where an actor with a good stage-presence can hold the eye; but not so good on the radio, where out of sound is apt to be out of mind. I have tried to get over this by (a) making references from time to time to the Prisoner's bearing and appearance; (b) giving as much warning as possible when he *is* about to break silence; (c) keeping him off the stage altogether in the scene with Herod.

(2) The scenes before Pilate have to keep popping in and out of the Praetorium. One must imagine a raised plinth or balcony, on which Pilate can stand with the Priests and Elders, above the level of the people in the street; from this he passes to interrogate Jesus inside the palace—doubtless through the usual heavy curtain which, by a convenient theatrical fiction, is deemed to be more or less impenetrable by exterior noises.

THE CHARACTERS

JESUS—Throughout the play, he never yields an inch. The interrogation before Annas is entirely irregular; he knows it, and says so. The evidence of the witnesses breaks down, and he will not assist the Court by engaging in any dispute. But the law does require him, as a pious Jew, to answer to the Oath of Testimony; silence here would be an admission of unorthodoxy; his answer is definite and uncompromising—naturally, for under this oath he is bound to speak the truth. . . . His first reply to Pilate ("do you ask this on your own account, or is this what they have told you about me?") draws attention to the fact that this is a new accusation—is he the prisoner of Rome on a separate charge, or have the religious authorities compromised their own political position? Having thus made clear the irregularity of the proceedings, he reassures Pilate on the point that is worrying *him* — "if I had intended rebellion, I should have come armed". This appears to satisfy Pilate; the further charges brought by the Priests Jesus leaves Pilate to take for what they are worth. . . . Flogging (and a Roman flogging was no joke) may exhaust his voice and body, but does not break his spirit; the tone of his reply ("you could have no power at all against me—") is exactly that of his rebuke to the Captain before Annas—the quiet assertion of what is, and is not, proper authority.

NOTE: that all this is as far as possible from that ostentatious insistence on martyrdom which Judas would have liked to see in him.

PETER—In the first little scene with John, Peter shows the weakness that will lead him to disown Jesus. He is distressed at his own behaviour, but is still

253

concerned to justify himself—"I should have been all right if only I'd been allowed to fight—and anyway he told us not to get killed". Also, he is nervous about getting into the High Priest's house, and so starts at a disadvantage. Then the support of John is withdrawn from him; and the question of the Portress (of the type which "expects the answer No") brings out the quick, nervous denial, and so makes easy the way for the second and third. Then he finds himself dragged into unwelcome prominence, in the presence of the men whom he assaulted in the Garden, and, under the direct challenge, he loses both nerve and temper.

JOHN—He had (I suspect) a fairly good excuse for running away—probably Brother James hauled him off bodily. But, having real humility, he is not concerned to excuse himself. Consequently, he is ready to combine candour with prudence by quietly taking the Portress into his confidence. He, too, does not seek martyrdom, for he has been told not to—but neither does he tell lies to escape it.

PORTRESS—A decent, good-hearted girl, ready to exchange backchat with the guards or do a good turn to a friend, without much thought one way or the other.

CAPTAIN OF THE GUARD—He is genuinely shocked by the Prisoner's manner to Annas, but not otherwise malicious. Nor are his men. They mean no real harm to Peter.

ANNAS—This old gentleman had been deposed from the High Priesthood by Pilate's predecessor, Valerius Gratus, and probably still considers himself the only properly constituted High Priest. In any case, having got an opportunity to assert himself, he does so, by conducting an irregular examination on his own account. His temper is not improved by the Prisoner's attitude.

WITNESSES—The 1ST WITNESS is a rather muddle-headed man, with no great gift of narrative. The 2ND and 3RD WITNESSES, being members of the Temple Guard (i.e. the ecclesiastical police), deliver their evidence with the routine glibness of the policeman in the witness-box.

NOTE: To make the Sanhedrim scene intelligible, it is necessary to remember that for a "valid testimony" Jewish law required the *exact verbal agreement* of at least two witnesses.

NICODEMUS and JOSEPH—These two are taking advantage of the above fact to obstruct the proceedings as much as they dare.

SHADRACH—He, as usual, displays far more brains than the rest of the Sanhedrim. It is his rooted conviction that nobody but himself can ever do anything properly. He is as malignant as any of them, but he cannot resist pointing out that they are making fools of themselves. He is more on the spot even than Caiaphas—he sees the snag about the Passover prisoner looming ahead, and has the wits to take steps about it in advance. This gives him unspeakable satisfaction.

CAIAPHAS is *determined* to get the thing put through. Everything seems to be in a conspiracy against him, but he will have his way or die for it. He knows the importance of getting the case watertight—yet when it comes to the pinch he will risk the dubious expedient of the Oath of Testimony; he knows the unpopularity of Roman rule, yet in the last resort he will openly acknowledge the authority of Caesar if that is necessary to his object (see also under PILATE). . . . With Judas he is uncomprehending and impatient. There is in this politician nothing of the priest, as we understand the word. The sight of a soul in torment is to him merely another irritating interruption, wasting precious minutes when he wants to hurry off to Pilate. Nothing of what Judas is saying means anything to him—how should it? since he is totally destitute of any sense of sin.

BARUCH—He too is an unscrupulous politician, but there is a good deal of decency in him. He has no use for failures—yet he can turn up to attend the execution of a couple of unimportant underlings who have been "unlucky", and he is the kind of man to whom such underlings are loyal. And, though impatient with the unpracticality of Jesus, he can genuinely admire his quality. For Judas he has every kind of contempt— that of the man of action for the intellectual, of the realist for the ro- mantic, of the loyal for the traitor, of the man without illusions for the self-deceiver, of the resolute man for the moral coward—and he is brutal without compunction.

JUDAS—At the opening of his scene with Baruch, Judas is probably already rather uneasy, and this very uneasiness makes him aggressive. The sight of Baruch creeping about Jerusalem in disguise is a relief—it persuades him that he was—he really *was*—quite right about the conspiracy, and he intends to be triumphant and self-righteous about it. Baruch pricks this bubble triumph. From now till the end, all his self-deceptions are peeled off successively, like the skins of an onion. His ghastly qualms of a few hours earlier prove only too well-founded—he was quite wrong about Jesus— stupidly, crassly and absurdly wrong; what is more, Baruch knows all about his "amateur spying", and thinks it ridiculous. Further, he now sees that he has been Baruch's dupe; Baruch, who first undermined his faith, now despises him for his lack of it. . . . At this point he tries to take refuge in the idea that Jesus may be acquitted. Baruch makes short work of this piece of wishful thinking, and proceeds to show him that all his talk about purgation by suffering has been mere romanticism—he has never envisaged it as a reality, or conceived of its happening to *him*. With a rough hand, Baruch strips away the romance and shows the reality—and here Baruch is probably more brutal than he knows, because Judas has brains and imagination. He has just *seen* Jesus; and that sight, and the details which Baruch is rubbing into him, produce together a nightmare picture which he cannot face. Finally, by some intuition, Baruch pounces on the act of betrayal, which, seen through his eyes, no longer looks like the performance of a public duty, but like a very dirty and cowardly piece of work. . . . He escapes from Baruch, and during the trial before the Sanhedrim has time to make his own further acquaintance.

Baruch's assessment of the situation, though shrewd, is shallow. So far, Judas has only got to the point reached by de Stogumber in *St. Joan* — he sees the ugliness of the thing he has done, and realises that no end or motive can justify a thing like that. The next scene takes him farther.

In the first few minutes with Caiaphas he is still buoying himself up with the notion that he can get rid of his sin by putting the matter straight. But he comes up against a blank wall. Smoothly and suavely he is informed that once more he has only been the dupe and tool of others. Jesus has been convicted, not of sedition, but of blasphemy, and the scruples of Judas are absurd and irrelevant. . . . And now, as he goes down, step after step, into hell, he is haunted by his victim, so that he echoes his words — "Scribes and Pharisees, hypocrites" — "whited sepulchres" — "the man who hates his brother is a murderer". He sees the truth about himself — the itch for suffering that was only an inverted cruelty; the refusal to believe in innocence that was rooted in the envy and hatred of innocence; the farther he goes, the more he finds hatred — he hates Caiaphas and Jesus and God and himself. He sees the truth, not only about himself, but about sin — he sees the need for the untainted priest and the spotless sacrifice; he even knows obscurely who is the untainted Priest and Victim who could do for him what Caiaphas cannot do — but he cannot be saved because he *will* not be saved. He goes on, down and down to the lowest pit of all, where sits the devil of pride that makes the sin unforgivable because the sinner resents and hates and refuses the forgiveness. At the bottom of that pit is only himself and his self-hatred, and here there is no place of repentance. So he goes to his own place.

And let us, my darlings, have no reservations or inhibitions, but a good, big, thundering piece of theatre in the grand manner — not too loud till we get to the final outburst — but with pace, pace, pace and passion.

HEROD ("The fox") — There is nothing to this degenerate son of Herod the Great — only a drawling, languid, rather effeminate voice and an empty mind, idle, vicious, shallow, luxurious, petty, contemptible and cruel.

"Let Jesus be the peacemaker between us" — is there any vision behind this remark? None whatever; the great wind has passed over him, and he nods and dances before it, but he has no idea why. He is perfectly frivolous, with just enough cunning to avoid even the shadow of any responsibility for anything.

PILATE, on the other hand, is interesting. He is neither knave nor fool; his trouble is that he is an ambitious government official, who has blotted his own record in the past by tactless dealing with the people he rules and despises. At first, nothing is in his mind but the infuriating nuisance of having to get up at dawn to perform a piece of official routine. He is aware that his wife is distressed about the matter, but this influences him only so far as to start him with a vague antagonism to the whole thing. He is not inclined to take the reports of the Prisoner's seditious activities very seriously—he knows, of course, that Jesus has aroused "feeling" in the province, but so far as the police reports go, this has all been about religion or something. Still—there it is—the man is a focus of trouble, and if the Sanhedrim wants him put out of the way, and the thing is legal, probably it's all for the best. But down underneath, something in him is on the alert, and Claudia's letter, with its emphasis and its touch of superstitious terror, is the reagent which crystallises his vague distrust and antagonism. Also, he likes the look of the Prisoner. And he does not, when he comes to look at them, like the look of the depositions. He is a Roman, and law and justice do mean something to him. Also he is obstinate by nature and more than willing to obstruct the Jews. From the moment that he decides to re-try the case, the Sanhedrim are faced with the task of forcing the thing through against the determination of the Governor.

1st *Phase of the Conflict:* Pilate takes evasive and delaying action. He begins by setting aside the blasphemy conviction as (a) irregularly obtained and (b) irrelevant to Roman interests. This brings out an open statement about the charge of treason and sedition. The political aspect of the Messianic claim is presented to him. He examines the Prisoner about his claim to kingship, and decides that he is probably a harmless crank. He therefore tells Caiaphas he can take no action in the matter, unless he receives a proper indictment in form on the new charge. (Incidentally, if he can get this, it will be a valuable weapon against the Jews, since it amounts to a *de jure* recognition of the Imperial suzerainty.) Caiaphas, on his side, wants to evade doing any such thing. He offers various other charges (which Pilate refuses to receive in this irregular manner) and deprecates any delay in getting rid of Jesus. Here, a casual statement gives Pilate a legal loophole. He can push the whole affair off on to Herod. If Herod likes to pass the death-sentence then it will not come back for ratification to Pilate. (Presumably it would go to Rome direct, or perhaps Herod could carry it out himself, as he did with John Baptist.) Up to this point, Pilate feels able to treat the whole thing rather cavalierly.

2nd *Phase of the Conflict.* Herod lets Pilate down by sending back the Prisoner (through another legal loophole) with the implication that no charge lies against him so far as Galilee is concerned. Pilate realises that he must now take the matter seriously, and presumably conducts a further examination in more detail (just before the opening of Sc. 5). Meanwhile, he has thought of another get-out. Without actually refusing to do what the Sanhedrim demand, he will satisfy justice and the people and himself by releasing this popular prisoner according to custom. This attempt to make the best of both worlds is disastrous; the move has been foreseen and countered. Pilate is now beginning to take the thing as a personal matter and is violently set on getting his own way, and ready even to run risks in doing so. This phase leads up to an accusation which sounds quite new to Pilate; the Prisoner has claimed to be the Son of God. This is the supernatural side of the Messianic claim, to which—while it appeared to be only something to do with the ecclesiastical definition of blasphemy—he had paid no great attention. But "a son of the gods" is an actual possibility to a Roman, and he remembers his wife's dream. He sends hastily for the Prisoner, and he is afraid.

3rd Phase of the Conflict. The struggle in Pilate is now between his fear of Caesar and his awe of the supernatural. Also, he is furious with Caiaphas and Co. and will turn the weapon of "treason" against them if he can. The shout "we have no king!" gives him an opportunity. He rounds on them instantly, and with savage delight extorts from them the admission of Caesar's imperium. But the thing comes back at him like a boomerang: "If you let this man go, *you* are disloyal to Caesar". The accusation is broadcast to his own soldiers—to the Roman citizens in the crowd; and he cannot face that. They have beaten him. He is humiliated, and he is afraid—before God and men he washes his hands of the thing—in the hope that in this way he may contrive to "have nothing to do" with this innocent man.

But though beaten, he has one shot left in his locker. He goes down with his guns firing—and his last act is to fling a deadly insult at the men who have outfaced and outfought him; he writes the insolent superscription: "This is the King of the Jews". (But for Heaven's sake, take the Prisoner away, because he cannot bear to look at him—and he must face the wrath of the gods, and the terrors of Claudia.)

Harsh, overbearing, obstinate, superstitious, decent in his way, but not big enough to smash his way out of a compromising situation, Pilate is at a disadvantage from the start because of his past history. (He has been in trouble three times already for over-riding the Jews too roughly.) But he is friendly to the Prisoner—and pays him the greatest compliment he knows how to pay: "He should have been a Roman". The thing to be borne in mind is the aspect of all these scenes as a cut-and-thrust duel between Pilate and Caiaphas.

NOTE: For various reasons I have made Pilate pretend at any rate to be too grand a person to speak Hebrew. He speaks Latin to Flavius and Marcus, and some popular form of Greek to everybody else. I don't want this difference conveyed by broken English; but the actor may contrive to indicate it by a little increase in pace and fluency when he is supposed to be speaking Latin.

ROMAN SOLDIERS—These men have no animus against Jesus. Custom has made them callous, and flogged and fainting prisoners are all in the day's work. If a criminal collapses under punishment one jabs or kicks him into consciousness—not because one particularly enjoys inflicting pain, but because that is the kind of handling appropriate to criminals. The Centurion, who is a judge of human material, is ready to administer a reproof when this sort of thing shows signs of becoming barbarous and un-Roman. Of course, any opportunity to indulge in horse-play and make fun of the Jews is always welcome; even the Centurion will unbend so far as to take part in the joke—jokes break no bones. . . . The soldier's song is intended to represent the popular sentimental ballad of the period; the other soldiers can join in raggedly—and if it can be sung "live" by the actors concerned, so much the better. Let it be as rough and ready as possible; we do not want a concert-platform performance—nor need it be tidily finished up.

THE CROWD is so important in this play that it must be quite clear in its collective mind what it is doing. The antagonism of the people to a person so popular as Jesus seems quite inexplicable and unconvincing till we really grasp what the situation is.

NOTE that, from the Sanhedrim point of view, the presence of the Crowd is an annoying accident. The whole object of the hasty trial was to *avoid* all publicity. The Crowd only has time to collect because of a whole series of unforeseen delays: (1) the time taken in getting Sanhedrim and witnesses together and communicating with Pilate beforehand; (2) the hold-up of the trial by the lack of agreement among the unrehearsed witnesses; and the obstructive tactics of Joseph and Nicodemus; (3) Pilate's unexpected decision to re-open the case; (4) his sudden brain-wave about handing the baby to Herod. But, since the Crowd is there, it becomes the strategic pivot of the campaign, and both sides bend all their efforts to capture it.

The first thing to remember is that when first the Crowd arrives *it does not know anything about the arrest of Jesus.* It has been in bed while the fate of God was being debated. A few early passers-by may have noticed that something is going on outside the palace, and at one point they will have seen Jesus there, evidently undergoing some sort of examination. These people will start gossiping, and various rumours will be bandied about. But there is a large section of the Crowd which has come there for the express purpose of demanding the release of the Passover prisoner, and *most of these are already prepared to call for Barabbas.* Their minds are full of Barabbas; Jesus is sprung upon them without the slightest preparation— and by whom? *By the Roman Governor,* whose office and person they resent and dislike.

Even so, a few of them are ready to think the thing over and shout for Jesus; but the CHEER-LEADER is skilful and quick to exploit their nationalist feeling and make the issue one of *demanding their rights as against Rome.* Barabbas was arrested because he had joined with others to stir up sedition, and had committed murder in the process. It does not do to think of him as just "a robber" or "a murderer"—we must think of him as a member of the I.R.A., arrested during "the troubles"; with Jesus as the rival candidate presented *by the English Governor-General* for the kindly consideration of a Dublin crowd!

The demand for crucifixion is at first comparatively mild and half-hearted. But during the flogging-scene, the CHEER-LEADER has had time to work the Crowd up into a frenzy of excitement; and when at last Jesus is brought out to them, the howl of execration must hit one like a blow in the face. (The expression "A'arrh!" indicates that frightful wild-beast noise made by Nazis and boxing-fans—a sort of rhythmic blood-yell.)

NOTE: The fact that Pilate's Hebrew is deemed not to be very good makes it possible for the CHEER-LEADER to make bolder appeals than he otherwise might to nationalist feeling, and to get all he can out of those words and actions of Jesus which appear to the people to be definitely un-Jewish.

SCENE I (THE TRIAL BEFORE ANNAS)

SEQUENCE I (THE STREET: AND THE COURTYARD OF THE HIGH PRIEST'S HOUSE)

THE EVANGELIST: Then the band and the captain and officers of the Jews took Jesus and bound him and led him first to Annas, that was father-in-law to Caiaphas the High Priest. But Peter followed him afar off; and so did another disciple.

(Sound of the band of guards passing; it fades away ahead)

PETER: Keep them in sight, John. We *must* see the end of this.

JOHN: I know what the end will be.... So does he. "Strung up on the gallows." ... Oh, Peter—we said we would die with him. What right have we to be alive?

PETER: He didn't want us killed. He told them to let us go.

JOHN: That doesn't make me feel any better. We ran away.

PETER: I could have died fighting.

JOHN: He neither fought nor ran. He faced fear empty-handed.... Look! They're going to the High Priest's house.

PETER: That's done it. We can't get in there.

JOHN *(suddenly stimulated by finding a situation he can tackle):* Oh, yes, we can. I've been there before. The servants know me.

PETER: Why, of course—you're a Zebedee, of the priestly line. Do you think they'll let us both in?

JOHN: We can but try. I'll run and catch up with the party.... *(voice fainter)* Wait for me outside.

(Fade in the sound of footsteps as he catches the party up)

CAPTAIN: Halt there!

(They halt, rather raggedly. CAPTAIN *knocks at the gate, which opens)*

PORTRESS: Who's there? ... Oh, Captain Elihu. That's right. The Lord Annas says to take the prisoner straight up. The staircase on the left.

CAPTAIN: Good! ... Here, men! Half a dozen of you bring him along. The rest wait in the courtyard. That all right, miss?

PORTRESS: They're welcome. There's a good fire burning.

(Scuffling noise as they pass in. PORTRESS *and* GUARDS *exchange greetings:* "Evening, Joel. ... Same to you, lass. ... Evening, Tabitha. ... Evening, Malchus—cold enough for you? ... Hullo, bright-eyes. ... Go along with you!" *etc.)*

Why, John bar-Zebedee! Haven't seen you for ages. Since when have *you* joined the Temple police?

JOHN: I haven't. But I want to come in.

PORTRESS: Of course. Why not? You're a friend of the house.

JOHN *(in a low tone):* I'm a friend of the prisoner.

PORTRESS: Oh! . . . Well, I've had no orders about that. . . . Look here. If you slip up that staircase and stand behind the curtain at the end of the gallery, you'll see and hear what's happening.

JOHN: You're a kind girl, Tabitha. By the way, I've got another man with me.

PORTRESS: Bring him in too.

JOHN: May I? Thank-you . . . *(Calling softly)* You there, Peter? The portress says you may come in.

PETER: That's very good of you.

PORTRESS: I can't let anybody upstairs I don't know. But you can come and sit by the fire in the courtyard.

PETER *(nervously):* There's rather a crowd there.

PORTRESS: Oh, it's only the police. . . . Run along, John bar-Zebedee. We'll look after your friend. . . . Up the stairs and along the gallery. You can't miss it. . . . *(to* PETER*)* Poor boy—he looks all in. How did he get mixed up in this? *You're* not a follower of this man Jesus, are you?

PETER *(hastily):* No, no, no—just a friend of John's.

PORTRESS: Well, you must keep him out of trouble. . . . I wonder what's going on up there. . . .

(Fade into next sequence)

SEQUENCE 2 (A ROOM ON THE UPPER FLOOR)

ANNAS: Is that the prisoner? Bring him forward. . . . H'm. . . . I think, Brother Shadrach, we might ask a few preliminary questions, just to clear the ground. . . . Now then, my man—By the way, I suppose he knows where he is and who I am? Eh, Hezekiah?

HEZEKIAH: I should hope that everybody knew your Reverence. . . . Prisoner, you understand that you are in the presence of the Lord Annas, head of the high-priestly family, and himself former High Priest and High Priest Emeritus of Israel.

JESUS: I know where I stand.

ANNAS: Very well. Jesus bar-Joseph, you have been accused of breaking the Law of Moses, of practising witchcraft, and of aiding and abetting others to do the same. Now answer me. What exactly is the doctrine you preach? And why have you surrounded yourself with this gang of followers? What is behind all this?

JESUS: *I* make no secret of what I do. I have always preached and taught openly in temple and synagogue where all the world could hear me. Why question *me?* You know very well it is illegal. There are plenty of people who know what I said. Your proper course is to call witnesses and interrogate *them.*

CAPTAIN: Is that the way to speak to his Reverence? Take that, fellow *(smacking him over the face)* and mend your manners.

JESUS *(quietly):* If what I said was wrong, then go into court and give evidence about it. But if I was right, why do you strike me?

ANNAS: You see what the man is—obstinate and insolent.

SHADRACH: Quite so. Unfortunately he seems to know something about court procedure. It is *not* legal to invite a man to incriminate himself. Evidence is *not* legal unless we have the agreement of two witnesses. And it is *not,* strictly speaking, correct for the police to hit the accused in the face.

ANNAS: Brother Shadrach—are you defending the man?

SHADRACH: Dear me, no. I only suggest that we are wasting valuable time.

ANNAS: Prisoner, I hoped you would see reason, and explain yourself informally to these gentlemen and myself. But since you are recalcitrant, and insist on a formal trial, you shall have it. We will proceed to the Sanhedrim, where you will find we have witnesses enough and to spare. . . . Captain, bring the accused to the Gazzith. . . .

(Fade into next sequence)

SEQUENCE 3 (THE COURTYARD)

IST GUARD: Br'rr! Put another log on, Malchus. These spring nights are chilly. What time is it?

MALCHUS: Getting on to cock-crow.

2ND GUARD: It's always coldest just before dawn. Here, stranger—you're shivering. Come nearer the fire.

PETER: Thank you—I'm quite all right here.

IST GUARD: I say, Malchus, how's your ear?

MALCHUS: I'd forgotten about it. That fellow Jesus healed it all right.

IST GUARD: Witchcraft, cousin, that's what it is. I'd get the priests to look at it if I were you. It might go bad on you. . . . I say, stranger, you're a Galilean by your accent. What do you know about this Jesus? You're not one of his people, are you?

PETER: Of course not. I don't know what you're talking about.

2ND GUARD: Oh, rot! You must have seen something of him in Galilee. . . .

3RD GUARD: Come on, give us the low-down on it!

4TH GUARD: Speak up, my lad! . . . He's shy!

2ND GUARD: Stand forward, let's have a look at you. . . . I believe you *are* one of the prisoner's men!

IST GUARD: Didn't I see you in the garden with him? . . . Malchus, look here—

PETER: Damnation! Leave me alone! I tell you I don't know the man. I never set eyes on him. I never—

(A distant cock begins to crow; the sound is taken up by another, close at hand; one after another all the cocks of the neighbourhood join in)

1ST GUARD: Well, you can see him now. Come on, lads—they're bringing the prisoner down.

THE EVANGELIST: And the Lord turned and looked upon Peter. And Peter remembered the word of the Lord, "Before the cock crow thou shalt disown me three times over". And he went out, and wept bitterly.

SCENE II (THE TRIAL BEFORE THE SANHEDRIM)

SEQUENCE I (IN THE STREET)

THE EVANGELIST: And at dawn, the elders of the people and the chief priests and the scribes were assembled, and Jesus was brought before the council.

BARUCH: Hey, there! Judas Iscariot!

JUDAS: Who's that? . . . Baruch! I didn't recognise you in that disguise. . . . You'd better clear out of this. Your conspiracy's off. They've arrested Jesus. He is coming up for trial now, before the Sanhedrim.

BARUCH: Is he indeed?

JUDAS: Pilate has promised to ratify the findings.

BARUCH: Then I suppose he's for it. Well, you were right. Jesus was incorruptible. I was always afraid he might be. . . . Much good it's done him. I knew what would happen when he refused my offer.

JUDAS: What do you say? Jesus refused?

BARUCH: Of course he refused. *(contemptuously)* Didn't you find out that much, with all your amateur spying? . . . I told him: "If you come in war, take the horse; if in peace, take the ass". He took the ass. The more ass he.

JUDAS: Are you lying to me? *(With swift suspicion)* Then what are you doing here?

BARUCH: Two poor lads of mine being turned off today. They were unlucky. They got caught. But they'll die without squealing. And they'll know I'm somewhere about to say good-bye to 'em. . . . Well, it's a pity. If Jesus had listened to me—

JUDAS: So he was innocent after all!

BARUCH: Why, what did you think?

JUDAS: I thought—

BARUCH: You thought he'd fallen for it? No more faith in him than that, after all your fine words? . . . Look! They're coming out of the High Priest's house. There goes Messiah, with his hands bound, to answer for his follies. . . . Well, let him die. We've got no room for failures.

JUDAS: Perhaps they will acquit him.

BARUCH *(sarcastically):* Perhaps the cat will acquit the mouse! . . . *(brutally)*

Here, what's the matter with you? You wanted him to suffer, didn't you? Now he's going to suffer. I hope you're pleased. If you had any guts, you'd be suffering with him. Why aren't you in court, making a noble speech and clamouring to be martyred in the cause? . . . But talking's one thing, suffering's another. . . . Going to Pilate, is he? That means the cross. Ever seen a man crucified? There's nothing poetical about it, and it hurts, Judas, it hurts. . . . Now's your moment to practise what you preach. Will you stand by your Messiah? Will you testify from the cross? Will you be eloquent from *that* pulpit about the value and blessedness of pain? Skewered up there in the broiling sun, like an owl on a barn door, with your joints cracking and your head on fire and your tongue like leather? Will you say from there what you said to me . . . ?

JUDAS: Damn you, be quiet!

BARUCH: Can't face it, eh? — He's facing it. I know that quiet sort. He'll walk up to death with his eyes open and his mouth shut. All *you* can do is to cringe and squeal. . . . Yes! And how did Jesus get taken? Somebody squealed then, I fancy. Who was it? *Who was it,* Judas Iscariot?

JUDAS *(in a stifled voice):* Let me go!

BARUCH: Bah! What filth! . . . Run, rat, run! *(Voice more distant)* You can't run away from yourself. . . .

SEQUENCE 2 (THE SANHEDRIM COURT)

THE EVANGELIST: And they brought many witnesses against him, but their witness agreed not together. . . .

CAIAPHAS: Tell the court again exactly what he said.

IST WITNESS: He said: "Which is easier? To say 'Your sins are forgiven' or to say, 'Get up and walk'? But to show you that the Son of Man has power on earth to forgive sins" — then he said to the paralysed man —

SHADRACH: I'm getting confused. Who said what to whom?

IST WITNESS: *Jesus* said to *us:* "Just to show you that the Son of Man has power — "

NICODEMUS: Did he say *he* was the Son of Man?

IST WITNESS: I don't think he actually said so.

IST ELDER: We have a witness here who says he did.

IST WITNESS: Well, I won't swear to the exact words. But he mentioned the Son of Man.

JOSEPH: It is scarcely a crime to *mention* the Son of Man.

CAIAPHAS: Witness, you can stand down. . . . We must have agreement about the words.

SHADRACH: You should have had a reporter on the spot.

CAIAPHAS: Brother Shadrach, pray spare the Court these sarcasms. Call the next witness, please. . . . Brother Joseph and Brother Nicodemus, I do not like to suggest that you are being deliberately obstructive —

NICODEMUS: And I don't like to suggest that the Court is trying to wrest the evidence.

CAIAPHAS: I hope not.

JOSEPH: But agreement is essential if a case is to be made out.

SHADRACH: Quite so. It's no use presenting Pilate with a case that's as full of holes as a colander. To use your own words, most Venerable, we want the thing water-tight.

CAIAPHAS: I quite agree about *that*. . . . Well, who is this witness, and what accusation does he bring?

2ND WITNESS *(briskly)*: My name is Abraham ben-Levi. I am a member of the Temple Guard. I accuse the prisoner of witchcraft and sacrilege. Three years ago, at Passover-time, I was in the Temple when this man caused a riot by interfering with the market. I heard him say: "I will destroy this Temple made with hands, and in three days I will build another, made without hands".

SHADRACH: You did, did you?

2ND WITNESS: Yes, and so did you, reverend sir. You were there at the time.

SHADRACH: I am not a witness—fortunately.

CAIAPHAS: Have you any one else to confirm you, ben-Levi?

2ND WITNESS: Yes. One of my comrades is here. He'll bear me out.

CAIAPHAS: Very well. . . . Call him in. . . . Is this the man? What is your accusation?

3RD WITNESS *(glibly)*: I accuse the man Jesus of witchcraft. Three years ago, at Passover-time, I was in the Temple and heard him say: "I am able to destroy this house of God, and build it again in three days".

NICODEMUS: Did he say he *would* destroy it, or only that he *could*?

3RD WITNESS: He said he could. If that isn't witchcraft, what is it?

IST ELDER: Did he say anything about rebuilding it without hands?

3RD WITNESS: No. My friend, Abraham ben-Levi, said that. "He'd have to build it without hands", he said. But I said, "He'd build it by the hands of demons".

CAIAPHAS: It doesn't matter what you and your friend said. You don't agree about what the prisoner said.

SHADRACH: As a matter of fact, you're both wrong. What he said was neither "I will" nor "I can" but: "Destroy this Temple, and in three days I will build it again". I remember it distinctly.

3RD WITNESS: Well, sir, you may be right. But that's not how I remember it.

CAIAPHAS: There is agreement at least about the claim to rebuild the Temple in three days. Prisoner—you hear these witnesses. Have you any defence to make against the charge of witchcraft? . . . Still silent? . . . This obduracy will do you no good.

IST ELDER: Is there much more of this kind of evidence?

ANNAS: Some twenty or thirty witnesses waiting.

IST ELDER: Because at this rate, between witnesses who all say different things and a prisoner who says nothing, we shall be here till tomorrow.

CAIAPHAS: I will interrogate the man myself.

NICODEMUS: My lord, that is barely legal.

CAIAPHAS: *Barely* legal, Brother Nicodemus, is still legal. He shall answer under the Oath of Testimony. If he still refuses to speak he is self-condemned.

JOSEPH: And if he exculpates himself?

CAIAPHAS: In that case, Brother Joseph, we shall call the other thirty witnesses.... Put the prisoner forward.... Jesus bar-Joseph, as you are a true Israelite, hearken and answer to me upon oath. I adjure you by the living God, that you tell us whether you are the Messiah, the Christ of Israel.

JESUS: I am. And you shall see the Son of Man sitting on the right hand of the Power of God, and coming in the clouds of heaven.

(Sensation)

CAIAPHAS: Do you then say you are the Son of God?

(Wail of Horror)

JESUS: I am.

CLERK TO THE COURT *(in a sort of formal recitative):* Alas: Alas! It is blasphemy! The High Priest has rent his garments.

CAIAPHAS: What further need is there of witnesses? You have heard his blasphemy. What do you think of it?

ALL: He is guilty of death.

CAIAPHAS: Jesus bar-Joseph, out of your own mouth you stand convicted of blasphemy in the highest degree, and are condemned to die, by sentence of the Court.

(Fade out on this)

SEQUENCE 3 (THE SANHEDRIM COURT)

THE EVANGELIST: Then Judas, when he saw that he was condemned, came again to the Chief Priests and Elders....

CAIAPHAS: Well, reverend brothers, considering it was done in such a hurry, that didn't go too badly. I had my doubts at one point, but all's well that ends well. Now we have only to see it safely past Pilate, and then we can look forward—

JUDAS *(off):* Let me pass, I say!

ANNAS: What's happened now?

JUDAS: I must see the High Priest!

CAIAPHAS: It's the man Iscariot.... All right, Levites, let him in.... *(To the ELDERS)* Come for more money, I daresay.

ANNAS: Don't give it him.

CAIAPHAS: Certainly not.... Well, my good man, what is it?

JUDAS: I have sinned. I have betrayed the blood of the innocent.

CAIAPHAS: Come now, come now. You are naturally distressed—

JUDAS (over-running him): Jesus is guiltless. He was never false to himself. He was never false to Israel. Rome has nothing against him. He consented to no conspiracy.

CAIAPHAS (curtly): He was not tried for conspiracy. He was tried for blasphemy.

IST ELDER: And duly condemned by the proper authority.

SHADRACH: We are not officially interested in his attitude to the Roman question.

JUDAS: You acted on my information.

ANNAS: All we needed from you was the opportunity to secure his person.

CAIAPHAS: And we are greatly obliged to you for your assistance.

JUDAS: Scribes and Pharisees, hypocrites!—How well he knew you!... Listen to me, you whited sepulchres! I have done a thing so hideous that hell itself is ashamed. The vilest thieves have some loyalty, and a scoundrel's dog can be faithful to him. But my Master was innocent, and I slandered him; innocent, and I accused him; innocent, and I betrayed him.

CAIAPHAS: You came to us of your own accord—and with the highest motives, I am sure.

JUDAS: I came because I hated him. "The man who hates his brother is a murderer"—I have murdered the Christ of God for hate.... It was written that he must suffer—Yes! And why?—Because there are too many men in the world like me.... I was in love with suffering, because I wanted to see him suffer. I wanted to believe him guilty, because I could not endure his innocence. He was greater than I, and I hated him. And now I hate myself.... Do you know what hell-fire is? It is the light of God's unbearable innocence that sears and shrivels you like flame. It shows you what you are.... Priest, it is a fearful thing to see one's self for a moment as one really is.

CAIAPHAS: What is all this to us? Your conscience is your affair.

JUDAS: What is it to you?—You are the High Priest. Day by day, week by week, month by month, you make the sacrifice for sin—the burnt-offering and the peace-offering and the trespass-offering. Year by year, on the Day of Atonement, you enter the Holy Place and pour out blood before the Mercy-Seat for the redemption of Israel. What can your priesthood do for me? Will the blood of bulls and of goats wash out my stain? You that are steeped to the lips in the same crime with me, can you stand there red-handed and offer up for both of us a spotless and acceptable sacrifice? There is no priest, no victim in all the world that is clean enough to purge this guilt.... Is God merciful? Can He forgive?... What help is that?— Jesus would forgive. If I crawled to the gallows' foot and asked his pardon, he would forgive me—and my soul would writhe for ever under the torment of that forgiveness.... Can anything clear me in my own eyes? Or release me from this horror of myself? I tell you, there is no escape from

God's innocence. If I climb up into Heaven He is there—if I go down to hell, He is there also. What shall I do? Caiaphas, High Priest of Israel, what shall I do?

CAIAPHAS: We cannot listen to this raving. You have done your service, and we have paid you well.

JUDAS *(quietly):* Is that your last word, fellow-murderer? *(loudly)* Take back your money, with the curse of Cain upon it. *(He flings down the pieces of silver)* I am going to my own place.

CAIAPHAS: Stop him! He's mad.

LEVITES: Halt, there!

(They bar his way with their pikes)

JUDAS *(bursting past them):* Hands off! I am unclean! . . . Unclean and accurst. . . . Unclean. . . . Accurst. . . . Accurst. . . . Accurst. . . .

(His voice dies wailing into the distance)

THE EVANGELIST: And he departed, and went, and hanged himself.

SCENE III (THE FIRST TRIAL BEFORE PILATE)

THE EVANGELIST: Then led they Jesus into the hall of judgment, and delivered him unto Pontius Pilate the Governor. And it was about three o'clock in the morning.

FLAVIUS: Excellency—are you dressed? These Jews are here wanting their sentence ratified.

PILATE *(yawning):* Oh, yes, curse them. . . . Come in, Flavius, and give me a hand with my cloak. . . . Kept up half the night and now full military dress at crack of dawn—who'd have my job? . . . I suppose they've brought all the papers.

FLAVIUS: Yes. Are they to come into the Praetorium?

PILATE: Oh, no! I've got to go out to them. If they came in here they'd be defiled, and couldn't hold their confounded ceremonies. . . . Have you lugged my clerk out of bed?

FLAVIUS: Yes, here he is.

PILATE: Ah!—Morning, Marcus. You look as though you had a thick head. You drink too much.

MARCUS *(with a feeble snigger):* Oh, sir—

PILATE: All right. Tell 'em to bring in the prisoner and hand me the report of the trial. . . . By the way, Flavius, did you get anything from the police about that Zealot—Baruch, whatever his name is?

FLAVIUS: Oh, yes. He's known to be seditious. He's had a bunch of malcontents lying up in the hills all last month. But they seem to have broken up the very day this Jesus entered Jerusalem.

PILATE: Doesn't look as if there was much in that part of it, then . . . *(Flicking over the report)* Ye gods! What's all this stuff?—Blasphemy, sabbath-breaking, witchcraft, law of Moses—pages of it. I suppose they know what it's all about.

(Tramp of a couple of soldiers)

Yes, come in, sergeant.

SERGEANT: The prisoner, sir.

PILATE: Good. Bring him along. Let's have a look at him. . . . H'm. Well set-up fellow. Looks you straight in the face. I like the appearance of him. Pity he's got to be executed. We could do with a man like that in the army. . . . Oh, well! Have you got the warrant made out?

MARCUS: Yes, Excellency.

PILATE: I take it it's in order. Let's see . . . "Jesus bar-Joseph, of Nazareth . . . carpenter . . . 33 years old . . . convicted before the Sanhedrim . . . 14th Nizam . . . blasphemy, and all the rest of it . . . sentence of death . . . delivered to me . . . take and execute. . . ." All right. Give me a pen *(Knock)* Oh, *come* in!

SLAVE: Your pardon, Excellency. A note from her Excellency the Lady Claudia. She asked it should be delivered *immediately,* wherever you were.

PILATE: Oh, thanks. . . . Now what in the—*(In a changed tone)* Here, Flavius. What do you think of this?

FLAVIUS: "Have nothing to do with that good man. I have had a terrible dream about him." . . . That's brief and emphatic, Pilate.

PILATE: Scored with such urgency, the stylus has gone clean through the wax—"have nothing to do with him". What am I to make of that?

FLAVIUS: Well, Pilate, Her Excellency is a woman. Some ladies have soft hearts for handsome preachers.

PILATE: Flavius, you were born a slave, and you have the vulgar mind of a slave. Learn to bear yourself like this peasant and keep your mouth shut, and some day you may get mistaken for a gentleman. Not otherwise. . . . Where's that report? It's just occurred to me that—Yes, I thought so. The prisoner was convicted, not by the agreement of witnesses but out of his own mouth, upon oath, under question from the court. Marcus, you're the expert on this sort of thing. Is that good Jewish law?

MARCUS: I don't say there's no precedent for it. But it's certainly rather irregular.

PILATE: And their tale about Baruch seems doubtful. Why all this hurry and hugger-mugger? I don't like it. I think they're up to some game. Marcus!

MARCUS: Excellency?

PILATE: I shall not sign the warrant. I'm going to re-try this case. . . . Is Caiaphas there?

MARCUS: Yes, sir, he's outside with a bunch of Elders.

PILATE: Very well, we'll go out to them. . . . The prisoner can wait here. . . .

(Cross-fade to the court outside)

IST ELDER: What a time the Governor's taking! He has only to sign his name. I sincerely hope nothing has gone wrong.

CAIAPHAS: So do I.

IST ELDER: Ah! He's coming out now.

SHADRACH: I don't see the warrant. I'm afraid the worst has happened.

ALL: Good-morning, Excellency.

PILATE *(abruptly):* Good-morning. What is your accusation against this man?

SHADRACH *(softly):* The worst *has* happened.

CAIAPHAS: If he were not a criminal, we should not have delivered him to you.

PILATE: As far as I can see this is an entirely Jewish question. Take him and deal with him according to your own law. It is not a matter for Rome.

CAIAPHAS: By our law he has already been convicted and condemned to death. But by Roman law we are denied authority to execute the sentence.

PILATE: By what offence has he incurred the death-penalty?

CAIAPHAS: He pretends to be the Messiah.

PILATE: What does that mean?

CAIAPHAS: It amounts to a claim to be king of all Israel.

PILATE: There is nothing about that in your court proceedings. I understood he was condemned for blasphemy.

CAIAPHAS *(controlling himself):* To *us,* such a claim is blasphemy, but in Roman eyes it is presumably treason.

PILATE: I see. This is a new charge: treason to Rome. I will go and interrogate the prisoner and see what his claim amounts to. . . . Marcus!

MARCUS: Yes, Excellency. . . . Had I better send for an interpreter?

PILATE *(with a groan):* Oh, yes, I expect so. . . . *(As they pass inside)* Wait a minute. I'll find out. . . . Here, you, fellow—you have no Latin, of course? . . . Can you speak Greek?

JESUS: Sufficiently.

PILATE: Good. That saves trouble. . . . Now then. What do you call yourself? Are you the King of the Jews?

JESUS: Are you asking me that on your own account? Or is that what they have told you about me?

PILATE *(contemptuously):* Am I a Jew? Your own nation and your own priests have delivered you up to me. What have you been doing? What is all this about being a king?

JESUS: My kingdom is not an earthly kingdom. If it were, I should have come with men and arms to protect me from my countrymen. But my kingdom does not rest upon force, or any human authority. It is not of this world at all.

PILATE: But you *are* a king of some kind?

JESUS: As you say, I am a king. That is your word and not mine; but it is the right word — in one sense.

PILATE: What is *your* word for yourself?

JESUS: The end for which I was born and came into the world was that I should bear witness to truth. Every one that has the truth within him recognises my voice as the voice of truth.

PILATE: Truth? What is truth? . . . You know, Flavius, I don't believe there's any harm in the fellow at all. I think he's just a crank. He reminds me of my old Greek tutor. He and his cronies were always wrangling about truth and the world of ideas, and that sort of thing.

FLAVIUS: Yes — metaphysics and philosophy and so on.

PILATE: Philosophy bores me stiff. . . . All right, Marcus. You needn't put that down. Anything I say in Latin is off the record. . . . I'm going to tell Caiaphas there's nothing in it. . . . Sergeant, fetch the prisoner along. . . . We'll get rid of this business and go to breakfast. . . . *(Outside)* Well, now, worthy Caiaphas, here's your man. I've examined him and I find no fault in him at all. There's nothing I can take action about.

CAIAPHAS: There is a whole list of subsidiary charges against him. Read his excellency the charge-sheet.

1ST ELDER *(rapidly):* In addition to the blasphemy of which he was convicted, he has violated the rights of property, having from time to time destroyed a valuable herd of swine and a fig-tree, interfered with the Temple market, and caused a riot thereby.

2ND ELDER: He has offended against public morals and the Jewish law, by breaking the Sabbath, denying the validity of oaths sworn at the altar, instigating young people to defy parental control, consorting with dissolute persons, and attempting to undermine the authority of Sanhedrim.

3RD ELDER: He is either a charlatan or a sorcerer, professing that he can perform miraculous cures, raise the dead, and destroy and rebuild the Temple by magic.

4TH ELDER: He foments political dissension, calling for the establishment of an independent Jewish kingdom, and when challenged about the payment of Imperial tribute, he returned an equivocal answer.

PILATE *(good-humouredly):* Prisoner, you seem to have committed every crime in the calendar. Do you want to make any reply?

JESUS: No.

PILATE: By the gods, Flavius, this man's a marvel. He can hold his tongue and keep his dignity. He ought to be a Roman. . . . My Lord High Priest, I cannot receive a case presented in this hasty and irregular manner. I will discharge the prisoner with a caution, and in the meantime —

CAIAPHAS: It is not safe to leave him at large. He has been preaching sedition up and down the country, beginning in Galilee and ending in Jerusalem itself.

PILATE: Galilee? Yes, by Pollux! — He's a Galilean, isn't he? He comes from

Nazareth. Why, he's not in my jurisdiction at all. . . . Here, Sergeant—take Jesus of Nazareth along to the Tetrarch, with my compliments and my humblest apologies for having unintentionally usurped his prerogative. . . . Sorry, good Caiaphas, but I cannot possibly ratify your sentence. It's *ultra vires*, if you know so much Latin. Good morning to you . . . *(going away)* Well, Flavius, if only I'd had the wits to think of that last night. . . .

(They fade off, laughing)

CAIAPHAS *(furious):* Well! Of all the—

SERGEANT: Now then, prisoner. You're to go to Herod, d'ye hear? Step lively, my lad. . . . March him off, you men. . . .

(They march the Prisoner off)

SCENE IV (THE TRIAL BEFORE HEROD)

THE EVANGELIST: When Herod saw Jesus, he questioned him in many words, but he answered him nothing. And Herod with his men of war set him at naught, and mocked him. . . .

HEROD: Slave, bring me a cup of wine. . . . Well, now, Techelles, have you addressed that letter to Pilate?

TECHELLES: Yes, Illustrious.

HEROD: I hope you have put in plenty of flourishes. He is a vain man. Go on, now: "I am deeply obliged to your Excellency for sending me Jesus bar-Joseph. I had long been anxious to see him, having heard many sensational stories. Alas! He was a disappointment. I asked him all the questions I could think of—my poor brain never functions very well before breakfast—but he was sullen and refused to speak—not nearly such good entertainment as his cousin John Baptist, whom I regretfully beheaded last year, and who could always be relied on for a rousing hell-fire sermon. . . ." Am I going too fast?

TECHELLES: Not at all, Illustrious.

HEROD: Good. . . . "Understanding that Jesus was a miracle-worker, I invited him to perform a few prodigies for our amusement. But no! He would only shake his head, and stare at me with those large eyes of his, till I was quite out of countenance. As for the kingship of Israel"—Techelles, why are you making all those faces?

TECHELLES: I beg your pardon, Illustrious—Ow!—Your Highness' pet monkey is tearing out my hair by the roots.

HEROD: Clever pet! Let the poor beast have his fun, Techelles. . . . Where was I?

TECHELLES *(in a voice of suppressed agony):* "As for the kingship of Israel. . . ."

HEROD: Oh, yes.... "so far as I am concerned, he is welcome to it. But I fancy that Imperial Caesar might find him unco-operative. So pray receive him back with my good wishes, since I find that he belongs to you after all. Though brought up in Nazareth, he is a native of Bethlehem in Judaea—the place, incidentally, where the Christ is supposed to be born. Indeed, I believe that this accidental circumstance, working upon a flighty brain, has engendered in him all this Messianic fantasy. The purple robe I have put upon him, I beg you to keep for Herod's sake. We have been quarrelling too long about a foolish trifle. Let Jesus be the peacemaker between us."—That will do, Techelles. Write it out fair, and embellish it with what compliments you think fit.... You may give me the monkey.... Come, my poppet, come to your master, and you shall have a piece of sugar.... Heigh-ho!... Why does nothing ever happen of the slightest importance in this tedious and intolerable life?

SCENE V (THE SECOND TRIAL BEFORE PILATE)

SEQUENCE I (WITHOUT THE PRAETORIUM)

(There is now the background noise of a considerable CROWD)

IST ELDER: How much longer is this going on? I don't think Pilate's satisfied with the evidence. He's gone in to consult with his clerk.

CAIAPHAS: I don't know what's come over him. He was perfectly all right yesterday.

SHADRACH: He's in a dangerous temper now.

2ND ELDER: And there's a nasty crowd collecting—the one thing we wanted to avoid. The story's got about.

SHADRACH: It's probably getting about. But I fancy a lot of them have come to demand the release of the Passover prisoner.

CAIAPHAS: What! Great heavens, I'd forgotten that.

SHADRACH: Yes. But Pilate will remember. Or that sharp lawyer of a clerk will remind him.

IST ELDER: If the people ask for Jesus, we're done! Somebody must go down into the crowd and get up a good outcry for—for—who's a likely choice? ... Dysmas.... Gestas.... No, they're small fry ... some one more important—

SHADRACH: The brigand Barabbas is the popular favourite.

CAIAPHAS: The very man! Violently nationalist, and a bluff, attractive rascal. Now, who can we get to—?

SHADRACH: Don't worry, most Venerable. I have engaged a good agitator already. I can see him down there.

CAIAPHAS: Shadrach, you are a genius! You think of everything.

IST ELDER: S'sh! Here comes the Governor.

PILATE *(formally):* My Lord High Priest, and members of the Sanhedrim. You have brought me this man, Jesus of Nazareth, accused of fomenting sedition among the people. I have examined him both in your presence, and privately, and can find no substance in these accusations. Further, I sent him to Herod, the Tetrarch of Galilee, who reports that nothing done by Jesus in that province renders him liable to the death-penalty. The most I can establish is that his behaviour has been rather indiscreet. I will, therefore, have him flogged, to teach him a little caution, and discharge him. . . . Officer! Take the prisoner out and give him the cat.

SERGEANT: Very good, sir.

CAIAPHAS: That will not satisfy us.

PILATE: It will satisfy justice. And it will satisfy the Passover custom. . . . Marcus, speak to the people, will you? You can talk their confounded lingo.

MARCUS: Attention, you Jews! This is your Festival, and as you know, it's your privilege to demand the release of a prisoner.

CROWD: Hear! Hear! That's right! Give us our right! That's what we're here for, etc.

MARCUS: The Governor is here in person to see that you get your rights.

CROWD: Hurray! Hurray for the Governor!

MARCUS: He'll speak to you himself. Silence for the Governor!

PILATE: Men of Jewry! I am here, according to custom, to release a prisoner to you. The choice, of course, rests with you; but there is a man brought here to-day —

CHEER–LEADER: Barabbas! He's the man we want! Give us Barabbas!

CROWD: That's right! Barabbas! Barabbas!

PILATE: Wait a moment!

(As he holds up his hand the CROWD *becomes silent)*

You may not all know it, but I have here another prisoner, whom the Sanhedrim have sentenced to death. The man called Jesus of Nazareth.

CROWD: What's that? What did he say? Jesus of Nazareth? Nonsense! That's right, he was arrested last night. What for? Sedition. . . . Witchcraft. . . . Blasphemy. . . . I don't understand this. . . .

PILATE: They haven't all got that, Marcus. Tell them in Hebrew.

MARCUS: Jesus of Nazareth has been sentenced to death by the Sanhedrim.

CROWD: Jesus of Nazareth? What a shame! What's he done? We must have Jesus. How about Barabbas? Jesus . . . Barabbas . . . Jesus . . . Barabbas. . . . *(The* CROWD *shows signs of splitting into two factions, one shouting, "We want Jesus!" and the other "We want Barabbas!")*

CHEER-LEADER: Barabbas! Barabbas! Come on, lads, you won't let Barabbas down? He's a real Jew! There's no nonsense about Barabbas!

CROWD: Good old Barabbas!

VOICE: Barabbas is a murderer! —

CHEER-LEADER: Barabbas is a patriot! *(Cheers)* He's fought for Israel *(Cheers)* and he'll fight again! *(Cheers)* Barabbas doesn't blow hot and cold! *(recklessly)* He wouldn't tell you to pay tribute to Caesar! *(Cheers) He* doesn't hob-nob with tax-collectors! *(Uproar)*

MARCUS: Quiet, there!

PILATE: Which of the two do you want released? Barabbas the robber? Or Jesus, whom you call Christ?

CROWD: Barabbas! Barabbas!

PILATE: Then what shall I do with Jesus called Christ?

CROWD: Anything you like! Take him away! We don't want him, we want Barabbas! Give us Barabbas!

PILATE: But Jesus is innocent. He has done no harm to anybody.

CHEER-LEADER: Who cares! Give us our rights! *(Cheers)* We won't be dictated to! *(Frenzied cheers)* We don't want Jesus! We won't have him! To the cross with him! Crucify him!

PILATE *(angrily):* These people have been got at.

CROWD: Crucify! Crucify!

FLAVIUS: Pilate, Pilate—you can't do it! There's going to be a riot.

PILATE *(passionately):* I don't care. I will have justice. . . . Be quiet there, you Jews!

(Momentary lull)

Why should Jesus be crucified? What crime has he committed?

(Confused clamour)

CHEER-LEADER: Ask the High Priest!

(Silence)

CAIAPHAS: We have a law, and by that law he ought to die, because he claims to be the Son of God.

PILATE: The son of a god?

CHEER-LEADER: Do you want this blasphemer who calls himself Son of God?

CROWD: No! No! Crucify! Crucify!

PILATE: What is all this? . . . A son of the gods? My wife sees visions—and they say he raises the dead!—Officer! Fetch me the prisoner. I must know what this means. . . .

SEQUENCE 2 (WITHIN THE PRAETORIUM)

(The swish and thud of a heavy whip)

CENTURION: Eighteen . . . *(Swish)* . . . Nineteen . . . *(Swish)* . . . Twenty . . . That'll do. . . .

(Pause, broken only by the gasping of the Prisoner)

Has he fainted?

IST SOLDIER: No, sir.... But he's shivering a lot....

CENTURION: Shove a cloak on him, one of you. We don't want him to pass out.

2ND SOLDIER: Here is the robe Herod sent with him....

3RD SOLDIER: Some garment! Whee! Look at the gold embroidery—

IST SOLDIER *(mockingly)*: Come on, King of the Jews.... Here's your majesty's royal robe. Permit me the honour—A'rr, stand up there, can't you! Publius, give him a jab in the ribs....

CENTURION: Here, stow that. He's game enough. I've seen some of you make more fuss over a flogging. Let him sit down.

3RD SOLDIER: A throne for the King of the Jews!—chuck us that stool, Lucius!—Hey, Publius—what are you doing there?

4TH SOLDIER: Making a crown for the King of the Jews.... Curse these thorns.... I've pricked my finger.

2ND SOLDIER: Give it here! There you are, my gallows-bird. King of the Jews—and the right king too for that lousy lot.

(Laughter)

CENTURION *(joining in the game)*: You've forgotten to give him a sceptre. Take my cane.

IST SOLDIER: Thank-you, Centurion!... Hail, King of the Jews!

2ND SOLDIER: What is your majesty's pleasure?

3RD SOLDIER: Will you please to declare war on Caesar?

(Loud laughter)

4TH SOLDIER: Or receive an embassy from the Queen of Sheba?

IST SOLDIER: Come on, lads! Music for his majesty....

> *(Sings)* Bring me garlands, bring me wine,
>   Lalage, Lalage,
>   A crown for you and a crown for me,
>   I'd rather have the rose than the laurel-tree.

SERGEANT: Centurion!

CENTURION: Quiet, there!... What is it, Sergeant?

SERGEANT: Pilate wants the prisoner. Sharp!

CENTURION: Very good. Now lads, stop fooling. Pick him up if he can't walk.

2ND SOLDIER *(not unkindly)*: How about it, mate?

JESUS: I can walk.

CENTURION: Right you are.... Carry on.

SEQUENCE 3 (WITHIN AND WITHOUT THE PRAETORIUM)

(CROWD noises outside)

PILATE: I tell you, Flavius, I've never had much use for religion. But those old stories . . . They say the gods have walked the earth before now—

FLAVIUS: Pull yourself together, Pilate. They're bringing the man in. . . . Do you think the gods look like that?

PILATE: Heaven help me, I don't know. His face frightens me. . . .

FLAVIUS: That's human blood upon it. Not the celestial ichor that runs in the veins of the immortals. Use common-sense. *(Aside to* MARCUS*)* I've never known the Governor lose his nerve before.

PILATE: Come here, Jesus Messiah. . . . I command you—I beg you—to tell me what you are and where you come from. . . . Will you not speak? . . . Man, don't you understand that I have power to crucify you or set you free?

JESUS: You could have no power at all against me, if it were not given you from above. God set you in authority. But the man who delivered me to you to procure an abuse of injustice—his sin is the greater.'

PILATE: Will nothing move you? Do you know what you are in for? . . . Come out here. . . .

(As they come out into the open, there is a yell of execration)

CROWD: There he is! There he is! A'rrh! A'rrh! A'rrh!

MARCUS: Quiet, there! Look upon the prisoner!

PILATE: There stands the man.

CROWD: Crucify! Crucify! Crucify!

PILATE: Shall I crucify your king?

CHEER-LEADER: We have no king!

CROWD: A'rrh! A'rrh! Crucify!

PILATE: Silence!

(Noise dies down)

You hear that, Caiaphas, "We have no king". Will you stand by that, you Priests? . . . Take down their answer, Marcus—Caesar will be interested. . . . Speak, Caiaphas. . . .

CAIAPHAS *(slowly)*: We have no king . . .

PILATE *(dangerously)*: Aha?

CAIAPHAS *(furious)*: We have no king—but Caesar.

PILATE *(with savage satisfaction)*: Ah! Caesar will be pleased to know it.

CAIAPHAS: Caesar will be pleased to know other things. This fellow calls himself a king. *We* deny it. Do *you* admit it?

SHADRACH: To claim the crown is treason to Caesar.

IST ELDER: If you let this fellow go, you are a traitor too. . . . Mark that, you soldiers! . . . You in the crowd there! How many of you are Roman citizens?

(Uproar and cries of "Treason!" *and* "Hail Caesar!"*)*

FLAVIUS: Pilate—it's madness. You can't go on. They'll denounce you to Rome.

PILATE: Jews, hear reason. I have examined this man Jesus—

CROWD *(intoxicated with excitement):* Crucify! Crucify! Crucify! A'rrh! A'rrh! A'rrh!

PILATE *(to* MARCUS*):* Bring me water.... *(Shouting over the tumult)* Listen to me, you fools! Rome has nothing against this man. If you send him to the cross, it is your responsibility. Look, now!

(Water poured)

Bear witness, all of you! *I wash my hands of this case.* I am innocent of the blood of this guiltless man. On your heads be it.

CHEER-LEADER: We'll see to it, Pilate! You can't scare us! His blood be upon us and upon our children!

CROWD: A'rrh! A'rrh! Crucify! Crucify! Crucify!

(Fade out, as PILATE *goes inside)*

PILATE: They've beaten us, Flavius.... Give me the warrant.... For God's sake take this man away, and give them that brute, Barabbas.... Get on, Centurion, get on—What are you waiting for?

CENTURION *(woodenly):* The label, sir, for the cross.

PILATE: Oh, yes—the title and accusation ... *(writing)* Yes. Take this and let them all see it.... I'll show these swine what I think of them.

THE EVANGELIST: Then they took Jesus and led him away to be crucified. And over his head, this superscription written, in Hebrew and Greek and Latin: "Jesus of Nazareth, the King of the Jews". Then said the chief Priests unto Pilate: "Write not, *The King of the Jews,* but that he said, '*I am the King of the Jews*'." Pilate answered: "What I have written, I have written".

KING OF SORROWS

CHARACTERS

The EVANGELIST.
CAIAPHAS, High Priest of Israel.
SHADRACH } Members
NICODEMUS. { of
JOSEPH OF ARIMATHAEA. { Sanhedrim.
ELDER. }
JESUS.
JOHN BAR-ZEBEDEE, disciple to Jesus.
MARY VIRGIN.
MARY CLEOPHAS.
MARY MAGDALEN.
BARUCH the ZEALOT.
GESTAS. }
DYSMAS. } Robbers.
SIMON of CYRENE.
CENTURION ("Marcellus"). }
CHILIARCH. { Roman
ADJUTANT ("Bassus"). { Soldiers.
PROCLUS. }
CAIUS PONTIUS PILATE, Governor of Judaea.
CLAUDIA PROCULA, wife to Pilate.
PHOEBE. }
CALPURNIA. { Romans of
FLAVIUS. { Pilate's
GLAUCUS. } household.
BALTHAZAR, King of Ethiopia.
1st SOLDIER. }
2nd SOLDIER. { of the
3rd SOLDIER. { 1st Quaternion.
4th SOLDIER }
1st SOLDIER. }
2nd SOLDIER. { of the
3rd SOLDIER. { 2nd Quaternion.
4th SOLDIER. }
1st MAN.
2nd MAN.
A BRUTAL VOICE.
1st WOMAN.
2nd WOMAN.
1st BOY.
2nd BOY.
CROWD.

281

NOTES

THE PLAY

The technical difficulty throughout has been the arrangement of perspective. Note that we begin with the crowd streaming along the road; then go and join the procession, which we subsequently follow, picking up the friends of Jesus where we left them at a point of vantage on the roadside and taking them along with us. A certain amount of crowd background on the phonograph should, I think, accompany us the whole way up the road.

In the scenes at Calvary, the action moves each time from the circumference to the centre: first the crowd, then the soldiers, then the group at the foot of the cross, then up to the crosses themselves. In Sc. II, Seq. 3, the two Maries and John carry this movement with them as they proceed from the crowd, through the soldiers, to the cross; and the same order is repeated in Seq. 5, and in Seq. 8.

The passages with the Maries and John have been slightly stylised, so as to keep a focus of restraint and dignity among the realistic brutalities of the soldiers and crowd, and to lead up to the lyrical and fantastical note introduced at the end, where Balthazar reappears to link this play up with the first of the series. In Sc. II, Seq. 3, Mary Magdalen's protests to the crowd are adapted from the Reproaches sung at the Good Friday Mass of the Presanctified.

THE CHARACTERS

JESUS—I have thought it best to add nothing whatever to the Seven Words from the Cross. This is hard on the actor, who has to make his effect each time "from cold", in about a dozen words. I have done my best to prepare him some sort of "entrance" in each case; and the two great cries—the *"eloi"* and the *"tetelestai"*—are solemnly ushered in by the Evangelist.

JOHN has one terrifically important moment in Sc. II, Seq. 5, where he has three lines in which to get across the ghastly implications of the *"Eloi, lama sabachthani"*. Otherwise, he is straightforward. The operative words for his state of mind are those in Sc. I: "My heart is dead. It died last night in the garden."

MARY VIRGIN—Restraint, dignity, strength—and that stillness and prenatural lucidity which sometimes accompany extreme anguish of mind. Her two big speeches in Scene I are spoken without any violent emphasis or emotion—the first with a sort of settled acceptance of the intolerable; the second with the clairvoyance of prophecy. She and John in their granite self-control are like pillars framing and supporting the wild luxuriance of Mary Magdalen's grief. (The effect is intended to suggest those pictures in which Our Lady and John stand upright on either side of the crucifix, while the dishevelled Magdalen crouches at the foot. Similarly, in the final

Calvary scene, there is the suggestion of a Pieta. Here Mary's words, "Give me my son into my arms", are an echo from *Kings in Judaea.)*

MARY MAGDALEN—Passionate, emotional, purely human, despairing. In her "wailing" at the roadside, and in the "reproaches" she wants a touch of the "keening" note which we used for the stylised "keening" of the Mourners in *The Light and the Life.* Without being in the least insincere, Mary tends naturally to dramatise her own grief a little—she sees all life dramatically. In her scene with the Centurion (into whose previous relations with her we need not go too closely) and the Soldiers we see again the old Mary who "danced and delighted them all with garlands of lilies in the red braids of her hair", deliberately recapturing the past in order to gain the present. In her last scene she is altogether collapsed, sobbing wildly and hysterically till soothed by Our Lady.

CAIAPHAS—This play is the apologia of Caiaphas. For once, he is completely sincere, and speaks as a true prophet. He puts his finger on the central weakness of Jewry, and his speech is that of a man who clearly foresees the failure of his own lifework. In his own way, he echoes Herod the Great at the end of *Kings in Judaea.* At this point, and at this point only, we ought to feel sympathy with Caiaphas.

NICODEMUS—As always, he wavers. He has the insight to glimpse a tremendous theological truth—but his reaction, as ever, is to cry "I dare not!" "Impossible!" and "How can these things be?"

JOSEPH OF ARIMATHAEA—He is not, I think, alert to theological truth. But he does, in a flash of imagination, see the "spiritual" truth about the Kingdom, with all its enormous social and political implications. He almost sees that whereas the way of Caiaphas is doomed to failure by its inherent limitations, the way of Jesus might have succeeded. . . . Ironically, he takes Caiaphas at his word about adapting himself to Rome, politely approaches Pilate to beg the body of Jesus, and so becomes Pilate's instrument for dissociating himself from the responsibility of guarding the sepulchre. . . . It is, of course, Joseph who reports to Caiaphas John's words about the rising from the dead (thus getting over an exegetical difficulty of which too much has been made by the critics of St. Matthew).

THE ROMANS—FLAVIUS, as we know, is Pilate's freedman; PHOEBE and CALPURNIA are probably slaves, but of the pampered and refined type who lived on terms of familiarity and almost equality with their owners. They represent, in fact, the *soubrettes* of French classical comedy, and are genteel, aping the manners of the fashionable. GLAUCUS, I fancy, is also a freedman—at any rate he is not above associating with Claudia's waiting-women. He is educated, vain, heartless, and full of airs and affectations. A very intolerable young man.

BARUCH is there, as he promised in *The Princes of this World,* to bid good-bye to Dysmas and Gestas—but as he is there incognito, his greetings are delivered in the guise of rough jesting. He is at his old game of fomenting ill-feeling against Rome; but across the fierce bitterness of his mood there breaks one great flash of generous enthusiasm—the man of action's admiration for sheer physical courage, even in a Messiah who has failed him.

THE ROBBERS—Coarse peasants, GESTAS, plain brute, foul-mouthed (so far as may be), vindictive, with a natural contempt for all the gentler virtues.

DYSMAS has the more engaging qualities of the 18th-century bully. He would adorn a Hogarth print of a Tyburn hanging.... I have affronted all the preachers and commentators by making his "Lord, remember me—" an act, not of faith, but of charity. It seems incredible that this robber who, so far as we know, had had no opportunity of close contact with Jesus or His teaching, and had certainly not been moved by what he knew of Him to any amendment of life, should have been so impressed by "the bearing of the Prisoner" as suddenly to conceive the idea, not of the Messianic kingdom, but of that spiritual kingdom which was a mystery to the disciples themselves until after the Resurrection. The wording of his phrase almost suggests a person asking for a place at court—it seems exactly what one would say to please and humour some one who imagined that he was Napoleon. If one looks at it that way, the request becomes an expression of pure human kindness, gratuitously offered out of the depths of acute physical suffering, and instantly recognised and accepted as such—"your charity to the harmless lunatic was literally and indeed charity to Me".

It then becomes easier to imagine that the answer and the accompanying look provide a "springboard" for a real act of faith and conversion. There is the dim apprehension of something unimaginable, bringing about an instant conviction of sin and of that which redeems sin, as the untutored mind gropes back to childhood and innocence. He is confused between the crucified man, of whose weakness it would be selfish to demand one added agony, and the eternal Christ, of whose strength he is half-aware, and with whose sufferings he seems to be mysteriously identified, so that in some strange way each is bearing the pain of the other.... but it is all too difficult for Dysmas—the only certain thing is the togetherness and the promise that is like the comfort of cool water....

SIMON OF CYRENE—I have not adopted the suggestion that he was an African, attractive as it is, since I do not want to anticipate the effect of Balthazar's African voice at the end of the play. I have therefore made him just a foreign Jew, come home for Passover—perhaps the very man we heard talking on the road in *Royal Progress*.

THE CHILIARCH—This young man is a commissioned officer—a patrician youth doing his customary period of military service as "captain of a thousand". (I have kept the classical title, since "colonel", to which it roughly corresponds, suggests to us a much older man—this lad is in his early twenties.) He is a pleasant "public-school" type, nicely and properly embarrassed at having to order the sixty-year-old Proclus about, and too inexperienced to deal with the veteran's distress, except by falling back on discipline and "K.R."—after which he returns thankfully to take refuge in the regimental sports programme.

THE CENTURION ("Marcellus")—The same who presided over the flogging in *The Princes of this World*. Much younger than Proclus—a man of 30 or so. Decent, sensible, soldierly, concerned to do his job with just so much brutality as is necessary and no more, and not to get into trouble. He can be sentimentally moved by Mary Magdalen's appeal (in both senses)—and off duty I dare say he is a bit of a lad. But he is not insensitive—the noontide darkness gets on his nerves, and he is glad when Proclus comes to relieve him.

SOLDIERS—Two separate quaternions are to be distinguished. All the men are much of a muchness, but it would be better to have two different sets of voices. They are carrying through a routine job in a routine way, and are not particularly savage about it, except, perhaps, IST SOLDIER of the First Quaternion, who is put out by having his eye blacked by Gestas, and disposed to take his annoyance out on Jesus.

PROCLUS—Quite straightforward and in character for the most part. At the end, however, the earthquake, and the meeting with Balthazar, coming on top of what he knows of Jesus, do drive home to him that there is something supernaturally queer about all this. There he is—the most decent, plain, practical person imaginable—yet involved in some huge web of destiny, stretching over more than 30 years, and touching eternity, as it were, at both ends. He is in the centre of the facts, yet only at the circumference of their meaning; still only an outsider and spectator. And from that position, this looker-on registers his opinion of the game—"Son of God he called himself—and so I believe he was". . . . Having done so, he must just turn to and carry on and deal with the visible people and events, with all the tact and decency and natural delicacy characteristic of the man.

CLAUDIA—She tells her dream very straightforwardly, not "acting" it, but just relating it. The terrifying thing about the dream is that nothing in it is obviously angry or menacing. Claudia reports the "Captain" as speaking quite simply and sweetly, as one would remind a child of a forgotten lesson—"Don't you remember? They crucified him. He suffered under Pontius Pilate" (Like saying—"Oh, but you know that. Everybody knows it. He came over in 1066.") The voices of the "Passengers" are merely repeating an established fact by rote; the unearthly "Voice" is quite bodiless and impersonal; the "winds and waves" are not emphasised; and only provide a background for the voices to grow out of; the whole thing scarcely rises above an undertone. It is all *taken for granted*, and that is what is so frightening.

For Claudia, the terror-point of the dream is that in some mysterious way it seems to menace her husband, to whom she is devotedly attached. Her emotional focus is now not Jesus but Pilate. It is *he* who is being softly and relentlessly condemned by gods and men.

CROWD—The crowd-characters call for no special remark, except that 2ND

WOMAN is another Hogarth type, and, if we only knew it, probably a trifle drunk. . . . THE WOMEN ("Daughters of Jerusalem") are sentimental and sloppy — the sort of people who "feel things dreadfully" and wallow in it — to the point at which, with a quite sublime egotism, they demand that Jesus should "console" them for his own sufferings.

SCENE I (THE ROAD TO CALVARY)

THE EVANGELIST: And when Pilate had delivered Jesus unto the soldiers, they took off the purple from him, and put his own clothes on him, and led him out to crucify him.

(Background noise of people passing)

IST BOY: Benjie! Sam! Come on! there's some chaps goin' to be crucified.

2ND BOY: Oo-er! Comin' up this way?

IST BOY: Yus. I got some rotten eggs to chuck at 'em!

2ND BOY *(whooping)*: Whee! Hurry up, everybody!

SHADRACH: Get away, you disgusting urchins!

ELDER: 'Morning, worthy Shadrach! Coming to see these men turned off? They've got a fine day for it.

SHADRACH: Too hot. Turn to thunder presently.

ELDER: No, there's a lovely breeze. Glorious weather. It's good to be alive.

SHADRACH: Ah, yes! *(sarcastically)* When you're old and ailing it's satisfactory to see strong young men being killed before their time. One likes to feel superior to somebody.

ELDER: Especially if "somebody" has been boasting that he is superior to death.

SHADRACH: Of course. We all fear death. It's very bumptious to pretend that death doesn't exist or doesn't matter.

ELDER *(acidly)*: If Jesus thinks that, now's his chance to prove it.

SHADRACH: And wouldn't you be annoyed if he did! Suppose he were to step down quietly from the cross and say, "You can't kill me. I've broken the curse of Adam and banished death from the world."—You would be simply furious.

ELDER *(alarmed)*: You don't think there's any danger of that?

SHADRACH: Danger?—No, I was only joking. Jesus will die, and so will you—what a comfort that is, to be sure! . . . Dear me! look at the crowd! Romans as well as Jews—quite a popular event. We'd better be getting along. . . .

PHOEBE: Oh, look, dear: there's Glaucus!

GLAUCUS: Why, Phoebe! and the fair Calpurnia too! May Venus and all her doves attend you! Hullo, Flavius! where are you all going?

FLAVIUS: To see the execution. Will you join us?

GLAUCUS: I'm sick of executions. When you've seen one you've seen the lot. If it was wild beasts or gladiators, yes!—Has Claudia given her ladies a holiday?

CALPURNIA: Claudia is sick, she has had bad dreams.

PHOEBE: She is troubled about the Jewish prophet. She sent us to see him and bring back word how he died. Pilate said Flavius might escort us.

FLAVIUS: Pilate has a fit of the sulks.

PHOEBE: He scowled all through breakfast, and boxed his slave's ears because a fly got caught in the honey. Then my lady burst out crying and went to her room, where she lies calling upon Apollo.

GLAUCUS: She has looked upon Pan in the moonlight. You should keep her bedroom curtains drawn. The full moon is unhealthy when it shines on a dreamer's face.

FLAVIUS: The Panic terror is on Pilate too. They said that Jesus claimed to be Son of God! Then Pilate trembled and asked him whence he came. But he was silent.

PHOEBE: Son of God? . . .

GLAUCUS: I've changed my mind. I'll come with you. There ought to be some novelty about crucifying a god. . . .

JOHN: Mary, Mother of Jesus, are you determined to go on?

MARY VIRGIN: To the gallows' foot, John bar-Zebedee.

JOHN: Speak to her, Mary, sister of Lazarus. Tell her she should not come.

MARY MAGDALEN: Dear Mother Mary, spare yourself. John is a man and I—I have lived in the world and seen many bad things. But for you it is very different.

MARY VIRGIN: Yes, Mary—it is different. All of you are his friends, but I am the mother who bore him.

MARY MAGDALEN: She will not heed me. Mary Cleophas, see if you can persuade her.

MARY CLEOPHAS: Mary, my sister! The sight will break your heart.

MARY VIRGIN: Mary Cleophas, have you forgotten the words of Simeon the Prophet? Three and thirty years ago he told me: "This child will divide all Israel, and his name shall be a scandal and an offence. Yes—and a sword shall pierce through your own soul also."—You see, it has all come true. . . . Look! Far down the road there is a little cloud of dust. Who will come up this flinty path to the scaffold?

MARY MAGDALEN: Our Master.

JOHN: Our friend.

MARY CLEOPHAS: The Holy One of Israel.

MARY VIRGIN: My child. When he was small, I washed and fed him; I dressed him in his little garments and combed the rings of his hair. When he cried, I comforted him; when he was hurt, I kissed away the pain; and when the darkness fell, I sang him to sleep. Now he goes faint and fasting in the dust, and his hair is tangled with thorns. They will strip him naked to the sun and hammer the nails into his living flesh, and the great darkness will cover him. And there is nothing I can do. Nothing at all. This is the worst thing; to conceive beauty in your heart and bring it forth into the world, and then to stand by helpless and watch it suffer. . . .

MARY MAGDALEN: How can you speak so calmly?

MARY VIRGIN: While we await the stroke, our minds are confused, wondering how it will come. But when once it has fallen, we are quiet, because there is nothing left to look for. Then everything becomes suddenly very clear—each fact distinct and lucid with its truth. . . . I know now what he is, and what I am. . . . I, Mary, am the fact; God is the truth; but Jesus is fact and truth—he is reality. You cannot see the immortal truth till it is born in the flesh of the fact. And because all birth is a sundering of the flesh, fact and reality seem to go separate ways. But it is not really so; the feet that must walk this road were made of me. Only one Jesus is to die today—one person whom you know—the truth of God and the fact of Mary. This is reality. From the beginning of time until now, this is the only thing that has ever really happened. When you understand this you will understand all prophecies, and all history. . . .

IST MAN: Who are the two men that are to die with him?

BARUCH: The robbers, Dysmas and Gestas.

2ND MAN: You see what a world we live in, where robbery and righteousness go to the cross together.

IST WOMAN: That's true. Jesus was a good man.

IST MAN: He was a blasphemer. The Sanhedrim did well to condemn him. He was more dangerous than any robber.

BARUCH: Dysmas and Gestas are not condemned for robbery, but for sedition against Rome. Jesus is not condemned for blasphemy, but for sedition against Rome. The wise fools of the Sanhedrim have made themselves the catspaws of Caesar.

2ND MAN: Stranger, who are you that speak so rashly? . . . *(In a low tone)* I think you are Baruch the Zealot.

BARUCH *(in a low tone)*: Lock that thought in your heart, and throw away the key.

(CROWD noise approaches)

(aloud) Look now! here they come—each man staggering beneath the weight of the bloody Roman cross—a fine burden for a Jewish back! Each man labelled with his name and the name of his offence. . . .

(Noise louder)

Read the titles: "Gestas: Robber and Rebel"—rebel against whom? Against Caiaphas?

IST MAN: Against order and the nation.

IST WOMAN: What a dreadful brute he looks!

2ND WOMAN: A hulking ruffian! I love a brave bully!

CROWD: Beast! . . . robber! . . . murderer! . . . Stones! . . . Stones! . . . Take that, you dirty thief. . . . Hurray! got him on the mouth! . . . Good shot! . . .

(Yells and laughter)

GESTAS: Hell seize you! The devil burn your bones, you lousy rats! If I could lay hands on you—!

IST SOLDIER *(impassively)*: Get on, fellow!

GESTAS: They've knocked my blasted teeth out!

IST SOLDIER: You won't need teeth where you're going. . . .

(Laughter)

Move on, will you!

BARUCH: Go on, Gestas! Give it 'em back! Use your mouth to spit with! . . .

(Laughter)

Look again. "Dysmas—Robber and Rebel"—robber to you, my friends, but rebel to Rome. . . . Hey, Dysmas, you old cattle-thief! Stealing again! What are you carrying there?

DYSMAS: A wooden horse with one leg.

(Laughter)

VOICE FROM THE CROWD: Why, you great fool! The horse should be carrying you, not you the horse.

(Laughter)

DYSMAS: I'll mount him at the road's end, cully, and look down on the ruddy lot of you.

(Renewed laughter)

2ND MAN: This fellow's a wag.

2ND WOMAN: He's well-plucked. I like 'em plucky. There's a flower for you, villain!

DYSMAS: Thank'ee, lass. I'd rather have a pint of beer.

(Laughter)

2ND SOLDIER: Oy! stir your stumps there!

DYSMAS: Excuse me, girls—I've got a date. Drive on, coachman, and to hell with Caesar!

2ND SOLDIER: Shut your mouth, fellow!

DYSMAS: I say, to hell with him! I'm a dead man, ain't I? I can say what I like! Down with dirty old Tiberias and his rotten empire!

(The CROWD mutter uneasily, not caring to associate themselves with this demonstration)

CENTURION: Whips, there! whips!

(They whip DYSMAS forward)

BARUCH: God save Jewry, where only the dead can speak freely! . . . Here comes the master-criminal, with all his sins on his head, "Jesus of Nazareth, King of the Jews"—do you relish the jest, good people?

IST MAN: It's a damned insult.

BARUCH: What can Jews expect but insult?

CROWD *(jeeringly)*: Hail, Jesus!... Hail to the crazy Messiah!... Fool!... Madman!... Carpenter!... Boo!

IST WOMAN: Poor soul! How white he is. He can hardly stagger along.

2ND WOMAN: He's got no spirit. Give me a jolly fellow who can laugh on the road to the gibbet.

CROWD: Come on, King of Israel! Do us credit! *(Laughter)* ... Give us a speech!... Prophesy! prophesy!... Give him a cheer, boys!... *(Booing and derisive yells)* ... Hosanna!... hosanna!... Palms for the mad Messiah!... Hey, lad! you've forgotten your donkey! *(Loud laughter and cat-calls)*

IST WOMAN: It's a shame to go on so.

2ND MAN: Only a week ago nothing was too good for him.

IST WOMAN: He's stumbling. He's going to fall.

IST MAN: No—he's set his teeth and gone on.

CENTURION *(shouting from a little way ahead)*: Oy, there! can't you get that man on faster?

3RD SOLDIER *(shouting)*: We'll try if you like, Centurion. But he's been down once already. *(To JESUS)* Come on now, put your back into it.

IST WOMAN: He's shaking his head, poor thing.

BARUCH *(explanatory)*: To get the sweat out of his eyes.

2ND WOMAN *(viciously)*: I hate a weakling.... Get on, with you!... Be a man ...

BARUCH: Hold your tongue, you shrieking harridan! You don't know a man when you see one.... To bear the unbearable—to go on when the thing is impossible—that's courage.... *(In a great shout, and with the utmost sincerity)* Hosanna, Son of Man! Hosanna!

JOHN: Mary, Mother of Jesus, be brave—they are coming.

MARY VIRGIN: I shall not give way, John bar-Zebedee.

JOHN: Prepare yourself. Gaze first on these two robbers, that you may see how men look when they are going to the cross.

MARY VIRGIN: God help you, poor lads!

MARY MAGDALEN: Three men—but where is our Master?—Oh, God! John—is that he?

MARY VIRGIN: Jesus, my son!

MARY CLEOPHAS: He didn't answer. He didn't look at you.

JOHN: He cannot, Mary Cleophas. He is walking blind. If he turned his head, he would fall.

MARY VIRGIN: Be still, sister, be still. We have no need of words, my son and I.

MARY MAGDALEN: I never thought he could look like that. *(Wailing)* O swift feet! O strong hands! O face that was the beauty of Israel! Where are the lips that laughed away our sorrow? Where is the voice that called back Lazarus from the grave? Kneel down, kneel down with me! Throw dust upon your heads! for the light of the world is gone out.

JOHN: Come, Mary.

MARY MAGDALEN: Are you not ashamed to stand upright when the lord of love is brought so low? Where is your heart, John bar-Zebedee?

JOHN: My heart is dead. It died last night in the garden. I can feel nothing.

MARY VIRGIN: Rise up, Mary my daughter. We must be strong for his sake.

CROWD: See where he goes, the crazy prophet! ... the saviour of Israel! ... the son of David! ... the Man born to be King!

(Booing and laughter)

MARY MAGDALEN: O cruel! cruel! Is there no grace in Israel? No hand to help? No heart to pity?

JOHN: Yes, there is one. Look! A poor woman has stepped forward with a handkerchief, and wiped the sweat from his forehead.

MARY VIRGIN: Oh, that was kindly done. I must speak to her.... Madam, I am his mother. I thank you. It will be remembered in the Kingdom.

CROWD: Listen to that! ... What kingdom? ... The woman's as crazy as he is!

(Outburst of noise ahead)

Oy! what's happened? ... He's fallen.... Get out of the way.... Let's have a look....

CENTURION *(shouting)*: Come on! come on! What's the matter now?

3RD SOLDIER: Prisoner's down again, Centurion.

CENTURION: Well, don't stand staring. Get him on his legs again.

CROWD *(helpfully)*: Chuck a bucket of water over him.... Let him get his breath back.... Give him a drink.... He's only shamming.... Take the whip to him....

CENTURION: Stand back, there!

BRUTAL VOICE: Come on, magician! Do your stuff! Take up your cross and walk!

(Laughter)

4TH SOLDIER: Nothing doing, Centurion. He's all in.

CENTURION: Sure? Let's have a look at him.... Now, my man, it's no good trying it on.... No, Publius, you're right.... Let him be a moment.

3RD SOLDIER: I think we flogged him too hard.

CENTURION: M'm. That's the worst of those well-plucked 'uns. They stick it out, and you think they can take it—and then they collapse on you afterwards.

4TH SOLDIER: He's coming round.

CENTURION: That's a mercy. If he died on our hands we'd be for it. Law says they must be crucified alive—*(sotto voce)*—poor devils!

SIMON OF CYRENE *(shouting from the crowd)*: And a wicked law it is! Roman law. Bloody and cruel. There was no such law in Israel before the Romans came.

(Sympathetic reaction from CROWD)

CENTURION: Quiet, there!

SIMON: I've seen enough of your law in Africa. I come back home to keep Passover—and here it is, defiling the very Feast.

CENTURION: That'll do, my lad! You Jews! You'll stone and burn and strangle—but that don't shed blood, so you call it civilised. A pack of hypocrites! . . . Can he walk now? . . . Wait . . . steady . . . give him a hand, he can't see where he's going.

3RD SOLDIER: What's he groping about for?

4TH SOLDIER: He's stretching out his hands for the cross.

3RD SOLDIER: Well, I'll be—

(The SOLDIERS *laugh, not unkindly)*

CENTURION: This is the most willing prisoner I ever saw. Goes like a lamb to the slaughter.

SIMON: Slaughter's the word for it!

3RD SOLDIER: All right, prisoner. What's the hurry? You'll get it fast enough.

(They laugh again)

CENTURION: Nonsense. He can't carry it. We'll have to find somebody—somebody with a hefty pair of shoulders. Here! where's that fellow that was bawling so loud?—Yes, you! What's your name?

SIMON: Simon. I come from Cyrene.

CENTURION: Well, lay hold of this and carry it—see? By the time you've lugged it up the hill you'll have no breath for bawling. Come on, now. No back-chat.

SIMON: I'll see you damned first!—*(With a sudden change of tone)* All right, I'll carry it for him.

CENTURION: That'll teach you to be so dashed sympathetic. . . . Now then, prisoner! We've taken the weight off you. . . . Can you manage now? . . . All right, then. . . . Carry on there!

(Fade CROWD *out and in again)*

JOHN: Mary, Mother of Jesus, give me your hand. We are nearing the end of the road, and the way is steep and stony.

MARY: I have your strength to lean on—but he must go unaided.

MARY CLEOPHAS: He is walking firmly now, sister. His head is lifted towards the hills.

JOHN: And the people have grown quieter. Perhaps they are feeling sorry. See! there's a group of women wailing and lamenting.

WOMEN: Alas! alas! . . . Poor man! . . . He preached so beautifully. . . . He spoke so sweetly. . . . He healed the sick. . . . He fed the hungry. . . . He was always so kind to children. . . . How sad, how sad to die so young! . . . Barely thirty years old, and handsome as young King David! . . . Cut off in the flower of his strength. . . . Oh, dear! oh dear! how sad it all is—I can't help crying. . . . Jesus! Jesus of Nazareth! We're all so sorry! . . . Speak to us! . . . Let us hear your voice again. . . . Comfort us, comfort us, son of consolation! . . .

JESUS: Daughters of Jerusalem, shed no tears for me. Weep for yourselves and for your children. For the time is coming when they will say, "Happy is the woman that never bore a child, and the empty arms that have no one to love or care for". And they will flee to the hills; and creep into the earth for hiding, and cry to the mountains: "Fall down on us! fall, and cover our misery!"

WOMEN: Alas! what kind of comfort is this?

JESUS: Do you weep for what you see now? The evil days are only beginning. If they do these things while the tree is green, what will they do when the timber is grown and seasoned?

WOMEN *(yielding to the spell of the voice)*: Have pity, Jesus, have pity! Lord, have mercy upon us!

CENTURION *(asserting his authority)*: That'll do, my man, that'll do. If you can talk you can walk. Get on with it.

(The procession moves on)

SCENE II (CALVARY HILL)

SEQUENCE I (AT THE FOOT OF THE CROSS)

THE EVANGELIST: And when they were come to the place which is called Calvary, there they crucified him, and the robbers, one on the right hand and the other on the left.

IST SOLDIER: Whew! . . . well, that's two of 'em.

2ND SOLDIER: That Gestas is a sturdy rogue. We had to break his fingers to make him open his fists.

3RD SOLDIER: Yes—he put up a stiff fight. You'll have a black eye, Corvus.

(Laughter)

IST SOLDIER *(vindictively)*: He'll ache for it. We strung him out tight as a bowstring.

2ND SOLDIER: Come on, come on, let's have the next . . . got him stripped?

3RD SOLDIER: Yes. Here you are.

4TH SOLDIER: This one won't give trouble.

3RD SOLDIER: Dunno about that. He wouldn't drink the myrrh and vinegar.

IST SOLDIER: Why not?

3RD SOLDIER: Said he wanted to keep his head clear.

IST SOLDIER: If he thinks he can make a get-away—

4TH SOLDIER: Ah! he's only crazy. *(Persuasively)* Here, my lad—don't be obstinate. Drink it. It'll deaden you like. You won't feel so much. . . . No? . . . Well, if you won't you won't. . . . You're a queer one, ain't you? . . . Come on, then, get down to it.

IST SOLDIER *(whose temper has been soured by the black eye)*: Kick his feet from under him.

2ND SOLDIER: No need. He's down. . . . Take the feet, Corvus.

IST SOLDIER: Stretch your legs. I'll give you king of the Jews.

2ND SOLDIER: Hand me the mallet.

JESUS: Father, forgive them. They don't know what they are doing.

(His voice breaks off in a sharp gasp as the mallet falls. Fade out on the dull thud of the hammering)

SEQUENCE 2 (THE HIGH PRIEST'S HOUSE)

NICODEMUS: Is your mind at ease about this matter, my Lord Caiaphas?

CAIAPHAS: Why not, Nicodemus?

NICODEMUS: I will not argue with you about the person of Jesus. His attitude at his trial has shaken me. I was ready to believe him a great teacher, a great prophet, perhaps the Messiah. I can do so no longer. He has claimed to be the Son of God—not in a figure, but literally—the right hand of the power and equal partner in the glory. That is either an appalling blasphemy, or else a truth so appalling that it will not bear thinking of.

CAIAPHAS: Are you saying that it might be truth?

NICODEMUS: I dare not. For in that case, what have we done? We have conspired in some unimaginable manner to judge and murder God.

CAIAPHAS: Just so. You have only to state the case to expose its absurdity. God is one, and God is spirit. Do you think there is a host of gods and half-gods walking the earth, and subject to human frailty, as in the disgusting fables of the heathen?

NICODEMUS: No.

CAIAPHAS: Then what have you to object to? Or you, Joseph of Arimathaea?

JOSEPH: Not the deed so much as the manner of it. Was it necessary, most Venerable, to lick the feet of Rome in public? admit the sovereignty of Caesar?

NICODEMUS: Was it wise to threaten Pilate with the Emperor? The power you invoked against Rome was still Rome.

JOSEPH: There is but one way with Rome—to slam the door against her; for let her squeeze in so much as a finger, and she will follow with the whole arm, till Jewry is no longer Jewry.

CAIAPHAS: Joseph and Nicodemus, let me tell you something. Jewry has gone for ever. The day of small nations is past. This is the age of empire. Consider. All through our history we have tried to slam the door. Jewry was to be a garden enclosed—a chosen race, a peculiar people. But the door was opened. By whom?

NICODEMUS: In the strife between the sons of Alexander, when Hyrcanus appealed to Rome.

CAIAPHAS: True. That strife brought us Herod the Great—the creature of Rome, who for thirty years held Jewry together in his gauntlet of iron. And when he died, what? New Strife,—and the partition of Israel, with Pilate the Roman made Governor of Judaea. Under Herod a tributary nation; after Herod, three tributary provinces. With every Jewish quarrel, Rome takes another stride. One stride—two strides—the third will be the last. . . . I have killed this Jesus, who would have made more faction; but for one pretender crucified, fifty will arise. . . . One day, the Zealots will revolt and the sword will be drawn against Caesar. Then the ring of fire and steel will close about Jerusalem; then the dead will lie thick in the streets, and the tramp of the Legions will be heard in the inner Sanctuary of the Temple. I, Caiaphas, prophecy.

JOSEPH (impressed): What would you have us do?

CAIAPHAS: Accept the inevitable. Adapt yourselves to Rome. It is the curse of our people that we cannot learn to live as citizens of a larger unit. We can neither rule nor be ruled; for such the new order has no place. Make terms with the future while you may, lest in all the world there be found no place where a Jew may set foot.

JOSEPH: Strange. You echo the prophecies of Jesus. But he, I think, would have enlarged the boundaries of Israel to take in all the world. "They shall come", he said, "from east and west and sit down in the Kingdom of God." Samaritans, Romans, Greeks—he received them all. . . . Is it possible that he saw what you see, and would have chosen to fling the door wide open? Not to exclude, but to include? Not to lose Israel in Rome, but to bring Rome into the fold of Israel?

NICODEMUS (shocked): Impossible! Israel can have no dealings with the Gentiles. He must have been mad to imagine—

CAIAPHAS (drily): Quite mad. It is the duty of statesmen to destroy the madness which we call imagination. It is dangerous. It breeds dissension. Peace, order, security—that is Rome's offer—at Rome's price.

JOSEPH (gloomily): We have rejected the way of Jesus. I suppose we must now take yours.

CAIAPHAS: You will reject me too, I think. . . . Be content, Jesus, my enemy. Caiaphas also will have lived in vain.

SEQUENCE 3 (AT THE FOOT OF THE CROSS)

(Excited CROWD-noise, out of which VOICES emerge)

VOICES: Who was going to destroy the Temple and build it in three days? ... Looks as though the Temple 'ud see you out! ... Come to that, why don't you destroy the cross? ... Split the wood, melt the iron ... that's nothing to a fellow who can overthrow the Temple. ... Go to it, miracle-man! ... Show us your power, Jesus of Nazareth. ...

MARY MAGDALEN: Is it nothing to you, all you that pass by? What has he done to you that you should treat him like this?

VOICES: He said he was the Messiah. ... King of Israel. ... Son of David ... greater than Solomon. ... Does Israel get her kings from the carpenter's shop? ... or out of the common gaol? ... Will you reign from the gibbet, King of the Jews?

MARY MAGDALEN: He would have made you citizens of the Kingdom of God—and you have given him a crown of thorns.

VOICES: Where are all his mighty works now? ... He saved others, but he can't save himself. ... Come on, charlatan, heal your own wounds. ... If you are the Son of God, come down from the cross.

MARY MAGDALEN: He gave power to your hands and strength to your feet—and you have nailed his hands and feet to the cross.

VOICES: Are you hungry, are you thirsty, Jesus of Nazareth? ... Where's the water you talked about? ... Where is the never-failing bread? ... Nothing up your sleeve now, conjurer? (Laughter) Loaves and fishes! Loaves and fishes!

MARY MAGDALEN: He fed you with the bread of Heaven and the water of life freely—and you have given him vinegar to drink.

VOICES: Charlatan! ... Sorcerer! ... deceiver! ... boaster! ...

MARY MAGDALEN: John—can't we get closer? It will be some comfort to him to have us near.

JOHN: I don't know if the soldiers will let us through. But we can ask them.

(CROWD background)

CENTURION: Pass along, there! pass along, please! ... Now then, my lad, stand back—you can't come any closer.

JOHN: Pray, good Centurion, let us pass. We are friends of Jesus of Nazareth.

CENTURION: Then you'd best steer clear of trouble. Take those women away. It's no place for them.

MARY VIRGIN: Sir, I am his mother. I implore you, let me go to him.

CENTURION: Sorry, ma'am. Can't be done. ... Corvus! keep those people moving! ... Now just you go home quietly.

MARY MAGDALEN: Marcellus—do you know me?

CENTURION: No, my girl. Never saw you in my life.

MARY MAGDALEN: Has grief so changed my face? ... Quick, you Maries, pull off my veil, unpin my hair! ... Look again, Marcellus! Is there another woman in Jerusalem with red hair like mine?

CENTURION: Mary of Magdala!

SOLDIERS: Mary!...Mary of Magdala!...Where have you been all this time, Magdalen?

MARY MAGDALEN: By the feet that danced for you, by the voice that sang for you, by the beauty that delighted you—Marcellus, let me pass!

MARCELLUS: Beauty! that's for living men. What is this dying gallows bird to you?

MARY MAGDALEN: He is my life, and you have killed him....

(The SOLDIERS *laugh)*

Think what you like—laugh if you will—but for old time's sake, let Mary of Magdala pass.

1ST SOLDIER: Oh, no, you don't, my lass!

2ND SOLDIER: Not without paying.

3RD SOLDIER: Sing us one of the old songs, Mary!

SOLDIERS: That's right!...Give us a tune....Sing, girl, sing!...Make us laugh, make us cry, Mary Magdalen!

MARY MAGDALEN *(distracted)*: My songs?...I have forgotten them all.... Wait....Wait....I will try....What will you have, lads? "Roses of Sharon"? "Dinah Dear"? "Home Again"?

SOLDIERS *(applauding)*: "Home Again"! "Home Again"!...S'sh!

(As MARY *sings,* SOLDIERS *and* CROWD *listen quietly)*

MARY MAGDALEN *(sings)*:

Soldier, soldier, why will you roam?
The flowers grow white in the hills at home,
Where the little brown brook runs down to the sea—
Come again, home again, love, to me.

(Here the SOLDIERS *join in the chorus)*

Pick up your feet for the last long leagues,
No more pack-drill, no more fatigues,
No more roll-call, no more bugle-call,
Company halt! and stand at ease.
Sunlight, starlight, twilight and dawn,
The door unbarred, and the latch undrawn
Waiting for the lad that I—

(She breaks down)

I can't go on.

CENTURION: All right, Mary....Let her through, lads...and the mother and the friend....That'll do....No more....Keep back, there....Move along, now, move along....Yes, Publius?

4TH SOLDIER: The prisoners' clothes, Centurion.

CENTURION: Oh, yes. They're your perquisite. Take 'em and share 'em out evenly.

SOLDIERS: Three pairs of sandals. . . . Four into three won't go. . . . We ought to have had Barabbas to make it square. . . . Who wants a cloak? . . . Me! . . . me! . . . You can both 'ave it. . . . Nah, then, don't grab. . . . fifty-fifty. . . . Tear it at the seam. . . . This tunic's full of 'oles. . . . Gestas, you mean thief! Why didn't you put on something decent?

GESTAS: May it rot your flesh, Roman dog. I wish it were steeped in vitriol. . . . Curse these filthy flies!

IST SOLDIER: Temper, temper! . . .

SOLDIERS: Ah! here's a nice bit of stuff—the Nazarene came from a good home. . . . Fair shares! fair shares!

4TH SOLDIER: 'Ere, wait a bit! It's a shame to tear it up. It's a lovely piece of wool and woven right through without a seam.

2ND SOLDIER: Toss for it, then.

3RD SOLDIER: Anybody got the dice?

IST SOLDIER: Here you are.

2ND SOLDIER: Luck, Lady Venus. . . . *(throws dice: laughter)* Hades! I've thrown the dog. Here, Publius. . . .

(The dice rattle again)

3RD SOLDIER *(humming to himself)*:
"Pick up your feet for the last long leagues . . . "

MARY VIRGIN: Jesus, my son, I am here—Mary, the Mother who loves you. The pain is sore, my darling, but it will pass.

MARY MAGDALEN: Jesus, Rabboni, I am here—Mary the sinner who loves you. Kneeling at the feet that I once washed with my tears. I will kiss them very lightly, for fear the touch should hurt you.

JOHN: Jesus, my lord, I am here—John bar-Zebedee, the friend who loves you. We ran away from you, Master. We refused the cup and the baptism, not knowing what we asked, and the places on your right hand and on your left have been given to these two thieves.

MARY MAGDALEN: Oh, look and see if there is any sorrow like this! The Master and King and Christ of Israel—crucified like a common felon!

GESTAS: Hold your tongue, blast you! Ain't hell's pains bad enough without all that caterwauling?—Tell 'em to shut up—d'ye hear!

DYSMAS: Aw, Gestas, leave him be. There's no 'arm in him. You and me was askin' for it. Broke the law and got what was comin' to us. But this poor blighter ain't done nothing. *(Whimpering)* Gawd! I got the cramps something cruel!

GESTAS: Christ and king—arr'h! a ruddy fine mess you're in, ain't you, with all your cant and pi-jaw? Slobbering about forgiving your enemies—I'd tear the throats out of the whole pack of 'em—and I'd start with you, you son of a dog!

DYSMAS: He's looney, that's all. Let 'im think he's Goddamighty, if it makes him feel any better. . . . You're all right, mate, ain't you? Of course you are. This 'ere's just a bad dream. One o' these days you'll come out in a cloud of glory and astonish 'em all. . . .

GESTAS: T'chah!

DYSMAS: There! he's smiling. He likes being talked to that way. . . . *(In a deeply respectful tone, humoring this harmless lunacy)* Sir, you'll remember me, won't you, when you come into your kingdom?

JESUS: Indeed and indeed I tell you—to-day you shall be with me in Paradise.

DYSMAS *(after an astonished pause and in a changed tone)*: You're not mad! . . . You're . . . I don't know what you are! . . . Don't look at me like that. . . . I been bad—bad all through—you don't know how bad. . . . Yes, you do; you know everything. . . . Near Jordan, I was born, near Jordan, and the water cool to the feet. . . . It's a long way, but you won't leave me. . . . Stay with us, Jesus, stay with us on the cross—go on looking at me. . . . I'm sorry—that's selfish . . . keeping your head upright—like red-hot pincers in your neck. . . . Give me the pain—it's all I'm fit for—but I think it's you that's bearing mine—somehow. I'm all muddled . . . and the water is cool to the feet.

(His voice dies away into a kind of muttering which sounds like delirium)

SEQUENCE 4 (THE ROMAN BARRACKS)

CHILIARCH: Well, Bassus, what is it? another chit?

ADJUTANT: Programme of the regimental sports, sir.

CHILIARCH: Oh, yes. I want to see that.

ADJUTANT: And by the way, sir—isn't it about time we relieved those chaps on Gallows Hill?

CHILIARCH: Eh? Oh! Yes. How long have they been on duty?

ADJUTANT: Since 6 a.m., sir.

CHILIARCH: H'm. Have we got a centurion we can send? Who is there?

ADJUTANT: Well, sir—there's old Proclus.

CHILIARCH: Proclus?

ADJUTANT: From Capernaum, sir. Attached for special duty during the Feast. Very reliable man, sir.

CHILIARCH: Right. Send him in.

ADJUTANT: Yes, sir. *(At door)* Orderly! Tell the Centurion Proclus he's wanted by the Chiliarch. *(Returning)* The boxing match should be pretty good, sir. I'd lay a few sesterces on Tiger Balbus.

CHILIARCH: Plenty of punch, but no style. Pompilius will beat him on points if he goes six rounds. . . . I see you've put Favonius down as a heavy-weight. I should have thought—ah yes!—this is Proclus, isn't it? . . . Centurion, I want you to take four men along to Gallows Hill to relieve Marcellus and his bunch. Keep the crowd moving—and see that the followers of this Jesus don't make a disturbance.

PROCLUS *(startled out of his military propriety)*: Gallows Hill, sir—I—I—I— *(recovering himself, in a stifled voice)* Very good, sir.

CHILIARCH: What's the matter, Centurion? You look as if you didn't like the job.

PROCLUS: Beg pardon, sir. You see, sir—I know the man.

CHILIARCH: What man? Jesus of Nazareth?

PROCLUS: Yes, sir. He was very decent to me, sir. Cured my batman.

CHILIARCH *(rather taken aback)*: I see. . . . I'm afraid there's no one else available. . . .

PROCLUS: I quite understand, sir.

CHILIARCH: Old legionary, aren't you?

PROCLUS: Yes, sir. Forty years service, sir. Drafted to the sixth. Seconded to King Herod's Guards, sir—seven years. Fifteen years active service in Germany. Remained on as a veteran. Ten years regionary in Galilee, sir.

CHILIARCH: Good record. . . . Well, Centurion, it's bad luck—but duty's duty, isn't it?

PROCLUS: Yes, sir. Sorry I forgot myself, sir.

CHILIARCH: By the way—the bodies are to be off the cross before sundown, because of the Jews' sabbath. If they're not dead by then, put 'em out. . . . All right, Centurion, carry on. . . . Damn it, Bassus, I hate ticking off these veterans. Forty years' service. Old enough to be my grandfather.

ADJUTANT: Yes, sir. . . . Queer thing—that Jewish prophet—making an impression on an old tough like that.

CHILIARCH: Extraordinary. . . . Well, well! what were we saying? Oh, yes— the heavy-weight contest. . . .

SEQUENCE 5 (AT THE FOOT OF THE CROSS)

CALPURNIA: What's the time, Flavius?

FLAVIUS: It must be close on noon.

CALPURNIA *(yawning)*: This is a very slow entertainment.

GLAUCUS: It's not meant to be quick.

PHOEBE: These coarse peasants don't feel things as we should. How long does it take as a rule?

CLAUCUS: Sometimes they linger on for three days.

CALPURNIA: That's absurd! We can't wait all that time.

GLAUCUS: Your man won't last so long. Three hours, more likely.

FLAVIUS: The god will die, then?

GLAUCUS: The god is dying. He has the marks upon him—the pinched nostrils and hollow face, sunken about the temples, and the skin dry and dusty like parchment. The countenance of death, as old Hippocrates taught.

PHOEBE: I can't see properly. It's coming over very dark.

CALPURNIA: The colour's gone out of everything—it reminds me of the day of the great eclipse.

FLAVIUS: It's a sort of blight, I think.

GLAUCUS: Perhaps the gods are angry after all.

FLAVIUS: Hadn't we better get home? We've seen all there is to see. The soldiers are looking at the sky and muttering. . . .

(Rattle of dice)

IST SOLDIER: Publius, you owe me fivepence. . . . What's happening to the weather? I can scarcely see the pips on the dice.

2ND SOLDIER: Better chuck the game. . . . How much longer are we going to stick here? I'm getting damned hungry.

4TH SOLDIER: What's it going to do? Rain?

IST SOLDIER: I wish it would. Stifling hot, and not a breath of wind. . . . I hate this beastly climate.

2ND SOLDIER: Better down here than up there. It's taken the kick out of Gestas, even. . . . Is the Nazarene dead?

3RD SOLDIER: Going home fast, I fancy. . . . I wish the relief would come. . . .

MARY MAGDALEN *(whispering)*: John, John—is it the darkness? or is there a change in his face?

JOHN: Yes, Mary—there is a change.

MARY VIRGIN: My son is dying.

MARY MAGDALEN: The whole world is dying. He is going out into the night and has taken the sunlight with him. He is so far, so far that our voices cannot reach him. O love, O love—will you not come again? . . .

MARY VIRGIN: Hush, he is trying to speak.

JESUS: Mother!

MARY VIRGIN: Yes, dear?

JESUS: Let John be a son to you now. . . . John—she is your mother.

JOHN: Yes, Master. I will take care of her. I promise.

MARY VIRGIN: And I will love him as though he were my own.

MARY MAGDALEN: He is dying. . . . I could not believe it. But he is dying.

(Pause)

JOHN: It grows darker and darker. . . . All the people are drifting away. . . . Soon there will be only the soldiers and ourselves. . . . When everything else has perished, love and duty still keep watch. . . .

(Silence. Then, from a great distance, the sound of a small troop of men marching. It comes nearer and nearer till it reaches the foot of the cross)

PROCLUS: Squad, halt!

(MARCELLUS steps forward to meet him and the two CENTURIONS perform the usual movements for changing the guard)

MARCELLUS: Proclus?

PROCLUS: Yes.

MARCELLUS: I am glad you have come.... Squad, 'shun.... by the left, march!

(*The first quaternion moves off. The tramp of their departing feet recedes to an infinite distance*)

THE EVANGELIST: And there was darkness over all the land until the ninth hour. And about the ninth hour, Jesus cried with a loud voice:—

JESUS: Eloi, eloi, lama sabachthani!

IST SOLDIER: Gods; what was that?

2ND SOLDIER: It startled me.

3RD SOLDIER: It was the Nazarene.

4TH SOLDIER: I thought he was dead.

PROCLUS: What did he say?

IST SOLDIER: I don't know, Centurion—he spoke Hebrew.

2ND SOLDIER: He called on Elias for help.

PROCLUS: Elias?

2ND SOLDIER: He's a national hero, or a demi-god of some kind, I think. Ask the young man there, he's a Jew.

PROCLUS: Young man, what did your master say?

JOHN: He said: "My God, my God, why hast Thou forsaken me?"—What horror could wring that cry out of him? He was always one with God.

PROCLUS (*worried*): If there was anything I could do—consistent with my duty, that is—

JESUS: I am thirsty.

PROCLUS: Have we any water?

2ND SOLDIER: Ah! let be. Perhaps Elias will come to help him.

IST SOLDIER: There's some vinegar here in the jug, Centurion.

PROCLUS: Better still.... Dip a cloth in it, and hold it to his mouth.

IST SOLDIER: I can't reach so far.

PROCLUS: Put it on the end of my cane.... It's so dark, I can hardly see his face.... Is he taking it?

IST SOLDIER: I can't tell.... I think he's going....

SEQUENCE 6 (THE GOVERNOR'S PALACE)

PILATE: Claudia, Claudia, tell me—what was this dream of yours?

CLAUDIA: I was in a ship at sea, voyaging among the islands of the Aegean. At first the weather seemed calm and sunny—but presently, the sky darkened— and the sea began to toss with the wind....

(*Wind and waves*)

Then, out of the east, there came a cry, strange and piercing . . .

(Voice, in a thin wail:

"Pan ho megas tethnéke—
Pan ho megas tethnéke—")

and I said to the captain, "What do they cry?" And he answered, "Great Pan is dead." And I asked him, "How can God die?" And he answered, "Don't you remember? They crucified him. He suffered under Pontius Pilate." . . .

(Murmur of voices, starting almost in a whisper)

Then all the people in the ship turned their faces to me and said: "Pontius Pilate." . . .

(Voices, some speaking, some chanting, some muttering, mingled with sung fragments of Greek and Latin liturgies, weaving and crossing one another: "Pontius Pilate. . . . Pontius Pilate . . . he suffered under Pontius Pilate . . . crucified, dead and buried . . . sub Pontio Pilato . . . Pilato . . . he suffered . . . suffered . . . under Pontius Pilate . . . under Pontius Pilate. . . . ")

. . . in all tongues and all voices . . . even the little children with their mothers. . . .

(Children's voices: "Suffered under Pontius Pilate . . . sub Pontio Pilato . . . crucifié sous Ponce Pilate . . . gekreuzigt unter Pontius Pilatus . . . " *and other languages, mingling with the adult voices: then fade it all out)*

. . . your name, husband, your name continually—"he suffered under Pontius Pilate".

PILATE: The gods avert the omen.
CLAUDIA: This day is like my dream, Caius—this darkness at midnoon. . . . Hark! What was that?
PILATE: Nothing, Claudia . . . there is nothing to hear. . . . Come away from the window.

Sequence 7 (AT THE FOOT OF THE CROSS)

THE EVANGELIST: And when he had received the vinegar, Jesus cried with a loud voice:
JESUS *(loudly)*: It is accomplished! *(softly)* Father, into Thy hands I commend my spirit.
THE EVANGELIST: And he bowed his head, and gave up the ghost.

(Earthquake)

And the earth did quake, and the veil of the Temple was rent in twain from the top to the bottom. And when the Centurion, and they that were with him, saw this, they were afraid.

(Earthquake repeated, and dying away. Pause)

SEQUENCE 8 (AT THE FOOT OF THE CROSS)

BALTHAZAR: Centurion!

PROCLUS: Sir?

BALTHAZAR: For whom are these gallows erected?

PROCLUS: Why, don't you know? ... I see by your complexion you are a foreigner. ... Two of the men are robbers. And the third is Jesus of Nazareth, whom they called the King of the Jews.

BALTHAZAR: Jesus, King of the Jews. Then the stars have led me aright—and I have found him as my dream foretold, by the tall tree on the hill. ... I think I recognize you, Centurion, though it is thirty years and more since we met.

PROCLUS: Indeed, sir? Where was that?

BALTHAZAR: At the court of King Herod.

PROCLUS: I remember. You are Balthazar, King of Ethiopia.

BALTHAZAR: I am. And there is the child that was born King of the Jews, at whose coming the great star shone.

PROCLUS *(astonished)*: Is that he? ... Herod told me to slay him and I refused. But you see they have killed him at last—and here I stand. ... Son of God he called himself—and so I believe he was.

BALTHAZAR: King of the Jews; king of the world; king of Heaven. So it was written; so it will be.

PROCLUS: As he died, the darkness lifted. It is very strange. ...

IST SOLDIER: Excuse me, Centurion.

PROCLUS: Yes?

IST SOLDIER: A Jew called Joseph of Arimathaea is here with an order from the Governor. He is to have the body of the Nazarene for burial. And you said that all the men were to be taken down tonight, so we broke the legs of the two robbers to finish them off, but as Jesus was dead already we left him as he was.

PROCLUS: Quite right.

IST SOLDIER: Yes, Centurion. But that young woman is hysterical and clinging to his knees—

PROCLUS: I'll come. ... Good evening, sir. You are Joseph of Arimathaea, I take it. Very good. ... Now, my girl, I'm sorry—you don't want him left hanging there, do you? We're going to take him down, and this kind gentleman will see him properly done by.

MARY MAGDALEN: Go away—don't touch him! He's not dead! Jesus! Lord! Master! Speak again! Tell them you are alive!

JOHN: Mary, Mary!

PROCLUS: Are you sure he is dead, you men?

2ND SOLDIER: He's dead enough, Centurion. But a spear-thrust will make sure. There!

PROCLUS *(angrily)*: What did you want to do that for?

MARY MAGDALEN: Oh! what have you done! He is living! See how the blood runs down.

PROCLUS: No, my poor lass! If he were living, the blood would leap—but this creeps dark and sluggish, clotting as it falls. He broke his heart, I think, in that last cry. . . . Excuse me, ma'am, but we must do our job—can you do anything with her?

MARY VIRGIN: Mary, my dear—come to me. There, there! . . . You will handle my son gently, Centurion?

PROCLUS: We will, ma'am. You are a brave woman.

JOHN: Mary—let me tell you a thing that he once said to us. . . . Are you listening? . . . He said, "The Son of Man is only a week-end guest in the house of death. On the third day he will rise and go."

JOSEPH: Did he say that indeed?

JOHN: He did, sir. I do not know what he meant.

PROCLUS: Carefully, men, carefully. . . . lower him by the knees and shoulders . . . . Have you the winding-sheet ready?

MARY VIRGIN: Give me my son into my arms. . . . I know you, King Balthazar. These are the baby hands that closed upon your gift of myrrh. This is the fair young head, crowned once with gold by Melchior, but now with thorns to be a king of sorrows. The third gift is yet to come.

JOHN: What was the third gift, Mother?

MARY VIRGIN: Frankincense.

THE EVANGELIST: Now in the place where he was crucified, there was a garden; and in the garden a new sepulchre, wherein was never man yet laid. There laid they Jesus; and they rolled a great stone to the door of the sepulchre. And the sabbath drew on. And the Chief Priests and Pharisees came together to Pilate.

SCENE III (THE GOVERNOR'S PALACE)

PILATE *(abruptly)*: Yes, Caiaphas. What is it now?

CAIAPHAS: Excellency, that lying charlatan Jesus of Nazareth—

PILATE: I want to hear nothing more about Jesus of Nazareth.

CAIAPHAS: Something has just come to our knowledge. During his lifetime, it seems, he boasted that if he were killed, he would rise again on the third day. It is surely advisable that the tomb should be carefully guarded. Otherwise, some of his followers may steal the body and give out that he has risen from the dead—thus starting a new superstition, infinitely more damaging than the first.

PILATE: Well?

CAIAPHAS: I suggest that you order sentries to be posted.

PILATE: It has nothing to do with me.

CAIAPHAS: The bodies of criminals are Roman property.

PILATE: A member of your Sanhedrim applied to me for the custody of this particular body. I was happy to oblige him. The thing has now become a Jewish affair. Rome is not concerned.

CAIAPHAS: Excellency —

PILATE: You have your own guards. Take whatever precautions you think fit. . . . Slave! Show these gentlemen out.

(A party of SOLDIERS *passes in the distance, singing)*

. . . "No more pack-drill, no more fatigues,
No more roll-call, no more bugle-call. . . . "

THE EVANGELIST: So they went, and made the sepulchre sure, sealing the stone and setting a watch.

THE KING COMES TO HIS OWN

CHARACTERS

The EVANGELIST.
JESUS.
JAMES BAR-ZEBEDEE.
JOHN BAR-ZEBEDEE.
SIMON PETER.   Disciples and
ANDREW BAR-JONAH.   apostles of
PHILIP.   Jesus.
NATHANAEL.
MATTHEW, the Tax-Collector.
THOMAS DIDYMUS.
SALOME, mother to James and John.
CLEOPHAS.   Disciples
MARY CLEOPHAS, his wife.   of Jesus.
MARY MAGDALEN.
CAIAPHAS, High Priest of Israel.
SHADRACH.
NICODEMUS.
JOSEPH OF ARIMATHAEA.   Members
IST ELDER.   of
2ND ELDER.   Sanhedrim.
3RD ELDER.
4TH ELDER.
ELIHU, Captain of the Temple Guard.
JOEL, a Levite.
A FLOWER-GIRL.
EUNICE, a Syro-Phoenician woman.
CAIUS PONTIUS PILATE, Governor of Judaea.
CLAUDIA PROCULA, wife to Pilate.
FLAVIUS, freedman to Pilate.
A ROMAN GUARD.
GABRIEL.   Archangels.
RAPHAEL.
A SLAVE.
LICTORS.

NOTES

The problem here has been to present, in one way or another, no fewer than nine supernatural appearances, without tedious repetition, and without suggesting either Surrey melodrama or the more lily-livered kind of Easter card. The treatment has been varied as frequently as possible between narrative and direct presentation; and an attempt has been made to distinguish between two elements which appear mingled in the narratives about the Risen Body—a queerness on the one hand and an odd kind of homeliness on the other. Though It appeared and vanished in a startling manner, and though Its identity was never immediately recognisable, the Body does not seem to have surrounded Itself with any atmosphere of numinous horror, and indeed took pains to establish Its essential humanity, by eating and allowing Itself to be handled. Only at Its appearance by the Sea of Galilee (presumably towards the end of the 40 days, when It was preparing to leave the earth) does the queerness become dominant over the homeliness.

As against this, the Angels seem on at least two occasions to have established a genuine supernatural awe—the women at the tomb "were afraid and bowed down their faces" and the "keepers trembled and were as dead men".

I have tried to set the key for this in the remark made by the Levite Joel: "The thing (the Risen Body) that passed us in the garden was human, but this (the Angel) was not".

Mechanics of the Resurrection: While it is unnecessary, either for faith or morals, to have any fixed views on the physical mechanism of the Resurrection, it is better for the artist to have some sort of consistent picture in his mind. The operative elements in the problem are (1) the open sepulchre, (2) the undisturbed grave-clothes. Why this conjunction?

(1) It seems clear that the rolling back of the stone by the Angel was not done to let the Body out. A form that could pass through barred doors or vanish into thin air from the supper-table was not going to be baulked by a few hundred-weight of stone. The door was opened in order to draw the attention of the guards and the disciples to the fact that the Body was gone.

(2) But since the removal of the stone destroyed the evidence of the unbroken seals and lent itself to a naturalistic explanation of the miracle, the grave-bands were left still in their windings for inspection.

Consequently, we can presume that when the Angel rolled back the stone, it was to disclose the tomb *already empty.*

We may therefore suppose that the physical body was, as it were, dissolved into its molecular elements, drawn out through the grave-clothes and through the stone, and reassembled outside—this phenomenon being (not surprisingly) accompanied by a violent "electrical" disturbance, perceptible as a kind of earthquake.

This, at any rate, is the picture which I have tried to give. The guards feel the tremors, and, on touching the stone, are sensible of some sort of molecular disturbance; and in the next moment this "electric storm" passes out through the stone, flinging them apart with the shock. At nine feet the Body is materialised sufficiently to flatten the flame of the torch as It passes over it. At thirty paces, It is already assembled into form and solidity.

There is no reason to imagine that the Body was obliged always to carry Its original physical components about with It. Presumably It could build Itself up from any atomic material that happened to be handy. But the disappearance of the original earthly body was obviously necessary *as evidence.*

It is also clear that the materialisations were always rapid. There are never any slow twirlings and thickenings of gaseous matter, as in the ectoplasmic manifestations of the spiritualist seance. Nor do subsequent appearances seem to have produced any of the "electrical" phenomena that attended the first.

It seemed desirable to establish a terrestrial and commonplace background to this supernatural story by inserting a couple of ordinary human scenes—the Sanhedrim scene and the little scene before the Governor's house—showing the reactions of Jews and Romans to the Resurrection.

Otherwise, the only point to note is that this play contains a good deal about doors, and knockings at doors. It is, in fact, a play about the door between two worlds.

I have supposed that the Zebedees had some kind of lodging in Jerusalem and that this was the place to which St. John led Our Lady when "from that hour" he "took her unto his own home". This, therefore, provides a focal point from which Salome, Peter and John can set out for the sepulchre, after being joined by Mary Magdalen, who has come in from Bethany. I have also supposed that when "all the disciples" (except Peter and John) "forsook Him and fled" on the night of Maundy Thursday, they fled to Bethany. This would be their natural course, since they obviously would not dare to enter Jerusalem, and yet were sufficiently close at hand to reassemble *in* Jerusalem on the night of Easter Sunday. They would not, of course, know till Mary returned after the Crucifixion what had happened to Peter and John and the rest of the party and would be under the liveliest apprehensions. (How Mary came to be present at the Crucifixion we do not know—but presumably she rushed off to Jerusalem on the Thursday night when the nine remaining disciples stumbled back to Bethany with the news of their Master's arrest.) All this fits in very well with the various Resurrection stories, and seems quite reasonable in itself.

THE CHARACTERS

JESUS—What is said above about the two elements of queerness and homeliness in the Resurrection appearances more or less covers this part. I have used the words "My girl, what are you crying for?" instead of the formal "Woman, why do you weep?" in his address to Mary Magdalen, to establish the "humanity", distinguish him from the Angels, and give colour to Mary's mistaking him for the Gardener. The homely side is stressed again when he asks for food in Scene II, Seq. 2. As the Ascension draws nearer, the language becomes more definitely formal, remote, and Biblical, to produce a sense of gradual withdrawal.

I have kept the gradation, which is plain in the Greek, of the three questions addressed to Peter, with the difference in wording between the first two questions and the last, and having thus abandoned the symmetry of the A.V., I have altered Peter's replies accordingly, so as to emphasise the meaning and Peter's mounting distress. "Are you more my friend *than any of these?*" (i.e. you who said that if everybody else deserted me, you would not). "Indeed, Lord, you know I love you" (i.e. I can never again make that claim, and I dare not even call myself your friend, but you know I love you). "Are you in truth my friend?" "I love you, indeed I do" (i.e. but that other word is not for me). "Then you do love me a little?" (i.e. I accept your word, if that is all you dare say of yourself—but can I be sure of that, at least?)—"Lord you know everything—look into my heart and see." (Temple translates *agapas* "do you love?" and *phileis* "are you my friend?" but I have ventured to reverse this—"friendship" seems to me to suggest, in this context, something more on an equality than "love". "Are you devoted to me?" might be even nearer *agapas,* but has something a little smug about it.)

DISCIPLES AND FOLLOWERS—I have tried to distinguish carefully the various degrees of faith, sorrow, despair, etc. in the most important characters. It seems to have been a general rule that the *more* faith you had, the *less* you needed convincing by supernatural appearances. It was at moments of doubt that the reassuring evidences were offered, and I have made a special point of this in Scene II, Seq. 2.

THE MEN

JOHN—The Crucifixion has left him in almost as deep a state of depression as any of the rest. It is he and Mary Magdalen who have to sustain the most acute sense of human loss, and he has temporarily lost sight of the hope which lingered in his mind at the end of Play II. But it is still there, not very far under the surface. And his mind and heart are open—he is ready to "do the next thing", to give some thought to the problem of Judas and to do what he can for Peter—he is not selfish or self-absorbed. Consequently, the moment he hears that the body is gone, he is ready to believe. The sight of the grave-clothes convinces him instantly. "John needs no angel." . . . At the first appearance in Jerusalem (Scene I, Seq. 2) he is startled—not so much by the visitation itself as by the manner of it—and recovers almost immediately, to take the lead in treating the Risen Lord almost exactly as he would have treated the human Jesus. His first words are an apology for mere bad manners, and almost playful; his hesitation to grasp the extended hand arises not from fear of the supernatural, but from the knowledge that it bears the print of the nails; his protest about the demand for food is a perfectly simple and almost childlike acceptance of the new conditions— vanishing is a thing quite natural and to be expected, but he does hope it won't happen. (I have suggested that the vanishing at Emmaus is connected with the failure of Cleophas and his companion to recognize Jesus, and that where he is readily recognized and trusted, the Lord is prepared to stay.) . . . At the second Jerusalem appearance (Scene II, Seq. 4) John is prepared, and feels the presence of Jesus before he actually sees him. So also at the Lake of Galilee (Scene III), he has a pretty good idea who the Stranger is even before the draught of fishes makes it a certainty, and has to be exhorted to "wake up" and attend to the boat.

PETER—From what the others say of him, it is plain that his denial of his Master and the catastrophe of Good Friday have plunged him into a state of settled melancholia, so that his friends are really alarmed, and watch him closely lest he should commit suicide. From this torpor he is aroused by the call to action, and runs to the sepulchre, where he is able to take note of the disposition of the grave-clothes, but is too completely shattered to draw the right deduction. Also, absorbed in his own remorse and having altogether abandoned hope, he is not able (as John does not need) to see the Angels. Nothing less than a private and personal visitation is necessary to convince him. And one must suppose that whatever Our Lord then said to him was of a "sharp, stern and bracing" kind, for though, at the next two appearances, he has recovered his old faith and eagerness, he is still not fully reinstated in the old relations. Only at the end, when his three denials have been atoned by his threefold affirmation, is he comforted with the promise of martyrdom. Even the last word to him is a gentle rebuke. Let him not trouble about what John or anybody else is doing—let him still look to himself. (For the "threefold affirmation" please see what is said above, under JESUS.)

THOMAS—It is unexpected, but extraordinarily convincing, that the one absolutely unequivocal statement, in the whole Gospel, of the Divinity of Jesus should come from Doubting Thomas. It is the only place where the word "God" is used of him without qualification of any kind, and in the most unambiguous form of words (not merely *theos* but *ho theos mou* with the definite article). And this must be said, not ecstatically, or with a cry of astonishment, but with flat conviction, as of one acknowledging irrefragable evidence: "2 + 2 = 4", "That is the sun in the sky", "You are my Lord and my God".

JAMES is, I think, quite ready to believe, but he, too, requires evidence, and betrays a slight anti-feminine prejudice, not unusual in the young male. Perhaps this comes from having lived too much with Salome, or perhaps he is anxious that his little brother John should not buoy himself up with unfounded hopes and suffer disappointment.

MATTHEW is, as usual, quite human in his reactions; but he too has difficulties—this time of a psychological kind. The human aspect of the thing troubles him: he is shrewd enough to spot a difficulty which has bothered other critics since him. But once he is convinced, he is ready to accept the Risen Lord as simply as he accepted him in the days of his flesh.

CLEOPHAS has only to tell his story straightforwardly, without painting it too much, except at the moment when he describes how they recognised the wounded hands.

THE WOMEN

NOTE that, for the WOMEN, there is, on an occasion such as this, the consolation of being able to *act*. The male disciples are lethargic because they have come to a dead end; the women can occupy themselves with funeral details, and get a certain mournful satisfaction out of them. The bustle of preparing spices, of collecting towels and basins, of the early morning excursion—the contemplation of fine grave-clothes, a rich casket, a beautiful tomb—it all soothes and braces them. At births and deaths, women come into their own and can *do* something, while men can only sit about helplessly. Melancholy as it all is, the women are on top—it is *their* adventure.

SALOME—She is a nice, shrewd, sensible woman, with a fund of the human wisdom that belongs to mothers of families, who have looked after babies, and dealt with bereaved people, and laid out corpses all their lives. She is a determined sort of person, and inclined to take charge of any situation.

MARY CLEOPHAS—She is rather quieter and more timid than Salome, but placidly resolved to go on and do what has to be done. The suggestion that she was the "other disciple" in the Emmaus story comes from the Bishop of Ripon, and besides being charming and natural in itself, has the advantage, dramatically, that it avoids the sudden introduction of two totally unknown characters at a late stage in the story. It is supposed by some commentators that she was in fact the sister of Our Lady, and this makes it natural for her to be staying in the Zebedees' house, though she and Cleophas apparently lived at Emmaus. We may, if we like, suppose that Cleophas came into Jerusalem on Easter morning to fetch his wife and was escorting her home when the meeting with Jesus occurred.

These two women have a simple, ready faith of their own. They accept the message of the Angels, and the appearance of the Lord is not needed to convince them. Mary Cleophas is, however, not sufficiently in tune with Christ to recognize him instantly in his later appearance. These two are typical of a rather matter-of-fact, exterior kind of faith, without intimate religious experience—the sort that reads its Bible and gets on with its work, and yet is, just occasionally, "visited".

MARY MAGDALEN—She is still in a strung-up state of nerves. She has recovered from the violent hysteria of the end of Play II, and, with her usual passionate love of people and things, is able to laugh a little at Martha, to take a sympathetic interest in the other disciples, to give John wise and experienced advice about Peter, and to find dramatic satisfaction in the idea of tending the Lord's body. But it is all very much touch and go with her. Her love, as the Angel says, is still set upon "the mortal flesh she knew", she is living for the moment, for "the next thing", clinging to the comfort of performing those last services; and the disappearance of the body flings her into a state of agitation in which she can see no angels—she cannot *wait* to see them—she must run somewhere, fetch somebody, *do* something. Having done it, she abandons herself to grief and can't even pay attention to angels when she does see them. She has lost contact with the other world—she can only be reached by the Jesus who is of this world also.

CAIAPHAS—I think Caiaphas, in what he calls his heart, knows what he is up against. He is fighting a rear-guard action with superb coolness and the most unscrupulous skill. Cutting sarcasm, barely disguised menace, blackmail, bribery—he knows how to use them all to keep the Sanhedrim from stampeding. "A daring pilot in extremity" he is here at his most brilliant worst; and with cynical effrontery he does not even bother to pretend that the story he proposes to circulate bears any relation to the facts. . . . And he is beaten, for within a few hours somebody has talked, and the rumours are flying about the City.

ELIHU and JOEL—They have already told their story once; they have now pulled themselves together, and are making a coherent report. They must make it with precision and without excitement, for they are telling a thing difficult to believe, and they are rather on the defensive. They offer fact, details—so many paces, such and such dispositions, so much light—an orderly narrative with no more comment than is extracted from them by questioning. Until they come to the Angel, and then the uncanniness of the garden with its moonlight and torchlight and shadows creeps into their voices; the tone remains level, and the narrative steady—but "Somebody laughed"—"it was not human"—"the tomb was empty"; *numen est.*

NICODEMUS—In Play II, Nicodemus has glimpsed the theological truth about Christ, only to repudiate it, because it is a thing which his reason cannot admit and live. Now, the nemesis of a timid intellect has overtaken him. He is confronted with the unimaginable thing, and his reason cracks under the strain. There is no need to suppose that he becomes permanently insane, but for the moment he is mad, or inspired, or both. . . . The words "Son of God" pull, as it were, a trigger in his mind, and his shrill cry cuts like a knife across the wrangle that is going on. He keeps this note up as far as "Curse ye Meroz, saith the Lord!"—then sinks to a disjointed babbling. Then, prophetically and almost ecstatically, "Rise up, O Lord, into Thy resting-place. . . . " and finally, to the Sanhedrim, with menace and terror, he repeats the words of Christ at the trial, "And you shall see the Son of Man ... ", in the middle of which he collapses and is carried out.

JOSEPH OF ARIMATHAEA is of tougher stuff. In the last play he refused to take any line about the Divinity of Christ, and he can truthfully say that he never asserted it. He is, of course, the immediate object of everybody's suspicions, and reacts energetically under this stimulus. But he sees very well indeed what the effect of all this is likely to be; his last words are a challenge to Caiaphas, and the last words of Caiaphas are, in their way, an admission of defeat.

THE ELDERS—IST ELDER is belligerent as usual. SHADRACH, sarcastic as usual, amuses himself by playing his own little comedy with Caiaphas, 2ND ELDER is born out of his due time; he obviously has a bent for scientific explanations and for mystery fiction. "Vaporous exhalations" is a good suggestion, and Caiaphas adopts it (it is a pity that the good gentleman had not the advantage of being able to talk about "gases" and "electricity"; he would have made a great play with them). But the ingenious idea of substituting a new corpse is ruled out as impracticable to (I am sure) his great disappointment.

The whole Sanhedrim scene must be played swiftly and as high comedy (except, of course, for Nicodemus's lines).

THE ROMANS and EUNICE—This little scene needs no commentary, except to note the lyrical suggestion in the Flower-Girl's street-cry, and that Claudia's "Merciful Apollo!" is not a mere exclamation, but a real prayer for mercy to the god who was at once the destroyer and the healer of men.

THE ANGELS—Should be strongly stylised. I have kept their speech as close as possible to the Bible, thinking the formal style suitable to their angelic nature. In their conversation together they execute a reverent little anti-phon every time their Lord is mentioned, and hail his appearance with the murmuring of the Holy Name; all this should be quite quiet and done as, so to speak, a matter of heavenly routine.

The name Raphael should be given its full three syllables: Raph-a-el, just like "Gabriel".

SCENE I (THE TOMB)

THE EVANGELIST: On the first day of the week, very early in the morning, cometh Mary Magdalen to the sepulchre, with Mary Cleophas, and Salome the mother of James and John, bringing the spices that they had prepared.

SEQUENCE I (THE LODGING OF THE ZEBEDEES IN JERUSALEM)

(A soft knocking on the door)

JOHN: Is that you, Mary?

MARY MAGDALEN: Yes, John.

JOHN: Come in. My mother will be down in a moment.... How did you find them all at Bethany?

MARY MAGDALEN: With heart and spirit broken. But a little comforted to know that all of us were safe. They were dreadfully anxious, thinking you and Peter had been arrested, and wondering what would happen to your mother and Mary Cleophas, and the mother of our dear Lord, left unprotected in Jerusalem. Martha scolded me terribly for having run into danger, crying and kissing me all the time, and breaking off every few minutes to fly to the kitchen and cook some little tempting dish or other to comfort us.

JOHN: Dear funny Martha!

MARY MAGDALEN: And when we couldn't eat, exclaiming that she was a wicked woman, and had broken the Sabbath for us, all to no purpose! And Matthew said without thinking, "Don't you worry — the Sabbath was made for man—" and that just about finished us.

JOHN: I know. A familiar word — the echo of a laugh — it is like a stab in the heart. Yesterday I found a pair of old sandals, moulded by the feet that wore them. We hid them from Peter.

MARY MAGDALEN: Peter is here with you?

JOHN: Like a sick animal that has crawled home to die. He can't eat. He can't sleep. He can't forgive himself. *(With passionate self-reproach)* It was my fault. I knew he was frightened, yet I left him alone in the house of Annas. Dear Lord! was there none of us you could trust for five minutes?

MARY MAGDALEN: Poor Peter! He takes his failures hard.

JOHN: He calls himself a worse traitor than — I can't speak the name. It is like poison in me. I can't say our Master's prayer. "Forgive us our trespasses, as we forgive"—no, it's impossible.... You heard what became of him?

MARY MAGDALEN: Yes. John, you can't hate him worse than he came to hate himself. His self-hate murdered him.

JOHN *(slowly)*: If I hate him, I am his murderer too.... Oh, God! there is no end to our sins! Do we all murder Jesus and one another?

MARY MAGDALEN: John, dear, you don't hate Judas — not really. You can't

318

bear the idea of hurting him. You don't understand his sin or his despair, but that's because you've never been truly wicked. The Master's the only good man I ever met who knew how miserable it felt to be bad. It was as if he got right inside you, and *felt* all the horrible things you were doing to yourself. . . . But I don't suppose Judas ever let him in. He was too proud. I think it was harder for him than for people like Matthew and me and that poor robber on the cross. We know we're so awful anyhow that it's no good pretending we're not, even to ourselves. So it doesn't matter if other people come in and see what we're like inside.

JOHN: Blessed are the humble, and the wretched and the poor—

MARY MAGDALEN: And the lost sheep and the sinners. You know, when the Rabbi said that, he really meant it. . . . Don't fret too much about Peter. He's not proud. He'll never go the way of Judas. . . . Only, don't be soft with him. The Rabbi wasn't soft—he was sharp and stern and bracing, and never let you pity yourself. Peter must face what he did, and learn to put it aside and do better next time.

JOHN: What next time? Our Master is dead. When you anointed him in the house of Simon the Leper, it was for his burial, as he said. And here comes Mary Cleophas and my mother, bringing the spices that they have prepared. . . . Mother, Mary Magdalen is here.

SALOME: Good morning, Mary dear.

MARY MAGDALEN: Dear Salome. Dear Mary Cleophas.

MARY CLEOPHAS: God bless you, Magdalen. Mary the mother of Jesus sends you her love.

MARY MAGDALEN: How is she, poor lady?

MARY CLEOPHAS: Worn out with grief, but wonderfully brave and calm. She said very sweetly that she commended her son's body to our love. And she gave us this to take with us.

MARY MAGDALEN: Oh, but what is it? I never saw such a beautiful casket. The gold and jewels are fit for a king's treasure.

MARY CLEOPHAS: It came from a king's treasure. It is King Balthazar's gift of myrrh, that he brought to Jesus at Bethlehem. It has waited for him three-and-thirty years.

MARY MAGDALEN: It shall lie above his heart where the soldier's spear smote him. . . . I have brought aloes and cassia. . . .

SALOME: Palm-wine for the washing; cloves and balm of Gilead. . . .

MARY CLEOPHAS: Labdanum, camphire, nard, and oil of sandal and cedar.

MARY MAGDALEN: We shall need a basin.

SALOME: Here it is. And a comb and scissors. . . . Have we towels enough?

MARY CLEOPHAS: I think so. And a clean linen garment. And fresh gravebands.

MARY MAGDALEN: We shall find those at the sepulchre. Joseph of Arimathaea brought them; a new garment, white as snow; and we dressed our Master in it and swathed the long cloths about him and bound his head with a fine napkin. The richest nobleman could have no better.

SALOME: Take them, all the same. It is well to be prepared. . . . Are the gates of the city open? Mary, how did you get in?

MARY MAGDALEN: I made a little present to the watchman. He is expecting us and will let us out by the postern.

SALOME: Then we had best be starting. . . .

JOHN: I don't like your going alone. Hadn't I better come too?

SALOME: No, dear. We shall be safer without you. Nobody will interfere with three women bound on an errand of mercy. Besides, this is a woman's business.

JOHN: I wish there was something I could do. I feel so helpless and hopeless.

SALOME: It's always so, my son. Men make a bustle in life, but women wind the swaddling-bands and the grave bands for all of them. . . . Come and see us out, and bar the door after us.

JOHN (meekly): Yes, Mother. . . . The moon's still up. You'll be able to find your way.

MARY CLEOPHAS: And the sun will rise soon. It's close on cock-crow.

JOHN: That's a bad time with Peter. I must go up to him.

MARY MAGDALEN: That's right, John. Peter's your job. Do your best for him.

JOHN: I will, Mary. . . . (He unbars the door). . . . Wait a moment. . . . All's quiet. Not a soul in the street. . . . Go quickly, and God be with you!

(He bars the door again)

SEQUENCE 2 (FROM THE GARDEN TO JERUSALEM)

(The cocks begin to crow. Then the sound of three heavy earthquake shocks. Next, from a distance, the feet of men running in disorder. They draw near and die away. Then a heavy knocking, repeated with haste and urgency; and a frightened voice crying — "My Lord Caiaphas! My Lord Caiaphas!"*)*

SEQUENCE 3 (THE GARDEN)

MARY MAGDALEN: Salome! Do you think we could go on now?

SALOME: Yes, dear. The earth-tremors seem to have passed.

MARY CLEOPHAS: I'm not really frightened of earthquakes. What I didn't like was those Temple Guards dashing past. They looked as though they were coming from the Garden.

SALOME: Never mind. They've gone now.

MARY CLEOPHAS: There might be some more. . . . Let's go round to the other side. There's a back way in, near the gardener's cottage.

MARY MAGDALEN: Oh, yes! And then we shan't have to pass the—the crosses.

MARY CLEOPHAS: And this way's really quicker. Just round here and along the wall. . . . There ought to be a gate just about here. . . .

SALOME: I've found it . . . unguarded . . . and open.

MARY CLEOPHAS: Thank God for that. . . . Hush! . . . Don't let the latch click back.

SALOME: Which way now?

MARY MAGDALEN: Go on till you come to the well in the middle of the garden. . . . It's dark under these olive-trees.

SALOME: We shall soon be through them. . . . I don't think there's anyone about.

MARY MAGDALEN: If we hadn't been able to get in, I should have died. So long as one can *do* something, it keeps one from thinking. . . . At least we shall see our Master's face again and kiss his feet for the last time, and remember, when we are desolate, that our love was with him to the end.

SALOME (seeing that MARY MAGDALEN is losing her self-control): Yes, dear. But later on you will find it easier to think of him as he used to be. That is God's merciful way. We forget the still body and the cold, waxen face, and our dead are given back to our remembrance alive and happy. . . . Here we are at the well.

MARY MAGDALEN: Now along this winding path to the eastward. The tomb is cut from the living rock, with a tall cypress on either hand. And twining above the door — Oh, Salome!

SALOME: What is it?

MARY MAGDALEN: I had forgotten! The door is closed with a great stone. Who will roll it away for us?

MARY CLEOPHAS (dismayed): Oh, dear! We should have brought John after all.

MARY MAGDALEN: It took four men to set it in place.

SALOME (firmly): I'm not going to turn back now. We might get help from the gardener. He's sure to be about soon, and if —

MARY MAGDALEN (interrupting her): Oh, look! There is the tomb. . . . But the stone has been rolled away.

MARY CLEOPHAS: Somebody's been before us.

SALOME: Are you sure it's the right tomb?

MARY MAGDALEN: How could I ever forget? . . . There are the cypresses and the wild vine over the door —

SALOME: Perhaps Joseph of Arimathaea —

MARY CLEOPHAS: Of course, that's it.

MARY MAGDALEN (dashing off): I'll run ahead and see.

SALOME: It's sure to be Joseph. He wouldn't be expecting us to come, and he'd want to see things done properly. A good man. I believe this was his own sepulchre that he'd prepared for himself, and certainly it's a most beautiful —

MARY MAGDALEN (calling as she runs back to them): Mary! Salome! He's gone!

SALOME: Gone?

MARY CLEOPHAS: Who's gone?

MARY MAGDALEN: The Master!—there's no one there, and the body's gone! —He's been stolen!—They've taken him away!—Where is he?—We must find him!—Oh, Rabboni, Rabboni, what have they done with you?

SALOME *(who, with* MARY CLEOPHAS, *has been uttering little cries of dismay)*: But, Mary dear!

MARY MAGDALEN: Let me go! I must fetch John and Peter!

MARY CLEOPHAS: Wait a moment, Mary!

MARY MAGDALEN *(crying as she runs)*: Rabboni! Rabboni!—Where are you?

MARY CLEOPHAS: It's no good. You can't catch her. . . . This is very strange, Salome.

SALOME: She's made a mistake. She can't have looked properly.

MARY CLEOPHAS: We shall soon see. . . . Well!

SALOME: The tomb's been opened, that's certain.

MARY CLEOPHAS: And the body's vanished—that's certain too.

SALOME *(with a horrified gasp)*: Tomb-robbers?

MARY CLEOPHAS: Oh no! That's too horrible.

SALOME: The Master's body stolen!—what will his mother say?—And John! *(In sudden alarm)* Oh, Mary! Those two men there, in white.

MARY CLEOPHAS: They don't seem like robbers.

SALOME: They seem more like—I am afraid of them.

GABRIEL: There is nothing to be afraid of.

MARY CLEOPHAS: Sirs, whether you are angels or men—

RAPHAEL: Why look for the living among the dead?

SALOME: Alas, sir, we were looking—

GABRIEL: I know. You are looking for Jesus of Nazareth, whom they crucified. He is risen; he is not here. Behold the place where they laid him.

SALOME: He is risen?

RAPHAEL: As he said. Go now and tell his disciples—and Peter—that he has gone before them, to lead them as of old into Galilee.

GABRIEL: There shall you see him. That is the message we were charged to deliver.

SEQUENCE 4 (THE ZEBEDEES' LODGING)

(A violent knocking)

MARY MAGDALEN: John! John! Open the door! *(She knocks again)*

JOHN: Coming! *(He unbars the door)* Mary! . . . Where are the others? For God's sake, what's happened?

MARY MAGDALEN: They've taken away the Lord out of the Sepulchre, and we don't know where they have laid him!

JOHN: Taken him away?

MARY MAGDALEN: Oh, do come quickly!

JOHN: Of course. At once. . . . *(calling)* Peter! . . . Run up and find him, Mary!

MARY MAGDALEN: Run, John, run! . . . *(She goes off calling)* Peter! . . . Peter!

SEQUENCE 5 (THE SANHEDRIM)

CAIAPHAS: Elders of the Sanhedrim. I have called you together at this early hour, because there is something you ought to hear. Captain Elihu and these three Levites were on duty last night at the tomb of the Nazarene . . . Captain, kindly repeat to these gentlemen the report you made to me.

ELIHU: We kept watch, two by two. And towards the first cock-crow Joel and Saul were lying some thirty feet from the sepulchre, with a brazier of coals between them, because the night was chilly. Abner and I stood leaning on our spears on either side of the door.

CAIAPHAS: You could see clearly?

ELIHU: The setting moon was over against us, and we had also a torch placed in a cresset on the ground about three paces distant.

CAIAPHAS: You hear that, gentlemen? . . . Yes?

ELIHU: I had just said to Abner that it was time to change the guard when we felt the earth move under us, and one of the sleeping men woke up and cried out. There came another tremor, and another, still more violent. I put my hand to the door to steady myself, and my arm tingled to the shoulder as happens sometimes when you touch iron in a thunderstorm. Then, suddenly—

1ST ELDER: Go on, man, go on!

ELIHU: We were flung apart with a great shock, so that we fell to the ground. And the flame of the torch streamed out flat, as though a wind had gone over it from the sepulchre.

2ND ELDER: Some vapour of the earth, discharged from a vent in the rock.

ELIHU: Joel can tell you the thing that happened next. Speak, Joel.

JOEL: I heard a pebble spin from the path, as if a foot had struck it; and something passed between me and the brazier, blotting out the light of the fire.

3RD ELDER: Had it form as well as substance?

JOEL: It went very swiftly. But the shadow that followed it was the shadow of a man.

2ND ELDER: Did you lay hold of it?

JOEL: No, sir.

1ST ELDER: This is a fine soldier—to be frightened of a shadow.

JOEL: I was startled, sir, but not afraid. . . . Then I heard a shout, and saw Abner and the Captain lying on the ground, with Saul running towards them. So I ran too, and we lifted them up. They were not hurt, but their bodies were numb where the shock had struck them.

3RD ELDER: And after that?

ELIHU: We took up the torch, and examined the stone and the seals, but found everything secure. And while we looked and wondered—somebody laughed behind us!

IST ELDER: These men were drunk, or dreaming!

JOEL: We turned about quickly, and saw a young man.

SHADRACH: The same person, or another?

JOEL: Another.

2ND ELDER: Did you see him plain?

JOEL: Yes. He was tall and fair, dressed in a short tunic belted about the waist; with sandals on his feet, and his hair curled close and bound with a fillet. His skin and his garments were whiter than the moonlight, and his face beardless, very fresh and smiling. In all my life I never saw anything so terrible as that smiling face.

IST ELDER: Why was it terrible?

JOEL: I cannot tell, but we were as dead men for fear of it. It was not like that other.

SHADRACH: What do you mean?

JOEL: Sir, the thing that passed us in the garden was human, but this was not.

2ND ELDER: Did the—apparition speak?

ELIHU: No, sir. It went forward and stood before the sepulchre. The moon was behind it, yet it cast no shadow on the face of the rock. Then, as though the great stone had weighed no more than a bubble, it rolled it back with one hand and sat upon it, smiling still. And the moonlight and the torchlight shone through the open door. And the tomb was empty. . . .

SEQUENCE 6 (THE GARDEN)

JOHN *(he is out of breath)*: Peter! Peter! it's true. . . . I got there and looked in. . . . There's nobody there. . . . Nothing. . . . Only the linen clothes lying on the grave-slab.

PETER: Where are the women?

JOHN: Heaven knows!—gone out by the other gate, perhaps. . . . Come and look, Peter. . . . Look there! . . . the Lord's body is gone.

PETER: Who can have taken it?

JOHN: *Did anybody take it?*

PETER: What's that you say?

JOHN: I don't know what I'm saying.

PETER: I'm going in to see.

JOHN *(whispering to himself)*: Oh, Master, Master—is it possible? . . . This is the third day. . . . No! I daren't say it. . . . I daren't think it. . . .

PETER: John! . . . there's something queer about this. . . . The grave-clothes are here. *The grave-clothes.* . . . What sort of robbers steal the body and leave the grave-clothes behind?

JOHN: Let me come.

PETER: See there, where the body lay. . . . The grave-bands, crisscrossed and wound together from breast to foot . . . and the napkin—not tossed with the rest, but wrapped up by itself—just where his head must have been. . . . Who can have arranged them like that—and in Heaven's name, why?

JOHN: Nobody!—nobody!— . . . Can't you see?—They have never been unwound. . . . Look! here is a bundle of myrrh still fast among the folds.

PETER: Never unwound?—You are mad! How could the body have passed—?

JOHN: Risen and gone! Risen and gone!—O Jesus! my friend and my living Lord!

SEQUENCE 7 (THE SAME)

THE EVANGELIST: Then the disciples went away again into their own home. But Mary Magdalen returned to the sepulchre and stood without, weeping. And as she wept, she stooped down, and seeth two angels in white sitting, one at the head, and the other at the foot, where the body of Jesus had lain.

RAPHAEL: Gabriel, messenger of the Most High, is our joyful errand done?

GABRIEL: Nearly done, Raphael, son of consolation.

RAPHAEL: Did those women understand us? They were very much afraid.

GABRIEL: They understood more than the soldiers. And in time, they will understand everything.

RAPHAEL: Those disciples did not see us at all.

GABRIEL: John son of Zebedee needs no angel. For his heart is close to the life of the Blessed—

RAPHAEL: To whom be glory—

GABRIEL: And dominion for ever—

RAPHAEL: Amen.

GABRIEL: And the eyes of Peter are darkened with sin and shame. But to him the All-Beautiful will speak—

RAPHAEL: Whose delight is in mercy—

GABRIEL: Amen.

RAPHAEL: But what of this woman, who stands and weeps without?

GABRIEL: We will show ourselves to her. Yet she will not heed us. For her love still clings to the mortal flesh she knew. . . . Woman, why do you weep?

MARY MAGDALEN: Because they have taken away my Lord, and I don't know where they have laid him.

(She turns away sobbing)

RAPHAEL: She has turned away.

GABRIEL: Say nothing. He is coming, before whose feet the wilderness breaks into blossom—

THE ANGELS *(together softly)*: Eloi, Eloi, Eloi. . . .

(MARY MAGDALEN *continues to weep*)

JESUS: My girl, what are you crying for?

MARY MAGDALEN: Oh, sir! What has become of him? . . . Are you the gardener? I beg you, if you have hidden him—if he must not lie here in your garden—tell me where you have put him and I will come and take him away. . . . Please—please—I beseech you—

JESUS: Mary!

MARY MAGDALEN *(with a wild cry)*: Rabboni!

JESUS: Do not hold me—do not cling to me now. Not yet. I have not yet gone to the Father. Till then you cannot possess me wholly. . . . Go now, run to my brothers and say to them: I am going home to my Father and to your Father, and to my God and your God.

THE EVANGELIST: Then Mary Magdalen came and told the disciples that she had seen the Lord. But the words seemed to them as idle tales, and they believed them not.

SCENE II (JERUSALEM)

SEQUENCE I (THE SANHEDRIM)

THE EVANGELIST: And the chief priests, being assembled with the elders, took counsel. . . .

1ST ELDER: Joseph of Arimathaea! Do you mean to stand there and tell us—?

JOSEPH: As God is my witness, I had no hand in it. I am as much amazed as you are.

2ND ELDER: That's a likely story!

3RD ELDER: You had access to the body—

4TH ELDER: The sepulchre was yours—

JOSEPH: You sealed the stone yourselves, and set the guard!

1ST ELDER: Yes, and you bribed them—

JOSEPH: How dare you?

3RD ELDER: You were a follower of Jesus. Can you deny it?

2ND ELDER: You have taken his part throughout—

1ST ELDER: Backed up his seditious and treasonable attempts—

JOSEPH: That is a lie! I said he was a prophet—

4TH ELDER: And the Messiah! What about that?

JOSEPH: How would stealing his body prove him to be the Messiah?

3RD ELDER: You have condoned his blasphemies—

JOSEPH: No!

2ND ELDER: And now you stage this fictitious miracle, to bring the Law into contempt—

JOSEPH: I deny it—

IST ELDER: And insult the All-Holy with the filthy and abominable pretence—
JOSEPH: Of what? Of what?—Prophets do not rise from the dead! Messiahs do not walk out of their graves! Of what are you accusing me? When did I ever say that Jesus was the Son of God?
NICODEMUS *(shrilly and hysterically)*: We have slain the Lord's annointed! He has risen in vengeance, with a mighty hand and with an outstretched arm!
CAIAPHAS: Brother Nicodemus!

(Hubbub)

NICODEMUS: Curse ye Meroz, saith the Lord!... *(His voice sinks to a rapid mutter)* Will not the Lord be avenged on such a nation as this?...A wonderful and horrible thing is come to pass in the land ... wonderful and horrible ... horrible....
2ND ELDER: This is shocking!
3RD ELDER: We must stop it somehow.
4TH ELDER: In God's name, Nicodemus—
NICODEMUS *(loudly)*: Rise up, O Lord, into Thy resting-place, Thou and the ark of Thy strength!... And you shall see the Son of Man sitting at the right hand of power, and coming—and coming—

(He collapses with a groan)

SHADRACH: All this is exceedingly painful.
3RD ELDER: He's in a fit of some kind.
CAIAPHAS: Get him out. Take him home, under medical supervision. Tell his family he is out of his mind. Convey our sympathy....

(NICODEMUS is removed)

Reverend brothers, let us hasten to forget this distressing scene.... I think nothing is to be gained by open scandal, or by accusations which cannot be substantiated.... You, Joseph of Arimathaea—if you are wise, you will fall in with our policy.
SHADRACH: And what is our policy, Most Venerable?
CAIAPHAS: Can you ask?... Naturally, we shall deny the story.... The weakness of our position, of course, is that we cannot produce the body.
IST ELDER: We shall leave no stone unturned!
CAIAPHAS: Certainly. But in case it should prove undiscoverable—
2ND ELDER: Undiscoverable! It must be somewhere.
CAIAPHAS: I said, *in case.*
3RD ELDER: Can't we just re-seal the tomb and pretend that nothing has happened?
CAIAPHAS: In a public garden? In broad daylight?... And suppose Pilate should hear rumours and order the tomb to be examined?
2ND ELDER *(brilliantly)*: Why not substitute another corpse?

CAIAPHAS: Having first crucified it, I suppose, by way of lending verisimilitude. . . . It would be simpler to stick to the truth.

SHADRACH: The truth being—?

CAIAPHAS: Really, Brother Shadrach! . . . The body was stolen, of course. . . . Unless anybody agrees with poor, afflicted Nicodemus. . . . No? . . . Then we must deal at once with these Levites. . . . Clerk, ask Captain Elihu to step this way. . . . Incidentally, gentlemen, pray note that this discussion has not taken place. No record of it will appear in the minutes. There will be a trifling disbursement from the Temple funds to be accounted for. It had better, perhaps, be debited to—er—educational purposes. . . . Ah! Captain Elihu!

ELIHU: Most Venerable?

CAIAPHAS: We are inclined to believe that your report was made in good faith. Needless to say, we cannot accept the supernatural interpretation you seem disposed to put upon it. You will realise that if the story were circulated in its present form, very serious doubts might be cast upon your sanity, or loyalty, or both. We suggest that the earthquake and the—er—thundery state of the weather produced some kind of—er—vaporous exhalation which stupefied you all, and that the disciples of the Nazarene profited by this to open the tomb and remove the body. The—um—apparitions you describe were doubtless members of the gang, whom, in your confused state, you mistook for—er—demons.

ELIHU: My Lord, I can only say—

CAIAPHAS: Better say nothing. We have taken a lenient view. . . . To avoid misunderstanding by the ignorant and superstitious it will be advisable for you to admit, if questioned, that you fell asleep at your posts.

ELIHU: My Lord! that would be a most dishonourable admission!

CAIAPHAS: It will prevent the drawing of other, and still more damaging conclusions. In view of the shock—and—er—nervous wear-and-tear sustained in the performance of your duty, we are willing to pay you something extra—

ELIHU: Thank you, my Lord.

CAIAPHAS: On condition, of course, that you refrain from—er—gossip.

ELIHU: Excuse me, my Lord. Crucified bodies are Roman property. If this should come to the Governor's ears—

CAIAPHAS: You shall not suffer. We will make it right with him. . . . Now, you quite understand?

ELIHU: Yes, Most Venerable.

CAIAPHAS: Very good. You may go. . . . Reverend Brothers, the Sanhedrim is adjourned. . . . Brother Joseph, one moment. . . . I mentioned no name to those Levites. I said "his disciples". I hope it will not be necessary to suggest names. But I shall make a general order that any one spreading malicious rumours is to be put under arrest. Is that clear?

JOSEPH: Perfectly. . . . Caiaphas, as man to man, what do you think you have done?

CAIAPHAS: The best I could for Israel.

Sequence 2 (The Lodging of the Zebedees)

THE EVANGELIST: Then the same day, being the first day of the week, the disciples were assembled in Jerusalem, with the doors barred for fear of the Jews....

JOHN: Then you still don't believe what we say?

JAMES: I should like better evidence, John. Mary Magdalen's a dear girl, but very excitable, and she's worked herself up into such a state—

JOHN: And our mother, James? The most practical, prosaic person that ever walked? And Mary Cleophas?

JAMES: What did they see? Two people in white, who might have been anybody. And after all, they're women. Now, if you and Peter—But no *man* has seen anything.

ANDREW: Peter has seen something.

JAMES: What's that, Andrew?

ANDREW: I went to him just now, and found him stretched upon the floor. He said: "The Lord is alive; I have seen him". I said, "What, here?" He answered, "Yes". "Well," I said, "what did he say to you?" Peter answered, "Don't ask me".... I laid him on his bed, and he fell instantly into a deep sleep, like a child. He is asleep now. Thomas is sitting with him.

PHILIP: It was a vision, maybe, or a dream. Our Lord is dead.

JOHN: Yes, Philip, I said that too, God forgive me.... Yet did we not see the widow's son raised up and Lazarus called from the grave? And what did our Lord say to you at that last Passover supper?

PHILIP: He died, nevertheless.

MATTHEW: Well, I dunno. I'd like to believe you, John. If I thought he was alive, I'd be that 'appy I wouldn't know what to do with myself. All the same—here's two people sees angels, and Mary and Peter say they've seen the Master, but you ain't seen nothing.

JOHN: I saw the grave-clothes.

MATTHEW: Granted. That's not what I mean. If it was really our Master, same as we knew him, who'd he go to first? Why, you, of course. You was the one he loved.

JOHN: He loved us all, Matthew.

MATTHEW: I know he did. But not quite the same way. You was his best friend. And God knows, when they killed him, it must have hit you 'arder than any of us. And if he was here alive, the very first thing he'd say would be, "Where's John?"

JOHN: He knows I'm here whenever he wants me.

MATTHEW: Yes, but it's not kind. It's not like him. Why should Mary and Peter come before you?

JOHN: Perhaps they needed him more.... Needed to *see* him, I mean. *I know* he's alive. I knew it the minute I got there.... I was *certain*.... And besides—

MATTHEW: Well?

JOHN: Peter's more important. The church was to be founded on Peter.

JAMES: There again—No offence, Andrew, but that's always puzzled me. Why on Peter and not on you, John, who were his special friend?

JOHN: Perhaps because of that. I don't think you can found a church on personal friends and special cases. It's got to be less exclusive—more—what's that Greek word?—more catholic.

NATHANAEL: What is the church? The thing we looked for was the Kingdom. Is that going to come now? or isn't it? You say he's alive, John—

JOHN: I know he's alive, Nathanael.

NATHANAEL: Well, what's he doing? And what are we to do?—You know there's an order gone out that anybody who repeats this resurrection-story will be put in prison, and—

(Knock at the door)

What's that?

ANDREW: They've come for us.

(Knocking repeated)

JAMES: I'll see who it is.

PHILIP: Take care, James!

JAMES *(at the door)*: Who's there?

CLEOPHAS *(outside)*: Cleophas and Mary.

JAMES: Oh!—wait a moment.... *(He unbars the door)* ... We thought you were the police.

CLEOPHAS: James—John—everybody! We've seen the Master!

DISCIPLES: What? ... You have? ... How? ... When? ... etc.

ANDREW: James, bar the door. *(Door barred)* Now—tell us!

CLEOPHAS: We were walking home to Emmaus—you know, our own village, about seven miles out—and discussing all these strange events, when a man came up with us—

JAMES: Where from?

CLEOPHAS: Wife, where *did* he come from?

MARY CLEOPHAS: From behind, I suppose, or out of a side turning. He just seemed to be there.

CLEOPHAS: He asked what we were talking about, and why we seemed so sad about it. So I said, "Are you a stranger in Jerusalem, that you don't know the things that have been happening there?" He said, "What things?" "About Jesus of Nazareth," I said, "who was a great prophet and did many wonderful works before God and the people. But the chief priests and the Roman officials condemned him to death and crucified him. And we are sad, because we had believed he would be the saviour of Israel. But they killed him three days ago. And now," I said, "some of the women who were with us—my wife here was one of them—astonished us this morning by saying that they had visited the sepulchre and found the body gone, and that they'd seen a vision of angels who told them he was alive."

ANDREW: Cleophas! that was awfully risky. The man might have been a spy.

CLEOPHAS: I didn't think of that. But I said that some of us had been to the tomb and found it empty, just as the women said, but we hadn't seen *him.* . . . Then the man said . . .

PHILIP: What was he like?

MARY CLEOPHAS: It's a queer thing, but it's as if we never really looked at him properly—did we, husband?

CLEOPHAS: I don't think we did, somehow . . . Well, anyway, he said: "How foolish you are! and how slow to believe what the prophets told you! Don't you see that the Messiah *had* to suffer all these things, and so enter into his glory?"

MARY CLEOPHAS: And then he began at Moses, and went through all the prophets, explaining what they'd said about the Christ,—how he was to be strangely born, and to be despised and rejected, and to know bitter grief and pain, and have his hands and feet pierced—oh, yes! but he was to ride into Jerusalem on an ass, like a king coming in peace—and he was to tread the winepress of God's wrath alone—and oh! lots of things! He made it all so clear.

CLEOPHAS: And how he should rise up again, like a plant out of the stony ground, and return as a loving shepherd and a great prince to sit on the throne of David and bring his people back from the grave. With much more. And we saw how all the prophecies fitted together like the incidents of one great story.

MARY CLEOPHAS: We could have listened for ever. And when we got to Emmaus, the sun was set, so we said: "Come in and stay with us, for night is falling". And he came in, and I got supper ready, and we all sat down.

CLEOPHAS: Then he took the bread, and blessed, and broke it. And as he held it out to us, we saw his hands—and the marks of the nails were in them.

MARY CLEOPHAS: And we looked in his face, and knew him. . . . It was as if we'd been blind all the time.

CLEOPHAS: Just in a flash, it came to us. . . . And then he was gone. There was nothing there, but the bread lying broken upon the table.

NATHANAEL: It was an apparition—

ANDREW: A vision—

CLEOPHAS: The bread was broken.

MARY CLEOPHAS: And I said, "Husband, didn't our hearts burn within us while he talked to us on the road?"—Because, looking back on it, the voice—and the things he said—we seemed to have known him all along.

CLEOPHAS: So we ran back all the way to Jerusalem to tell you. . . . It's true, you see, after all.

MATTHEW: It's frightening, that's what it is. Uncanny. That's not the Master we knew. Appearing like that, and vanishing and you not recognising him—

PHILIP: It's a phantom—how do we know it isn't an evil spirit? . . . I don't like it. . . . Supposing it was to come in on us now—

JESUS: Peace be unto you!

(Consternation)

PHILIP *(in a terrified gasp)*: It's here!

ANDREW: Heaven deliver us!

MATTHEW: Lord have mercy upon us!

JAMES: Blessed angels protect us!

(Babble of alarm)

JESUS: Children, what are you afraid of? Why do you doubt? . . . *(A little reproachfully)* John!

JOHN *(recovering himself)*: Oh, my dear! Forgive us for being so stupid! . . . You startled us—coming in like that, so suddenly, through the locked doors—we thought you were a ghost. . . . Dear Lord, is it really you?

JESUS: Feel me and see. Take my hand.

JOHN *(shrinking a little—not because he is afraid, but remembering the Emmaus story)*: Your hand?

JESUS: A ghost has not flesh and bones as I have—haven't I?

JOHN: Your hands are warm—and strong—and they are wounded. . . . How dared they use you so? . . . I stood and saw it. Each blow went through my heart.

JESUS: My heart was pierced also. Look!—Don't let that terrify you, children. You see—you can feel—that I am alive.

JAMES: You are alive.

MATTHEW: Master, it's wonderful to have you back.

ANDREW: It seems too good to be true.

PHILIP: Our Master and our friend—dear, dear Lord Jesus!

NATHANAEL: I can hardly believe it yet.

JESUS *(with reassuring simplicity)*: I should like something to eat. What have you in the house?

JAMES *(a little apologetically—it is his house, and there doesn't seem much to offer)*: There's some broiled fish left from supper—and bread, of course.

JESUS: That will do well.

JAMES: Come and sit down—won't you?

MATTHEW: Why, this is like old times.

JOHN: Here's a piece of honeycomb—new and unbroken. I'm so glad we kept it. . . . *(thought strikes him)* Master!

JESUS: Yes, John?

JOHN: You—you're not going to leave us yet?

JESUS: Why should I leave you?

JOHN: Cleophas and Mary—you did not eat with them. . . . O Master, stay a little—only a few minutes longer!

JESUS: Do you know me, John bar-Zebedee?

JOHN: I know you. I trust you. Stay or go as you will, Lord. Your will is ours. . . . Oh! but it's good to see you eat. It's so real. . . . Master, where have you been these three days?

JESUS: With the souls in prison.

JOHN: Did they know you? Are you their Master too?

JESUS: I am the good shepherd. I know my sheep and am known by them. All of them. From the beginning of the world, and for ever. . . .

SEQUENCE 3 (A STREET IN JERUSALEM, BEFORE THE GOVERNOR'S PALACE)

(Slight CROWD *background)*

FLOWER-GIRL: Buy my flowers! Who'll buy my sweet spring flowers?—Roses of Sharon and lilies, all a-growing and a-blowing! . . . Garlands! garlands! . . . Who'll buy my garlands? . . . Yes, lady?

EUNICE: Tell me, good woman—this crowd before the Governor's door—with the carriages and the lictors . . . is Pilate leaving Jerusalem?

FLOWER-GIRL: Yes, dear—he's off! I'll lose customers by it—they use a lot of flowers in the palace.

EUNICE: Does his lady go with him?

FLOWER-GIRL: Yes, dear. If you wait you'll see them start. . . . Buy a sweet nosegay, dearie? . . .

EUNICE: Give me all the lilies you have—a big bunch of them—Here's a silver piece—

FLOWER-GIRL: Yes, dearie. . . . That's a kind lady—Beautiful, ain't they, all a-growing and—

EUNICE: Quick! Quick! the doors are opening. . . . I must run—

FLOWER-GIRL: There you are, dear! . . . Bless you, lady! . . .

EUNICE: Pray let me pass, good people!

GUARD: Now then, miss! What do you want?

EUNICE: I've brought some flowers for the Governor's lady.

GUARD: All right. She's just coming down. Stand near the carriage and you can give them to her. . . . Guard, 'shun! . . . Present arms!

SLAVE *(at the top of the steps)*: Make way for their Excellencies! Room for the Governor! Room for the Lady Claudia Procula!

PILATE: Claudia, my dear—you are sure you feel strong enough for the journey?

CLAUDIA: Yes, Caius. I am quite well. I am glad to be leaving Jerusalem.

PILATE: So am I, by Pollux! Always hated the place. Eh, Flavius?

FLAVIUS: A detestable hole, Pilate.

EUNICE: Madam! Madam!

PILATE: What's this? What's this?

FLAVIUS: Come, girl! You mustn't trouble her Excellency.

CLAUDIA: Why, it's my little friend Eunice, the masseuse at the baths! I must say good-bye to her. . . . You go on, Caius. . . . Are these lovely flowers for me? Thank you, child. That's sweet of you!

EUNICE *(in a whisper)*: Madam! Have you heard what they are saying in the City?

CLAUDIA *(in a whisper)*: No. What?

EUNICE *(in a whisper)*: The Nazarene is risen from the dead.

CLAUDIA: Merciful Apollo!

FLAVIUS: Madam! Are you unwell?

CLAUDIA: It's nothing. A little giddiness. . . . Hand me in. . . . The air will revive me. . . . Thank you, Eunice. . . . Bid them drive on.

FLAVIUS: Drive on!

LICTORS: Make way! make way! Make way for the Governor! . . .

(The carriages and escort roll away)

FLOWER-GIRL *(in the distance)*: Who'll buy my flowers? Sweet spring flowers! Lilies and roses of Sharon!

SEQUENCE 4 (JERUSALEM—THE LODGING OF THE ZEBEDEES)

THE EVANGELIST: Now Thomas called Didymus was not with the disciples when Jesus came. And after eight days, they were together once more, and Thomas with them.

THOMAS: You can all say what you like. Seeing's believing. I tell you again— unless I see in his hands the print of the nails—no, seeing's not enough! Until I have felt with my finger the print of the nails—until I grasp and hold him and thrust my hand into his side, I'll believe nothing.

MATTHEW: Reely, Thomas! Anybody'd think you didn't *want* it to be true.

THOMAS: Wishful thinking won't do. I want proof. And when I say proof—

JOHN: Hush, Thomas. He's here.

JESUS: Peace be unto you.

DISCIPLES: And to you.

JESUS: Come here, Thomas. Put out your finger and feel my hands. Reach out your hand and thrust it into my side. And doubt no longer, but believe.

THOMAS *(with absolute conviction)*: You are my Lord and my God.

(The crucial word is spoken at last, and received in complete silence)

JESUS: Thomas, because you have seen me, you have believed. Blessed are they that have not seen, and yet have believed.

PETER *(who has suddenly become aware of some appalling implications)*: Master—

when I disowned you—when we disbelieved and doubted you—when we failed and deserted and betrayed you—is that what we do to God?

JESUS: Yes, Peter.

JAMES: Lord, when they mocked and insulted and spat upon you—when they flogged you—when they howled for your blood—when they nailed you to the cross and killed you—is that what we do to God?

JESUS: Yes, James.

JOHN: Beloved, when you patiently suffered all things, and went down to death with all our sins heaped upon you—is that what God does for us?

JESUS: Yes, John. For you, and with you, and in you, when you are freely mine. For you are not slaves, but sons. Free to be false or faithful, free to reject or confess me, free to crucify God or be crucified with Him, sharing the shame and sorrow, and the bitter cross and the glory. They that die with me rise with me also, being one with me, as I and my Father are one.

JOHN: This, then, is the meaning of the age-old sacrifice—the blood of the innocent for the sins of the world.

JESUS: Draw near. Receive the breath of God. As the Father sent me forth, so I send you. The guilt that you absolve shall be absolved, and the guilt that you condemn shall be condemned. And peace be upon you.

SCENE III (THE SEA OF GALILEE)

THE EVANGELIST: After these things, Jesus showed himself again at the Sea of Galilee. There were together, Simon Peter, and Thomas, and Nathanael, and the sons of Zebedee, and two other of his disciples. Simon Peter saith unto them, "I go a-fishing". They say unto him, "We go also with thee". They went forth and entered into a boat immediately, and that night they caught nothing.

JAMES: Still no fish in the nets, and the dawn is breaking.

PETER: No good, boys. . . . The weather looked right, and I hoped for a catch. . . . Well, that's all there is to it. We'd best make for home.

JAMES: There's a man standing on the beach.

THOMAS: Perhaps he wants to be taken over. We'll put in there.

JESUS (calling from a distance): Hey, lads! Have you had a good haul?

PETER (calling back): No, sir! No luck, I'm afraid.

JESUS: Cast on the right side of the boat. There's a shoal there.

ANDREW: What's that?

THOMAS: What's he know about it?

PETER: No harm in trying, Thomas. . . . Come on, Andrew . . . get the net down. . . . Mind your helm, John. . . . Over! (the trawl goes out with a splash) . . . Pay out, there, pay out. . . . Let her run. . . . Wake up, John— keep her before the wind. . . .

(Wind in the sail, and the water rippling from the bow)

Look out, lads!... haul away....

JAMES: The net's full—there was a shoal, as he said.

JOHN: It is the Lord.

PETER: What?—Of course! Here, give me my coat—I'm going to swim ashore—

THOMAS: Here, Peter—I say!—

JAMES: Let him go, Thomas.

(PETER *dives off with a splash)*

We can see to the net, Andrew, give a hand.

ANDREW: It's too heavy to get in.

JAMES: Better heave-to, and tow the net in with the dinghy.

THE EVANGELIST: So they came in and landed, for they were but a hundred yards from shore.

JAMES: Look, John—there is a fire of coals, with fish laid upon it—and bread. He is busied with it—I wish I could see his face.

JOHN: And Peter sits there watching.... *(He calls softly)* Peter!

PETER *(not to them, but to that other)*: The boat is in.

JESUS: Bring some of the fish that you have caught.

PETER: Andrew—have you brought the trawl?

ANDREW: Tied to the stern of the dinghy....

PETER: Find me one of the best....

JAMES: Here you are.... You'll want a knife....

PETER *(going)*: Thank you....

NATHANAEL: Are we to go with him?

JOHN: Better stay here, and count the fish.... They are big ones....

(Brief pause)

THOMAS: ... twelve, fourteen, sixteen ...

NATHANAEL: He is cooking them together upon the fire ... our catch, and those he brought with him ... twenty, twenty-two.... Do you think we dare ask him who he is?

JOHN: We know very well who he is.... How many do you make it?

JAMES: Seven-score here.

ANDREW: And thirteen. A hundred and fifty and three. All great fish.

JOHN: And this time the net was not broken.

JESUS: Fishers of men—come and have breakfast.

JOHN: The sun has risen. Do you see now who it is?

THE EVANGELIST: And when they had eaten, he speaketh unto Simon Peter....

JESUS: Simon, son of Jonah—are you more my friend than any of these your brothers?

PETER: Indeed, Lord—you know that I love you.

JESUS: Feed my lambs. . . . Simon, son of Jonah, are you in truth my friend?

PETER: Indeed, Lord—I love you—you know I do.

JESUS: Tend my sheep. . . . Simon, son of Jonah, do you love me then a little?

PETER *(distressed)*: What can I say? . . . Lord, you know everything. Look in my heart—my cowardly, faithless heart—and read there how I love you.

JESUS: Feed my sheep. . . . Indeed and indeed I tell you, when you were young you girded yourself and walked as you chose. But when you are old, you will stretch out your hands and others will gird you and carry you to a place that is not of your choosing.

PETER *(guessing what he means)*: Lord, as they did to you?

JESUS: Follow me.

PETER: Yes, Lord—to what end you will. . . . See, John is following too. . . . What is to happen to him?

JESUS: If I choose that he should abide until my coming, what is that to you? Follow me.

THE EVANGELIST: And after forty days, Jesus led his disciples unto the Mount of Olives, and there he spoke unto them, saying—

JESUS: All power is given to me in Heaven and on earth. For thus it was written that Christ should suffer and rise from the dead. And you are witnesses of these things. Stay therefore in Jerusalem, till you receive the promised power from on high. Then go and teach all nations, baptising them in the name of the Father, and of the Son, and of the Holy Ghost. And lo! I am with you always, even unto the end of the world. Amen.

THE EVANGELIST: And he lifted up his hands and blessed them. And while he blessed them he was parted from them, and a cloud received him out of their sight. And behold! two men stood by them in white apparel, which said to them—

GABRIEL: Ye men of Galilee, why stand ye gazing up into Heaven? This same Jesus, which is taken up into Heavens, shall so come in like manner as ye have seen him go into Heaven.

THE EVANGELIST: Amen. Even so come, Lord Jesus.

These things are written that ye might believe that Jesus is the Christ, the Son of God. And there are also many other things which Jesus did, the which, if they should be written every one, I suppose that even the world itself could not contain the books that should be written.